International Human Resource Management: A Cross-cultural and Comparative Approach

Edited by Paul Iles and Crystal Zhang

Chartered Institute of Personnel and Development

Chartered Institute of Personnel and Development
Published by the Chartered Institute of Personnel and Development, CIPD House,
151 The Broadway, London, SW19 1JQ
First published 2013

Designed and typeset by Exeter Premedia Services, India

Printed in Great Britain by Ashford Colour Press
British Library Cataloguing in Publication Data

A catalogue of this publication is available from the British Library
ISBN 978 1 84398 3002

The views expressed in this publication are the authors' own and may not necessarily reflect those of the CIPD.

The CIPD has made every effort to trace and acknowledge copyright holders. If any source has been overlooked, CIPD Enterprises would be pleased to redress this in future editions.

Chartered Institute of Personnel and Development, CIPD House,
151 The Broadway, London, SW19 1JQ
Tel: 020 8612 6200
Email: cipd@cipd.co.uk
Website: www.cipd.co.uk
Incorporated by Royal Charter
Registered Charity No. 1079797

International Human Resource Management: A Cross-cultural and Comparative Approach

Edited by Paul Iles and Crystal Zhang

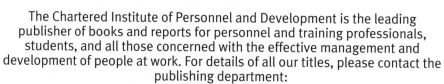

The Chartered Institute of Personnel and Development is the leading
publisher of books and reports for personnel and training professionals,
students, and all those concerned with the effective management and
development of people at work. For details of all our titles, please contact the
publishing department:
tel: 020 8612 6204
email: publishing@cipd.co.uk
The catalogue of all CIPD titles can be viewed on the CIPD website:
www.cipd.co.uk/bookstore

Contents

List of figures and tables

Authors' biographies

THE EDITORS

Paul Iles, Chartered FCIPD, is Professor of Leadership and HRM at Glasgow School for Business and Society, Glasgow Caledonian University. He is a chartered psychologist, Associate Fellow of the British Psychological Society, and Chartered FCIPD. He has a particular interest in leadership development, coaching, international HRM and talent management, and has published a number of articles on these issues in recent years in leading refereed journals.

Paul has designed and delivered leadership and change programmes for many clients in the public, private and voluntary sectors, including for the Rover Group, Littlewoods, the Civil Service and local government, as well as with banks and other companies in China. He has also worked on applied research programmes with the Learning and Skills Council, British Council and Standards Board for England.

Dr Crystal Zhang, Academic MCIPD, is a Senior Lecturer in HRM and Organisational Behaviour (OB) at Leeds Business School and teaches at the executive level in the UK, China and Africa. She has also delivered the management development programme for Sinopec in China and the MA HRM for the NHS in the UK.

Dr Zhang received her doctoral and master's degree in HRM and OB from Leeds University Business School. Her research interests are in international human resource management, cross-cultural learning, career development for ethnic minorities and talent management in China, and she has published in the area of learning theories and practice, cross-cultural HRD, graduate employment, global leadership and managing HR in India and China.

THE CONTRIBUTORS

Dr Niki Kyriakidou is a Senior Lecturer in Human Resource Management and Organisational Behaviour with a doctoral and master's degree in HRM and a bachelor's degree in political sciences and public administration. Dr Kyriakidou's research interests revolve around international human resource management, leadership and career development. Her current publications are in the areas of: leadership and management; learning theories and practice; workplace learning; cross-cultural HRD; graduate employment; managing human resources in the Middle East and Mediterranean region. She has also contributed to numerous book reviews in professional and academic journals, and currently acts as reviewer and referee for a number of publishers and academic journals.

Shakiya Nisa, Academic Assoc. CIPD, is a Senior Lecturer in Human Resource Management and Organisational Behaviour at Leeds Metropolitan University. Shakiya is an Associate Member of the Chartered Institute of Personnel and Development and she joined Leeds Business School in 2010. She teaches on the MA in HRM and MBA graduate programmes and on related undergraduate courses.

Her main area of expertise lies in the emotional experience of HR practitioners in the changing world of work, including the area of work–life balance. Shakiya's recent research interests are around postgraduate employment prospects of south Asian graduates and international HRM in India. Shakiya has previously worked as an HR practitioner in the retail and banking sector as well as in the public sector.

Tingting Jiang has a master's degree in management from Zhejiang Sci-tech University, Hangzhou, China. She is co-author of the paper 'Employee-based Brand Equity, Organizational Attractiveness and Talent Management in the Zhejiang Private Sector', published in the *Journal of Technology Management* in China, 2011. As a team leader, she proposed the project 'Fun door: an open door for your better future career' for the CEEMAN 2012 Global Challenge Future Competition and obtained a top-30 team award in the final, participating in the Grand Summit funded by CEEMAN and UNESCO in Slovenia. She currently works in securities futures in Hangzhou, China.

Xiaoxian Zhu is a doctoral researcher at Salford Business School, the University of Salford. She has a particular interest in talent management, employability and international human resource management. She assists in the PMI2 project at Leeds Business School. Previously she was awarded a master's degree in International Trade and Finance by Leeds Business School. She previously worked as marketing executive at the Porsche Center China.

Acknowledgements

To Teresa, for her support throughout this project.

In loving memory of my parents, Albert and Ruby, who always supported my educational career.

Paul

Walkthrough of textbook features and online resources

LEARNING OUTCOMES

At the beginning of each chapter a bulleted set of learning outcomes summarises what you can expect to learn from the chapter, helping you to track your progress.

 MERGERS AND ACQUISITIONS IN NIGERIAN BANKS

CASE STUDY 7.1

M&As are growing in Africa, especially in South Africa and the Nigerian banking sector. This is prompted by government regulation enforcing consolidation of the sector, but is an under-researched area. In Nigeria mergers involved merging 70 previously independent banks to create 19 new banks. As elsewhere, the human factor and HRM are critical to success. Such HRM issues as cultural due diligence (undertaking an assessment of the different cultures involved and their potential for clash or complementarity), pre-merger communication, management and employee due diligence (for example the different HR policies and practices and staff skills, competencies, age levels, demographics, experience, qualifications, etc) and future rewards all play a role in merger success.

Within the Nigerian banking sector, these measures led to large job losses and continued monitoring by the Central Bank of Nigeria. Banks anticipated acquiring other resources such as IT and talent, enhancing capability, achieving complementarity and widening their regional coverage within Nigeria. In many cases prior relationships, family connections and informal personal links

origins of senior managers in the new merged bank.

Communications through seminars, emails, packs, training and the intranet played a key role in helping overcome resistance, enhance interaction and build understanding and integration. Some banks were much more 'open' and 'transparent' than others over issues such as what came next – some restricted information to top management only and some employees only got information from the local newspaper!

Nine banks followed an *assimilation* approach, where one or more of the combined firms adopted – voluntarily or by coercion – the identity, name, culture and policies of one partner. Four banks followed a *novation* approach, involving high levels of reorganisation and restructuring, often renaming themselves to symbolise 'combining the best of all parties'. Here HRM policies and practices played a particularly important role. Three followed a *structural integration* approach, where banks maintained high levels of autonomy, identity and separateness. This seemed particularly the case when merging banks came from both the

CASE STUDIES

A range of case studies from different countries illustrate how key ideas and theories are operating in practice around the globe, with accompanying questions or activities.

REFLECTIVE ACTIVITY 1.2

1   Who do you think has most responsibility for ensuring a supply of skilled labour to enterprises: the state/government, enterprises/employers or individuals?

2   Why do you think this?

3   What is the general stance taken in your country?

4   If it has shifted in recent years, why is this?

(adapted from Gold et al 2009)

However, this is not a static picture, as Case Study 1.1 shows – in recent years there has been much change in these systems, often towards a more 'voluntarist' or 'demand-led' market-oriented system and away from the 'supply-led' interventionist system of earlier years.

REFLECTIVE ACTIVITIES

In each chapter, a number of questions and activities will get you to reflect on what you have just read and encourage you to explore important concepts and issues in greater depth.

LEARNING SUMMARY

This chapter has discussed the role of IHRM in international mergers and acquisitions, joint ventures and alliances, distinguishing between equity and non equity partnerships or combinations. Such combinations are of growing importance in developing new products, accessing new markets and securing new resources, including human resources and talent, but pose a number of challenges if they are to be successful. Issues of culture and people management are central to success at every stage, from planning the combination and selecting a partner to integration of the parties into a new company or alliance, but HRM is often ignored, making a contribution only at the integration stage. Here such issues as communication, training and development are key. The chapter discussed some of the HR issues involved and how their neglect may lead to problems for the combination, as well as examples where HRD and OD techniques such as future search may have a role to play in ensuring success.

LEARNING SUMMARY

End of chapter summaries bring together the main themes of a chapter.

ONLINE RESOURCES FOR STUDENTS

- Additional chapter – *Issues and New Directions in International HRM*.

- Annotated web links – access a wealth of useful sources of information in order to develop your understanding of issues raised in the text.

- Self-test questions – multiple-choice and true/false questions test your knowledge, tracking learning and highlighting any areas of development.

ONLINE RESOURCES FOR TUTORS

- PowerPoint slides – allow you to design your programme around ready-made lectures, including figures and tables from the text.

- Lecturer's guide – provide guidance on how to use the book in your teaching, discussing the context of each chapter and responses to in-text learning features.

- Additional case studies – offer a selection of activities to encourage application of theory into practice, for use within class or as independent study. All cases are accompanied by discussions points and guidance for tutors.

For online resources, please visit www.cipd.co.uk/orl

PART 1

INTRODUCTION AND CONTEXT

CHAPTER 1

International HRM, National Differences and the Transfer of HRM

Paul Iles

LEARNING OUTCOMES

By the end of this chapter, you should be able to:

- Identify approaches to international, comparative and cross-cultural HRM.

- Define the concepts of institutional theory and national business systems.

- Appreciate national differences in HRM policy and practice.

- Consider and analyse some key theoretical perspectives on institutional theories and national business systems, with particular respect to the employee relations and national vocational education and training systems.

- Evaluate the implications of the above perspectives on international HRM.

- Evaluate the usefulness of neo-institutionalist explanations of global diffusion, adoption and adaptation of HRM policies and practices.

- Evaluate approaches to understanding the convergence, standardisation and transfer of IHRM practices.

INTRODUCTION

This chapter outlines the approach the book will take and analyses national differences in IHRM from a critical perspective of *institutional systems* (for example institutional theories and national business systems). For this chapter, 'institutionalist' perspectives and approaches will be the main focus; Chapter 2 explores competing or complementary 'cultural' theories of national difference, whereas Chapter 3 looks at IHRM policies of the enterprise, and in particular discusses the global 'transfer' of HRM practices. In doing so, it offers a more developed critique of both institutionalist and culturalist explanations through a discussion of neo-institutionalist theories. The following sections explore each of these areas in more depth.

The aim of Chapter 1 is to familiarise the student with an understanding of institutional theories of national business systems in different national and regional contexts to provide a contextual framework for an understanding of international, comparative and cross-cultural HRM. IHRM has become increasingly significant for countries, firms and individuals. Not only are Western and Japanese companies increasingly operating globally, but companies from the BRICS countries – Brazil, Russia, India, China and South Africa – are also rapidly internationalising (O'Neill 2011).

While many textbooks focus on mobile international managers/expatriates, all staff in international/multinational companies (MNCs) and public sector/voluntary agencies, for example non-government organisations (NGOs), will also have to display an international mindset. This book therefore does not just focus on MNCs, but on public sector/third sector agencies as well as educational bodies, collectively referred to here as IEs (international enterprises). This book therefore focuses on specific HR issues faced by international enterprises (IEs) in the context of international business, as international human resource management (IHRM) and cross-cultural HRM (CCHRM) have become increasingly significant for countries, firms and individuals.

As Dowling et al (2008) point out, the field of IHRM is often characterised by three broad approaches:

1 **comparative HRM**, describing, comparing and analysing HRM systems in various countries or regions

2 **cross-cultural management**, focusing on organisational behaviour in an international context

3 **international HRM**, focusing on aspects of HRM in IEs.

This is an approach taken by Garavan and Carberry (2012) to international HRD (IHRD); they distinguish between the 'international HRD trajectory' (HRD research in the context of the MNC – we explore this area further in Chapters 4 and 16) and the 'cross-cultural HRD trajectory' (analysing how national culture can influence IHRD; again, this is explored further in Chapters 4 and 16). In this chapter we discuss their third dimension on IHRD, the 'comparative HRD trajectory' or comparative analyses of HRD approaches across nations, and how societies can develop what is usually called 'national HRD', describing characteristics of national systems and how they influence national and organisational HRD practices (G. Wang 2008; Wang and Swanson 2008).

Our textbook therefore incorporates all three perspectives of international HRM, at national, firm and individual levels. It aims to provide a comprehensive and up-to-date overview of international HRM; analyses of and recommendations for solutions to global and cross-cultural challenges are discussed in Part 2, while an in-depth analysis is presented in Part 3 of some of the emerging economies in Eastern Europe, the Middle East, India, Africa and China, as well as the EU, USA and Japan. In Part 4, the IHRM policies of the enterprise in their institutional and cultural context are discussed.

In this book we therefore distinguish three levels of analysis, discussed in more detail in Part 1:

1   **Country/region level:** *comparative HRM.* This involves an analysis of different national/regional business systems and employment systems. This analysis tends to employ macro-level theories, for example institutional theory. Many UK/European texts are located here, and we discuss IHRM at a regional level in Part 3. We clearly cannot cover every country and region, so we have been selective in our focus. We primarily focus on the major economies – USA, UK, European Union (EU) and Japan – in their regional context and on the major 'emerging economies'. These include the so-called BRICS countries – Brazil, Russia, India, China and South Africa – and some of the leading 'Next 11' or N-11 countries, such as Nigeria and Mexico, all of which are likely to have an increasing impact on the world economy in the forthcoming decades (O'Neill 2011).

2   **Individual level:** *cross-cultural management/OB.* This involves an analysis of such organisational behaviour (OB) topics as leadership, communication, teamwork, motivation, conflict, communication and negotiation from the perspective of the individual manager; here we tend to use OB/organisational psychology perspectives and theories of culture. Part 2 of the book focuses on this area in more detail.

3   **Firm level:** *international HRM.* This level of analysis focuses on company policies and practices such as recruitment/selection, training/development, reward/compensation, talent management, employee relations and performance management. The focus is often on international staff, especially expatriates, and their management and development. Analyses tend to employ meso-level theories; many US texts are located here. We discuss enterprise IHRM policies in their institutional and socio-cultural context in Part 4.

First we explore institutionalist approaches to national differences in HRM policy and practice at the country/region level (comparative HRM) after introducing what we mean by IHRM and why it is important. Chapter 2 introduces the individual level of analysis (cross-cultural HRM) and Chapter 3 the firm level (international HRM).

REFLECTIVE ACTIVITY 1.1

1   So, what is IHRM *and*

2   Why is its study important and worthwhile?

If possible, discuss these questions in pairs or a small group, and try to arrive at a consensus view.

Some points you may have mentioned include:

a)   What is IHRM?

- HRM examines the way that organisations recruit, reward, train and motivate their most important resource – their staff.
- IHRM explores HRM processes from a comparative and international perspective.
- IHRM is about strategies for competitive edge.

- IHRM is about exploiting human capital to the full around the world.
- IHRM involves such issues as recruitment, reward, training and development ... **but also** issues such as cooperation, commitment and motivation, which means cultural competency and cultural understanding are important.

b)   So why study IHRM?

You may have mentioned:

- Business and management **has** globalised, so HRM needs to also become more international.

- Management should be international and outward looking.
- There is a requirement for enterprises to compare and learn from different nations and cultures.
- MNCs need international management skills and knowledge transfer to subsidiaries.
- There is a global spread of best practice and diffusion.
- Strategic and governmental processes are international and global.
- Industrial relations are internationalising to reflect global business.

You may have come up with other interesting ideas on these two questions!

SO HOW DOES IHRM DIFFER FROM DOMESTIC HRM?

The difference between international and domestic or national HRM does not lie in the activity or function of HRM; in both, similar activities and functions are carried out (for example recruitment and selection, HRD, career management, performance appraisal/management, reward, etc). The difference lies in other areas – one is the *location* in which HRM is being performed: is it in the home or the host country? This brings in issues of cultural and institutional differences, as well as geographical dispersion and differences in time zones.

Another key difference lies in which group of *employees* are involved; there are three main categories here:

- **HCNs** – host-country nationals or locals
- **PCNs** – parent-country nationals (of which expatriates are a major sub-category)
- **TCNs** – third-country nationals, neither locals nor expatriates but citizens of a third country.

As an example, if Guinness Nigeria employed Irish expatriates as, say, the CEO or finance director, these would be PCNs (as Guinness is headquartered in Ireland); Nigerians, probably the bulk of the workforce, are HCNs, or locals. If a British or Dutch employee was the operations manager, or a South African the HR director, they would be TCNs. We explore the management of these three categories in Chapter 3.

There are other differences, such as the amount of risk involved, including health and security risks, and the role of the state, which is likely to be more extensively involved in IHRM than in domestic HRM. A particular issue is the *separation by time and distance* of international operations; IEs are attempting to manage operations not only physically distant, but often *culturally different and distant* too. This is explored in more depth in Chapter 2; here we explore the differences in *institutions* between countries and regions, which also raise challenges for

IHRM. To do this, we use 'institutional' theories, in particular the concept of differences in 'national business systems'.

THE 'NATIONALITY THESIS' IN COMPARATIVE HRM: HOW DO WE BEST UNDERSTAND DIFFERENCES BETWEEN COUNTRIES AND REGIONS?

In comparative HRM, the 'nationality thesis' argues that globalisation – which we explore further in Chapter 3, especially in terms of its implications for IHRM – does not necessarily force countries, sectors and firms towards a *convergence* in their structure, culture, patterns of behaviour and HRM policies and practices. Institutional and cultural legacies exert a structuring influence, and national patterns still show *divergence* in their HRM systems; US firms, for example, differ from German firms in the strategic role played by HR, the role of unions and the commitment to training and development. Different frameworks have been developed to analyse and examine the relationship between social context and behaviour; the most significant contributions to the debates which we will explore have come from 'culturalist' and 'comparative institutionalist' approaches.

Culturalist perspectives explain organisational structure and practice as a collective enactment of beliefs and values or of shared cognitive structures, ideas and understandings (for example Hofstede 2001, 2002); we explore these in detail in Chapter 2. Here we look at institutionalist perspectives, which argue that culturalist approaches typically fail to consider cultural patterns as dynamic and emerging characteristics linked to historical development, or as having close relationships with material institutions and social groups. We will also, in contrast, explore the global *transfer* and standardisation/convergence of HRM practices using an institutionalist theory lens in Chapter 3 when we look at the firm level.

INSTITUTIONALIST APPROACHES AND NATIONAL BUSINESS SYSTEMS

Institutional perspectives see firms and institutions as socially constituted, and reflecting national distinctiveness: dominant national institutions tend to be integrated and mutually reinforcing. National institutional arrangements tend to be robust, demonstrating significant inertia in the face of pressures for change. Such approaches seek to establish a conceptual framework that allows comparative study of different 'national business systems' firmly anchored in empirical research, allowing cross-country comparisons. Here we will focus on one main institutionalist theory, the 'national business system' approach; as with cultural theories, this too takes the 'nation' or 'region' as the key unit of analysis, but focuses on a broad range of institutional factors. Specific contexts foster distinctive forms of business and market organisation, influencing how companies operate (Ferner 1997; Tempel and Walgenbach 2007; Gamble 2010).

NATIONAL BUSINESS SYSTEMS APPROACHES

Institutionalist analyses focus on macro-level societal institutions, in particular those that govern 'access to critical resources, especially labour and capital' (Whitley 1999: 47). They look to differences in the organisation and the activities of the state, the capital, labour and financial systems, and the route taken by different countries to industrialisation and modernisation (especially the role played by the state). Systematic analysis of the major national institutions and the interactions between these institutional arrangements is termed the 'national industrial order' by Lane (1992) in her analysis of British financial versus German production-oriented capitalism. 'National business systems' is the term employed by Whitley (1999) in his analysis of divergent capitalisms and the different paths taken by nations in terms of coordination and control; this is the term we will use here.

There are some differences in claims as to what the 'dominant social institutions' actually are; sub-systems considered as a significant part of a national business system by some might be excluded by others. Lane's framework (1992, 2000), for example, consists primarily of the state, the financial system and, interestingly for our purpose, *the system of education and training*; this institution we will explore in more depth. To a lesser extent, she also includes the network of business associations and the system of employee relations.

For Lane (1992) the most significant national institutions therefore are:

- the state
- the financial system
- the network of business associations
- the system of employee relations
- education and training systems.

The state

This is particularly influential in shaping business systems, as it exerts both a direct and an indirect influence through its shaping of other institutional organisations (Lane 1992), such as education, finance, business associations and IR systems. Furthermore, the role of the state during industrialisation in implementing and enforcing development policies and creating and maintaining a stable and supportive political and economic environment for enterprises is crucial. German enterprises, for example, tend to have close relations with banks, insurance companies and the state, with much evidence of cross-shareholdings and interlocking directorates. Greater commitment to union consultation and worker participation, employee training involving unions and extra-firm bodies, such as employer associations, and employment security is also evident, termed 'Rhenish capitalism' by Albert (1993), or the 'social market' model. The USA and the UK, in contrast, give more emphasis to the market, to shareholder interests and to 'flexibility' in labour markets.

The financial system

The financial system affects both the ability of the state to support and guide business development and the nature of enterprises' strategic business choices and risk management, as well as relations between banks and firms.

The network of business associations

Differences between associations in powers and breadth of functions and services affect enterprise strategy. For example, in Japan, business networks link industrial, commercial and financial firms in complex networks of relationships, creating stable, long-term relationships among firms. On the contrary, in Britain, trade associations are not subject to uniform regulation and often compete for membership. This situation results in lower membership, a less secure financial basis and a voluntarist position, inhibiting the width and depth of functions they are able to perform and leaving firms more institutionally isolated (Lane 1992).

The system of employee relations

National systems of IR influence business organisation both through their structural relations and through underlying employer–employee relationships (Lane 1992). The strength of trade unions directly determines the role of unions in collective bargaining, the effectiveness of conflict resolution, the degree of flexibility in labour deployment and the nature of negotiated bargains. The national system of IR ultimately places constraints on the strategic choices that enterprises can adopt. We explore this further in Chapter 20.

Education and training systems

The development and competitiveness of countries is influenced by the nature, scope and quality of their education and training system. There are major differences between nations in the organisation and structure of formal educational institutions and their links to labour markets, with consequences for recruitment, promotion and training policies, as well as the division of labour (Lane 1992). We will discuss this area shortly.

Whitley (1999) identifies three 'ideal types' of national business systems:

- **Particularistic:** here firms lack trust in formal institutions, with a weak or predatory state; weak collective intermediaries/norms govern transactions; and firms exercise paternalistic authority relationships. This type is characterised by flexibility and *opportunistic hierarchies*; the control exercised by the owner is typically direct and personal; coordination is highly personal and non-routinised; and flexibility is a response to the unpredictable environment. Examples might include family firms, especially in developing countries.
- **Collaborative:** here, interlocking institutions encourage cooperative behaviour, as in Japan and Germany. This leads to 'cooperative hierarchies' and corporatist/interventionist approaches. Owners and managers share authority more with employees and partners; skilled manual workers are typically integrated into the organisation as core members.
- **Arms' length:** here there is flexible entry and exit within an institutionalised formal system. Competitive capital markets exist and the state acts as regulator. Training, for example, is seen as a matter for individual firm investment, not for coordinated collaboration between the state, employers and unions, as in the USA or the UK. This approach leads to 'isolated hierarchies'.

Whitley (1999) compared the role of the state in South Korea and Taiwan in economic development (see also Green et al 1999; Walter and Zhang 2012). In South Korea, the state directly managed the dominant industrial networks, known as *chaebol*, through agencies and fiscal control (an interventionist position). *Chaebol* are financed by state banks and government-controlled trading companies. On the other hand, the Taiwanese government adopted a more US-style *laissez-faire* attitude towards the development of large firms. Without government support, the difficulty of obtaining bank loans and high bank interest rates, family firms and the business group are the dominant organisational forms throughout the economy, especially in the export industry.

Various typologies of institutionalist frameworks and the outputs of these systems exist. They are helpful in comparing a national business system with other systems and in identifying the critical institutions which influence the structure and behaviour of economic enterprises. This focus on national business systems shows that there are different national varieties of capitalism globally; we examine these in greater detail in Part 3 on regional differences in HRM:

- **US/UK:** liberal market model, shareholder-based, short-term orientation, explored in Chapter 8
- **Continental European:** Euro Rhenish/communitarian/corporatist model, stakeholder-based, long-term orientation, explored in Chapter 8
- **Japanese:** *kairetsu*-based, with interlocking networks
- **Korean:** *chaebol* family-based enterprises/conglomerates
- **Chinese:** family firm and state-owned enterprise, explored in Chapter 14.

Others add Arab management as a distinct model (Al-Suleimany 2009; Weir 2000a, 2000b), explored in Chapter 10. Such types of capitalism show differences in terms of the role of the state, financial institutions, education and training systems, nature of the labour market, system of labour relations, roles of chambers of commerce, banks, equity markets and other institutions. Analyses of 'comparative business systems' (Whitley 1992) show many such national institutional differences, from the nature of the firm to the nature of markets to the types of control systems. Examples include the nature of systems of control, the nature of firm and markets (for example whether cooperative, as in Japan or Germany, or competitive, as in the USA); the role of intermediaries such as trade associations or chambers of commerce; and the type of integration, trust and relationships found within organisations. We explore this issue in more detail in Chapter 8 on HRM in the USA and Europe.

Some of these differences, for example over time-scale or collectivism, also reflect cultural differences, which we explore further in Chapter 2. Whether institutions affect culture, or vice versa, or whether there is mutual influence, is an open question. Other national business systems, for example China and India, will display even more divergence from the US model, as we shall see in Part 3.

However, there is a danger of over-generalisation in these explanations; for example, Whitley (1999) claims that Japan and Germany are both examples of collaborative business environments generating 'cooperative hierarchies', but there are significant differences between the Japanese and the German education and training systems. The development of the internal labour market and in-company training in large Japanese firms as opposed to the greater support German firms have from the system of education and technical/vocational training focusing on skill development responsive to economic needs is one example (Lane 1992, 2000). There may also be transitions from one system to another, as we shall see with respect to China in Chapters 3 and 14 with respect to vocational education and training (VET) systems.

There are other approaches to national business systems; for example, Orru et al (1997) distinguish 'alliance capitalism', with both horizontal flexibility and vertical efficiency facilitated by the state, as in Japan, from 'familial capitalism', where there are strong horizontal linkages but a comparatively weak state with fragmented interests and weak planning, as in Taiwan. 'Dirigiste capitalism', where there is an emphasis on vertical integration and state leadership, centralised planning and targeted capital flows, is also found, for example in South Korea. Nations pursuing such policies would appear on the interventionist (corporatist/centralised) pole in Figure 1.1. Differences in vocational training and development systems usefully illustrate this point, so we turn to these next.

NATIONAL HRD AND THE VOCATIONAL AND EDUCATIONAL TRAINING SYSTEM

National HRD (NHRD) is a relatively new term for how a nation or country sees the role of skills development and utilisation in its economic and social life (McLean 2004; Gold et al 2009) and is expressed in the policies and practices of the state and its agents, for example parastatal organisations owned or controlled by the state or quasi-non-governmental organisations (QUANGOs). National HRD shows government interest in workforce development as a strategic issue and interest in the importance of HRD and its contribution to a country's development (McLean 2004) with roots in economic development theory and in the measurement of human capital (G. Wang 2008; Wang and Swanson 2008). Governments that accept its importance believe that investment in skills by national governments will be a lever for economic development. We explore this theme more fully in Part 3 with comparisons of how China, India, Russia and Brazil have approached this issue (Ardichvili et al 2012).

The market for skills may fail; incentives for firms to acquire skilled workers and/or bear the costs of training may not be effective. National governments may then intervene to address this 'market failure' in ways that vary from country to country, influenced, as national business systems theorists insist, by specific cultural and institutional factors.

A distinction often made is between *voluntarism*, where government sees its role as encouraging organisations to take responsibility for skills acquisition and training, and *interventionism*, where governments seek to influence corporate decision-making (Gold et al 2009). Figure 1.1 shows this distinction, and points to the possibility of changes to the system of VET (which can occur in both directions).

Figure 1.1: Voluntarism and interventionism in organisational HRD

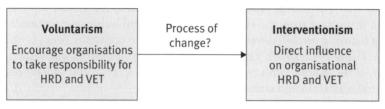

(adapted from Gold et al 2009)

For example, governments may impose a training levy on organisations to fund training and development, as in France (annually as a proportion of payroll). If an organisation provides training, it receives a grant, resulting in an increase in training expenditure (Greenhalgh 2001). However, the downside is the creation and maintenance of an expensive system for administering levies and grants, and the main benefits often accrue to already highly trained, mobile workers and training providers with a ready-made market. The UK had a levy system in the 1980s, but as part of a move by the Government towards a more voluntarist approach, it put more responsibility on decision-makers in organisations to invest in training to create skilled employees.

In many continental European countries there is a tradition of state support for VET following compulsory schooling in the form of infrastructure, regulation and funding. This position may become politically accepted by all parties (for example in Scandinavia and much of north-west and central Europe), resulting in a consensus between the 'social partners' of government, employers and trades union organisations – the 'cooperative hierarchy' or 'collaborative' type of national business system discussed by Whitley (1999).

REFLECTIVE ACTIVITY 1.2

1   Who do you think has most responsibility for ensuring a supply of skilled labour to enterprises: the state/government, enterprises/employers or individuals?

2   Why do you think this?

3   What is the general stance taken in your country?

4   If it has shifted in recent years, why is this?

(adapted from Gold et al 2009)

However, this is not a static picture, as Case Study 1.1 shows – in recent years there has been much change in these systems, often towards a more 'voluntarist' or 'demand-led' market-oriented system and away from the 'supply-led' interventionist system of earlier years.

VOCATIONAL EDUCATION AND TRAINING IN SWEDEN

Sweden has long enjoyed a social democratic political and social model with a historically well-funded education system (including VET). Reforms in 1993 sought the integration of academic and vocational education in upper secondary schools. 'Traditional' apprenticeships all but disappeared, alongside an aspiration for a 50% rate of university participation. There is a generally positive social and cultural attitude towards education, with approximately 97% staying on after compulsory secondary education.

Strong employer–union collaboration coincides with the Government playing a supportive, facilitative, funding role rather than driving change in a clearly structured VET system, but there is flexibility at local, regional and school levels. New initiatives from the new non-socialist government elected in 2006 focused on specific labour markets or social needs and improving employer–school links (but there is scope for further improvement). Essentially there is 'rolling reform' of the system within a relatively stable institutional framework.

(Johnson et al 2008, http:// www.lsc.gov.uk/ and http:// ffe.lsc.gov.uk/)

Questions

1 Why do you think there has been change in Sweden? What do you see as the relative advantages and disadvantages of voluntarist and interventionist VET systems?

In East Asian 'tiger economies' (for example South Korea, Singapore) there have often been similar examples of 'collaborative' or 'cooperative' national business systems, with their VET system often showing some degree of coordination over the supply and demand for skills to help their nations move up the skills and technology ladders (in Part 3 we look more closely at this – Ardichvili et al 2012). The state here often plays a strategic role in economic growth and the transformation of skills; the longer-term nature of returns to investment in skills, including the social as well as economic benefits, also seems linked to the cultural value of 'long-term orientation', which we discuss in greater depth in Chapter 2.

2 What are the advantages and disadvantages of such an approach to NHRD/VET? How does it compare with the system in operation in your own country?

Garavan and Carberry (2012) points out that many studies of NHRD have been of Asian countries, exploring relationships between government, employers and trade unions, labour market characteristics, and the regulation of the employment relationship. However, there has been a lack of studies addressing the convergence or divergence of national approaches to HRD. Of course, hybrid positions may exist, showing different mixes of voluntarism and interventionism. Between the extremes of centralisation and voluntarism are various efforts to gain the benefits of both in such European countries as Austria, Germany and the Czech Republic. These have traditionally taken a more corporatist approach, seeking to generate agreement between the key stakeholders/ social partners, but, as in Sweden, have adopted more business-driven and free-market policies, including towards VET, in recent years. There are also efforts to move from one model towards another; for example, the Czech Republic has sought a transition from a centralised model towards a less interventionist corporatist model, whereas in France there are efforts to move in the direction of a more market-oriented, demand-led model (Gold et al 2009).

This section has pointed out the issue of change in one aspect of a national business system, with countries attempting to benchmark and learn from other national systems. Gamble (2000, 2003, 2010) points out several limitations in the national business systems approach; he claims it resembles 'culturalist' explanations in that both ignore heterogeneity, both between and within industries; both fail to allow space for firm-level agency; and both fail to account for organisational outcomes between firms. In particular, both are poor at explaining how organisational practices change, or are transferred globally – they can account for wholesale transfer or no transfer, but not partial transfer or hybrid outcomes. We next turn to this area and an alternative institutionalist approach: neo-institutionalism.

GLOBAL STANDARDISATION AND CONVERGENCE IN IHRM?

How are HRM practices diffused or standardised globally? Are they converging across the globe? The 'national business system' approach highlights 'how business continues to be influenced by the national institutional frameworks in which it is embedded' (Tempel and Walgenbach 2007: 2) but 'it downplays the effects of transnational developments on national patterns'. Another 'institutionalist' perspective, *'neo'*, or *'new'*, *institutionalism*, in contrast, emphasises the global diffusion of practices and the adoption of these by organisations, but pays little attention to how such practices are interpreted or 'translated' as they travel around the world (compare Czarniawska 1997; Czarniawska and Joerges 1996). What is needed is a framework which moves beyond the convergence/divergence dichotomy to capture signs of both global standardisation and continued persistence of differences in IHRM.

Neo-institutionalist explanations of the global standardisation of organisational forms (Tempel and Walgenbach 2007; Gamble 2010; Iles et al 2010c) seek to explain how global forms of HRM are diffused and standardised. What Greenwood and Hinings (1996) label the 'new institutionalism' emphasises legitimacy and the embeddedness of 'organisational fields' of key suppliers, resource and product consumers, regulatory agencies, and other organisations that produce similar services or products. For Tempel and Walgenbach (2007: 2) 'particular organisational forms exist not because they provide an optimal input–output balance, but because they correspond to institutionalised expectations'. The focus is on attaining legitimacy within the institutional environment by adopting its expectations of structure and practice, including IHRM practice.

DiMaggio and Powell (1983: 143; 1991) introduced the *homogenisation* phenomenon: organisations become increasingly similar to each other as managers try to change them. *Isomorphism* best captures this process: organisations in the same or similar social, economic and political contexts come to resemble each other over time (Iles et al 2010c). DiMaggio and Powell (1983) distinguish two types of isomorphism: *competitive* and *institutional*. Competitive isomorphism emphasises market competition and fitness measures, but IEs also face institutional pressures from government regulators, professional associations such as the CIPD and social networks, competing not only for resources and customers, but also for political power and institutional *legitimacy*.

Three institutional mechanisms influence organisational decision-making: *coercive*, *normative* and *mimetic*. *Coercive* mechanisms arise from pressures exerted by political contexts and the challenge of legitimacy and from formal and informal pressures exerted by other organisations upon which they are dependent, experienced as force, persuasion or invitations to collusion (Meyer and Rowan 1977).

Normative mechanisms refer to the articulation between management policies and the professional backgrounds of employees in terms of educational level, job experience and craftsmanship; in many cases, the influence of the professions *per se* can be as strong as that of the state. Professional networks, such as professional and trade associations (for example the CIPD in the UK), help define and promulgate norms about organisational and professional behaviour, and normative mechanisms create pools of individuals who not only share common expectations, but also occupy similar positions across a range of organisations and possess a similarity of orientation and disposition. This 'normative isomorphism' is reinforced by filtering personnel, as many professional career tracks in organisations are carefully controlled and monitored, both at entry and throughout the career path. Individuals in similar positions across organisations tend to have similar biographies in terms of education, skills, work experience and ideology, and similar patterns of thought about organisational practice; through this global discourse, HRM ideas and concepts are diffused globally.

Finally, *mimetic* mechanisms refer to imitations of the strategies and practices of competitors as a result of uncertainty; these are the mechanisms most often referred to in discussions of management *fashion-setting* (Abrahamson 1991). Management fashions need to be not only novel, but also appear to be rational, solving problems for the organisation. Management fashions are developed by fashion-leaders such as consultants, academics and leading MNCs, and marketed to 'fashion-followers' such as local companies through books, publications, seminars, websites and training courses. Organisations may model themselves on other similar organisations in their field, perceived to be more legitimate or successful. Later, fashionable managerial techniques may be 'diffused unintentionally, indirectly through employee transfer or turnover, or explicitly by organisations such as consulting firms or industry trade associations' (DiMaggio and Powell 2002: 172). This may occur internationally through the global or regional rotation of personnel, as we shall see in Chapter 3; through expatriates 'transferring technology', through employees studying common concepts on education or training courses, reading similar textbooks, and from global consultancies preaching a common message, as well as the deliberate actions of

IEs themselves in standardising operations; or through popular management books and the management consulting industry (Fincham and Evans 1999).

Isomorphism thus results from adopting institutionalised elements, in particular expected structures and management practices. The fashionable practice may become institutionalised over time as a regular practice, adopted 'ceremonially' perhaps in name only or simply as a re-labelling of an existing practice without substantive change, or rapidly dropped in favour of the next fashion or fad.

How do transitory management fashions in IHRM become institutionalised or taken for granted? Perkmann and Spicer (2008: 812) comment that '... managers' decisions to embrace new ideas are often informed by collective beliefs about rational or progressive managerial practice, shaped by idea providers such as consultants or gurus'; fashionable management concepts may acquire permanence when anchored within field-wide institutions. *Institutional entrepreneurs* such as consultants can act as agents, purposefully working towards changing existing or creating novel institutions; for Scarbrough (2002), institutionalisation is driven by the 'translation' of practices into specific organisational contexts through the actions of professional groups and consultants, and while business 'gurus' may legitimate a body of knowledge, large consulting firms will engage in its commodification and colonisation, and business schools in due diligence and innovation through critical analysis.

Building these institutions requires different types of institutional work: political work to reconfigure rules and boundaries; technical work to suggest, recommend or prescribe certain courses of action; and cultural work to establish or reframe belief systems and values and link practices to more widely anchored discourses. Political work involves advocacy and is more likely to be carried out by politicians, trade unionists, lobbyists and industry associations. Technical work involves theorising, standardising and education, developing theories, standards, models and world-views and providing education and training, and is more likely to be carried out by consultants, academics and professional bodies such as the CIPD. Cultural work involves the construction of normative networks and identities and is more likely to be carried out by journalists, public relations and advertising specialists, professional bodies and social movements, perhaps in contestation with other professional groups, as well as in constructing professional identities (for example the current debate about the emerging coaching industry as a profession and its implications for HRD – Hamlin et al 2008). Such actors seek to 'promote discourses that associate practices with widely accepted norms and values' (Perkmann and Spicer 2008: 829).

Figure 1.2 shows how this might work in the IHRM field. In Chapter 17, we discuss how this might happen with reference to a specific HRM practice – the global diffusion of 'talent management' (Iles et al 2010c).

Figure 1.2: IHRM and the new institutionalism

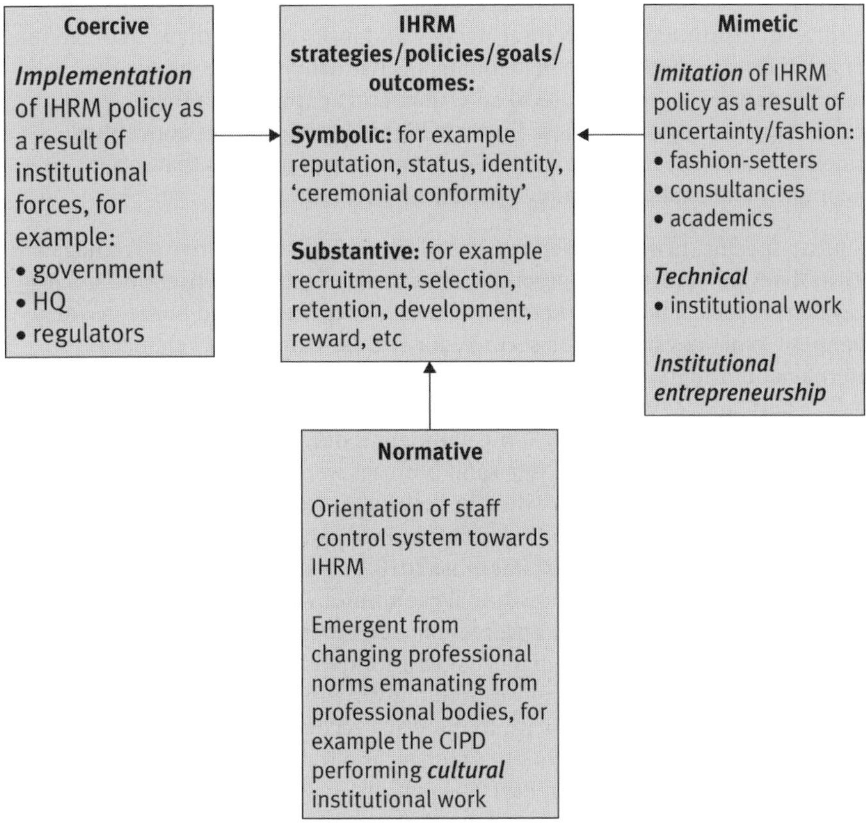

Coercive	IHRM strategies/policies/goals/outcomes:	Mimetic
Implementation of IHRM policy as a result of institutional forces, for example: • government • HQ • regulators	**Symbolic:** for example reputation, status, identity, 'ceremonial conformity' **Substantive:** for example recruitment, selection, retention, development, reward, etc	*Imitation* of IHRM policy as a result of uncertainty/fashion: • fashion-setters • consultancies • academics *Technical* • institutional work *Institutional entrepreneurship*

Normative

Orientation of staff control system towards IHRM

Emergent from changing professional norms emanating from professional bodies, for example the CIPD performing *cultural* institutional work

adapted from Iles et al (2010c: 140)

However, emphasising the adaptation of organisations to their societal and cultural (particularly institutional) environments, and the global diffusion and adoption of practices, downplays the role of national cultural and institutional differences and how such practices are locally interpreted or translated as they diffuse, an area we develop in Chapter 7 on international mergers, acquisitions and joint ventures (Czarniawska and Joerges 1996; Iles and Yolles 2002a, 2002b, 2003b; Iles et al 2004; Yolles and Iles 2006). There may be diffusion of a common global language, such as 'empowerment' or 'customer service', but leaving leeway for local interpretation and practice. In some countries, 'good customer service' may be signified by the use of first names; in others, titles. In some, 'networking' may signify playing golf with key contacts, in others, joining chambers of commerce, attending sports events or beach barbecues or joining local officials in karaoke and banquets. 'Impact' may signify participative leadership styles in some countries, authoritative direction in others, as we shall see in Chapter 5 on leadership. An 'over-socialised' view of actors leaves little scope for agency in the role actors play as 'interpreters', 'synthesisers' and 'hybridisers' in the local interpretation and implementation of globally diffused practices.

Gamble (2010: 728), in his study of the extent to which Japanese retail companies in China 'transferred' home practices, argues that existing theories, including culturalist, institutionalist, sectoral, agency and international division of labour perspectives, are shown to be inadequate, individually, to account for the complex patterns of transfer, local adoption, and adaptation in these multinational companies. These findings highlight the value of conceptual bricolage and multi-level analysis for developing explanations that can encompass and explicate complex patterns of hybridisation.

Context-specific, firm-level perceptions of sources of competitive advantage are key motives for transferring practices, constrained by the practices and norms prevalent in local labour markets. Some companies transferred home-country 'Japanese' practices such as job security for regular employees, reliance on internal labour markets and customer service, but did not often transfer others, such as part-time employment, careful recruitment, slow promotion, seniority pay or use of male supervisors. Some companies did, however, try to transfer some practices. In China, staff fines and bonuses were often introduced, absent in Japan. 'National' explanations, whether cultural or institutionalist, 'leave us with static, overly homogenised, and over-determined models' which 'neglect the extent of sub-national diversity' (Gamble 2010: 711–12) and 'transfer by multinational companies to transitional economies with high levels of deinstitutionalisation illustrates problematic dimensions for various theoretical perspectives, including influential neo-institutionalist models' (ibid: 705). The claim here is that it is increasingly difficult, given rapid change in a 'deinstitutionalising' environment, to discern a recognisable 'Chinese model' of work organisation and employment practice, and that various forms of 'hybrid' practice exist. Later chapters in Part 3, especially in relation to Africa and Latin America, explore whether this is a claim that can also be made about other emerging or transitional economies.

LEARNING SUMMARY

In this chapter we began by discussing the scope of IHRM and the particular focus taken in this book. Though IHRM is defined in various ways, and different writers draw different boundaries around it, the core areas concern getting the right people with appropriate experience, skills, knowledge and other attributes in the right place at the right time on a global scale. These activities, whether conducted by large multinational companies, small companies or public service organisations, are carried out in a rapidly changing global context. We discussed how IHRM differs from domestic HRM in being concerned with global location, national and cultural differences, and different categories of staff – HCNs, PCNs and TCNs. We then analysed a particular approach to analysing national differences based on institutional theories such as the 'national business systems' approach, and illustrated this with particular reference to institutions concerned with vocational education and training or national HRD. We also explored the value of neo-institutionalist explanations in addressing issues of global convergence or divergence in IHRM practice and the diffusion or transfer of

IHRM across national boundaries, with a discussion of the limitations of this and other theoretical accounts prevalent in the field.

An alternative, or perhaps complementary, approach to analysing national differences is extensively discussed in Chapter 2 when we explore theories of culture and their implications for HRM. We then begin to analyse IHRM policy at the firm level in Chapter 3, with particular reference to the 'international orientation' of the firm.

National Difference, Culture and IHRM

Crystal Zhang and Paul Iles

LEARNING OUTCOMES

By the end of the chapter, you should be able to:

- Understand the concept of culture.
- Appreciate the importance of culture to international human resource management.
- Explain Hofstede's and Trompenaars' models of national culture.
- Appreciate the difficulties in conducting cross-cultural research.
- Critically analyse the contribution of concepts of culture and culturalist perspectives to IHRM.

INTRODUCTION

Cross-cultural management is not a new topic. Cross-cultural research can be traced back as early as the tenth century from the Arab scholar Abu al-Rayhan al-Biruni (973–1048), possibly the earliest pioneer in cross-cultural studies in the anthropology of religions. He compared human behaviour and culture as influenced by different religions, arguing that all cultures have unique common human elements which make them distinct from all other cultures (Rosenthal 1976).

The study of culture has remained a vital field in anthropology, psychology and OB, analysed and debated by the early anthropologists from the nineteenth century. From the 1950s to the 1970s, there was rigorous theoretical development in the anthropology discipline on the understanding of culture. Keesing (1974) distinguished between the *ecological* and the *ideational* theory of culture; in the former perspective, culture is conceptualised as adaptive systems, while in the latter aspect, culture is seen as cognitive, structural and symbolic systems. In 1980, with the publication of *Culture's Consequences*, Hofstede (1980) initiated a fundamental shift in how culture would be viewed and studied, leading to an explosion of empirical investigations into cross-cultural differences.

In Chapter 1, we pointed out that, despite globalisation (Chapter 3), national differences – especially in organisational forms, managerial practice and HRM systems – remain pervasive; why should this be? We introduced two main perspectives on this – culturalist and institutionalist approaches – and discussed in some detail one institutionalist approach to this question, the 'national business systems' perspective. In this chapter, we discuss in more depth 'culturalist' explanations of national differences and their implications for IHRM.

But what is culture? And why is it such an important driving force in our daily life? Why is it important for us to understand culture? Human beings are social animals who live in social groups; we are also an adapting species, given the diverse civilisations we have created over thousands of years. Each individual has a unique background, history, upbringing and personality. Even though there are common values and behaviours, these differences lead to different forms of social interaction and form the unique identity of a group; unwritten rules on how to do things, how to behave or how to adapt into a group are referred to as its 'culture'. Culture can be represented by symbols, signs, heroes, religions, taboos, laws, rituals, customs, etc. How to adapt into a new group or culture is a fundamental challenge to all human beings, especially with globalisation, migration and the growth of international business. With increasing globalisation and social mobility (Chapter 3), it is therefore important to understand the origins and historical development of this controversial, paradoxical and evolving concept, and its impact and implications for cross-culture management theories and practices and IHRM (Bird and Fang 2009). It is equally important to equip ourselves, and employees, with those skills and competence to be able to survive in this new era. This chapter will therefore lay the foundation stones of some of the fundamental milestones in the research of culture as a concept, before ending with a critical discussion of its value to IHRM research and policy. In Part 2 we explore this in greater depth by reference to the contribution of cultural theories to a series of topics of great relevance to IHRM.

OBSERVING AND ANALYSING CULTURE

In one sense, cultural research can be easily conducted: one simply needs to open their eyes and observe the surroundings. Below is a quotation from social anthropologist Kate Fox about her training as a cultural explorer (or ethnographer). It succinctly summarises what to look for in culture: rules, which include both the official and the hidden sets on how to behave, to do things and to fit in with the observed culture:

> By the time we left England, and I embarked on a rather erratic education at a random sample of schools in America, Ireland and France, my father had manfully shrugged off his disappointment over the chimp experiment, and begun training me as an ethnographer instead. I was only five, but he generously overlooked this slight handicap: I might be somewhat shorter than his other students, but that shouldn't prevent me grasping the basic principles of ethnographic research methodology. Among the most important of these, I learned, was the search for rules. When we arrived in any unfamiliar culture, I was to look for regularities and consistent patterns in the natives' behaviour, and try to work out the hidden rules—

the conventions or collective understandings—governing these behavior patterns. (Fox 2004: 7)

However, to understand culture, you need tools guiding you as to what to look for; and different theories provide different answers to this question.

THE CONCEPT OF CULTURE

La culture, c'est ce qui reste quand on a tout oublié.

(Culture is what is left if you forgot all else.)

This quote comes from Edouard Herriot, a French politician and pioneer of European unity, and sums up one view of the concept of culture. It is not a material 'thing' that can be touched or held in the hand, but something within us. It can represent the values of a country, or the elitist aspects of a society's achievements, as in the use of the term 'high culture' to refer to art, classical music and opera, for example, and an appreciation of good literature, music, art and food. The word itself comes from the Latin for 'cultivation' and was introduced into English in the fifteenth century to represent the cultivation of the soul or mind, in the same manner as the cultivation of the land by a farmer. Thus culture in this sense enhances our appreciation of life and is an intrinsic part of it.

CULTURE FROM AN ANTHROPOLOGICAL PERSPECTIVE

A nation's culture resides in the hearts and the soul of its people.
(Mohandas Gandhi)

For anthropologists and other behavioural scientists, culture refers to the full range of learned human behaviour patterns, and more extensive work on cross-cultural studies was carried out in the nineteenth century. The term was first used in this way by Edward B. Tylor, the first professor of anthropology at Oxford University, in *Primitive Culture* published in 1871 (note the title reveals an issue bedevilling much debate on culture, as 'difference' easily slips into 'deficient'; many people, including researchers, judge 'different' cultures as 'deficient' ones, emphasised by the early twentieth-century German use of the term 'Kultur'). He defined culture as 'that complex whole which includes knowledge, belief, art, law, morals, custom, and any other capabilities and habits acquired by man (sic) as a member of society' (Holden 2002: 21).

Sir Francis Galton became the first to introduce the problem of cultural group independence in his work on correlation (Bird and Fang 2009). His critiques on Tylor's study involved claims that the processes of culture transfusion created relationships that cannot be easily disentangled, and culture groups could not be regarded truly independent from one another (Lindridge 2005, quoted in Bird and Fang 2009). We return to this argument in Chapter 3 when we discuss the concept of 'hybridisation', or 'cross-vergence', in IHRM; HRM systems and practices are complex mixtures of home- and host-country practice, as we explore in Part 4 when we discuss HRM in China, Africa, India and Latin America in particular.

Another important point is that cultures are dynamic and constantly evolving; for example, the Oxford English Dictionary is updated every year, adding new words to reflect vibrant changes in language and culture. Many 'English' words, such as bungalow, shampoo, chintz, chutney, jute, juggernaut, thug, pyjamas and gymkhana originate from Indian languages; others, such as tycoon, tea, typhoon or ketchup, from Chinese languages, reflecting great linguistic hybridisation. Acronyms used in text and Internet instant messages, such as OMG, LOL and FYI, were officially added to the dictionary in 2011. Our written and spoken languages, governments, buildings and other man-made things are the products of culture, not culture in themselves, but given meaning by culture. For this reason, archaeologists cannot dig up culture directly in excavations; broken pots and other artefacts of ancient people are only material remains that reflect cultural patterns, things that were made and used through cultural knowledge, skills and concepts.

Similarly, the material things around us represent our culture; a retrospective look at the evolution of the mobile phone, for example, would arouse a smile and memories from those who had experienced/used/seen the first brick-like portable phones. Artefacts act as reminders and triggers; when people see them, they think about their meaning and hence are reminded of their identity as a member of the culture, and, by association, of the rules of the culture. In the book *The Man in the High Castle* by Philip K. Dick, one of the characters discusses the concept of history associated with an item: '"I mean, a gun goes through a famous battle, like the Meuse-Argonne, and it's the same as if it hadn't, *unless you know*. It's in here." He tapped his head. In the mind, not the gun.' In this example, a gun was just a gun, unless *you know* its history and that it was a gun used at a famous battle. Then that gun would trigger a completely different feeling. Another example would be the Elgin Marbles, in the British Museum, which would arouse very different feelings from the British and the Greeks, or the Turks, who first sold them to the British when Greece was part of the Ottoman Empire. A Ming or Qing porcelain vase associated with an emperor will have much greater monetary value to a contemporary Chinese buyer than an equally beautiful one whose provenance is debated, as Gammack and Stephens (1994: 73) claim: 'rather than viewing knowledge as a disembodied commodity that can be removed from its context for independent analysis, the explicit construction of knowledge is seen as a process meaningful to the knowers involved in producing it'.

One of the strengths of the 'cultural' perspective is that it reminds us that the social world is a world of inter-subjectivities and 'multiple constructed realities' (Lincoln and Guba 1985: 295) and participant actions explained by understanding the subjective dimensions of their behaviour (Corbin and Strauss 2008), arguments key to symbolic interactionist (Mead 1934) and social constructionist (Berger and Luckmann 1967) accounts of social and organisational reality. It draws attention to the role of 'symbols', triggers to remind people of rules, beliefs and expectations, shorthand ways to keep people aligned and indicate status within a culture, including clothing. When working with Rover, one of us (Iles) noticed that the engineers during the 1990s alliance with Honda wore, like everyone else, the same uniform, symbolising the 'equality of functional contribution' often stressed in Japanese companies, but they quickly switched to smart suits to indicate their higher status under the BMW acquisition, where engineers were now the privileged group!

Office decor and layout and non-verbal communication (for example open-plan offices or 'hot-desks' as opposed to larger, better-furnished offices being associated with higher organisational status; the depth of the bow in Japan being tied to status) also serve as cultural symbols. Status symbols signal the 'correct behaviour' with respect to others in the hierarchy, alerting users of prescribed behaviours appropriate to status and position. For example, the Mercedes-Benz logo is an icon representing a high-value automobile brand, but that symbolism would be lost to someone not familiar with the culture.

A danger here is that 'culture' is seen in a deterministic, monolithic way, neglecting possibilities of change, challenge and resistance; if explanations of human action derive from the meanings and interpretations of actors under study (Gill and Johnson 2010: 61–2), are they not better accessed through qualitative methods and induction, often used by anthropologists, to understand the meanings and interpretations of participants rather than the positivist survey methods often employed in the study of culture (for example Hofstede 2001)?

Organisational members deploy meaning 'in making sense of their worlds and which influence their ongoing social construction and accomplishment of meaningful action' (Gill and Johnson 2010: 62; Glaser 1978; Ritchie and Spencer 1994; Alvesson and Deetz 2000). Highly structured methodological approaches may impose an external logic distorting access to subjective domains, including cultural meanings. Monolithic accounts of 'culture' may tend to play up false concepts of fixity and stability, and play down subcultures and conflicting cultures within a given society.

Within discussions of organisational behaviour (OB) a distinction is often made between those who see organisational culture as a variable, a 'part' of the organisation (culture is something that an organisation has, one entity that adds to the organisation as a whole, able to be manipulated and altered depending on leadership and members) from those who see it as 'the same as the organisation', a 'root metaphor' for something that the organisation is and created through communication and symbols, or competing metaphors (Modaff et al 2011; Smircich 1983; Brewis 2005). Hofstede (2001) takes a 'culture as variable' stance; national culture is something a nation 'has', a basically functionalist and unitarist perspective.

Romani (2011) has extended this 'interpretive' perspective focusing on meaning, symbol and inter-subjective understanding to national culture through a discussion of the usefulness of cultural metaphors, such as fine wine for France or American football for the USA, to help people make sense of their realities and contexts. A conference involving two organisations engaged in a merger (Chapter 7) may use, in addition to individual and group work and presentations, creative drama and imagery such as drawings of how participants saw their respective organisational cultures and skits dramatising incidents illustrative of organisational cultures to obtain large-group consensus on the kind of 'preferred culture' for the new organisation.

Romani (2011) also discusses 'critical views' of culture interested in issues of power, discourse and the silencing of some voices while privileging others. One example is 'postcolonial theory', questioning the 'reality' of cultural differences and asking what ends or agendas they serve. One example is the work of Jackson (2012a: 2901) on the informal economy in Africa, which we discuss further in Chapter 11. Cross-cultural perspectives should take in the geopolitical context of informal organisations and the power relationships involved, drawing on postcolonial theory to 'better understand the nature and role of such organisation within an interface of structural and phenomenological influences that question the nature of the "indigenous" as an artefact'. In Chapter 11 we also discuss China's growing involvement in Africa; Jackson (2012b) seeks to analyse China's previous anti-colonial relationship with Africa to understand the extent to which its engagement is giving voice to African management.

CULTURE FROM A NATIONAL LEVEL

In the 1994 Quentin Tarantino crime film *Pulp Fiction*, one of the characters recalls his experiences of Europe: fries with mayonnaise rather than ketchup, beer in bottles rather than plastic cups in cinemas and the iconic translation of the McDonald's hamburger *Quarter Pounder with Cheese* into *Royale with Cheese* in France. His partner on screen was amazed by these cultural differences; he would probably be even more amazed if he knew that he could order boiled rice instead of fries as a side order for a Kentucky Fried Chicken meal in Asian countries. Food is an intrinsic part of culture, and the little differences in food consumption can easily reveal differences among countries in the world. *Culture* here is and has often served simply as a synonym for *nation* without any further conceptual grounding, a point we shall discuss later. Thus, Italy is famous for pizzas and pastas, India for curries and China for rice.

 MCDONALD'S AND ITS INTERNATIONAL MARKET STRATEGY

CASE STUDY 2.1

McDonald's, the leading global food service retailer with more than 30,000 local restaurants, serves 52 million people in more than 100 countries each day. The golden arches form one of the world's most well-known and valuable brands, and McDonald's holds a leading share in the global market of fast food restaurant segments in virtually every country in which it operates (http://www.mcdonalds.com/corp/about.html).

Look at the website above. What do you think of the marketing strategy of McDonald's in different countries and how it has adapted its product offer in international environments? For further information on this, see below.

Further reading

Dash, K. (2005) McDonald's in India. *Harvard Business Review.* September.

Ko, S. and Woo, C.H.L. (2008) McDonald's: Is China lovin' it? *Harvard Business Review.* December.

Vignali, C. (2001) McDonald's: 'think global, act local' – the marketing mix.

British Food Journal. Vol 103, No 2. pp97–111.

Vrontis, D. and Pavlou, P. (2008) The external environment and its effect on strategic marketing planning: a case study for McDonald's. *Journal of International Business and Entrepreneurship Development.* Vol 4, No 3/4. pp289–307.

The invention of 'nations', political units into which the entire world is now divided and to one of which every human being is supposed to belong – as manifested by his or her passport – is a recent phenomenon in human history (Hofstede 2001: 13). Over decades, there has been increased movement of people across borders, looking for work and settling down in foreign countries; for example, Britain has had a large movement of immigrants from Second World War refugees from Europe, from Commonwealth colonies in Asia and in the Caribbean, and more recently from Central and Eastern European countries, changing and moulding British culture. The British staple of fish and chips came from Jewish immigrants, and curry is an undeniable part of current British culture. However, there are times when an indigenous culture may feel threatened by incoming cultures, prompting populist politicians to ask for immigration caps and provoke soul-searching over what constitutes a national culture and identity. As Queen Elizabeth II celebrates her 60 years on the throne, the notion of Britishness and British culture is under intense strain as Scottish politicians attempt to break away from the UK.

While the United Kingdom has now devolved into English, Welsh, Scottish and Northern Irish nations, European countries have been coming together to form a European Union, an eclectic and complex mixture of differing cultures from the 'cold industrious North' to the 'warm relaxed South'. During the current (2012) European financial crisis, cultural stereotypes (for example lazy Greeks, bossy Germans and chauvinistic French) have been used by the media as a short-hand way to explain the problems. In 2012, six leading national European newspapers undertook a joint project named Project Europa in an attempt to understand 'Euroscepticism' and national stereotypes (www.guardian.co.uk/world/series/europa).

The British were thought to be *drunken semi-clad hooligans or snobbish, stiff free-marketeers, and very obsessed with the world wars and the weather.* The Germans were considered to be *uber-efficient, diligent, disciplined and prone to steal the best sun loungers on holiday.* On the other hand, the Spanish were thought to be *macho men and fiery women prone to regular siestas, so that nothing ever gets done.* However, Spain is no longer a country of siestas, and the 38.4-hour Spanish working week is actually longer than those in Germany (37.7), Italy (38) and France (35.6), showing the persistence of cultural stereotypes.

 REFLECTIVE ACTIVITY 2.1

NATIONAL STEREOTYPES AND CHARACTERISTICS

The *Guardian* newspaper in the UK has joined together with leading European newspapers

(*Spiegel* in Germany, *Le Monde* in France, *El Pais* in Spain and *Gazeta Wyborcza* in Poland) to start Project EUROPA in order to understand the new Europe. In the United Kingdom, too often Europe is discussed and reported through its common institutions or purely in terms of its relations with Britain. Who are these neighbours in Europe? What are their lives? Their cultures? Their aspirations? And, more importantly, are these stereotypes true? Or should we be debunking them?

Questions

1   Describe national characteristics and stereotypes you think of within Europe. How true to reality do you think they are?

2   How useful do you think it is to describe national differences as 'cultural differences'?

3   What are the culture differences/ similarities between the UK (or another country) and another country of your choice?

4   Will these differences/similarities, if any, make it more difficult/easier for a British manager (or manager from your chosen country) to conduct business there?

Further reading

http://www.guardian.co.uk/world/series/new-europe

THE WORK OF GEERT HOFSTEDE AND ITS IMPLICATIONS FOR IHRM

Geert Hofstede, a Dutch cultural anthropologist, defined a very commonly used set of models for international cultures, defining two types of culture (Hofstede 1991). Culture 1 refers to anthropological culture, that is, civilisation, education, literature. Culture 2 refers to a broader and more fundamental human process, for example how people greet, eat, demonstrate emotions and keep a physical distance from others, also referred to as 'the collective programming of the mind which distinguishes the members of one group or category of people from another. Culture in this sense is a system of collectively held values.'

Using a unique database of responses from IBM employees throughout the world, Hofstede initially analysed cultural differences along four dimensions (Hofstede et al 2010) and rated 58 countries on each of them on a scale from 1 to 100. A further two dimensions were added to the initial four. The six dimensions were based on the following theoretical constructs:

1 POWER

Hofstede named this power distance (PD or PDI). It refers to the extent to which less powerful members expect and accept unequal power distribution. High PD cultures usually have centralised, top–down control. Low power distance implies greater equality and empowerment. Malaysia, Panama and Guatemala rated the highest in PDI. India, China, Russia and much of Africa and Latin America score highly on this dimension.

2 PREDICTABILITY

Hofstede named this uncertainty avoidance (UA or UAI). It defines the extent to which a culture values predictability. UA cultures have strong traditions and rituals and tend towards formal, bureaucratic structures and rules. Greece was number one here, followed by Portugal and Guatemala. Russia, France and Japan score highly on UAI, as do much of Latin America, but not China or Singapore.

3 SELF

Hofstede named this individualism versus collectivism (ID or IDV). In an individual environment individual people and their rights are more important than the groups they may belong to; in a collective environment, people are born into strong extended family or tribal communities and these loyalties are paramount. The US was first in IND here, closely followed by Australia and Great Britain; many Asian and African countries, such as Brazil, China and India, were more 'collectivist'.

4 GENDER

Hofstede named this dimension masculinity versus femininity (MAS). It focuses on the degree to which 'traditional' gender roles are assigned in a culture; that is, men are considered aggressive and competitive, while women are expected to be gentler and be concerned with home and family. Japan led the MAS list, followed by Austria and Venezuela; Nordic countries scored as much more 'feminine' (and, interestingly, have by far the greatest proportion of women in leading political and economic roles). India, Brazil and China also score highly on masculinity.

5 TIME

Hofstede named this long- versus short-term orientation (LTO). It is the cultural trait that focuses on to what extent the group invests for the future, is persevering and is patient in waiting for results. This dimension, also known as Confucian dynamism, was proposed following a Chinese value survey based on traditional Chinese cultural values, and represented Confucian values in Chinese and other East Asian societies influenced by Confucianism, such as Korea, Vietnam and Japan. As such, China led on this dimension, followed by Hong Kong and Taiwan. It refers to the capacity to adapt traditions to new situations, willingness to save, a thrifty approach to scarce resources, a willingness to persevere over the long term and subordinate one's own interests to achieve a purpose, and a concern with virtue (Bond 1988; Hofstede and Bond 1988). This dimension did not appear in Hofstede's original work, but was identified as important by Chinese scholars among Chinese employees.

6 HAPPINESS

Hofstede named this indulgence versus restraint; it is a newly added construct, loosely correlated to LTO, and focuses on gratification. In an indulgent society, there is relatively free gratification of 'natural' human desires related to enjoying life and having fun. In a restraint society, strict social norms control and regulate gratification. As might be expected, America and western Europe are indulgent societies, while many Asian and Muslim countries are more restrained.

Hofstede (2001) has emphasised that 'culture' is best seen as the set of commonly held and relatively stable beliefs, attitudes and values that exist within an organisation (organisational or corporate culture) or society (national or societal culture), influencing the way that it undertakes and implements its decision-making, resolves its problems and, in general, behaves. Culture is thus embodied in symbols, rituals and heroes, reflected in organisational communication: manners, dress codes, social rules and norms, and role models.

Like macroscopic (national) culture, microscopic (organisational) culture also comprises corporate values, norms, feelings, hopes and aspirations. For Hofstede (1987), national culture thus has *values* as its central component.

Hofstede has integrated these dimensions into national models: for example, the UK is said to resemble a 'village market', with low uncertainty avoidance, individualism and low power distance; Germany is a 'well-oiled machine', with higher uncertainty avoidance and power distance; France, with high power distance, is more of a 'pyramid'; and India, the Middle East and other Asian countries, with high collectivism and power distance, are more of a 'family'.

These dimensions have implications for comparative HRM, as we will explore in Parts 2 and 3. In the UK, there will be a stress on interpersonal, communication and negotiation skills in managers, perhaps assessed through assessment centres and psychometric tests; in Germany, a stress on technical competence, assessed through the education/apprenticeship system; in France, a stress on analytical skills and on 'elite' potential, assessed through the education system and background in elite institutions such as 'grandes ecoles'; in much of Asia and the Middle East, a stress on family connections. In the Nordic countries, with their high 'femininity' scores, both genders are more likely to pursue more personally satisfying rather than hierarchically oriented careers. As we shall see in Chapter 3, IEs from countries high in uncertainty avoidance (for example Japan) seem more likely to make extensive use of expatriates (parent-country nationals) to control overseas operations than those from countries low in uncertainty avoidance (for example USA, UK, the Nordic countries).

Hofstede's work has received sustained criticism, especially on the publication of the second edition of the original book (Hofstede 2001: 2), for example Smith (2002) and McSweeney (2001, 2002). Hofstede's analysis was carried out many years ago; it was done on a country-by-country basis; it may not hold in countries where there are strong subcultures based on ethnic origin or geography; it was done on a single company. Uncertainty avoidance did not emerge as a distinct dimension in his Chinese study, but long-term orientation did. Are four (or five or six) dimensions sufficient to capture the complexity of national culture?

There have been many critiques concerning the use of nation-states as the basic unit of analysis (McSweeney 2002; Soderberg and Holden 2002). In Canada, for instance, there is a distinct French Canadian culture with quite a different set of norms compared with English-speaking Canada. A Spanish firm from Barcelona investing in Perpignan in France will not experience cultural difference as much as one from Granada investing in Lens. In Italy, masculinity scores differ between north and south. Hofstede generalised national cultures into theoretical constructs; the dimensions identified are perhaps best regarded as approximations, although many would criticise the over-generalisation (for example Ailon 2008).

Hofstede appears to assume that national territory corresponds to cultural homogeneity, but China, as with many countries in Africa, or India, is not homogenous, with strong regional differences and minority ethnic/religious subcultures. There is also a problem with the use of some of his terms. For instance, the words 'individualism' and 'collectivism' appear to differ in meaning in different countries. As an instance of this, take employee loyalty (Mead 1994). Japanese employees may be seen to be loyal to their organisations, while Chinese and many Asian or African or Latin American employees may well be more loyal to their families. However, both adopt the principle of 'collectivism' that differs from Western individualism.

Hofstede himself has acknowledged the limits of his model (Hofstede 2011) and, in a speech in 2011, argued that cultural research suffers from seven deadly sins, one of which is 'level confusion' or confusion over value differences at individual, national or corporate levels.

REFLECTIVE ACTIVITY 2.2

Visit the following link and listen to Hofstede's recent speech: http://www.geerthofstede.nl

To what extent do Hofstede's dimensions reflect your understanding of your own culture? Provide two examples for your answers.

The fifth dimension (Confucian dynamism or LTO) has been particularly critiqued, though Hofstede has addressed the criticism through analysis of another dataset (the World Values Survey) instead of the Chinese values survey (Minkov and Hofstede 2012). Fang (2003) argued that the loose labels of "'short-term' and 'long-term' oriented" may not necessarily be appropriate, proposing to include the Chinese yin-yang philosophy as a bipolar dimension. Wu (2006) has also re-examined the significance of the LTO using Taiwanese and American respondents, demonstrating that work-related cultural values are not static and can be changed over time; there have been sufficiently influential political, societal and economic changes over the past 30 years to cause a change in people's values.

Fan (2002) has explored Chinese culture using Kluckhohn and Strodtbeck (1961), Hofstede (1980), and the 'Chinese Culture Collection' (Bond 1988) to develop a list of 71 values running across eight categories: national traits, interpersonal relations, family/social orientation, work attitude, business philosophy, personal traits, time orientation and relationship with nature. Confucianism provides both the behavioural and moral doctrine of human relationships, social structures, virtuous behaviour and ethics, extolling loyalty, duty, obedience, obligation, submission, seniority and trust.

However, recent organisational and HR reforms in China, such as performance-based reward and lower job security (Chapters 3 and 14), have led to generational differences in assumptions, beliefs and values between first-generation employees hired pre-reform and second-generation, younger employees hired post-reform

(Liu 2003). Younger workers, however, express greater unhappiness with regard to 'harmony' at the expense of poor performance, and see loyalty in less relational and in more conditional, contractual and calculative or 'transactional' ways.

Interestingly, not long ago the same 'Confucian' values supposedly promoting China's growth were held to be *holding it back* – which rather casts doubt on the value of these kinds of explanation! Other regions have shown similar patterns of cultural change; Arab cultures (Chapter 10) are often seen as masculine and middling on individualism, uncertainty avoidance and power distance, with family the cornerstone of social life and social identity, and loyalty oriented to the 'wider' extended family. However, there has been a diminution in size of the typical household and again, as in China, a tendency for younger generations to have a more independent life (Suliman 2006). In much of North Africa, more individualised work values have also emerged (Mellahi 2006; Yahiaouni and Zoubir 2006). Horwitz (2012) and Kamoche and Newenham-Kahindi (2012) argue that collectivist 'African values' like *ubuntu* (inter-connectedness and interdependence, to be discussed much more in Chapter 11 on HRM in Africa) hold more appeal for older, male employees than younger, female ones, indicating that different sections of the workforce did not share a common set of cultural values, as in China.

In summary, Hofstede's impact on the field has been at least fourfold (Bird and Fang 2009: 140): (1) theoretically and methodologically, by adopting nation/state culture as the basic unit of analysis, he succeeded in narrowing the concept of culture into more concise and measurable components; (2) he established culture values as a key impact on organisational behaviour; (3) his theory enhanced awareness of cultural variations; and (4) his culture paradigm inspired other scholars and practitioners in large-scale studies, such as the GLOBE project, which we explore in more detail in Part 2 when we look at leadership and leadership development (Chapter 5).

OTHER MODELS OF CULTURE: SCHWARTZ, TROMPENAARS AND HAMPDEN-TURNER

There has been much interest in understanding how to differentiate cultures ever since the work of Hofstede (1980), with a variety of approaches. Schwartz (1990) believed there are difficulties with Hofstede's classifications; collectivism/individualism has values that are common, and the dichotomy implies a polar distinction in which individual and collective goals cannot be coincident (Gouveia and Ros 2000). His main model includes seven dimensions: conservatism; hierarchy; mastery; affective autonomy; intellectual autonomy; egalitarian commitment; and harmony. Trompenaars (1997), perhaps the most-cited model after Hofstede (2001), classified cultures along a mixture of behavioural and value patterns, assimilating 30,000 responses from business executives selected and drawn from 55 countries to identify seven value orientations. The seven value dimensions identified were:

1   *Universalism versus particularism* (rules and procedures as opposed to relationships): universalism is about finding broad and general rules.

Particularism is about finding exceptions. When no rules fit, it judges the case on its own merits.

2   *Communitarianism versus individualism*: individualism is about the rights of the individual and sees group-focus as denuding the individual of their inalienable rights. In contrast, communitarianism is about the rights of the group or society, seeking to put the family, group, company and country before the individual. It sees individualism as selfish and short-sighted. Individualism is viewed as competitive while communitarianism promotes cooperation.

3   *Neutral versus emotional* (concealing emotions as opposed to showing emotions): a streamlined and machine-efficient culture prefers a neutral outlook where interactions are objective and detached and where there is less chance of emotions confusing the issue, assumed to be a characteristic of the colder north-western countries of northern Europe and America. In contrast, warmer southern European and many Latin American and African countries prefer to conduct business with emotions.

4   *Diffuse versus specific cultures* (superficial as opposed to deep relationships): similar to the previous dimension, as in diffuse cultures, everything is connected, and this integration helps construct the big picture, which is important for building trust. In contrast, specific cultures assume that separation of work and life is the way to success.

5   *Achieved status versus ascribed status*: that is, who one is as opposed to what one does. Achieved status is gained through performance, whereas ascribed status is gained through other means, such as seniority or gender or social class, by right rather than daily performance. It finds order and security in knowing where status is, and where it stays.

6   *Time as sequence versus time as synchronisation*: time as sequence sees events as separate items in time, sequencing one after another; time as synchronisation sees events in parallel, synchronised together, finding order in the coordination of multiple efforts.

7   *Human–nature relationship*: orientations to nature influence the way we conduct our day-to-day lives and businesses. If we believe we can and should control nature by imposing our will, we are described as inner-directed. In contrast, to believe that we should 'go with the flow' is to be outer-directed.

For Dahl (2004), individualism and ascribed status seem broadly consistent with Hofstede's (2001) individualism and power distance; the other dimensions focus more on effects of underlying value dimensions. Thus the neutral/emotional dimension describes the extent to which feelings are openly expressed, relating to normative behaviours rather than values. Universalism/particularism describes a preference for rules rather than trusting relationships, and could be interpreted as part of Hofstede's uncertainty avoidance dimension, as well as the collectivist/individualist dimension. The diffuse/specific value classification describes range of involvement. The human–time relationship appears to be Hall's (1984) polychromic/monochronic time perceptions, and the human–nature relationship closely connected with the human–nature relationship in Kluckhohn and Strodtbeck (1961).

Trompenaars and Hampden-Turner have also summarised their cultural factors into a model of corporate culture, assuming that differences in national cultures help determine the type of corporate culture chosen. The four corporate models are:

1   *incubator* (fulfilment-oriented)

2   *guided missile* (project-oriented)

3   *Eiffel Tower* (role-oriented)

4   *family* (person-oriented).

Figure 2.1: Trompenaars and Hampden-Turner's four corporate cultural models

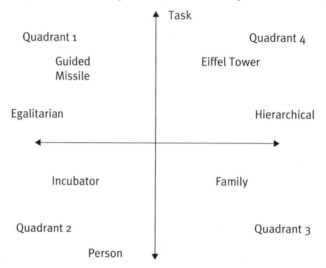

Each model represents a distinct characteristic in terms of relationship between employees, attitude to authority, ways of thinking and learning, attitudes to people and to managing change. These are summarised below.

RELATIONSHIP BETWEEN EMPLOYEES

Families, for example many Indian companies, show diffuse relationship to an organic whole to which one is bonded; Eiffel Towers, for example many French companies, show specific roles in a mechanical system of required interactions. Guided missiles, for example many German companies, show specific tasks in a cybernetic system targeted upon shared objectives, while incubators, for example many Nordic companies, show diffuse spontaneous relationships growing out of shared creative processes.

ATTITUDE TO AUTHORITY

In families, status is ascribed to parent figures who are close and all-powerful; in Eiffel Towers, status is ascribed to superior roles who are distant yet powerful. In contrast, in guided missiles, status is achieved by project group members who contribute to the targeted goal, and in incubators, status is achieved by individuals exemplifying creativity and growth.

WAYS OF THINKING AND LEARNING

Families show intuitive, holistic, lateral and error-correcting, in contrast to logical, analytical, vertical and rationally efficient Eiffel Towers. Guided missiles are problem-centred, professional, practical and cross-disciplinary, while incubators are process-oriented, creative, ad hoc and inspirational.

ATTITUDES TO PEOPLE

Families treat people as family members; Eiffel Towers as human resources; guided missiles as specialists and experts; incubators as co-creators.

MANAGING CHANGE

In families, the 'father' (boss) changes course; in Eiffel Towers, the rules and procedures are changed; in guided missiles, the aim shifts as the target moves; while in incubators, the focus is on improvisation and attunement.

When working in other countries and with people from other countries, Trompenaars (1997) recommends that their national culture is determined and taken into account during interaction and negotiation. To measure these dimensions, Trompenaars and Hampden-Turner use a variety of dilemma scenarios and questions, which ask the reader to choose between two opposite answers (for example, 'if your friend is driving and is involved in an accident, but speeds away, do you report him to the police?' is one measure of universalistic values). A combination of the responses from different questions gives a scale. Responses from managers from specific countries are collated and placed on scales of each dimension, and the score read to obtain an estimate of that country's inclination. Thus a typical US manager can be placed 65% along the universalistic–particularistic scale – which does not mean that 65% of US managers chose the universalistic option (Woolliams 1997, cited in Trompenaars and Woolliams 2004).

REFLECTIVE ACTIVITY 2.3

To what extent do Trompenaars' theories reflect your understanding of your own culture? Provide two examples for your answers.

Can responses to dilemma scenarios really provide a true picture of the dimensions? Rai and Holyoak (2009) suggest that moral dilemma scenarios are prone to biases originating from the researchers themselves, rather than the respondents. This point was initially raised by Hofstede (1996), who questioned the conceptual categories presented by Trompenaars as dimensions, the validity of the model and the paucity of data used to support the dimensions.

Nonetheless, the Trompenaars database is a unique database of social data which, with better analysis tools and refinements, may offer a detailed and accurate interpretation of cultural differences. We return to this issue in Chapter 6 when we look at ethics and corporate social responsibility.

Finally, let us refer to some general criticisms of culturalist explanations of national difference (we have already mentioned some specific criticisms of Hofstede 2001). As we saw in Chapter 1, cultural explanations predict inhibition of parent-country diffusion of HRM practices to foreign affiliates and enhance the need for local responsiveness and isomorphism, but they cannot account for change over time or divergence within national populations … they also ignore the potential to implement innovative practices in novel settings … frequently, 'culture' provides a convenient catch-all 'black box', deployed to explain why MNCs cannot transfer their parent country organisational practices … in a way that closes off further analysis or explanation. (Gamble 2010: 708)

This is also broadly true of the institutionalist 'national business systems' approach, reminding us that we do not have all the answers to questions in IHRM. We should beware of placing too much faith in static, overly homogenised and over-determined models that neglect the agency of firms and individuals to shape and influence IHRM practices – though not always in circumstances and contexts of their own choosing, of course. We need to seek to understand and analyse these actions and interpretations within the social, national, cultural, economic, historical and political contexts in which such actions take place.

REFLECTIVE ACTIVITY 2.4

How might cultural differences have an impact on one of the following: learning and training, perception and motivation, leadership, and teamwork?

LEARNING SUMMARY

Gelfand et al (2007) argue that the study of cross-cultural differences in the workplace 'has a long past but a short research history'. Hofstede, Lewis, Schwartz and Trompenaars have paved the way to an appreciation of cultural differences and its impact in a business setting, though not without criticisms, such as taking the nation as the unit of analysis, ignoring subcultures, perpetuating stereotypes, and downplaying change, instability and resistance. The 'valuing diversity' approach argues that cultural differences should be recognised as a resource and an asset for the organisation; dealing with cross-cultural conflicts successfully will improve creativity, innovation and adaptiveness, enhance productivity and improve competitive advantage. It is crucial that cultural theories are taken in their context and not applied to other levels for which they were not designed; they do not provide a complete analysis of national differences, but may complement other kinds of analysis, such as institutional approaches and national business systems approaches discussed in Chapter 1. Molinsky (2007) found that to operate effectively in unfamiliar and foreign cultural situations, one needed to be able to culturally code-switch, changing the 'cultural programming' to fit the local culture; ethnocentrism is probably not a good attribute in our global culture. The speed of communication and the scale of international trade mean that we and our cultures are interacting with each other on more occasions and levels than a decade ago. To effectively sail across the sea of cultures will require an awareness of ourselves in the world and an appreciation of others, a point we will develop in Part 2 as we apply culturalist theories to specific IHRM issues, in Part 3 as we explore specific regions, and in Part 4 as we analyse specific enterprise policies.

CHAPTER 3

Globalisation and IHRM Policies at the Enterprise Level

Paul Iles

LEARNING OUTCOMES

By the end of this chapter, you should be able to:

- Critically analyse the changing impact of globalisation on IHRM.

- Analyse the impact of globalisation and informatisation on organisations, and especially on IHRM.

- Critically evaluate different approaches to and frameworks in IHRM with particular reference to host country, country of origin and firm effects.

- Understand the IHRM policies of the international enterprise.

- Discuss the advantages and disadvantages of different orientations to IHRM, with particular reference to regiocentric approaches.

INTRODUCTION: IHRM IN CONTEXT: THE CHANGING WORLD OF WORK AND ORGANISATIONS

This chapter discusses the 'globalisation' thesis and its implications for IHRM policy and practice, especially the contention that in an ever-more globalised world, HRM policies and practices are diffusing and 'converging' to a standard model, despite the national, cultural and institutional differences explored in Chapter 1. We explore a selection of contextual themes relevant to an understanding of the changing nature of IHRM, in particular globalisation and 'informatisation', especially the rise of ICT (information and communication technologies) and their impact on HRM. We do not attempt in this chapter to review all the factors in the business environment that may impact on IHRM, as some of this is dealt with elsewhere in the book, but we return to some of these themes when we look more closely at IHRM policies and operations in later sections (especially in Part 3 on the regional context). We do, however, discuss various theoretical frameworks to understand the *firm, home- and host-country contexts* of IHRM, as well as *contingent* factors impacting on IHRM, and especially the role of managerial 'international orientations'. We also explore the value of neo-institutionalist explanations in addressing the issue of global convergence or divergence in IHRM practice and the diffusion or transfer of IHRM across national boundaries.

REFLECTIVE ACTIVITY 3.1

What do you see as the current concerns and challenges facing global organisations today, and in the near future?

THE GLOBAL BUSINESS ENVIRONMENT

Two major trends shaping the contemporary business environment are *globalisation* and the impact of information and communication technologies, which we shall refer to as 'informatisation'. These have increased the unpredictability and dynamism of the business environment, and many organisations have sought to transform their IHRM practices to respond to these challenges. Organisations throughout the world are passing through a process of social and cultural change that is transforming not only their traditional values and beliefs, but also the way that they make decisions, including HR decisions, as Figure 3.1 shows.

Figure 3.1: The impact of globalisation and ICT on IHRM

(adapted from Iles and Yolles 2006)

THE IMPACT OF GLOBALISATION

Globalisation is shown in Figure 3.1 as affecting organisational viability through its impacts on organisational fitness. Globalisation can refer to many different economic, political and social phenomena; exposed to global competition, the survival and viability of organisations is brought into question. With globalisation, enterprises can gain access to global markets, which may, if they are transformed, lead to enhanced viability. Globalisation also acts directly on enterprises by pushing them towards restructuring in the face of increasing competitive pressures. ICT can also, however, impact on organisational viability by potentially enhancing their effectiveness, helping restructure enterprises by enabling them to improve their efficiency. If organisations are to respond to these twin challenges, they will need to transform their management and HRM processes, including their IHRM processes. If they do this successfully, they may, as Figure 3.1 shows, improve their ability to manage the impacts of globalisation and ICT through enhanced efficiency and effectiveness, and therefore enhanced viability.

Globalisation also affects organisational fitness as organisations attempt to change their paradigms (ways of doing things, or success recipes) to meet new demands as the rules that condition and facilitate their operations change. We will explore this in particular with the case of changes in the HRM paradigms adopted by Chinese organisations as they have opened up to increased Western and Japanese investment, altered ownership rules and gained access to the World Trade Organization (WTO) in 2001; however, many of these influences and processes are similar with respect to other countries, especially developing countries and emerging markets.

THE IMPACT OF GLOBALISATION: THE CASE OF CHINA

Globalisation has also affected IHRM practice in other ways: foreign direct investment (FDI) has been encouraged in the UK, China and many other countries, increasing the internationalisation of the economy. Japanese investors and their associated HR practices have played a key role in both the UK and China (Gamble 2010). In recent years, the increasing international integration of global economies, the global power of multinational companies and increasingly diverse workforces as a result of increased labour migration have also had major effects.

Box 3.1 illustrates some of these changes, while Box 3.2 discusses the impact of ICT (seen here in terms of 'informatisation').

BOX 3.1: WHAT IS GLOBALISATION?

Globalisation involves:

- a stretching of social, political and economic activities across frontiers, regions and continents
- an intensification, or the growing magnitude, of interconnectedness and flows of trade, investment finance, migration, culture, and so on
- a speeding up of global interactions and processes
- the development of worldwide systems of transport and communication increases the speed of diffusion of ideas, goods, information, capital and people

- a growing extensity, intensity and velocity of global interactions, which can be associated with their deepening impact such that the effects of distant events can be highly significant elsewhere
- specific local developments coming to have considerable global consequences
- the boundaries between domestic matters and global affairs becoming increasingly fluid.

As such, globalisation can be thought of as the widening, intensifying, speeding up and growing impact of world global interconnectedness.

(adapted from Iles and Yolles 2006)

BOX 3.2: WHAT IS INFORMATISATION?

This may be seen as the process through which information technologies (for example communication technologies and the World Wide Web) have transformed economic and social relations such that cultural and economic barriers are reduced:

- The technological innovations provoke radical cultural and social changes that will be fundamentally different from the status quo.
- In the post-industrial, information-based society, knowledge will be the driving force of society, rather than industrial technologies.
- The convergence of technologies will precipitate further changes that promise to fundamentally alter the human landscape, a process of change that features the use of informatisation and IT to such an extent that they become the dominant forces in economic, political, social and cultural development.
- A means through which there is accelerating growth in the speed, quantity and popularity of information production and distribution.

Informatisation is therefore the process whereby information and communication technologies shape cultural and civic discourse, including not just computers and the Internet, but other related technologies that involve the transfer of information, including more traditional media technologies, such as film, satellite television and telecommunications. As societies and economies reorient themselves around technologies, there are likely to be deep consequences for IHRM.

(adapted from Iles and Yolles 2006)

GLOBALISATION AND CHANGING IHRM PRACTICES

One example of the impact of globalisation on IHRM is provided by China and how its HR policies have been impacted by both ICT and by its accession to the World Trade Organization (WTO). Box 3.3 discusses the impact of WTO accession on Chinese organisations, a topic we will pursue further in Chapter 14 (Iles and Yolles 2006; Guo et al 2011).

BOX 3.3: WHAT IS THE IMPACT OF WTO ACCESSION IN CHINA?

- helps to encourage effective competition in organisations
- brings challenges; companies will have to transform themselves to enable them to deal with them. This will not only involve a change in management approach, but much more fundamental changes

- encourages international cooperation to help develop companies
- requires that organisations will have to pass through a transition due to the new set of international regulations and practices that WTO will bring
- trade liberalisation
- more privatisation and reduced state trading
- changes in economic and regulatory behaviour
- internationalisation of product standards
- rights for international import/export trading, leading to new product markets
- new rights to invest and establish subsidiaries
- right to choose one's own joint venture partner
- cultural conflicts will appear as China's enterprises balance the use of political connections with commercial considerations
- changes in effectiveness and efficiencies of companies
- greater failure rate for enterprises that do not understand the meaning and implication of the regulations

(adapted from Iles and Yolles 2006; Guo et al 2011)

These changes will have significant impacts for IHRM, to be explored further in Chapter 14 on HRM in China, such as:

- enhancing competition and efficiency in Chinese companies
- putting pressure on companies to recruit and select high-skilled staff, and encouraging the growth of performance management and the sacking of less productive workers
- putting a greater premium on talent management and career development
- allowing inefficient companies to go to the wall, increasing pressures on welfare systems
- encouraging greater foreign direct investment and joint ventures in China, and encouraging Chinese companies to acquire Western companies and invest abroad (for example the acquisition of Rover by car companies from Nanjing and Shanghai or the attempts by the state oil company SINOPEC to buy US oil companies).

China's joining of WTO is therefore helping to encourage effective competition in Chinese organisations, bringing many challenges. Companies will have to transform themselves to enable them to deal with these, not only involving changes in management approach, but also much more fundamental changes, including encouraging international cooperation to help develop companies and requiring that organisations will have to pass through a transition due to the new set of international regulations and practices that WTO accession brings (*China Daily* 2002).

Recent enterprise, property and ownership reforms have affected state-owned enterprises (SOEs), but despite greater autonomy they are still subject to intervention by an array of local, regional and national state agencies. Not all pressures are pushing them in the direction of corporatising and marketising reform, as they are still expected to play a social role in avoiding unrest over rising unemployment by promoting stability and employment.

International division of labour perspectives provide a useful corrective to the overemphasis on 'national differences', whether cultural or institutional, discussed in Chapter 1 (Walter and Zhang 2012). They argue that firms' HRM practices reflect a plant's position within the international division of labour. Wilkinson et al (2001) found that MNCs in the developed East Asian countries are often engaged in transferring production to China and Malaysia, based on a common HRM model of Taylorist work organisation and low-trust, low-commitment and low-investment relationships. In part this is driven by parent control, and in part by low host-country HRM capability – factors we explore further in Part 2. With the recruitment of young, female, less educated workers and the avoidance of ex-SOE employees, firms are often characterised by low skill levels, insecure employment, automation, mass production and considerable constraints on local HRM, with only rudimentary training offered to employees. However, though this perspective usefully draws attention to similarities between firms located in the same position in the 'new international division of labour', it finds it more difficult to account for differences between them, or the kinds of complex patterns of hybridisation found in, for example, China and Latin America; such an approach tends to neglect both societal effects (Chapter 1) and firm-level agency effects, which we explore in relation to international orientations (Gamble 2010).

With respect to issues of global convergence or divergence in HRM practices, discussed in Chapter 1, there is little evidence that China, Japan and South Korea, for example, are converging to an 'East Asian' model of HRM in terms of employee relations, flexible resourcing, performance-based reward and employee development, despite geographical and cultural proximity. Indeed, China, in terms of a more market-based system (alongside the persistence of 'guanxi', or connections) has moved more quickly to a Western-type system than Japan, especially in IJVs (international joint ventures), FIEs (foreign-invested enterprises) and larger SOEs. As Gamble (2010: 707) puts it, 'until recently one could draw parallels between employment regimes in these two countries. … however, HRM practices in China's transitional economy have been accelerating away from this model'. WTO entry is likely to lead to even greater downsizing and restructuring, especially in SOEs and in manufacturing.

UNDERSTANDING THE IHRM POLICIES OF THE INTERNATIONAL ENTERPRISE

Internationalisation and the effective use of international human resources located outside the home or parent country are major issues affecting enterprises in an increasingly global economy. A key issue is why and how enterprises adopt different HRM policies and practices in such areas as training, talent management and career development.

 REFLECTIVE ACTIVITY 3.2

What do you think are the main issues affecting enterprise IHRM policy?

You may have mentioned such factors as:

- managing geographical dispersion
- managing cultural diversity
- managing multi-cultural teams
- developing international competencies
- convergence in or divergence in IHRM across the globe
- global transfer of IHRM policies and practices through the activities of such global actors as MNCs, MBAs or consultancies – not only do MNCs tend to introduce similar practices across the globe, consultancies do too; and students studying MBAs and master's degrees may follow similar courses and read similar textbooks, making it more likely HRM practices may converge
- continued divergence of IHRM due to cultural and institutional country-level differences, especially in terms of how HRM policies are interpreted and adapted.

One useful framework (Budhwar and Debrah 2001) draws attention to the influence of three general factors; an IE's HRM policies and practices are the product of an interaction between these three factors:

1   *National-level factors*, such as culture, institutions and the national business system, discussed in Chapters 1 and 2; home (parent) country factors include domestic cultural, legal, political and economic factors and a dynamic business environment. Multinationals may remain deeply rooted in the national business systems of their country of origin – often termed 'country of origin' effects (Ferner 1997).

2   *Contingent factors*, such as organisational age, size, structure, ownership, stage of internationalisation, life cycle stage, trade union presence and stakeholder interests.

3   *Organisational factors*, such as corporate and HRM strategies. Firm-specific factors include senior management's attitudes towards internationalisation and the international strategy, structure and corporate culture of the firm, as well as policies relating to primary HR functions and internal labour markets.

In analysing HRM in developing countries, Budhwar and Debrah (2001) in practice select four national factors as particularly important – national culture; national institutions; dynamic business environment; and industrial sector – which form the 'macro environment' of firms understood in a national context, as depicted in Figure 3.2. We primarily use these dimensions to explore IHRM in a regional and comparative context in Part 3, especially the role of national culture and institutions (building on our analysis of these in Chapters 1 and 2).

Figure 3.2: Factors determining cross-national HRM practices

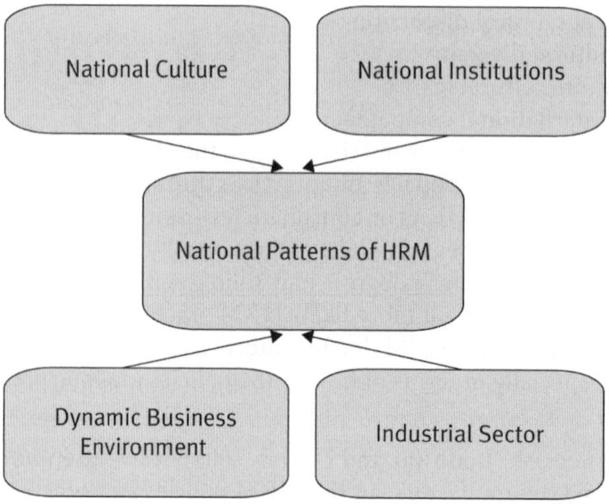

(adapted from Budhwar and Debrah 2001: 6)

An integrative model to study IHRM at the enterprise level – the concern of this chapter and Part 4, as HRM at the national or regional level is the subject of Chapters 1 and 2 as well as Part 3 – has been put forward by Shen et al (2005). This tries to move forward from a single-factor focus on factors associated with IHRM policy and practice, such as contextual factors such as the well-known PESTEL factors, or firm-specific factors such as international strategy, structure, culture, stage of internationalisation, mode of internationalisation, size, sector, reliance on international markets, top managers' perceptions or ownership type.

Evans and Lorange (1989) identified 'two logics' (product-market and socio-cultural factors) governing choice of IHRM policy; however, there are a number of intervening factors which may have a differentiated impact on IHRM policies and practices, such as:

- country of origin effects (Ferner 1997)
- host environmental effects: political, legal, economic and socio-cultural environments
- firm characteristics and other contingent effects.

Figure 3.3 presents an integrative framework for studying IHRM policy at the enterprise level, which we use in later sections of the book, based on Shen et al (2005).

Figure 3.3: An integrative IHRM framework

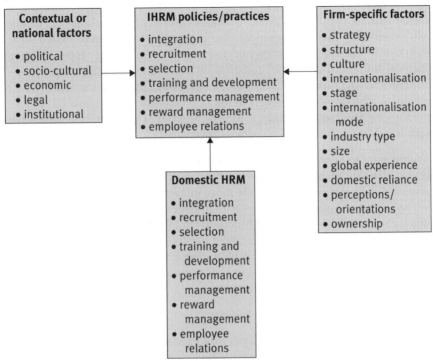

Contextual or national factors	IHRM policies/practices	Firm-specific factors
• political • socio-cultural • economic • legal • institutional	• integration • recruitment • selection • training and development • performance management • reward management • employee relations	• strategy • structure • culture • internationalisation • stage • internationalisation mode • industry type • size • global experience • domestic reliance • perceptions/ orientations • ownership

Domestic HRM

• integration
• recruitment
• selection
• training and development
• performance management
• reward management
• employee relations

(based on Shen et al 2005: 373; Budhwar and Debrah 2001)

There is empirical evidence for the influence of all of these factors; for example, Shen et al (2005) found that Chinese companies were affected by all the contextual factors outlined in Figure 3.3. Political factors influenced whether such companies set up operations in a particular country; Hong Kong and western Europe were seen as relatively safe and stable, for instance. HR policies for Chinese parent-country nationals (PCNs), based internationally, took account of 'Chinese values' such as respect for age, hierarchy and 'face'; but 'morality' and 'peer opinion' contributed less to host-country national (HCN) recruitment and appraisal than they did back in China; here experience and technical criteria were more influential. Companies did not feel they could transfer local 'Chinese' domestic HRM policies to foreign affiliates, partly because they saw these as socio-culturally based within a specific Chinese context, and partly as they saw them as inefficient, and not sufficiently market-oriented! However, political and cultural factors within China limited their ability to change such practices in China itself. Similarly, Gamble (2010) discovered that Japanese retail companies could introduce HRM practices such as more rapid promotion or performance-based pay rather than seniority-based pay into their Chinese operations, but found it more difficult in Japan itself due to cultural and legal restrictions.

Economic and legal factors (for example local pay rates, legal restrictions) also affect whether the company uses PCNs or HCNs for different positions. Firm-specific factors such as the firm's international strategy, structure, organisational culture and stage/mode of internationalisation also affect IHRM, especially the degree to which domestic HRM policies are transferred or localised (an issue pursued in more depth in Chapter 1). 'Power culture' organisations may be more likely to centralise their management of affiliates than 'role culture'-based ones. Those new to internationalisation may use more PCNs; industry type also has an influence, with multi-domestic industries such as trading and shipping companies relying more on PCNs than global growth industries such as electronics, which were more likely to use HCNs. Ownership is now less of an issue for Chinese companies than it used to be; even SOEs often now report low interference from central and provincial government.

It is important to note that the extent to which the factors identified in Figure 3.3 influence IHRM differs and that such influence can vary over time; reliance on international markets may contribute more influence than labour costs for some companies, but not other companies with greater reliance on domestic markets. Some factors may also affect some functions of IHRM more than others; the political, legal and economic environment locally or the firm's overall international strategy may have a bigger impact on staffing and reward practices than training and development practices, for example, as these may be more affected by the socio-cultural environment.

INTERNATIONAL ORIENTATIONS TO HRM

Shen et al (2005) point out that a firm's orientation to IHRM is influenced by its overall international strategy, organisational culture and stage/mode of internationalisation; for example, a 'differentiation' corporate strategy may require employing many local HCNs and giving the affiliate substantial autonomy. Adopting a divisional structure also influences choice.

A useful framework, which we will use throughout our discussion of IHRM policies in Part 4, is provided by the concept of the 'international orientation' of the enterprise. IEs can choose four generic orientations to IHRM, depending on their orientation to foreign people, ideas and resources. Perlmutter (1969) originally identified three different international orientations to staffing the MNE – *ethnocentric*: appointing mostly parent-country nationals (PCNs) to top subsidiary positions; *polycentric*: appointing host-country nationals (HCNs); and *geocentric*: appointing the 'best person', including third-country nationals (TCNs). Perlmutter and Heenan (1979) identified a fourth approach to structuring the operations of MNEs: *regiocentric*, employing 'regional nationals'. Here, managers are transferred on a regional basis, perhaps as a midway station on a journey to be fully geocentric. This approach employs a wider pool of staff than polycentric/ethnocentric approaches, but it is limited, in that employees generally only move outside their HQ within a particular geographic region (Reiche and Harzing 2011).

Again, note the interplay between different aspects of IHRM here; firms pursuing ethnocentric staffing are also less likely to provide management development for HCNs and more likely to export home-based appraisal systems as compared with polycentric approaches, which are more likely to use host-based approaches and more extensive management development of locals. Shen et al (2005) found ethnocentric Chinese companies often relied on generous pay for locals rather than providing extensive career or development opportunities offered to Chinese HCNs in order to remain competitive. We next discuss these orientations in more depth.

1 Ethnocentric

Here the IE takes an 'international' rather than 'global' approach, exporting the home system and making strategic decisions at headquarters (with mother–daughter relationships with subsidiaries). Key positions such as CEO and finance director are often filled with PCNs, that is, *expatriates*. This orientation has the advantage of *maximising global efficiency and standardisation* (Bartlett and Ghoshal 1989) but it minimises both *local responsiveness* (local managers who may know their local labour and product markets well are marginalised) and *worldwide learning* (all strategic ideas and initiatives tend to come from the home-country headquarters in a top–down manner, rather than bottom–up, as in subsidiary to HQ, or laterally, as in subsidiary to subsidiary).

2 Polycentric

Here the enterprise adopts a 'multinational' or 'multi-domestic' approach, adapting its IHRM policies to the local system (for example to the role of *guanxi* in China or *wasta* in the Middle East, Chapters 14 and 10 respectively). Local subsidiaries enjoy much autonomy as 'sisters', and host-country nationals (HCNs) occupy important positions. This strategy is more common in some sectors (for example advertising or food, where local responsiveness is important) and in enterprises from countries rated lower in uncertainty avoidance (for example many European countries). In addition, some positions, such as HR director, are also most likely to be filled by locals, as cultural differences in motivation and reward and communication with locals in their own language are seen as important. However, the strategy minimises standardisation, as each subsidiary can go its own way, reducing economies of scale and increasing costs. Worldwide learning is also inhibited, as ideas and innovations in one subsidiary tend to stay there and not flow up to HQ or laterally to other subsidiaries. One reason for this is that HCNs are unlikely to be promoted to positions in other countries, or to headquarters; training is also often conducted locally, rather than globally, so staff tend not to meet counterparts in other affiliates.

3 Geocentric

Here the enterprise takes a global approach to operations; through global sourcing of talent and global training programmes, it promotes employees to positions and subsidiaries regardless of nationality. It is likely to employ many trans-country nationals (TCNs) to maximise global standardisation as well as worldwide learning (using similar HRD vehicles to spread learning). It also seeks to enhance local responsiveness by using HCNs or 'cosmopolitan' TCNs rather than 'ethnocentric' PCNs. This strategy is characteristic of 'transnational' companies (Bartlett and Ghoshal 1989) seeking to maximise global efficiency, national responsiveness and worldwide learning. However, for most companies this remains an aspiration, rather than a reality. Firms may thus create new 'hybrid' IHRM systems, different from both home and local systems; German firms in China, for example, may introduce more performance-pay-based systems than in Germany itself, as may Japanese retail stores (Hartmann et al 2010; Gamble 2010).

4 Regiocentric

Here the enterprise adopts a regional approach, companies using managers from a particular region (for example Europe, East Asia, North America) and enjoying considerable regional autonomy. Common HRM policies are often developed across the region (but not globally); within Europe there may be regional sourcing of talent and pan-European mobility, but this may not extend to Asia or North America.

REFLECTIVE ACTIVITY 3.3

What are the advantages/disadvantages of these orientations? No option is without disadvantages, for the company or employee.

Essentially, these perspectives all involve different advantages and disadvantages, especially trade-offs between global or local advantage, global learning and integration or responsiveness (Perlmutter 1969). Some of these have been discussed above; we will explore these further with respect to regiocentric strategies, a growing, but less-studied, orientation.

REGIONAL INTEGRATION AND REGIONAL STRUCTURES

As we have seen, IEs seem to often retain distinctive features, often linked to 'country of origin' (Ferner 1997) despite the impact of globalisation and pressures towards 'global convergence', sometimes held to reduce the importance of local contexts (Meyer et al 2011). IEs need to exploit the differences and similarities in their multiple host locations; this is traditionally seen in terms of the need to balance *local responsiveness* with *global integration* within the overall IE structure (Bartlett and Ghoshal 1989). Most research has focused on the design and implementation of global strategies and the management of the tension between global integration and local responsiveness. Rugman et al (2011) argue that this fails to recognise the full complexity associated with adaptation to local contexts – each subsidiary needs to reconcile both parent and local business interests, and different stages of the value chain in subsidiaries will vary in their position on an integration–responsiveness spectrum. In practice, few companies pursue fully geocentric HR practices; as labour flows become increasingly intra-regional and cross-regional, does regionalisation help firms pursue transnational strategies?

To manage complexity, speed up knowledge flows, ensure strategic consistency and promote strategic initiatives, hierarchy and centralisation have recently been re-emphasised in IEs in the form of regional structures (for example, Nell et al

2006) with a growing trend for IEs to relocate activities to regional headquarters (RHQs). However, as Holt et al (2006) and Nell et al (2006) have pointed out, RHQs represent a relatively new area in international business research, and there is little literature concerned with the location or functions of RHQs within global structures leaving, as Nell et al (2006: 4) note, 'a conceptual lacuna for intermediate geographic levels between global (headquarters) and local (subsidiaries)'. So 'regional integration schemes – though key external drivers of strategic change in the MNE – have been underemphasised and occupy only a minor position in traditional conceptual frameworks on MNE strategy' (Rugman et al 2011: 266).

In part this growth in regional HQs may be due to a realisation that the local context is itself embedded in a broader regional context as 'the supra-national regional dimension has been gaining importance in determining national institutional frameworks' (Meyer et al 2011: 243); examples include the growing importance of regional bodies such as the EU and NAFTA or APEC.

IEs establish RHQs for different reasons; Holt et al (2006) found that RHQs established in order to be responsive to regional markets used significantly different criteria in making a decision as to where to locate from those established to facilitate global coordination. In addition, the selection criteria used by US-based IEs were significantly different from those used by Asian-based IEs. Location decision priorities also varied across industry sector. Some RHQs employ small numbers of staff and assume limited regional coordination roles; others manage sales, production, purchasing, finance and R&D for the whole region. RHQs therefore play different roles and perform different tasks, presumably providing different costs and benefits for IEs.

Tarique et al (2006) have pointed to the relatively high degree of independence often afforded to regions within a regional structure. Subsidiaries may be managed as interdependent units under the 'guidance' of RHQs, who may enjoy high levels of autonomy with regard to staffing and TM. Flows of PCNs may be lower than in structures using ethnocentric approaches, and reliance on TCNs may be higher in situations where IEs have established and well-developed regional structures. Regional integration may be a process of 'semi-globalisation' aimed at 'improved accessing, bundling, and leveraging location advantages for specific value chain activities' throughout the region (Rugman et al 2011: 256).

What do RHQs actually do? In China, RHQs were used to integrate HRM, not just to develop regional strategies but to function as implementation instruments and incubators for transnational HRM strategies. Most local Chinese managers reported not to the Japanese HQ, but to a regional HQ. Nell et al (2006) found RHQs were engaged in normative integration, enhancing interaction through workshops and meetings, and building intra-regional teams as well as allocating subsidiary managers regional tasks and engaging in intra-regional training and development. RHQs were often effective in introducing higher levels of vertical information processing, formalisation, centralisation and professionalism, but were also often accused of introducing bureaucratic overload.

RHQs may also present challenges in managing, with constant reorganisation regarding the mandates and scope of the regions. Regional groupings need a clear rationale to minimise instability and subsidiary dissatisfaction. RHQs may help the management of interdependencies *within* the region, between the RHQ and the various subsidiaries under its responsibility; however, their introduction may also increase the risk that interdependencies *across* the regions are not well managed.

For example, in one Irish-based US logistics company, management transfers were generally restricted to 'within region' transfers, with little opportunity for progression beyond the region; 'while there was ample opportunity to attain experience in other European locations, it was very rare for European expatriates to be transferred to the US operation' (Collings et al 2008). Here the deployment of US expatriates had been reduced in Europe owing to the increasing self-sufficiency of the European region, with the company placing more emphasis on international rotation at a regional level among high-potential staff. US-based MNEs in Ireland have increasingly employed not PCNs but HCNs and TCNs in key positions. Whereas US firms are often 'ethnocentric', imposing standardised formal practices globally, they tend not to use PCNs as widely as Japanese firms (perhaps for cost reasons, but also because of the high 'failure rates' often observed for US expatriates, or the reluctance of Americans to travel – Reiche and Harzing 2011). Some companies had adopted regiocentric strategies and introduced RHQs; TCNs socialised into the firm by experiences of working in RHQs may provide an alternative option to monitor and control subsidiaries as 'their broader experience within the regional structure may lead them to have a more balanced understanding of the subsidiary's role within the multinational firm' (Collings et al 2008).

Regio- and geocentric approaches may also enable HCNs to become involved beyond the local level, which may enhance identification to both the local and global firm (Caligiuri and Stroh 1995). Additionally, regional and international assignments, especially temporary but repeated transfers, are powerful mechanisms for socialising local employees into overall organisational values, thereby decreasing the salience of national cultural influences in favour of an integrating corporate culture. However, regiocentric IEs may still develop 'silo' mentalities at a regional level, each region attempting to hold on to its talent, thwarting a global perspective by limiting high-potential development to the regional level. Regiocentric strategies may therefore still limit talent sourcing outside the home region, so the best talent inside the IE is not fully utilised and knowledge flows are limited.

Case Study 3.1 helps illuminate some of these issues.

IHRM CHALLENGES IN ESTABLISHING A NEW REGIONAL HQ: THE CASE OF APHQ

ABC, a leading Japanese car company, has established six regional centres and regional head offices around the world over the last few years to devolve more power away from the company's head office in Japan. ABC has been experiencing problems through its own worldwide expansion; the emphasis on volume had somewhat compromised quality, resulting in an increase in defects, a decline in reliability and a less favourable perception of its vehicles. As a result, Japan HQ decided the company had to get back to 'traditional values', creating a delicate balance between the simultaneous need for centralisation and decentralisation, and tapping into local expertise, knowledge and experience.

One regional centre is APHQ, headquartered in a major Asian city, and covering south-east Asia and Australasia. ABC's Global Programme was already in place before APHQ was established; a key component was that the regions were to reflect the mix of nationalities and not to be dominated by any particular nationality. RHQs and constituent subsidiaries had been established some years before in North America and Europe, and there are indications of organisational learning from this, with senior staff moving between regions on a global basis, facilitating the passing on of previous RHQ experience. Here, Japanese nationals had initially been appointed to the senior positions in the RHQ (an ethnocentric orientation), and then gradually replaced by local nationals over time. This worried Japan HQ in terms of whether local nationals could perform the roles to the standard required. One way of dealing with this had been tight central control from Japan HQ through bureaucratisation and standardisation, with HQ devising

the rules and regulations. The European RHQ was seen as more challenging than North America because of the variety of nationalities it was important to represent in the RHQ; in Asia Pacific, the culture of the region may be even more diverse, from New Zealand to Pakistan.

APHQ followed the same pattern as in other already-established regional centres, initially having Japanese nationals make up the majority of staff, then replacing them by locals from the various countries making up the region through organisational restructuring, recruiting permanent staff from the region and recruiting seconded staff from the region. Questions included how to attract other nationals to APHQ, what they would do there, and how they would fit in when there. What was the 'exit strategy' for those on secondment? When secondees arrived at APHQ, they did not find themselves on a traditional Western form of development programme, but on a 'sink or swim' regime; being expected to struggle was seen as part of training/development.

Subsidiaries had questioned the value of the RHQ in the early days of the US RHQ, but over time acknowledged that they did make key contributions, such as identifying and sharing 'best operational practices', the creation of a regional talent pool, facilitating labour mobility around the region and developing and running training programmes relevant to a range of people from the affiliates. APHQ has also demonstrated its value to the affiliates by auditing training provision across the region, and 'best identified practice' was shared across the region.

The establishment of trust between RHQ and the affiliates and between the affiliates themselves was central to making such progress. Cross-region training programmes proved particularly valuable, but the extent of cross-regional collaboration was still limited, inhibiting cross-regional organisational learning.

APHQ was attempting to identify 'talented' staff from across the region with a view to bringing them in for the benefit of the region; however, it was experiencing problems in attracting middle managers, as junior staff were not yet ready for promotion. The plan was to attract them from affiliates in each country, give them regional experience, and then return them to an affiliate. An extensive amount of basic skills training was required in

management and teamwork, as many staff came from a production background.

(adapted from Preece et al 2013)

WHAT FACTORS AFFECT CHOICE OF INTERNATIONAL ORIENTATION?

There are several factors affecting the choice of which orientation, especially which category of staff to use, as described in Figure 3.3. These include the country/region of origin of the company, the nature of the host country, the type of industry sector, the age and performance of the subsidiary, and the type of position to be filled (Reiche and Harzing 2010; Harzing 2001).

'Country of origin' effects include Japanese MNEs historically using high numbers of PCNs in subsidiary organisations (Collings et al 2008) and European firms using a higher percentage of TCNs (Harzing 2001). Gamble (2010: 716) also found in China that Japanese retail stores 'made greater use of expatriates than comparable European and American firms'. The main role of the HQ IHRM function in Japanese companies is often to manage Japanese expatriates at their subsidiaries in Asia, with little involvement in the management of local HCNs, unlike US firms, where senior-level managers are usually included regardless of nationality. Almost all presidents are Japanese, and most senior positions also, as was the situation in RHQs in the early days with Case Study 3.1; the explanation given is often that this makes communication and liaison with Japanese HQ easier, and local skill levels may be seen to be lower. In contrast, the Japanese subsidiaries of US or European-based firms are usually headed by Japanese HCNs, who also make up most of the HR positions. If the home country shows high uncertainty avoidance, like Japan, PCNs may also be used as 'control' mechanisms; cultural distance may also be a factor, and if subsidiaries are located in 'distant' countries, enterprises seem to prefer to deploy PCNs (though these may be less willing to go in these situations!).

In addition, *subsidiary* characteristics such as *age*, whether an *acquisition* or a new greenfield site, and the *performance* of the company are all significant factors affecting choice; the longer a subsidiary has been in operation, the fewer PCNs may be used, as the need for 'control' may be diminished in long-standing, presumably successful, affiliates, and if acquired, existing local managers may be left in place. Greenfield sites in contrast may be initially staffed with PCNs.

There are also *industry* effects; ethnocentric approaches seem more common in some sectors, for example banking and finance than others, such as advertising, electronics or food industries, all multi-domestic industries where cultural responsiveness is important. The *host country* also has an influence: local education levels, level of risk and cost of living all have impacts on choice. So the use of PCNs is most common in Japanese companies, especially in banks, and in Africa/Latin America as a host region compared with western Europe/North America. PCNs are also most likely to be the financial director, managing director or CEO of the company. Locals are most likely to occupy the role of HR director and make up the bulk of the workforce.

 REFLECTIVE ACTIVITY 3.4

You are a company from an emerging economy seeking to staff one of your European subsidiaries and create a regional HQ. Which international orientation would you choose, and why?

LEARNING SUMMARY

This chapter has analysed the impact of globalisation and informatisation on international enterprises, in particular on their IHRM strategies. It has argued that both have impacts on organisational strategy and structure, and particularly on IHRM policies and practices. Different models and frameworks have been developed to identify factors affecting IHRM, usually citing home-country, host-country, firm-specific and other contingent factors. It argued that as IEs internationalise, different drivers – global integration, cultural responsiveness and worldwide learning – come to the fore and that different IHRM orientations (ethnocentric, polycentric, regiocentric and geocentric) have different advantages, disadvantages and implications for IHRM. We focused on regiocentric strategies, associated with regional structures and with the establishment of regional headquarters, as this seems to be a growing trend in international business but remains under-researched. The chapter did not attempt to review all the factors in the business environment that may impact on IHRM, as some of this is dealt with elsewhere in the book; we will return to some of these themes when we look more closely at IHRM policies and operations in later parts (especially Part 4).

PART 2

HRM AND NATIONAL CULTURE

CHAPTER 4

Cross-cultural Learning: Theories and Principles

Crystal Zhang and Paul Iles

LEARNING OUTCOMES

By the end of this chapter, you should be able to:

- Analyse the nature of learning in cross-cultural settings and its importance in the context of an organisation.

- Define 'learning' and explain the learning theories.

- Evaluate various models of learning styles and their complexity in cross-cultural situations.

INTRODUCTION

> Live as if you were to die tomorrow. Learn as if you were to live forever.
> (Mohandas Gandhi)

This quote from Gandhi encompasses the concept of learning. It is a universal and essential human activity which never stops. From children playing to formal and informal education and training, it is an important aspect of our growth and development. It is itself as much an experience as is the subject of the learning. We not only learn to improve *what* we know, but have the opportunity to 'learn *how* to learn' better or faster. Learning styles vary from country to country as each try to find the best methods for imparting knowledge. Hofstede (1991) argues that a country's culture shapes its people's preferred modes of learning through their socialisation experiences. Indeed, family, school and work are important media for the transmission of cultural values (Kolb 1984). Deconstructing this further, the family unit, the school and the work environment would have their own culture, which will shape learning style preferences. Thus the organisational culture will dictate its learning style. As Sadler-Smith (2006: 2) points out, 'learning is at the heart of *organization* … and … has the power to enable individuals and organizations to fulfil their personal and collective goals and ambitions'. With the increasing globalisation of the economy and the internationalisation of the workplace, an understanding of learning is therefore crucial for anyone involved in international HRM, such as trainers, consultants and facilitators, assessors of qualifications and, especially, managers and leaders. This is particularly more complex and challenging when the learning occurs in a cross-cultural context owing to the existence of individual differences in learning style across the countries and cross-cultural variations in training principles and evaluation.

This chapter introduces some of the key learning theories and principles and discusses the effects of culture on learning.

DEFINITION OF LEARNING

Learning:

[as noun]: the acquisition of knowledge or skills through study, experience, or being taught.

[as modifier]: an important learning process, knowledge acquired through study, experience, or being taught. (Oxford English Dictionary)

Learning is about the acquisition, processing and retention of knowledge or skills. It has happened when people can demonstrate that they know something that they did not know before (insights and realisations, as well as facts) and/or when they can do something they could not do before (skills) (Honey and Mumford 1996). The learning process is also an important aspect of learning, as we gain experience through doing things actively or passively (Kolb 1984).

LEARNING THEORIES

Much of our learning occurs in early childhood, when we learn about the social and physical environment around us. This 'non-formal learning' or 'mental progamming' occurs without conscious awareness (Eraut 2000). Learning theories were created to provide conceptual frameworks in our attempt to understand the learning process. We will focus on the main behavioural and cognitive theories which had been applied to management:

- *behavioural theories* – the learner sits and listens, or does as they are told
- *cognitive theories* – require mental involvement for the active thinking learner.

Behavioural theories

Behavioural psychology is best known for *Pavlov's salivating dog conditioning*, which is a method of learning through conditioning (reinforcement). Behavioural theories are independent of any internal cognitive or mental activities, as these could not be assessed. Instead, learning is said to have occurred when there is a change in the behaviour. The environment (for example a loud noise) shapes the behaviour and a certain amount of conditioning is necessary to strengthen the relationship between environment and behaviour.

Classical conditioning occurs where behaviour is learned through a stimulus. The classic experiment comes from Pavlov, who trained dogs to associate the ringing of a bell with food and to salivate if they heard a bell even though no food was visible.

Operant conditioning occurs when behaviour can be shaped by a reward or a stimulus. This was proposed by Skinner (1953) and is supported by experiments involving animals *operating* a lever to obtain food. Operating the wrong lever would either produce no food or, worse, a punishment. Thus positive (reward) or negative (punishment) reinforcements can be used to shape behaviour.

Behavioural theories can be crudely summarised as an input/output psychology and form the basis of the field of *organisational behaviour* when applied to improve individual and group performance. For example, employee behaviour can be positively reinforced (by money, promotion, recognition or positive feedback) or negatively reinforced (by demotion, criticism, threat of dismissal).

 REFLECTIVE ACTIVITY 4.1

Visit the following link for Pavlov's original experiments:

http://www.youtube.com/watch?v=hhqumfpxuzl

Cognitive theories

In the early 1920s, Lewin defined the general law of psychology, stating that a person's behaviour B is a function of a person's personality P and environmental situations E (that is, $B = f(PE)$). The environment refers not only to physical environment, such as directions and distances, but also to psychobiological factors, such as quasi-physical, quasi-social and quasi-mental structure. This conceptual framework took into account the relationships between individual and environmental factors and forms the basis of many cognitive theories. Contrary to behavioural theories, cognitive theories attempt to understand the mental processes occurring when an input is registered, processed and an output decided upon. Thus people can decide which inputs to give attention to and also which inputs to ignore, depending on their individual pattern. This pattern is sometimes termed either cognitive style, learning style, strategy or personality (Coffield et al 2004; Curry 1983; Riding and Rayner 2002). We present here some of the cognitive theories relevant to organisation learning – Jung's model of personality types, the Myers-Briggs Type Indicator, Witkin's field-dependent/independent dimension, Kolb's experiential learning model, Kirton's adaption-innovation (AI) dimension and Allinson and Hayes' intuitive-analytic dimension.

Jung's model of personality types

Carl Jung (1923) formulated a model of cognitive styles or personality types. He believed that people naturally pick up their own preference types to understand things and can be divided into two basic groups with different personality or attitude types: the introverted and the extroverted. Under these two basic psychological types, Jung identified four further essential 'functions types': thinking, feeling, sensation and intuition. Each of these four functions types can also be either introverted or extroverted. With more focus on the judgement, the types of thinking and feeling fit in the rational dimension, while sensation and intuition belong to an irrational dimension depending heavily on perception. Jung (1923: 406) argued that 'the auxiliary function is possible and useful only in so far as it serves the dominant function, without making any claim to the autonomy of its own principle'. There are thus eight subcategories developed and these correspond with the rational and irrational dimension. The eight types are extrovert feeling (EF), extrovert thinking (ET), introvert feeling (IF), introvert thinking (IT), extrovert sensation (ES), extrovert intuition (EN), introvert sensation (IS) and introvert intuition (IN). The first four types (EF, ET, IF, IT) link to the rational way of information processing, while the latter four (ES, EN, IS, IN) to the irrational manner. His work had a great impact on later researchers, for example Myers (1962) and Kolb (1976).

Myers-Briggs Type Indicator

Drawing from Jung's work on personality types, Myers and Briggs developed the theory further into a more accessible and measureable instrument called the Myers-Briggs Type Indicator (MBTI). The MBTI extended and redefined the Jungian concepts of 'rational' and 'irrational' and referred to them as 'judgement' and 'perception' respectively. The MBTI instrument has a series of questions (126 for the longest to 50 for the shortest) associated with four bipolar discontinuous scales: extraversion (E) and introversion (I), sensing (S) and intuition (N), thinking (T) and feeling (F), and judging (J) and perceiving (P). It also proposed the possible mixing of the different function types from Jung (1923) so that the possible matching of various types results in Myers' 16 distinct personality types, that is, ISTJ, ISFJ, ISTP, INTP, INTJ, INFJ, ISFP, INFP, ESTJ, ESFJ, ESTP, ENTP, ENTJ, ENFJ, ESFP, ENFP (Myers 1962). Thorne and Gough (1999) summarise the 10 most common MBTI types based on their positive and negative aspects in traits. For example, the positive traits for INFP are artistic, reflective and sensitive, while the negative traits are careless and lazy. As for ISTJ, the positive traits are calm, stable and steady and the negative traits are cautious and conventional.

Myers promoted her theory from a purely academic context to a wider audience in organisations, high schools and in the field of counselling and marital relations. As such, the MBTI has been widely accepted as a research instrument and one of most popular personality measures, and has been translated into a number of languages (Furnham and Stringfield 1993).

Witkin's field-dependent/independent dimension

Influenced by Lewin's concept of differentiation, Witkin (1978) started to research psychological differentiation and found that people differ in the way they orient themselves in space. In their study, Witkin and colleagues established the idea that different types of space orientation resulted from not just the difference in a person's perception, but from the individual's innate characteristics. Thus, the method by which people perceive the environment reflects their approach to the processing of information, and ultimately to adaptation. Witkin defined two ways of perceiving: *field-dependence* (FD) and *field-independence* (FI) based on the perception of an upright in space. Witkin and Goodenough (1981) referred to this work as the articulated-global field-approach dimension.

Individuals of the FD type heavily rely on the environment and are easily affected by any stimulus. They become more oriented to situations with a high number of interpersonal contacts and a structured environment. FD people would be classed as extroverts. On the contrary, FI people believe in their own subjectivity, without background influence. They are considered to be less interested in people and to show and demonstrate more physical and psychological distancing from people.

Based on his findings over a number of years, Witkin and Goodenough (1981) identified several characteristics of cognitive style. They believed cognitive style is the form rather than the content of cognitive activity; it is a pervasive dimension and reflects deep-seated personality; it is developed to fit the life situations with which the individual or group must cope; and it is bipolar, unlike intelligence or other abilities. The work of Witkin and his colleagues provides a significant theoretical foundation for the cognitive style construct and has influenced the development of other more recent measures (analytic-intuitive, serialist-holist, impulsive-reflective).

Kolb's experiential learning model

Influenced by Lewin's research and dissatisfied with traditional methods of management teaching, Kolb (1976) proposed his experiential learning model based on a 'learning cycle'. The keyword here is *experiential*, which means relating to or resulting from *experience*, as compared with *experimental*, which means related to or based on *experiments*.

Kolb proposes that experiential learning has six main characteristics:

1 Learning is best conceived as a process, not in terms of outcomes.

2 Learning is a continuous process grounded in experience.

3 Learning requires the resolution of conflicts between dialectically opposed modes of adaptation to the world (learning is by its very nature full of tension).

4 Learning is a holistic process of adaptation to the world.

5 Learning involves transactions between the person and the environment.

6 Learning is the process of creating knowledge that is the result of the transaction between social knowledge and personal knowledge.

Kolb's learning theory sets out four distinct learning styles, which are based on a four-stage learning cycle. In this respect, Kolb's model differs from others since it offers both a way to understand individual learning styles, which he named the 'Learning Styles Inventory' (LSI), and also an explanation of a cycle of experiential learning that applies to all learners. It is also a fluid model which enables the experiential learning to be 'a holistic process of adaptation to the world' (Kolb 1984). The stages in Kolb's learning cycle are concrete experience (CE), reflective observation (RO), abstract conceptualisation (AC) and active experimentation (AE) (Figure 4.1). Ideally, learners can involve themselves in new experiences openly and without bias (CE), reflect on it and observe it objectively from many angles (RO), formulate and generalise the observation into a logical concept (AC) and test the concepts in a new situation (AE). For each of the learning stages, the experiential learner needs to engage with the fundamental ability associated with that stage. The tension in the abstract–concrete dimension is between relying on conceptual interpretation or on immediate experience in order to grasp hold of experience, while the tension in the active–reflective dimension is between relying on internal reflection or external manipulation in order to transform experience (Coffield et al 2004).

To help individuals assess their approach to learning, Kolb (1976) developed the self-descriptive Learning Styles Inventory (LSI). The LSI provides information on the individual's relative emphasis on the four abilities in the learning cycle. The LSI's norms were obtained from a sample of 800 managers and management students. Four styles of learning were discovered and labelled 'converger', 'diverger', 'assimilator' and 'accommodator', each of which corresponds to one specific quadrant in the learning cycle (Figure 4.1). The convergers, found in the AC–AE quadrant, are good at applying ideas in practice, and prefer to deal with things instead of people. The divergers (CE–RO quadrant) are strong in imagination and brainstorming, tend to be emotional and favour dealing with people rather than with things. The assimilators (AC–RO quadrant) excel in synthesising facts into theory via inductive reasoning. Finally, accommodators (CE–AE quadrant) are more action-oriented, with their greatest strengths in carrying out plans and getting involved in new experience.

Figure 4.1: Kolb's experiential learning cycle and basic learning styles

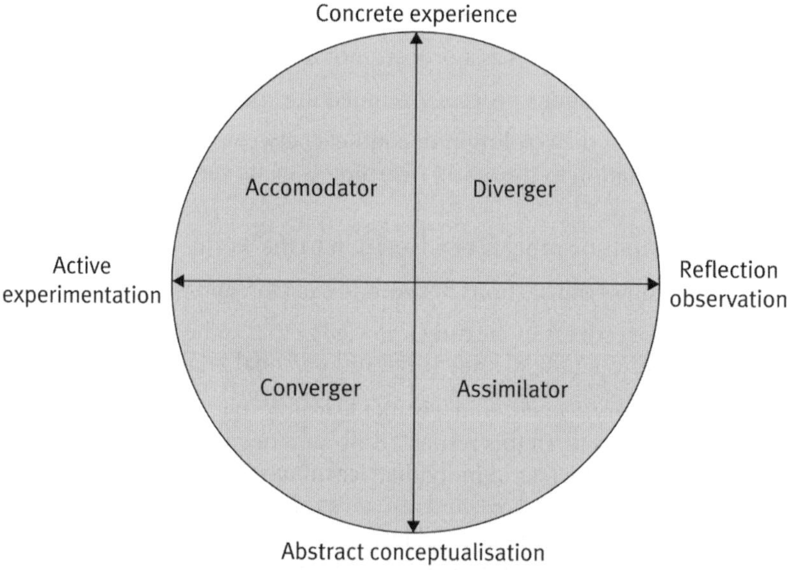

© 1995 Kolb learning style inventory (LSI), developed by David A. Kolb. Printed with permission from Hay Group, Inc. All rights reserved.

Source: adapted from Kolb et al (2001: 229)

REFLECTIVE ACTIVITY 4.2

Visit the following weblink to listen to Kolb's wisdom:

http://www.haygroup.com/leadershipandtalentondemand/video/details.aspx?id=303

Kolb's theory was further developed by Honey and Mumford (1982), who designed their own Learning Style Questionnaire (LSQ) specifically for managers.

The LSQ is proposed as a detailed practical manual with simple language for management people in order to make people aware of their strengths in the four types of learning styles. While basically the same as Kolb's model, the learning styles have been relabelled and redefined. Accommodators are now *activists* who are having an experience; divergers are *reflectors* who are reflecting on the experience; assimilators are *theorists* who draw their own conclusion on the experience; and convergers become *pragmatists* who put their theory into practice to see what happens. Table 4.1 summarises the differences in activists, reflectors, theorists and pragmatists. The authors also emphasise that 'no single style has an overwhelming advantage over any other. Each has strengths and weaknesses but the strengths may be especially important in one situation, but not in another' (Honey and Mumford 2000: 43).

Table 4.1: Strengths and weaknesses of the LSQ

Style	Strength	Weaknesses
Activists	– flexible and open-minded – ready to take action – like to be exposed to new situations – optimistic about anything new and therefore unlikely to resist change	– tendency to take immediately obvious action without thinking through possible consequences – often take unnecessary risks – tendency to do too much themselves and to hog the limelight – rush into action without sufficient preparation – get bored with implementation/consolidation/follow-through
Reflectors	– careful – thorough and methodical – thoughtful – good at listening to others and assimilating information – rarely jump to conclusions	– tendency to hold back from direct participation – slow to make up their minds and research a decision – tendency to be too cautious and not take enough risks – not assertive; not particularly forthcoming and have no 'small talk'
Theorists	– logical, 'vertical' thinker – rational and objective – good at asking probing questions – disciplined approach – grasp of the 'big picture'	– restricted in lateral thinking – low tolerance for uncertainty, disorder and ambiguity – intolerance of anything subjective or intuitive – full of 'shoulds, oughts and musts'
Pragmatists	– eager to test things out in practice – practical, down to earth, realistic – businesslike, get straight to the point – technique-oriented	– tendency to reject anything without an obvious application – not very interested in theory or basic principles – tendency to seize on the first expedient solution to a problem – impatient with indecision – more task-oriented than people-oriented

Kirton's adaption-innovation (AI) dimension

According to Kirton (1976), people *cannot* and *do not want to* change their fundamental and stable, preferred style of behaviour. He states that a person's preferred style has been found to be unvarying – it is behaviour that is flexible. The adaption-innovation theory is concerned with differences in the thinking style of individuals that affects their creativity, problem-solving and decision-making. These concepts will have particular relevance for managers, since they focus on the interaction between people and their often changing work environment, offering managers new information on, and insight into, the personality aspects of change in organisations. Kirton argues that when confronted with the need to make sense of a changing situation and decide how to act, some people appear to focus their attention on doing things better (adapting) while others perceive possibilities for doing things differently (innovating).

The Kirton A-I dimension is a single dimension construct measuring *creativity style* with scores ranging from 32 to 160 (Kirton 1994). Low scores would be adaptors while high scores would be innovators. Kirton (1994) presented a list of characteristics associated with A-I dimension. Briefly, adaptors are stable, predictable and sensitive, while innovators are risk-takers. Adaptors produce fewer ideas, but expect many of those to succeed. Innovators produce many ideas, but expect few to succeed. Organisational fit is more important to adaptors than innovators. Adaptors are most likely to stay in an organisation where they fit and most likely to leave when they don't fit. Innovators are less strongly motivated by considerations of organisational fit to stay or leave since they are less likely to pay attention to whether or not they are in fit.

In the A-I theory, it is the individuals who influence their groups and legitimise their culture into the organisational climate (or culture), as organisations cannot think. Thus group membership or person–organisation fit is crucial for cohesion. The appointment of a new leader would slowly change the organisational culture, such that people would leave if they do not fit and new members are brought in. The Kirton A-I can be used to estimate a person–organisation fit. In the model, people with similar alignment would work more cohesively. However, Kirton also stresses that group cohesion is not the same as group homogeneity. A group would usually consist of individuals of varying A-I scores, with a skewed majority average A-I score. Those outside the majority group would be marginalised, creating a cognitive gap, unless a *bridger* comes in to mediate and bridge the gap. Bridging is to reach out to people in the team and help them be part of it, so that they may contribute even if their contribution is outside mainstream (Kirton 2003). Bridgers usually have an intermediate A-I score between the majority and the outsider, are willing to undertake the role of bridger and are skilled in bridging.

Allinson and Hayes' intuitive-analytic dimension

Allinson and Hayes (1996) presented a test to differentiate those individuals who are predominantly intuitive thinkers from those who are predominantly analytical thinkers (which they ascribed to the dominance of the right hemisphere or left hemisphere of an individual's brain respectively). The Cognitive Style Index allows people to identify where they are along the intuitive–analytical gradient. The CSI has been widely used as a tool on a national and international basis. Importantly, CSI has been used in matching the cognitive styles of mentors or supervisors to their subordinates or protégés, such that similar cognitive styles improve the learning efficiency. Intuitive leaders may be less dominating and more nurturing than their analytic colleagues, and they are more liked and respected by analytic members than analytic leaders are by intuitive members (Allinson et al 2001; Armstrong et al 2002). With a growing number of companies turning to psychology-related testing for hiring purposes, such dyad matching in the formal mentor–protégé relationship is becoming increasingly feasible. Therefore, managers or career mentors can first review their cognitive styles and then make protégé candidate selections accordingly.

The Cognitive Style Index questionnaire has been translated into several languages (Lofstrom 2002) and the results used for cross-cultural studies. Coffield et al (2004: 138) argue that 'the CSI has the best psychometric credentials' out of 71 learning styles models that they reviewed and assessed. However, there has been criticism over its oversimplification of the intuitive–analytic continuum. Instead, it has been proposed that intuition and analysis are not contrasting opposites, but are two dimensions, ranging from high to low on each, which can be combined to generate four quadrants, such as high intuition and high analytic or low intuition and low analytic (Sadler-Smith 2006; Hodgkinson and Clarke 2007).

 REFLECTIVE ACTIVITY 4.3

Visit the following link for more discussion on learning styles:

http://www.arasite.org/RMdatabase/Coffield.pdf

THE EFFECT OF CULTURE ON LEARNING STYLE

The internationalisation of the workplace is now evident in the cultural heterogeneity of the colleagues we work with. While it used to be that our colleagues all came from a similar cultural background, it is rarely the case in this age of globalisation. Person–organisation fit is even more complex owing to the multitude of individual learning styles and culture under one organisational culture. Cross-cultural contacts are also experienced during short overseas trips to visit suppliers, customers, international divisions and expatriate assignments.

Traditionally, there has often been a distinction between East and West in the analysis of national cultures. Although there is no evidence to show biological or genetic differences, several studies have explored the cross-cultural differences in learning style between national groups. We will now review a cross-section of studies investigating such differences.

CULTURE AND KOLB'S EXPERIENTIAL LEARNING

Several studies have attempted to link cultural differences to learning style as measured by Kolb's LSI (Yamazaki 2005). Culture here was defined primarily by national boundaries. While Desai and Taylor (1998) showed a difference in the learning style between Australian and Asian students, Marriott (2002) and Loo (2002) instead argued that learning style was dependent on the discipline studies. One explanation could be that culture was a loosely defined term, and as such could not be correlated with learning style. To address this, Jaju et al (2002) investigated the relationship between LSI and culture according to Hofstede's dimensions, and provided the first empirical evidence for cultural differences in the learning style of undergraduate business students in the USA, Korea and India. A later study by Boland et al (2011) on accounting students found that Japanese students preferred learning-by-watching style (diverger) while Australian and Belgian students preferred learning-by-thinking style (assimilator). While these studies were performed on undergraduate student samples, a paper by Joy and Kolb (2009) attempted to investigate the effect of culture on the learning style of non-student adult respondents. In this study, culture was defined along the framework used in the Global Leadership and Organisational Effectiveness (GLOBE) survey (House et al 2004) and was divided into cultural dimensions, which included but was not limited to Hofstede's original dimensions. This study is significant as it attempts to compare respondents from seven different countries. However, the impact of culture was found to be only marginally significant (Joy and Kolb 2009). This could be that culture was never measured, but simply mapped to the House et al (2004) study. The authors instead found that the level of education and the area of specialisation had more impact than culture in shaping the learning style. In other words, learning style was dependent on the type of discipline or profession, and the length of time spent in that discipline, such as a postgraduate degree or employment, reflecting the earlier findings by Marriott (2002) and Loo (2002).

IS THE EAST INTUITIVE OR ANALYTIC?

Based on their study of Canadian and Japanese MBA students assessed using the MBTI, Abramson et al (1993) found that Canadians prefer a logical, impersonal and objective thinking-based cognitive style, while the Japanese prefer a more feeling-based cognitive style with a concern for group harmony and friendly human relations. They also suggest that the Japanese would seem to be particularly adaptable to new situations with their openness to new information. These studies find the East is more intuitive, while the West is more analytic. This was also the conclusion proposed by Kassem's study on service firms in the Arab region (1989), that is, the Arab manager tended to rely on market instincts instead of hard data like Western managers. This suggests that Western managers may be more analytic while Arab managers are more intuitive.

However, evidence also favours the opposite view. Kume (1985) studied the cultural difference between Japanese and North Americans in management practice. The results suggest that Japanese tend to have a consensus style of group decision-making while North Americans prefer a more individualistic and independent approach. The emphasis in the Japanese way is a sense of commitment, shared responsibility, interdependence and close coordination. The time spent in the process does not matter since the secured consequence of the decision is the main concern. In contrast, North Americans' decision-making style is more likely to be quick and even impulsive due to the motive of achievement and accomplishment. This suggests that the Japanese style tends to be more analytic, while the North American is more intuitive. In a study of 222 Chinese managers and 148 European managers, Furnham and Stringfield (1993) found a dramatically significant difference between the two cultures: Western managers tended to be more extroverted, more intuitive, more feeling and more perceiving whereas Chinese managers were more introverted, more sensing, more thinking and more judging. Indeed, in a later study on Japanese, Canadian and American managers, Abramson et al (1996) suggested that Japanese managers are slower decision-makers than their Canadian and American counterparts, implying a more analytic style for the Japanese.

Interestingly, in a study of 150 Chinese and American graduate students, Huang and Sisco (1994) found no differences in analyst and synthesist thinking styles. Instead, they propose that the Chinese students were more pragmatic than their American counterparts. Furthermore, in a study of 394 managers from six nations and 360 management students from five nations assessed on the Cognitive Style Index, Allinson and Hayes (2000) found that the British are more intuitive than people from Australia, France, Germany, Hong Kong, India, Jordan, Nepal, Russia and Singapore.

CULTURAL DIFFICULTIES TO ADAPTATION?

Branine (1996) and Warner (2004) reviewed training in China and propose reasons for the failure of Western-style management education in Chinese companies. They explain that the less intuitive learning style of Chinese managers would have been heavily influenced by strict government guidelines. Furthermore, the Chinese style of teacher-centred education would have caused their learning styles to be characterised by a rigid following of rules rather than free involvement and thinking. Hofstede (1991) previously suggested that the complexity of characters in Chinese script develops the children's ability at pattern recognition, but also imposes a need for rote learning. However, Sadler-Smith and Tsang's (1998) study of 183 Hong Kong and 225 British university students to test memory theory (deep/superficial learning) did not support the stereotype of 'Asian learner equals rote learner'.

In a study of three Japanese companies in the UK, Saka (2004) found that the Japanese management style and company practices were readily accepted when habitual routines and pre-existing organisational settings were 'Japanified' through extensive use of expatriate managers. A possible explanation for the successful Japanese–British ventures was that the Japanese and British cultural values are sufficiently compatible for the organisational learning to arrange compromises (especially in regard to the unionisation and attitudes of the British workforce). However, in a study looking at Japanese companies in China, Hong and colleagues (2006) found that the Japanese-style management did not work even though the two nations share similar core cultural values. Several explanations were offered to explain the incompatibility, such as the notion of power-distance and the use of interpreters/intermediaries.

LEARNING SUMMARY

Due to cultural socialisation and mental programming, learning styles can be considered to be culture-bound cognitive schemes and can vary from culture to culture. The various learning theories introduced in this chapter show diversity in the different styles for learning. Multinational or mismatched teams can have conflicting learning styles, which can cause cross-cultural irritations or problems if ignored. However, the diversity in learning styles should be embraced, as a cohesive and diverse team would be more likely to adapt and succeed through the synergy of styles. Understanding one's preferred learning style and that of others helps to understand areas of weakness and gives people the opportunity to work on becoming more proficient in other modes, or it helps to realise strengths, which are useful in cross-cultural training and management situations.

 TOYOTA WAS IN DENIAL. HOW ABOUT YOU?

CASE STUDY 4.1

by Professor Richard Tedlow, Harvard Business School

Published 8 April 2010, *BloombergBusinessweek* http://www.businessweek.com/stories/2010-04-07/toyota-was-in-denial-dot-how-about-you

A failure to deal with obvious problems was its biggest problem. But instead of just shaking your head, take a look at your own company.

In the past weeks we have learned two things about Toyota. First, when it comes to crisis management, the company stinks. Second, when it comes to manufacturing automobiles, Toyota isn't what it was cracked up to be.

It is that second item that came as the real shocker. Anyone questioning this company's level of quality a year ago would have had difficulty finding an audience. But today, Toyota finds itself having to recall more than 8 million vehicles, and it may soon have to pay the maximum fine the U.S. Transportation Dept. can levy for concealing safety information. As you surely know, a wide array of Toyota's vehicles must undergo repairs for a potentially deadly accelerator problem. Indeed, it has already cost lives.

Manufacturing defects can crop up at the best of companies. And Toyota was certainly counted among the best of the best. Anyone still interested in reading about the company's vaunted production system can go buy a book like *The Toyota Way* or *The Machine that Changed the World*. But evidence is starting to indicate that we were living in a 'Toyota reputation bubble,' comparable in its own way to the dot-com and housing bubbles.

In 2005, Toyota recalled more vehicles in the U.S. than it sold. Worldwide, nearly 1.5 million Toyota vehicles were recalled the following year. Why was there not a spate of articles about Toyota no longer being the company people thought it was? Outsiders writing about Toyota fell victim to what John Kenneth Galbraith many years ago called the conventional wisdom. We all saw Toyota through the prism of its supposed manufacturing superiority, a prism that distorted reality. When the accelerator recalls were followed by Prius recalls over faulty brakes, the jig should have been up. But to this day I know people who do not plan to take recalled Toyotas back to the dealer. They are still in denial.

Evidence of trouble was available to Toyota long before American consumers were told. The gas-pedal problem appeared in Europe a year before it started causing accidents in the U.S., as the company's brass knew full well. Acknowledging as much in congressional testimony, Toyota's top U.S. executive, Yoshimi Inaba, characterised the company's response this way: 'We did not hide it. But it was not properly shared.' What on earth were they thinking? Did they believe that the failure of this most public of products would pass by unnoticed?

I believe I know the answers to these questions. Toyota's top people were in denial, just as the public was. By denial, I mean that they stopped being honest with one another. And they stopped being honest with themselves. If Toyota's products were as fatally flawed as they were, that would be too awful to be true. Therefore, the awful truth was brushed away. I've seen this happen in so many companies that I was compelled to write a book about it. There's a highly valuable lesson for all businesspeople in the tragedy at Toyota: If denial can destroy the reputation of a company that was once so admired, it can destroy the reputation of your company, too. Unfortunately, organisations (and people) that are in denial have a hard time seeing through their own

smokescreens. Here are some questions you should ask yourself to help you avoid Toyota's fate:

What happens to the bearer of bad news? Does your company shoot the messenger rather than heed the message? There are indications that this may have been the case at Toyota.

Do the real issues of the day only come up in the hallways after meetings are finished?

Are you trash-talking your competitors' products? If so, how sure are you that yours are superior?

Is your company building a new large headquarters to celebrate itself? There is some evidence of the 'edifice complex' at Toyota.

Would you rather be conventionally wrong or unconventionally right? Toyota's top people chose the former.

If your answers to these questions make you a bit uneasy, think about how Toyota President Akio Toyoda must be feeling right about now.

Questions

1   What is your preferred learning style? Are you an intuitive decision-maker or analytical decision-maker?

2   Based on your observation and experience, to what extent does national culture have an impact on the learning style?

3   What are the limitations of behavioural and cognitive theories of learning?

CHAPTER 5

Cross-cultural and Global Leadership, Leadership Development and IHRM

Crystal Zhang and Paul Iles

LEARNING OUTCOMES

By the end of the chapter, you should be to:

- Analyse the importance of leadership in cross-cultural settings and its importance in the context of an international enterprise.
- Critically analyse various leadership theories and models.
- Critically analyse concepts of distributed and dispersed leadership.
- Understand the importance of global leadership to IEs and the role of global leadership development to IHRM.

INTRODUCTION

> A leader knows the way, goes the way, and shows the way. (John Maxwell, leadership guru)

What is a leader? Who qualifies? What makes a good leader? The opening quote from leadership guru John Maxwell summarises one version: he or she *knows the way*, that is, they have a vision of a preferred future; they *go the way*, that is, they have the courage and willingness to pursue the vision; and they *show the way*, that is, they have influence and the capacity to persuade others to follow them to achieve it. History has witnessed many leaders, some good, others less so, and much has been written to decipher the 'secret' of leadership; for example, with the death of iconic Apple leader Steve Jobs, his biography was the top-selling book in America, with 380,000 copies sold in the US during the first week (Kwok and Silverman 2012; Isaacson 2012).

What makes for leadership, especially in the globalised twenty-first century? This chapter introduces some important leadership theories and asks how relevant they are in the face of cultural differences, explored in Chapter 2. We also discuss cross-cultural leadership: can leaders transcend their own culture and move across cultures and boundaries to become a global leader? We then discuss recent, more collective theories of leadership, such as *distributed leadership*, and discuss the challenges and issues posed by global leadership and leadership development.

REFLECTIVE ACTIVITY 5.1

Alone, with a partner or in a small group, try to think of two people you associate with the term 'leader'.

1   In your view, what have they done that makes them a good leader? How are they similar to, or different from, each other?

2   Compare your responses with others and try to define what you mean by 'leader' and 'leadership'.

(adapted from Iles et al 2010b)

IS LEADERSHIP MANAGEMENT?

> From the moment of their birth, some are marked for subjugation and others for command. (Aristotle)

Who will lead and who will follow? Do we obtain leadership through divine blessing, or birthright? Through strength of arms, or wits? Could we make a hero from zero? These questions have been raised by philosophers such as Aristotle and writers such as Shakespeare throughout history. Managers may have the formal authority to be in charge of subordinates and influence others (Yukl 2010), but are leaders different from managers? As summarised in the often-quoted Bennis and Nanus (1985):

> Managers are people who do things right and leaders are people who do the right thing.

Nonetheless, managers must have leadership competencies in order to lead their team, and leaders, however charismatic or visionary, cannot succeed without management skills. In the 1980s burgeoning interest in management development in the UK, allied to the expansion of business schools and a proliferation of management courses such as the MBA, presented management as a rational, technical activity with underpinning skills, knowledge and 'competencies' that could be learned and applied through business education courses at universities and management development programmes in companies. The UK's relatively poor economic performance since the Second World War was often attributed to poor management, lack of modern management skills, and the low quantity and quality of management education and development in the UK as compared with its then leading competitors, the USA, Germany, France and Japan (Thomson et al 2000; Institute of Management 1997; Constable and McCormick 1987; Handy 1987; Mangham and Silver 1986).

Since the 1990s, the question has been raised in the UK and elsewhere as to whether management and management development were enough to drive organisational success. There has been renewed emphasis on leadership and leadership development and the transformational leadership abilities of individuals (for example, Bennis and Nanus 1985; Grint 2005; Storey 2004, 2011; CEML 2002).

Kotter (1990) claims that organisations need to promote both stability and change, requiring both leaders and managers. Mabey and Finch-Lees (2008), however, challenge this by arguing that de-layering, workforce fragmentation and greater flexibility mean that both 'leadership' and 'followership' are now necessary for most staff, at all levels; knowledge workers in particular cannot be managed, only led; and the concept of leadership is culture-bound and gendered, elevating the self-importance of corporate leaders (Mangham 2004). Calling for 'leadership competencies' (Salaman 2004) redefines the person, their expectations, how they see themselves and how they are seen by others, differentiated from mere 'followers' or 'managers'.

REFLECTIVE ACTIVITY 5.2

1   Are leaders the same as managers?   2   Do leaders require different skills?

LEADERSHIP THEORIES

Many theories have been put forward to understand the leadership process; here we provide a brief overview of some major leadership theories (Table 5.1), showing their evolution from understanding the traits of the leader (great man and traits theories) to the role of the leader in organisational performance (transformational theory). Figure 5.1 shows the evolution of these ideas, including newer theories such as servant leadership and distributed leadership, which we will discuss shortly. We discuss 'ethical' and 'authentic' leadership theories in Chapter 6.

Table 5.1: Main leadership theories

Great man theories for example, nineteenth, early twentieth century	Belief that leaders are exceptional people, born with innate qualities, destined to lead. Until the latter part of the twentieth century, leadership was thought of as a male quality, especially in terms of military leadership.
Trait theories for example, up to 1940s	Lists of traits or qualities associated with leadership continue to be produced, assuming that certain qualities, attributes and traits make someone better at leadership.
Behaviourist theories 1940s, 1950s	Focus on what leaders actually do, not their qualities as 'styles of leadership'.
Situational leadership 1960s, 1970s	Leadership as specific to the situation/context in which it is exercised; some situations may require an autocratic style, others a more participative approach.
Contingency theory 1970s	A refinement of the situational viewpoint: which situational variables best predict the most appropriate or effective leadership style in particular circumstances?
Transactional theory 1980s	Emphasises importance of the relationship between leader and followers, focusing on the mutual benefits derived from a form of 'contract', for example rewards or recognition in return for commitment or loyalty.
Participative theories 1970s, ongoing	Ideal leadership style takes the input of others into account, encouraging group participation and contribution.
Transformational theory 1980s, ongoing	Change and the role of leadership in transforming organisational performance are emphasised.

(adapted from Bolden et al 2003)

Figure 5.1: Evolution of leadership ideas

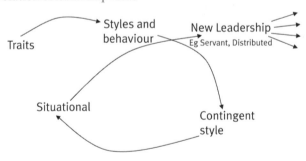

LEADER TRAITS, STYLES AND SITUATIONS

Early approaches to leadership focused on leader 'traits', failing to find much consistency across sectors and organisations; later leader behaviour or 'styles', such as concern for both people and production and attention to both task and socio-emotional/relationship dimensions, became more fashionable. Much research, however, was conducted on small groups and the behaviour (self-reported or reported by team members) of team leaders or supervisors, rather than top leaders of large organisations; the main measures of team performance were often attitudinal or perceptual rather than performance-related. More contingent or situational theories of leadership followed, arguing against the view that there was 'one best way' of leading in favour of 'it all depends on the situation', taking follower maturity or leader position power or relationships into account (Fiedler 1971, 1981).

In contrast, the 1990s saw more concern with 'creating corporate culture' and the need for *transformational leadership* in large organisations facing new global challenges, renewing interest in earlier, more political and sociological accounts of leadership (Burns 1978; Weber 1978). One influential model (Bass (1985, 1990) distinguishes 'transactional' from 'transformational' leaders, exercising idealised influence and inspirational motivation in a 'charismatic-inspirational' style and often more highly correlated with exertion of extra effort, satisfaction with the leader and perceptions of leader effectiveness (Bass 1985, 1990; Bass and Avolio 1993).

Recent work has extended this, stressing the importance of *emotional intelligence* to leadership, especially transformational leadership (Goleman 2000; Goleman et al 2002; Dulewicz and Higgs 2000a, 2000b). Goleman et al (2002) popularised the notion of emotional intelligence (or emotional quotient – EQ) for leaders; following Salovey and Meyer (1990), this involves competencies in self-awareness, self-regulation, motivation, empathy and social skill. EI involves understanding one's emotions and also the emotions of others, creating an environment of trust to build rapport.

 REFLECTIVE ACTIVITY 5.3

Go to:

http://www.personal.psu.edu/faculty/j/5/j5j/IPIP/

http://www.yourleadershiplegacy.com/assessment.html

1   How do you judge the usefulness of such leadership style/trait assessment tools?

2   What questions would you want to ask about them to help you evaluate their usefulness?

(adapted from Iles et al 2010b)

Closely related is the cultural quotient (CQ), 'a person's capability for successful adaptation to new cultural settings, that is, for unfamiliar settings attributable to cultural context' (Earley and Ang 2003). Cross-cultural leaders here need to be successful in terms of cultural adaptability, emotional and cultural intelligence, and the ability to be global and local at the same time (Alon and Higgins 2005).

Is it possible to identify different styles of leadership? Lewin et al (1939) identified three major leadership styles – *authoritarian, participative* and *delegative* – representing the level of empowerment within a group. An authoritarian style concentrates power within individuals (I want you to…), diffusing it to the group represents participative leadership (Let's work together to…), while a delegative style allows employees to make their own decisions (You take care of this while I…). See Table 5.2.

Table 5.2: Lewin's leadership styles

Authoritarian leadership (tells)	Leader tells employees what they need to do and how; decisions made by leader independently. Productivity is highest in this style, but it can stifle creativity and innovation.
Participative leadership (consults)	Leader makes decisions together with the followers. Members of the team can make suggestions but the leader makes the final decision. Creativity and innovations are highest but productivity is reduced.
Delegative leadership (delegates)	Delegative or *laissez-faire* leadership gives free rein to employees; it can be effective if employees are highly skilled, knowledgeable and trusted, but can lead to poorly defined roles and low motivation if not (contingency theory).

Lewin's leadership styles were further developed in terms of organisational performance by Litwin and Stringer (1968), who identified six leadership styles: coercive, authoritative, democratic, pace-setting, coaching and affiliative.

CRITICISMS OF THESE APPROACHES

However, in many studies, no practising organisational leaders are actually observed (often samples are in the military, education or students), and a confusing combination of emotional and rational constructs is often generated. Leadership researchers are also criticised for focusing on what leaders *should* do, not what they actually do, as in the prescriptive model of Kotter (1990).

Notice that each of the theories focuses on the *individual* as leader, rather than leadership as a collective or shared responsibility. Does this reflect their origins in very individualistic societies, especially the USA (Chapter 2)? An emerging field is *collective, shared, dispersed* or *distributed* leadership (Tamkin 2012). Note the *implementation* of collective leadership may, however, still lie within the remit of participative and transformational leaders.

DISTRIBUTED, SHARED AND DISPERSED LEADERSHIP

Traditional leadership theories concentrate on the differentiation of leaders and followers; leaders possess power, authority, influence and control through their personal traits, style or position. In contrast, *distributed leadership* blurs the boundaries between leader and followers; the leadership mantle shifts from an 'autocratic' to a 'democratic' style, and leadership power/influence is shared among individuals in a team, with employees given decision-making opportunities. Such leadership may be distributed among a small team (for example co-leaders such as chair and chief executive, or leadership trio) or more widely among team or organisational members, as Figure 5.2 shows.

Figure 5.2: Degrees of distributed leadership

(adapted from Ross et al 2005)

We argue that the models of leadership outlined in Tables 5.1 and 5.2 are de-contextualised and individualistic (Iles and Preece 2006), carrying the danger of once again proposing a 'one best way' of leadership common to early trait or style models. They are usually seen in terms of a set of individual leadership 'competencies' rooted in a strong US, male and private sector view of the 'heroic leader' (Alimo-Metcalfe and Alban-Metcalfe 2001, 2011) and neglecting issues of ethics, integrity and external networks (Chapter 6) as well as organisational and inter- organisational politics (Iles and Macaulay 2007). For Alvesson and Svenningsson (2003: 961), normative leadership research sees 'the leader as consistent essence, a centred subject with a particular orientation'; however, leaders are not 'the autonomous, self-determining individual with a secure unitary identity (at) the centre of the social universe' (Alvesson and Deetz 2000: 98).

This 'individualistic' orientation to leadership – 'leadership is what leaders do' – has implications for leadership development; leadership development is usually seen as about developing leaders. A typical leadership development programme may involve an initial assessment of the individual against a 'leadership competency profile', perhaps involving psychometric tests of ability, personality or emotional intelligence; a diagnosis of strengths and 'development needs'; the construction of a personal development plan (PDP); and the provision of a range of training and development experiences to address these development needs. These may involve coaching and mentoring (internal to the organisation, or with senior executives, more probably delivered by outside consultants), training, projects and secondments, and perhaps 'outdoor development' where participants are faced with unfamiliar leadership challenges 'outside their comfort zone' in a mountain, forest or marine environment. These may involve team exercises, role-playing or trust-building activities, with de-briefing, assessment and feedback. The chief executives studied by Iles and Preece (2006) in the north-east of England, for example, experienced a mix of master-classes on business-related topics, personal coaching, peer learning/action learning, online training, a weekend 'retreat' or residential course, and the opportunity of a 'global challenge' in a challenging environment in another country.

These activities may all be very useful for personal and human capital development; some, such as action learning, may even build social capital, *bonding* the group together in ways that may lead to continued business and personal relationships. They may also facilitate *bridging*, providing the participants with access to wider external networks. But are they sufficient to develop *leadership*, as opposed to *leaders*? (Iles and Preece 2006; Preece and Iles 2009; Day 2000).

Here we distinguish 'leader development' as a form of human capital development from 'leadership development' as a form of social capital development; just as manager development should not be conflated with management development (Dale and Iles 1992), leadership development should not be equated with leader development. A focus on developing *leadership* rather than *leaders* may be more helpful, viewing leadership development as involving the development of social as well as human capital (Bourdieu 1986; Iles and Preece 2006; Day 2000; Day et al 2004).

We propose that approaches to leadership development can be analysed using the axes 'individual–collective' and 'open/emergent–prescriptive/closed'; most current approaches are individual–closed/prescriptive, but other approaches are not just possible, but often appropriate (Iles and Preece 2006). See Figure 5.3.

Figure 5.3: Approaches to leadership development

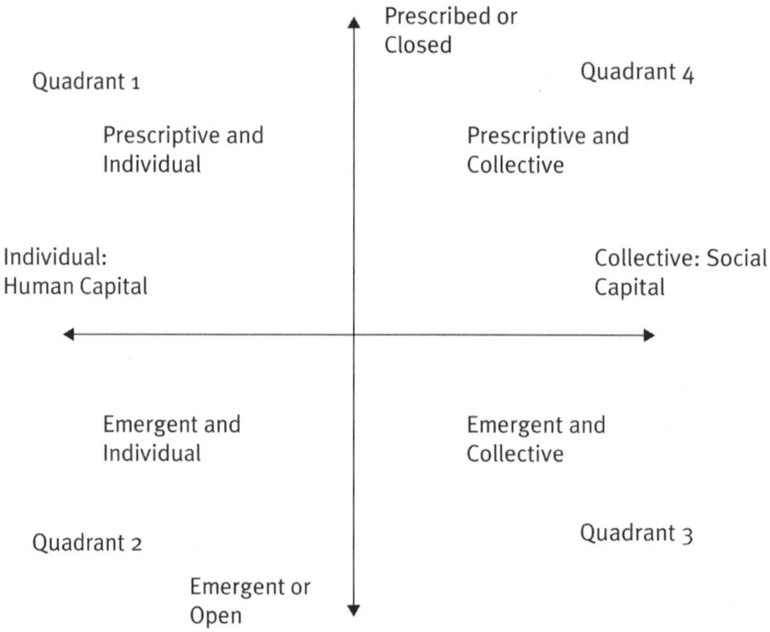

(adapted from Iles and Yolles 2003a; Rodgers et al 2003; Iles et al 2010b)

When solo leaders are seen as the main originators and directors of leadership, this may preclude us from getting 'accurate understanding of leadership practice, in particular the actual divisions of leadership labour which prevail in different contexts' (Gronn 2002: 425). Yukl (1999: 292–3) suggests that 'some leadership functions … may be shared by different members of a group, some leadership functions may be allocated to different members, and a particular leadership function may be performed by different people at different times'; leadership is 'a shared process of enhancing the collective and individual capacity of people to accomplish their work roles effectively … the leadership actions of any individual leader are much less important than the collective leadership provided by members of the organisation.' Similarly, for House and Adtja (1997: 457), 'leadership involves collaborative relationships that lead to collective action'.

Dissatisfaction with traditional 'solo' leadership has led to the development of more 'collective' approaches to leadership (Brookes 2006, 2008; Edwards 2011; Fitzsimons et al 2011) with *distributed* or *shared* leadership being the most fashionable terms; for Gronn (2000: 333) it is 'an idea whose time has come'.

Shared leadership (SL) is the term mostly used in the US literature, especially in healthcare (Pearce 1997, 2004; Pearce and Sims 2002; Ensley et al 2006). For Pearce et al (2008: 355) it is virtually interchangeable with *decentralised* leadership, for example 'three empirical studies have directly assessed the effects of centralised, vertical leadership and the effects of decentralised, shared leadership'. In SL, team members engage in simultaneous, ongoing, mutual influence processes (Pearce and Conger 2003), sharing or dispersing leadership enactments, including those associated with knowledge exchange, sharing and integration, in 'a dynamic, interactive influence process among individuals in teams for which the objective is to lead one another to the achievement of team or organisational goals or both … often involves peer, or lateral, influence and at other times involves upward or downward hierarchical influence' (Pearce and Conger 2003: 1). SL is therefore explicitly linked to 'the CEO's use of empowering leadership-leader behaviour specifically focused on the encouragement of leadership from below' (Pearce et al 2008: 354). This is similar to much 'leadership style' theory, especially 'participative' or 'democratic' leadership styles (Table 5.2).

Distributed leadership (DL) is the term most used in the UK, Scandinavian and Australian literature, especially in the education sector (Bolden 2011). Thorpe et al (2011: 241) define DL as 'a variety of configurations which emerge from the exercise of influence that produces interdependent and conjoint action'; it is a general, overarching label for these kinds of configurations, with shared, conjoint and dispersed leadership seen as specific dimensions of DL. Gronn (2009) identifies *hybrid* forms of leadership where DL is one 'leadership configuration' both within and between organisational units; collaborating agents may be coalitions of individuals and teams, acting in close proximity or across a number of sites. Distributed and focused leadership are seen as end points of a continuum, not separate categories; leadership aggregation is 'minimalist' DL, with responsibility shared among others in a 'leader-plus' manner (Spillane et al 2004) such as in co-leadership, or leader partnerships. DL is here characterised by interdependence, the complementary overlapping of responsibilities and the coordination and management of interdependencies; DL can be dispersed and 'numerical'; or conjoint and 'concertive'. The first numerical view suggests that all organisational members can be leaders at some time; leadership is an aggregated enactment among some or all of team/organisation members, or a sum of the parts of leadership from different members (Gronn 2002). The role of leader could change according to specialist expertise at each stage of an organisational process (Wenger 2000: 231; Gibb 1958: 103). The second concertive view emphasises the holistic aspects of developing collective leadership activities and processes; leadership results from conjoint, synchronised agency and actions and dispersed enactment. This can take three forms: *spontaneous collaboration, intuitive working relations* and *institutionalised practices.*

Spontaneous collaboration refers to occasional and voluntary leadership alignment, whether anticipated or unanticipated. Intuitive working relations can emerge over time; here 'leadership is manifest in the shared role space encompassed by their partnership' (Gronn 2002: 430). 'Co-leadership' is where two leaders, for example chair and chief executive, work side by side with equal responsibility and influence; institutionalised practices in contrast are related to formal arrangements of structural relations involving interdependent action between co-leaders, sometimes accompanied by tight role descriptions specifying areas of responsibility.

What is driving such interest in DL? Orthodox formulations of solo leadership may prescribe a division of labour which is rapidly changing with increased complexity, new technologies and team-based work structures (Ray et al 2004; Thorpe et al 2011). The rise of cross-functional and other teams, the need for speedy and relevant information, the increasing complexity of executive jobs and the importance of team-based knowledge work may require DL (Pearce 2004; Pearce and Conger 2003). Such practices require team members to share both tacit and explicit knowledge through such initiatives as establishing communities of practice, employee participation, participative leadership, and the building of social, as well as human, capital through knowledge-sharing. DL may offer a way of taking account of these structural changes taking place in many organisations (Thorpe et al 2011), coping better with the resulting ambiguities and tensions in flatter, matrix, networked, project and knowledge-based structures. The need for coordination and alignment in DL is often stressed, especially in highly interdependent tasks requiring knowledge and information exchange, sharing and integration, which suggests that these are key team processes and that important features favouring DL include task complexity and knowledge intensity (Iles and Feng 2011).

However, in the education sector, DL has often been introduced owing to external pressures and agendas, often as a rhetorical device to avoid staff consultation. Bolden et al (2008: 365–6) claim it 'may be used by those in positions of real power to disguise power differentials, offering the illusion of consultation and participation without obscuring the mechanisms by which decisions are reached and resources distributed … at best it is a rhetorical term to legitimise drawing upon the capabilities and motivations of a far wider range of constituents and better aligning leadership with the collective interests of organisational members'. Gordon (2002) asks whether 'under the guise of sharing leadership's power and control, dominant power holders will exercise their power through a network of compliant, so called, self-leaders'.

We agree with Thorpe et al (2011) that DL is an overarching term for different kinds of collective leadership, but feel there is a need to analyse different leadership practices and their distribution in different contexts, including national and regional contexts. Leadership does not just exhibit 'focused' patterns, but also involves shared, collective and distributed phenomena (Gronn 2000, 2002; Pearce and Conger 2003). Iles and Feng (2011) argue that DL may be more supported in 'collectivistic' cultures, for which there is some empirical support (Erdogan and Liden 2006). US teams whose members endorsed more collectivistic views exhibited higher levels of collective leadership (Hiller et al 2006).

Research on DL (Gronn 2002, 2008; Harris 2007, 2008, 2012) has failed to reach definitive conclusions on whether DL is effective; much evidence comes from the education sector (McBeth 2008). Some patterns of leadership distribution seem more effective than others (Leithwood et al 2006). 'Planful alignment' is associated with superior performance compared with situations where leadership was distributed with little or no planning. 'Spontaneous alignment', perhaps similar to 'spontaneous collaboration' or 'intuitive working relations' (Gronn 2002), is also positively associated with performance, in contrast to 'spontaneous misalignment' or 'anarchic misalignment'; see Figure 5.4.

Figure 5.4: Effectiveness of distributed leadership

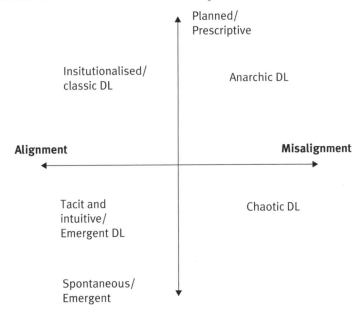

(adapted from Leithwood et al 2006; Thorpe et al 2011)

Mehra et al (2006) have also failed to support the claim that the more leadership is distributed across team members, the more effective the team; Iles and Macaulay (2007) found 'fragmented' rather than 'distributed' leadership of the 'ethical agenda' in local government (see Chapter 6 on ethical leadership). Not all dispersed or distributed leadership is effective, leaving a number of questions that require further attention (following Bolden 2011: 259–60):

1   What is being distributed? What leadership actions, tasks, decisions, responsibilities or functions?

2   Who is doing the distributing? The formal/focal leader? Others? Who controls this distribution?

3   To whom are leadership tasks/functions being distributed?

4   To what extent is such leadership being distributed?

5   How is leadership being distributed?

6   How is distributed leadership best developed?

7   Where can DL be best applied?

8   When is such leadership distributed? Under what conditions/situations is DL more likely to be found? Is it more common, appropriate or effective in some cultures and contexts than others?

GLOBAL LEADERSHIP

Developing global leaders is becoming a priority for IEs and an area of top management concern, as an insufficient supply of global leaders is often cited by top managers as inhibiting growth, especially in emerging markets and the BRIC countries (Mendenhall et al 2008). It is often linked to global talent management, to be discussed in Chapter 17. Evans et al (2011: 207) observe that 'rapid growth combined with a small pool of experienced leaders means that the lack of global leadership skills has been the primary workforce challenge for enterprises'. They also point out 'there is no accepted definition of the global leadership construct or established body of tested theory' (p208). There are several approaches to this area; here we will focus on three:

1   the relationships between leadership and culture

2   the attempt to identify 'global leadership competencies'

3   global leadership and leadership development policies and programmes in different contexts.

LEADERSHIP STYLES AND CULTURE

Depending on the context, leaders can choose to employ different leadership styles; cultural context is claimed to affect the optimum choice of leadership style. We can consider the implications of the three leadership styles from Lewin against Hofstede's dimensions, discussed in Chapter 2 (Hofstede 2001). The scores on the Power Distance Index (PDI) range from 11 to 104; the higher the score, the more authoritarian the leadership, while lower scores refer to a more delegating leadership style, as illustrated in Figure 5.5 (Dorfman et al 1997; Offerman and Hellman 1997; Ardichvili and Kuchinke 2002; Mazdar 2005). Therefore, countries with a high PDI, such as Malaysia (104), China (80) and India (77), will favour an authoritative leadership style, where employees defer to the leader and tend not to question their authority. On the other hand, countries with low PDI scores, such as Austria (11), New Zealand (22) and Ireland (28), favour delegative leadership, where everyone knows their responsibility and is able to approach and question authority. Mid-scoring countries such as the United States (40) and Greece (60) would favour a participative leadership style. Furthermore, employee empowerment is also proposed to be dependent on power distance; empowered MBA students from high PDI cultures performed less well than when they were unempowered (Eylon and Au 1999).

Hofstede (2001) proposes that leadership in collectivist cultures more often resembles authoritarian styles, where a dominating leader maintains close supervision of the group. Leaders in collectivist cultures may also be more supportive of employees, displaying affiliative leadership supporting group relations (especially long term), reducing group tension and offering care for employees' well-being. This is a 'paternalistic' style, often found in Latin America (Chapter 12) whereby leaders will take care of the followers, but will demand obedience in return. This correlation between collectivism and paternalistic leadership is found in several studies (Wendt et al 2009). Leaders in individualistic societies may be more likely to display participative and delegative leadership styles, where opinion is sought from followers. Indeed, van de Vliert and Smith (2004) showed that leaders in individualistic cultures tended to rely more on their subordinates for information.

Cultures with high uncertainty avoidance tend to show authoritarian leadership styles favouring control, rationality and lack of trust in employees; cultures with low uncertainty avoidance are said to adopt leadership styles that are more participative and delegative, and foster innovation (Dorfman et al 1997; Offerman and Hellman 1997; Shane et al 1995; Mazdar 2005). See Figure 5.5.

Figure 5.5: Leadership and power distance

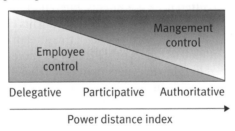

THE GLOBE STUDY OF LEADERSHIP STYLES

The Global Leadership and Organisational Behavior Effectiveness (GLOBE) programme is an ongoing large-scale global study of culture, leadership and organisations involving 170 investigators across 62 societal cultures (House et al 2004). Importantly, House et al did not divide culture across nations, unlike Hofstede (2001), but instead across common societal cultures; hence, for example, there is Canada (English-speaking) and Canada (French-speaking). They identified nine dimensions: performance orientation, uncertainty avoidance, humane orientation, institutional collectivism, in-group collectivism, assertiveness, gender egalitarianism, future orientation and power distance. House et al (2004) also identified six culturally endorsed implicit leadership theory (ILT) dimensions universally shared among all of the societal cultures they studied, that is, ways in which people distinguish effective and ineffective leaders. Different countries have both similar and dissimilar views on leadership; whereas being decisive, informed, honest, dynamic, administratively skilled, a coordinator, just, a team-builder, an effective bargainer, being dependable, a win–win problem-solver, planning ahead, being intelligent, and being excellence-oriented were universally acceptable traits, being ruthless, egocentric, asocial, non-explicit, irritable, non-cooperative, a loner and dictatorial were universally unacceptable. Culturally contingent traits included enthusiasm, self-sacrificing, risk-taking, sincerity, ambition, sensitivity, being self-effacing, compassion, uniqueness and wilfulness. As Osland (2008: 34) puts it, the major contribution is to show 'that national leadership styles have certain aspects in common as well as many cultural differences. Therefore, when global leaders have followers from different cultures, they have to be prepared to switch styles.'

GLOBAL LEADERSHIP COMPETENCIES

Recent models of 'global leadership' have often focused on leader characteristics or competencies (Black 2006; Osland 2008), emphasising inquisitiveness, embracing of duality, exhibiting character and demonstrating savvy. Mendenhall and Osland (2002) identify six core competencies: cross-cultural relationship skills, traits and values, cognitive orientation, global business expertise, global organising expertise and visioning , while Osland (2008) presents a pyramid model of global knowledge, threshold traits, attitudes and orientations, interpersonal skills and system skills. Organisations need to assess the fit between candidate competencies and present or future global leadership role.

A range of assessment instruments has been devised to assess and develop global leaders, such as cultural difference assessments, intercultural adaptability assessments and global leadership competency assessments (Bird and Osland 2004). As Osland (2008: 61) notes, virtually all of this stream of research 'is limited to opinion about global leaders or self-reports. There are no studies of their actual behaviour … the global leadership research has, for the most part, taken a content approach and focus on identifying competencies.'

One example of a global leadership competence assessment inventory is the INSEAD Global Executive Leadership Inventory, or GELI, by Kets de Vries, based on executive interviews, which uses 360-degree feedback: http://media.wiley.com/product_data/excerpt/42/07879698/0787969842-1.pdf . It identifies two broad roles of global leaders – *charismatic* (motivating) and *architectural* (systems and processes) – and 12 competency dimensions: visioning, empowering, energising, designing and aligning, rewarding and feedback, team-building, outside orientation, global mindset, tenacity, emotional intelligence, life balance and stress resilience.

However, these perspectives outlined above also see competence in essentialist, individualist ways as attributes of individuals, characteristic of the Anglo-Saxon conceptualisations dominant in most HRM models. Are such models of global, as well as domestic, leadership, as of competence and talent (as we shall see later in Chapters 15 and 17) also de-contextualised and individualistic (Iles and Preece

2006)? Is there another approach to 'global leadership'? Case Study 5.1 shows one such alternative.

 WORLDLY LEADERSHIP OR GLOBAL LEADERSHIP?

CASE STUDY 5.1

Turnbull et al (2012) argue for 'worldly leadership' rather than 'global leadership' to challenge the hegemony of Western business education, as 'postcolonial theory' discussed in Chapter 2 seeks to do. Leadership theories informing business education have largely been rooted in Western conceptions of leadership, with 'global leadership' often shorthand for exporting Western managers or leadership models. Ethical and sustainable leadership, and leadership for the common good, are also necessary (see Chapter 6), and giving voice to the disenfranchised or marginalised. Leadership wisdoms originating beyond the Western world can help support a radical transformation of global business education towards a more responsible and sustainable template building on indigenous and Eastern ideologies. Forty-five in-depth interviews with leaders from indigenous and non-Western cultures were conducted to gain insights into how their leadership identities, values and behaviours had been shaped by their societies and the oral wisdoms in their cultures, as well as interviews and observations of 26 executives participating in a class of the International Master's Program in Practicing Management.

> http://
> www.worldlyleadership.org/
> themes/

> http://
> www.leadership.org.uk/page/
> sharon_turnbull_s_articles

This MA programme involves the 'managerial exchange', where managers pair up and spend the better part of a week at each other's workplace. The programme is delivered in five countries (England, Canada, India, China and Brazil) by local faculty and in local organisations, and involves a diversity of organisations – corporate, SME, NGO, entrepreneurial – to facilitate authentic sharing of unique life biographies and insights. Each module – managing organisations, context, relationships, change and continuity – lasts approximately 10 days; participants move between concept-based training and real-life experiences, and also benefit from peer-to-peer learning, complementing observation, visits and feedback (http://www.impm.org/).

The research identified a number of embedded leadership wisdoms currently overlooked: a deep-rooted ethic of responsibility, conviction, stewardship and sustainability and a cosmopolitan mindset. This view challenges Western business schools to embed the knowledge found within those societies and communities towards a more sustainable response to our planet. Responsibility, humanity, benevolence, trusteeship, contribution, honesty and conviction are some of the core 'wisdoms' that can inform and frame a radical rethink of the norms of business school curricula; new forms of business education based on leadership wisdoms in indigenous and oral cultures and ancient texts have therefore much to contribute to radical mindset change in business education.

Question

1   Do you agree with Turnbull's views?

2	How would you bring such views into international	leadership development programmes?

To some extent, Turnbull's views share critiques of traditional leadership models put forward by proponents of such ideas as distributed, stewardship and authentic leadership. We look more closely at corporate social responsibility and ethical leadership in Chapter 6.

GLOBAL LEADERSHIP AND LEADERSHIP DEVELOPMENT IN DIFFERENT CONTEXTS

Is global leadership development different from 'domestic' leadership development? Evans et al (2011: 207) focus in particular upon what they call the 'intransitivity' of leadership in IEs, or 'the difficulties of translating leadership capability at one level to capable accomplishment at the next level'. With globalisation and regionalisation this has

> become more urgent, creating new leadership roles for senior managers. … Regional structures place particular demands on senior managers, as operating managers within their regions are often the ones to make strategic initiatives; regional managers will therefore need to develop extensive coaching skills to support them, coordinate their efforts and promote cross-border learning. …They must be able to stretch, and at the same time to support, the local units; facilitate cross-border learning; and to build strategy out of entrepreneurial initiatives. Finally, top managers need to be institutional leaders with a longer time horizon, nurturing strategic development opportunities, managing organisational cohesion through global processes and normative integration, and creating an overarching sense of purpose and ambition … more empirical research is needed to understand the skill requirements at different levels of multinational firms. (ibid: 207)

However, these features present challenges for global leadership development as

> many people who perform well in entrepreneurial leadership roles at the operating level will find it difficult to adjust to more ambiguous roles as lateral co-ordinators and integrators in business areas or regions. Those individuals who have the potential to master such a transition need to be identified, and appropriate developmental experiences need to be provided to build the new skills they will need. (ibid: 207).

This has important implications for leadership development and talent management, viewed as knowledge-sharing and knowledge-transfer mechanisms, if sustainable competitive advantage comes from building strong organisational capabilities that are hard for others to imitate. Leadership development is 'a powerful vehicle for global coordination' (ibid: 218):

> In a fast-moving, competitive global environment, strategic initiatives come from the operating-level managers, not from top management. The operating managers heading up business units and subsidiaries need to be aggressive entrepreneurs, creating and pursuing new business opportunities, as well as attracting and developing resources, including people. In contrast, the senior managers heading up businesses and countries/regions, to whom these entrepreneurs report, need to be integrative coaches with strong skills in lateral co-ordination, able to cope with the complexity of vertical and horizontal responsibilities simultaneously . (ibid: 208).

One issue is 'striking the balance' between top–down or organisationally driven initiatives and bottom–up or open-market, individually driven ones. 'Open job resourcing' initiatives for internal staff, accelerated by the global standardisation of HR processes through intranet e-HR technology, such as self-help/self-service technology services like e-learning and transparent career track management (for example IBM, Cisco), help people to continuously look for openings posted on the intranet themselves (Evans et al 2011). Usually senior-level leadership jobs are still managed top–down, leaving open the question of how far down or up to cascade these two approaches.

In general, corporate mobility and cross-functional moves are seen as vital in broadening perspectives; employees assume responsibility for results outside their function, building relationships, networks and social capital. However, 'if a company is to get out of its dependence on home-country expatriates … talented locals need experience in challenging line positions at headquarters that will provide them with the matrix perspective, the global mindset and the social networks to equip them for senior leadership positions' (Evans et al 2011: 218–19), leading to conflicts with high-potential PCNs competing for the same positions (Chapter 3).

Mendenhall et al (2008) argue that general leadership development methods suitable for 'domestic' leadership should be modified for global leadership development – for example coaching or mentoring by those with international experience, international job assignments and reflections on intercultural survey instruments. In addition, processes using *contrast, confrontation and replacement/remapping* should be used in a transformational process of *letting go* and taking on new constructs and models. This process can be facilitated by 'enabling competencies' such as tolerance of ambiguity and the provision of opportunities through experiential rather than didactic methods (that is, 'open' or emergent experiences, quadrants 2 and 3 in Figure 5.3). These experiences include travel, seminars, project teams, outdoor learning and inpatriation/expatriation assignments which confront 'normal' ways of behaving with 'different' ones, as well as helping build networks. Experiential methods such as simulations, planned field trips, global development centres and assignments carry higher potential for such 'remapping' than lectures or seminars (quadrant 1 in Figure 5.3).

In this chapter we have analysed the importance of leadership in cross-cultural settings and its importance in the context of an international enterprise, and critically discussed various leadership theories and models, particularly emerging frameworks such as distributed and dispersed leadership. We have sought to understand the importance of global leadership to IEs and the role of global leadership development – or perhaps 'worldly leadership development' – to IHRM.

Leadership styles and patterns currently differ among nations. Culture colours the way things are done, but less so what is done. In foreign operations, who do we assign to lead: expats or local talents? In increasingly multinational and multicultural teams, who do we assign as team leaders: PCNs, HCNs or TCNs (Chapter 3)? From what we have gathered in this chapter, we need global leaders, or perhaps worldly leaders, who can use a variety of leadership styles depending on the situation, *and* have high IQ, EQ and CQ. Where do we find them? Interestingly, these individuals may have always been around: the sons and daughters of immigrants, cross-country businessmen, and military, religious or business expatriates, who have been aptly named as *third culture kids* (Pollock and Van Reken 2009). They have grown in between two worlds as they follow their parents around the globe. Some settle in the host culture, others return home; all are neither from here nor from there. Having grown up in different cultures, they have the potential to empathise with the foreign and synergise home and away; they could well be the ideal future expatriates (Selmer and Lam 2004). An interesting observation was made when US President Barack Obama was elected: his father was from Kenya, his mother was from America and he grew up in Indonesia and Hawaii (Newton-Small 2007). Furthermore, his staff comprises many who share his experience as children from multicultural backgrounds and experience of living abroad (Van Renken 2008). Could it be that this is the way for cross-cultural leadership? Or is there still room for global or worldly leadership development initiatives, especially of the more emergent and open kind?

CHAPTER 6

Ethics, Culture and Corporate Social Responsibility

Paul Iles

INTRODUCTION

In chapters on HRM in different regions we often discuss the importance of corporate social responsibility (CSR) to HRM, in many developing countries in particular, with reference to 'multiple stakeholder management'. In recent years we have seen many failures in ethical corporate leadership, and globalisation is changing the ethical questions and problems faced by IEs and leaders. How can we help staff and managers recognise and be aware of ethical questions and issues?

Most discussions of CSR, ethics and HRM see it as about developing codes of governance, fairness, performance indicators and 'best practice' guidelines over such issues as the use of child labour, health and safety standards, and environmental pollution (Bevan 2007). Ethics and CSR have major roles to play in IHRM, in part as they directly relate to such issues as equal opportunity, diversity, discrimination in employment, recruitment and selection, appraisal, performance management and talent management, where the interests and rights of the individual or group may come into conflict with those of the organisation. They also play major roles in cross-cultural HRM, which is why we consider them here; what should a manager do when a practice viewed as wrong in the home country may be seen as legal and acceptable in the host country? Is a relativist, or an absolutist, perspective most appropriate? *Ethical relativists* may define the situation as 'what is right is what is right in the host country'; there are no absolute rights and wrongs. *Ethical absolutists*, in contrast, may seek to apply universal standards or principles, while *cosmopolitans* may seek to reconcile these extremes (Briscoe et al 2012).

After discussing these issues we go on to explore some approaches to ethics in HRM, from ethical and authentic leadership to integrity testing, as well as ethical issues in different contexts such as North America, the Middle East and English local government. We then move on to a related area of growing importance to IHRM – CSR – exploring such issues as what areas are covered by the term, what is driving interest in it, and the business benefits that may accrue to companies adopting it. We also look at the roles of voluntary self-policing, codes of practice and international labour law.

ETHICS, CULTURE AND IHRM

What works in domestic contexts may be seen very differently in another country, with different perceptions of unethical conduct – 'legitimate business relationships' in one country may be seen as 'collusion' in another with a different ethical climate. Should a manager use connections or bribery as an HR tool, or gift-giving to smooth relationships? Since these may seem culturally acceptable in some countries, what ethical issues are raised?

The Hofstede (2001) framework discussed in Chapter 2 places China with Spain in the 'moderate to high collectivism and high power distance' group (Jackson 2001: 1269). Chinese and Spanish managers at a Beijing business school both placed high importance on external relations and gift- giving and accepting, and both judged organisational loyalty issues as having high ethical importance; other national groups may take a different view. The Chinese, however, viewed pilfering supplies and taking extra personal time from work as less ethical. Jackson (2001: 1294) attributes this to China being 'likely to be higher in both collectivism and uncertainty avoidance than Spain' and that 'higher obligation-based culture and higher levels of regulation explain why managers attribute a higher ethical importance … to issues involving relations with the organisation'. Similarly, Chinese managers attributed high importance to group ethical issues, such as passing blame to others and claiming credit for others' work.

Problems of corruption/bribery remain, not just in developing countries, as issues central to IHRM; recent scandals in the UK over MPs' expenses fraud, phone-hacking and payments to public officials for information have demonstrated this. In the UK, the importance of connections and knowing the right people (for example family/school connections, 'the old school tie') in getting into universities, internships and jobs remains pervasive. Western or Japanese companies, and increasingly Chinese companies in Africa, may take advantage of foreign operations by employing low-wage workers, by moving operations 'offshore' or by outsourcing work to low-wage economies (for example Briscoe et al 2012). Multinational companies from differing countries of origin may use subcontractors using child labour or exploited, low-wage labour; for example, allegations have hit Gap, Banana Republic and Apple in China. Such practices are not unknown in Western countries, of course (for example exploitation of migrant labour, use of sweatshops and home-working).

ETHICS, ETHICAL THEORIES AND ETHICAL PRACTICES

Ethics is a nuanced arena of debate that often leaves it open to a broad range of interpretations. Managers and employees everywhere may operate from completely different ethical perspectives over values and what is classed as right or wrong, especially in culturally different regions. There are two main theories here (Iles and Macaulay 2007):

- *Consequentialists* look to the moral value of the *outcomes* of actions – who was hurt or helped? They are *utilitarian*, often adopting economic utility as the most important value; the happiness of the greatest number is the criterion by which to assess utility, and 'the end justifies the means' is a frequent justification invoked.
- Non-consequentialist or *deontological* theories tend to be rooted in Kantianism; human dignity is seen as an end in itself, with stress on universal moral rules and human rights and a focus more on motivations behind actions – what was the person trying to do?

We first discussed cultural differences of this kind in Chapter 2, where we compared 'universalistic' and 'particularistic' dimensions of culture put forward by Trompenaars (1997) in responses to such dilemmas as 'do you report your friend for a traffic accident'? Does it make a difference if the offender is your friend (or sister, spouse, partner, son, etc) compared with a stranger or slight acquaintance? In a similar vein, efficiency theory tends to stress shareholder value, while social responsibility theory stresses stakeholder value.

Ethical issues involve moral rights, as ethics is the study of morality and moral standards – those by which you judge right from wrong. The standards you use are influenced by the values you hold, so ethics is centrally about *values*. Organisations, like individuals, are often claimed to show values, as embodied in 'organisational culture'. These may be written in mission or value statements; at other times they are simply informal rules about how things get done in a given organisation. Values influence behaviour; therefore, the more clearly you understand your personal values and those of an organisation, the more likely you are to make the best decisions for yourself.

 REFLECTIVE ACTIVITY 6.1

1   What are your own personal values?

2   How do they influence your behaviour at work?

We will now turn to an examination of ethical issues and how they have been handled by HRM in different regions and cultures, beginning with North America.

ETHICAL ISSUES IN HRM IN NORTH AMERICA

In recent years there have been a series of corporate scandals in the USA, such as Enron, Worldcom and Tyco, as well as a series of banking scandals; top managers have often pleaded ignorance of any corrupt or unethical activities, leading to greater interest in corporate governance and ethical leadership (the UK has also had a range of banking scandals, ranging from Barclay's Bank attempting to fix the inter-bank lending rate (LIBOR) and Californian energy market to the alleged involvement of HSBC in Mexican drug money-laundering and Standard Chartered in laundering Iranian money despite US sanctions). Attention has been given to how to limit such actions by identifying, preventing and deterring illegal and unethical activities. Possible options include external regulations, compliance programmes and voluntary ethical initiatives, including psychometric testing (Kacmar et al 2011).

One typical approach has been through laws and regulations. The Sarbanes-Oxley Act (SOX) 2002 was designed to protect the public from executives allowing unethical and illegal behaviours to occur; CEOs and CFOs are required to sign statements making them personally responsible for quarterly financial statements, with fines and prison following conscious misrepresentation. Other external regulations in the USA include laws on compensation and overtime pay, discrimination and affirmative action laws, health and safety regulations, dismissal requirements and privacy issues.

In addition, company codes of ethics are often developed, signed, monitored and registered with the Securities and Exchange Commission (SEC), and 'whistleblowers' revealing details of corrupt activities receive protection. Corporate codes of ethics spelling out standards of acceptable behaviours and policies, such as over monetary values of acceptable gifts, and values statements describing the values the firm wants employees to adopt are also popular. Visible buy-in from the top is recommended as necessary, as well as wide dissemination and follow-up.

However, claims that companies such as Walmart continue to push low costs on to suppliers, requiring them to operate 'sweatshops' to survive, have led to repeated lawsuits by employees. Incidents of paying less than the minimum wage and unpaid overtime have also been subject to legal action.

Assessment of the *ethical climate and culture* (for example pressures for misconduct, prevalent attitudes); *training* in implementing a code of ethics; *appraising* ethical performance; *rewarding* individuals for ethical behaviour; and *communicating* the ethical message to the workforce are all recommended. The *costs* of unethical behaviour also need to be identified and communicated, including human costs (demotivation, loss of talent, lack of trust and loyalty) as well as monetary costs (in fines, loss of reputation and customers, damage to the brand, falls in share price).

REFLECTIVE ACTIVITY 6.2

See the Ethics Resource Center and Ethics Effectiveness Quick Test at

> www.ethics.org/ethics-today/
> archives.html

> www.asaecenter.org/Resources/
> ANowDetail.cfm?ItemNumber=38646

This test seeks to assess organisational cultures and climates in such areas as rewarding ethical behaviour, creating ethical principles and procedures, ethics training, and ethical leadership to identify areas of improvement. These include policies and procedures about allowing individuals opportunities to take advantage of situations, for example offers of gifts, hospitality, tickets to concerts and sporting events.

How appropriate are these to organisations in your own country?

See also:

> www.journalofaccountancy.com/
> Issues/2003/Feb/
> EnsuringEthicalEffectiveness.htm

However, policies are only useful if *enforced* through rewards and sanctions. Creating a corporate division responsible for the ethical agenda is one option (for example Ernst & Young developed a values statement in 2003 followed by a code of conduct and an ethics and oversight board and the appointment of an ethics and compliance officer). Given the 'individualism' that is a feature of US culture (Hofstede 2001), it is perhaps not surprising that two leading attempts to develop ethical HRM in the USA have involved seeking to recruit individuals with strong ethical characters through 'integrity tests' and selecting and developing 'ethical leaders'. We first look at the role of 'integrity testing', usually used for 'lower-level' staff.

ARE INTEGRITY TESTS THE ANSWER TO ETHICAL PROBLEMS?

There has been increasing interest in the concept of 'integrity': behaving in ways that reflect broadly shared values in areas such as trustworthiness, honesty and unwillingness to take advantage of others, often also associated with emotional intelligence. It is an over-simplification to believe that integrity is solely an attribute of an individual, however. Almost everyone will show integrity in some situations; almost everyone will be dishonest or untrustworthy in others. The *situation*, and especially the *norms* that operate in workplaces governing issues such as ethics, stealing, lateness and expense-fiddling will all influence how much 'integrity' is displayed by both employees and leaders.

However, people do seem to differ in the extent to which they show 'integrity' across a range of situations; honest people tend to show integrity behaviour across a wider range than dishonest people. Therefore, integrity seems to be a product of both *personal* (for example values, attitudes, beliefs) and *situational* factors (norms, opportunities, rewards and sanctions). To influence integrity at work, we can try to change the situation: introduce better monitoring and security procedures, change organisational norms, publicise efforts to reduce and isolate dishonesty, and ensure ethical leadership, often emphasising codes of conduct, registers of interests and monitoring. Or we can try to 'change the person': training, investigation and dismissal, and recruitment, assessment and screening. 'Recruiting for integrity' may be very important in situations with many opportunities for dishonest acts and organisational norms tolerating some degree of dishonesty (some corrupt police forces, for example). Employee theft and fraud is a major and growing problem in the retail and financial services industry, and integrity tests are often advocated as one strategy to minimise theft and other counterproductive behaviours (though often focusing on front-line staff rather than leaders). Their use is mainly in the USA, UK and Netherlands, especially in retail and banking, but they are rarely used for managerial and executive staff (despite the potentially much greater risks of dishonest and corrupt behaviour at this level?).

There are basically two kinds of integrity tests:

1   *Overt tests*: scales seek to assess admissions of dishonesty and employees' or candidates' perceptions of their own or others' dishonesty over issues such as drug use, theft and dishonesty, punitive attitudes towards dishonesty, and their thoughts regarding dishonesty. Questions might ask: 'Have you ever been convicted of theft?' or 'Should this company sack people convicted of stealing?'

The links below show one company's product, Vangent, with research reports on its use:

www.pearsonps.com/instruments/reidr.htm

http://www.vangent-hcm.com/docs/
842C96B4-92AA-299C-150B6A8759B849DF/Articles/
SIOP_Article_2011.pdf?

2   *Personality-based tests*, where employees and candidates are presented with items describing characteristic behaviours, interests and activities (for example the Employee Screening Questionnaire and the Hogan Personality Inventory (www.hoganassessments.com/HPI.aspx), often containing 'normal' personality dimensions and reliability scales. These seek to measure such dimensions as thrill-seeking, resistance to authority, and aspects of the 'Big Five' personality factors, such as conscientiousness, agreeableness and extroversion (see Chapter 5). Dishonest employees may, for example, score low on conscientiousness, risk-taking or responsibility. Scores are often correlated with measures of sabotage, lateness, substance abuse and theft, general measures of counterproductive work behaviour, overall job performance and measures of 'shrinkage' (losses attributed by stores to employee theft).

In general, both kinds of such tests show similar levels of validity for predicting relevant future performance comparable to other kinds of psychometric tests, with few major group differences except for women scoring higher on integrity in most tests than men (Van Iddekinge et al 2012). Overt tests tend to be validated against polygraph tests and indices of theft; personality tests against supervisory ratings or personnel data.

However, none of these, despite the apparent popularity in the USA of the polygraph, have been shown to be more effective than integrity tests. Honest but anxious people may fail such tests, whereas dishonest but calm people may pass them. Current employees may also have their behaviour monitored through surveillance systems of various kinds, especially shop-floor employees; these may raise other ethical issues such as invasion of privacy (managers and executives tend to have their privacy respected). However, organisational factors such as loose norms, socialisation of new recruits to tolerate or perform illegal acts, lack of any end-accountability for ethical behaviour, and scapegoating of whistleblowers reporting illegal or unethical acts usually have stronger impacts on dishonesty than personal variables (bad barrels have more impact than bad apples!), leading to concerns over 'ethical leadership' and ethical climates as leaders have significant impacts on the 'ethical tone', climate or culture of the organisation. They can support policies, structure, behaviour and beliefs to support ethical behaviour (Sims 2000) and enjoy greater discretion and autonomy in engaging in unethical behaviour than front-line staff.

ETHICAL AND AUTHENTIC LEADERSHIP

We discussed leadership in Chapter 5; many examples of unethical behaviour are related to ethical leadership (or lack of it). *Counterproductive leadership behaviour* (Jackson and Ones 2007) is an example of counterproductive work behaviour (CWB), intentional or volitional behaviour contrary to the legitimate interests of the organisation. Leaders have significant opportunities to steal, waste or cost their organisations huge amounts of money; both 'property deviance' and 'product deviance' are feasible, as well as interpersonal issues such as sexual harassment, bullying or abuse. Types of CWB include theft, property destruction, misuse of time and information and resources, unsafe behaviour, poor attendance, poor quality of work, alcohol and drug use, and inappropriate verbal and physical actions, some targeted at the organisation, some at organisational members.

They may also foster CWB among others through their own CWB, promulgating CWB as normal business practice. Leaders may rationalise misconduct by citing fear of failure, perceived norms, unshareable problems, denial of harm, unnecessary or unjust laws and regulations, corporate survival needs, expectations and pressures from others, perceptions that everybody else is doing it, and being deserving of the rewards/entitlements. Judgement calls, faulty rules and socially embedded norms are common reasons given for bending rules, as well as denial of victims (for example 'they deserved it/had it coming to them').

Ciulla (2006: 17) suggests that 'leadership is morality magnified'; leadership, management and organisation are practices that have an inherent ethical quality to them. Are the ethics and integrity of leaders what give their ideas and vision legitimacy and credibility (Mendonca 2001)? Minkes et al (1999: 328), for example, argue that both management and leadership are concerned with 'ought' questions. Ethical leadership has most commonly been associated with transformational models of leadership (Chapter 5); for Bass (1985), however, some leaders could become so transformational, and a leader's vision so strong, as to breed unethical behaviour; excessive charisma may lead followers to commit morally reprehensible acts. Bass and Steidlmeier (1999) categorised transformational leadership into two types: authentic, concerned with the development of followers and the needs of the organisation; and pseudo-transformational, displaying self-interest, seeking glory, personal power or individual reward. Such research is often prescriptive, building on philosophy and focusing on principles of 'ethical leadership'.

Other approaches are more descriptive, rooted in organisational and social psychology to assess how leadership is perceived as ethical (or not) in particular organisational settings. What particular ethical behaviours do leaders engage in?

Ethical leadership has been defined as 'the demonstration of normatively appropriate conduct through personal actions and interpersonal relationships and the promotion of such conduct to followers through two-way communication, reinforcement and decision-making' (Brown et al 2005: 120). Treviño et al (2003) identify seven characteristics: an outward-oriented people focus that seeks to develop followers; high visibility of good conduct by the leader; open communication and good listening skills; setting standards of self and others, with lapses in conduct not tolerated; being always accountable; seeing the decision-making process as an end in itself; and employing a broader understanding of issues and a greater ethical awareness of concepts such as the common good. Ethical leadership has both *moral person* and *moral manager* dimensions, involving more than traits such as integrity and transformational leadership to also include transactional components, such as using communication and reward systems to guide ethical behaviour and stand out against an ethically neutral ground.

Brown et al (2005) developed a model (Figure 6.1) where ethical leadership is influenced both by personal factors (for example the 'Big 5' attributes such as conscientiousness) and situational factors (the ethical context, culture and climate and exposure to ethical role models). Other factors moderate it, such as need for power or ability to monitor one's own behaviour.

'Ethical leadership' is thus both similar to, and different from, other influential perspectives, not just emphasising transformational-type behaviours such as self-awareness, concern for others, ethical decision-making, integrity and role-modelling ethical behaviour for others, but also using more 'transactional' and 'other-oriented' behaviours such as setting ethical standards and holding followers accountable through rewards and sanctions.

Figure 6.1: An ethical leadership construct

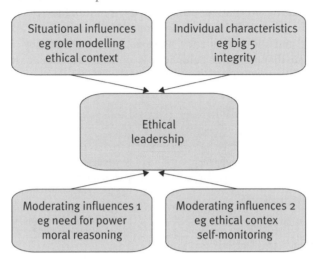

(adapted from Brown et al 2005: 596)

Resick et al (2006) use data from the GLOBE project discussed in Chapter 2 to assess four dimensions of ethical leadership: altruism, character/integrity, collective motivation and encouragement. Though universally supported, the degree to which each component was endorsed by respondents varied across cultures, suggesting that though 'ethical leadership' may be universal, the importance attached to key elements of it varies across cultures.

An alternative, or perhaps complementary, concept is *authentic leadership*, based on the classical Greek maxim 'to thy own self be true', and humanistic and positive psychology. It involves knowing, accepting and acting in accord with one's values, beliefs, preferences and emotions. Avolio et al (2004: 4) define authentic leaders as 'individuals who are deeply aware of how they think and behave and are perceived by others as being aware of their own and others' values/moral perspective, knowledge, and strengths; aware of the context in which they operate; and who are confident, hopeful, optimistic, resilient and high on moral character'. Authentic leadership is the 'root construct' underlying ethical, spiritual, servant and transformational leadership; authentic leaders develop authenticity in followers through enhancing self-awareness and self-regulation and positive modelling, involving four core elements:

- *self-awareness* – of values, identity, emotions, goals and motives, such as knowing when to re-evaluate positions
- *unbiased processing* or 'balanced information processing' from multiple perspectives, such as listening to different viewpoints before deciding
- *relational authenticity* or 'relational transparency', presenting one's genuine self and 'saying what you mean' through self-disclosure, sharing information with others to build trust
- *authentic behaviour and action* in accordance with values and needs, rather than to please others or avoid punishment.

For May et al (2003), authentic decision-making involves recognising moral dilemmas, evaluating alternatives transparently, intending to act authentically and sustainable authentic behaviour, developed by fostering 'moral capacity', 'moral courage' and 'moral resiliency' as aspects of 'moral efficacy'. Endrissat et al (2007: 217) argue that authentic behaviour is 'context-dependent': its value and meaning varies across cultures.

? REFLECTIVE ACTIVITY 6.3

See the following websites on authentic leadership:

www.authenticleadership.com

www.authleadership.com

www.authenticleadershipcenter.com

1   How American/'culture-bound' do these perspectives seem to you?

2   Is 'authenticity' always an important ethical value, or can it excuse bad/negative behaviour – 'this is just me/how I work/the real me/I'm not faking/pretending but being true to myself'?

There has been increasing interest in issues of trust, ethics and ethical behaviour in the public services in England in recent years (for example Lawton et al 2005; Iles and Macaulay 2007), especially with regard to local government, motivated by concerns over bribery and fraud, for example 'cash for questions' in Parliament, 'cash for access' to ministers and expense fraud by MPs.

LEADING THE ETHICAL FRAMEWORK IN ENGLISH LOCAL GOVERNMENT

Legislation in 2000 made four major recommendations for local authorities in England:

- a code of conduct
- a register of members' interests to avoid conflicts of interest in, for example, planning decisions
- a standards committee comprising elected members of the authority and independents to oversee ethical issues in general, and the code of conduct in particular
- an independent body, the Standards Board for England, to investigate alleged breaches of councils' codes of conduct and to promote high ethical standards.

Ethical leaders can be identified at the sub-local authority level (for example standards committees); at the central government level (for example government departments); and in national independent organisations (for example the Committee on Standards in Public Life, the Standards Board for England). A crucial role is the *monitoring officer* (MO), providing most training and advice on ethical issues and liaising between central bodies (particularly the Standards Board) and other local bodies, most notably the standards committee and parish and town councils (Lawton et al 2005).

Monitoring officers, usually lawyers, are the lynchpins of the new ethical framework, with new duties, functions and responsibilities concerned with local investigations and determination of complaints about alleged breaches of the code of conduct and responsibility for both the code of conduct and the register of interests. They may also serve as the leading officer to standards committees. This approach is more concerned with monitoring behaviour through codes of conduct than assessing personal integrity or selecting and developing ethical or authentic leaders.

There has also been interest in developing ethical frameworks in other regions, such as the Middle East, to which we next turn.

ETHICAL ISSUES IN HRM IN THE MIDDLE EAST

In much of the Middle East the influence of often family-based 'connections' (*wasta* or piston) affects HRM, especially in such areas as recruitment, selection, promotion and performance management (Chapter 10) (Weir 2003; Weir and Hutchings 2005). This may help humanise the workplace, creating a warm atmosphere and showing commitment to life beyond work; it may also lead to appointments on the basis not of merit, but of who has connections, raising ethical issues over nepotism, bribery and corruption.

Someone holding a 'relativist' ethical position may feel relaxed about this – it fits with Arab/Muslim 'collectivist' and 'particularistic' cultures (Hofstede 2001; Trompenaars 1997) where people are expected to put families and relatives first. Managers may feel pressured to appoint, promote or fail to discipline people who are poor performers but well connected to rich, powerful or high-status groups (not just an issue in this area of the world, of course!). However, many *within* the Middle East have challenged these practices in the name of more 'universalist' principles (Trompenaars 1997) such as fairness, transparency or meritocracy, as well as more 'utilitarian' principles such as enhancing efficiency and effectiveness. Such challenges have often been raised with regard to government and public service employment. Common ethical challenges here include setting and implementing anti-corruption and integrity standards; making anti-corruption institutional/procedural frameworks effective; and improving scrutiny over government and civil service action (Ashour 2004; OECD/UNDP 2006).

Some countries, for example Tunisia, Yemen and Dubai, have progressively reformed and modernised their civil services, introducing more flexibility and incentives, but in many others public sector pay structures encourage bribery and petty corruption, especially in agencies dealing directly with the public (Suliman 2006). Many countries lack effective ethics regimes and integrity provisions to control discretion and prevent conflicts of interest, allowing favouritism and nepotism to thrive. In some countries, such as Egypt, there are formal regulations, but these may be rarely enforced. Public sector HRM policies and practices in the Middle East can therefore be deficient in various ways (Ashour 2004):

1   Overall, institutional frameworks may not state and enforce basic ethical/ integrity principles or limit political and personal influences on HR decisions.

2   Lack of HR planning data and an overall HR policy may fail to emphasise merit and competence, leading to exclusion or disproportionate representation of groups.

3   Absence of fair, equal and transparent recruitment policies may lead to favouritism, nepotism and corruption.

4   Absence of sound selection and placement policies based on merit and competence may lead to invalid and biased selection criteria, subjectivity, favouritism and discrimination, and an absence of equal opportunity.

5   Weak performance management systems may reduce accountability through ill-defined jobs, reducing fairness in evaluation.

6   Discrimination in rewards based on personal or political factors such as personal, family or clan loyalty may be widespread.

7   Training and development may be subject to abuse and corruption through bribery, non-competitive contracts and favouritism in training nominations.

8   Promotions and career advancement may be based on personal or political criteria, or 'inducements'.

9   Disciplinary procedures may be subject to corruption and malpractice, lacking fairness or transparency.

10   Officials leaving employment may still seek to advance personal interest through bids for business or use of information and influence as consultants or contractors.

Many similar challenges exist in many developing countries, as well as in many advanced industrial countries, as shown in our discussion of ethical issues in the USA and the UK; many local HR researchers and practitioners have begun to recognise and address them. To avoid or minimise unethical practice, HRM strategy generally also needs to balance ministerial and organisational autonomy and accountability in HRM, as decentralisation may lead to increased discretion for corruption and favouritism (as Iles et al 2004 found in Mauritius). Alternative approaches to developing ethics/integrity regimes may need to be developed in more culturally appropriate ways, not just the transfer of Western models. Benchmarking initiatives against best practices worldwide, perhaps complemented by religious-based integrity efforts, where appropriate (for example Islamic-based ethical initiatives emphasising their ethical basis) may also be useful.

CORPORATE SOCIAL RESPONSIBILITY (CSR) AND IHRM

A more recent development in this area has been the principle of 'corporate social responsibility' (CSR) and an appreciation of the role HR can play in developing CSR initiatives. The focus has often been on clarifying the nature, limitations and implementation of CSR policies and practices. Company reports and websites now often routinely include sections on CSR, including areas such as fair trade, human rights and environmental protection and climate change. Sachdev (2006, 2011) points to such high-profile issues as the accusations against Shell of longstanding human rights and environmental abuses in the Niger Delta in particular, Tesco's role in poor pay and conditions for its South African fruit pickers, and Primark, Gap and Nike's alleged use of child labour in India. Many such abuses have occurred with the company's suppliers or subcontractors.

In China, many MNCs are often seen as 'good' corporate citizens, taking social responsibility seriously to protect their image, with wages and working conditions above the local average (Cooke 2011b); despite concerns over pollution, it is also a global leader in renewable and clean energy, solar and wind power (see http://www.worldwatch.org/node/5497 and http://www.bbc.co.uk/news/science-environment-17662973).

However, other MNCs dominate low-technology industries with low-skill and Tayloristic working practices (Wilkinson et al 2001), and concerns with CSR have also dominated recent news stories on IEs in China, as Case Study 6.1 shows.

 APPLE, CHINESE 'SWEATSHOPS 'AND CSR AT FOXCONN

CASE STUDY 6.1

Based on: http://www.fairlabor.org; http://somo.nl/publications-en/Publication_1963 www.guardian.co.uk/sustainable-business/fair-labor-investigation-apple-foxconn; http://lcbackerblog.blogspot.co.uk/2012/03/transparency-and-monitoring-corporate.html; *Guardian*, 12 March 2012)

Apple (makers of the iPhone, iPad and iPod) has recently been involved in reports that one of its most important manufacturing suppliers – Foxconn Technology – violates CSR standards and labour rights in China. Its supplier code of conduct requires suppliers to treat workers with dignity and respect and provide safe and healthy working conditions; the company is required to terminate its relationship with suppliers that do not adequately address problems within 90 days. However, Foxconn has continued to assemble iPads and iPhones, despite allegedly offering excessive overtime work, crowded living conditions, improper disposal of hazardous waste, falsifying records, disregard for workers' health and the use of child labour.

The Taiwanese giant Foxconn is China's largest exporter and, with 1.2 million workers, one of the nation's biggest employers, with plants throughout China assembling electronic devices for companies such as Amazon, Dell, Hewlett-Packard, Nintendo, Nokia and Samsung. The Fair Labor Association, an NGO, recently completed an intensive investigation of Foxconn at Apple's request. It and Foxconn have laid out an action plan and timeline that, if fully implemented, will have far-reaching impacts on its employees and on Chinese manufacturing as a whole, reducing working hours to Chinese legal limits of 49 per week while preserving current levels of pay by July 2013.

Does this policy shift reflect the recent loss of Steve Jobs, a dominant, charismatic CEO, a capitulation to pressure from NGOs and investors about the validity of autonomous reporting and self-policing, or a real shift in internal corporate culture? You can find an overall 2007 profile of CSR in Apple by the Dutch-based NGO SOMO (http://somo.nl/; http://somo.nl/publications-en/Publication_1963) and an assessment of its environmental performance from the US-based NGO As You Sow (http://

asyousow.org/sustainability/climate %2oIT%2).

Questions

1   Can Apple and Foxconn set an example so that other employers will be obliged to follow in order to attract and retain workers – a race to the top, rather than the race to the bottom, by becoming an employer of choice ?

2   Is global, lasting change only possible if all companies are held to the same standard and take responsibility for their role in the global supply chain?

3   What about those who 'supply the suppliers'?

4   Do consumers also have a moral obligation to demand high CSR standards from corporations to stop corporate misbehaviour?

Questions include the responsibilities of businesses beyond maximising profits and delivering shareholder value; issues of corporate governance now receive higher attention (for example ethical indices in many stock exchanges, ministers for corporate responsibility, and the reporting of CSR issues in company reports and websites). We address some of these issues elsewhere in the book, for example, when we look at developments and issues in HRM in Africa and Latin America (Chapters 13 and 14). Here we introduce the topic and outline some major principles and controversies, focusing primarily on the role of HRM in CSR.

WHAT IS COVERED BY THE TERM CSR?

Sachdev (2011) points to the 'conceptual confusion' in this area; the term covers a range of issues, including the environment, animal welfare, labour rights and impact on communities, as Table 6.1 shows.

Table 6.1: Some areas of interest to CSR

Animal rights
Social causes
Religious foundations
Human rights
Philanthropism
Cooperative principles
Employee involvement schemes
Avoidance of certain markets, for example tobacco, war, alcohol
Environment, for example green/ecological issues, climate change, deforestation, pollution
Fair trade
Organic food
Discrimination, diversity, equal opportunity
Health and safety
Pay and working conditions
Child labour
Collective bargaining and trade union recognition

CSR often involves responsible companies acting beyond purely legal obligations to ensure that commitments to multiple stakeholders are met – not just shareholders, but also employees, suppliers, customers and the wider societal/ community interest, as implied by McWilliams and Siegel (2001: 117): 'actions that appear to further some social good, beyond the interests of the firm and that which is required by law'.

Note that all of these terms are contested; for example, is 'fair trade' the same as 'ethical trade'? There is clearly some overlap between 'ethics' and 'CSR'; Janney and Gove (2011: 1563) discuss the US 'stock-option backdating scandal', where firms falsified the dates they had awarded stock options to employees in terms of CSR, but ask: 'Was this disclosure behaviour consistent with each firm's prior reputation for ethical behaviour?'

Does CSR refer to the continuing commitment by IEs not only to behave ethically but also to go beyond this by contributing to the economic and social development of the communities in which they operate, as well as that of their workforce (Briscoe et al 2012)? Should IEs not only meet the needs of shareholders, but also those of a wider range of stakeholders in a 'sustainable' way, not compromising the ability of future generations to meet their own needs? Can CSR be observed when companies integrate social and environmental concerns in their business operations and in their interaction with their stakeholders (European Commission 2011)? The European Commission defines CSR in terms of the responsibility of enterprises for their impact on society, integrating human rights, consumer concerns and social, environmental and ethical concerns into their business operations. Alternative terms include corporate responsibility, corporate citizenship and responsible business.

Carroll (2001) argues that companies have multidimensional responsibilities – economic, legal, ethical and philanthropic. CSR may be deployed defensively to protect reputation and profits; or proactively, to change culture and reputation with stakeholders. In some businesses, such as the Co-operative Bank and retailer, ethical issues and CSR have become mainstream concerns (Sachdev 2011).

CSR is therefore an evolving but disputed concept with potentially far-reaching implications for IHRM, especially as HRM is now often the implementer of many CSR programmes, particularly those involving the workforce. However, its practice is distinctly uneven, with codes of practice often being poorly monitored and poorly enforced.

WHAT IS DRIVING SUCH INTEREST IN CSR?

Most UK operations of MNCs are covered by a CSR code, mostly part of a wider international code; Sachdev (2011) points to growth in SRI, or socially responsible investment, as well as in legal requirements in many European countries, as partly driving CSR, which is also driven by the actions of ethical consumers and pressure groups. Anticipated benefits include avoiding risks (for example corruption, accidents); attracting capital and investment from ethical investors, social-venture capitalists, social investment firms and social entrepreneurs, and by desires to avoid government intervention and secure community and government support. Different agendas and concerns have driven interest in CSR, and different issues are stressed in different codes, often associated with country of origin. Lower priority is often given to collective bargaining in many US-based companies, or even outright opposition; in the UK there is often little union involvement, though in European firms, especially from Germany or Nordic countries, CSR codes may be negotiated with an international union federation or European works council (Sachdev 2011).

For some companies, drivers may be a concern for human rights; for others, social justice; for others, a business case, such as skill upgrading or productivity gains. For others, as in Case Study 6.1, NGO and media pressure seems crucial. However, some feel CSR distracts companies away from their core business of pursuing profitability, or that CSR harms economic development, leads to an unregulated informal sector, or its costs harm competitiveness (Cooke 2011b). For others, CSR neglects the role of power (Knights and O'Leary 2005, 2006). Banerjee (2010) argues that despite emancipatory rhetoric, discourses of corporate social responsibility are defined by narrow business interests and serve to curtail interests of external stakeholders; they are 'ideological movements that are intended to legitimise and consolidate the power of large corporations'.

Does a business case for CSR stack up? For many companies, CSR is of strategic concern because ethical/CSR approaches can affect profits, corporate reputation, branding and employer branding, and the recruitment and retention of staff. Stock exchanges such as the FTSE in the UK and the Dow Jones in the USA have created ethical indices, such as FTSE4Good, requiring minimum standards and good practice. EU laws have led the way in terms of the European Social Agenda and Directives, while Germany has a 2001 law in place requiring MNCs to report on social and environmental matters (Sachdev 2006, 2011).

Relationships between financial performance and CSR initiatives may, however, not be causal in the direction often claimed – firms may take such initiatives when financially viable, not that CSR generates 'business benefits'. CSR may signal 'quality' to investors, employees and commentators or analysts, signalling financial health, enhancing reputation and corporate identity and boosting employer brand (Janney and Gove 2011); CSR may help offset negative reactions to wrongdoing, making these appear 'aberrations'. From a neo-institutional theory perspective (Chapter 3), firms may undertake CSR because it is socially expected of them. Prior signals of ethical behaviour and values through CSR may exacerbate market reactions to later wrongdoing violations, exposing firms to greater scrutiny and charges of hypocrisy if caught, and thus greater market sanctions. For example, Body Shop in the UK presented itself as a champion of CSR initiatives (animal testing, environmental damage, etc) but as a result exposed itself to more journalistic investigations of violations. Rock stars Bono of U2 and Sir Bob Geldof have a high profile championing poverty and development issues, especially in Africa; as a result their tax avoidance strategies, for example, have come under greater scrutiny. However, self-disclosure of wrongdoing, rather than attempting a cover-up, may buffer the firm and ameliorate damage, perhaps because it is seen as consistent with CSR initiatives, trust and responsiveness (Janney and Gove 2011).

Why firms 'go green' has been a perennial issue; a response to *regulation*, *stakeholder pressure* or seeking *business benefits*? Crotty and Rodgers (2012) found that while 'because it pays' motives were persuasive for many Russian manufacturers, regulation and stakeholder pressure had only limited impacts on greening. To be sustainable, however, CSR needs HRM input, for example on ethical labour standards, equal opportunity and diversity, to be discussed in more depth in Chapter 20. Taking CSR seriously may also hopefully deliver HR outcomes, such as employee well-being, talent attraction and engagement, as well as organisational outcomes, such as higher productivity, customer satisfaction, local acceptance, reputation and higher profits/share price. Undertaking CSR initiatives may also generate suspicion over company motives: is it just PR? There may be a need for external regulation and enforcement, but this also creates tensions: do codes of conduct just shift blame for infringements away from the company and on to individual employees? For global companies, different localities have varying standards, codes, values and laws.

Other issues include whether CSR should be delivered in a top–down way or through participation and involvement, reward and appraisal, or communication, training and development. Bonus payments may be linked to environmental, health and safety, and employee satisfaction measures. A major debate is over the effectiveness of 'voluntary self-policing' by companies as distinct from a compulsory regulatory approach. Self-policing is open to abuse (for example PR spin, great-sounding policy rhetoric, but poor implementation or monitoring of effectiveness), and many inspectorates may be weak or powerless in the face of rich, powerful MNCs with armies of expensive lawyers and PR spin-doctors. Voluntary codes may work best when they produce standards that can be monitored, when embraced by companies willing to investigate stakeholder claims of violation (see Case Study 6.1) and when stakeholders can affect the consumer markets for companies. Can they help stakeholders, including NGOs, leap over the state 'middleman' and directly affect corporate behaviour in a targeted way? In Chapter 20 we discuss this issue further with respect to labour rights, employment relations and the role of the International Labour Organization (ILO) in particular.

LEARNING SUMMARY

This chapter has reviewed issues of ethics, corporate social responsibility and labour standards, laws and regulations and their implications for IHRM. It has looked at the role of HRM in ethical behaviour and specifically discussed ethical behaviour in the Middle East and North America, in leadership and corporate governance, and in English local government. Concepts of ethical and authentic leadership have been discussed, as well as how to reduce or eliminate unethical behaviour, including the role of integrity tests, codes of conduct, training and monitoring. It has also examined the concept of corporate social responsibility (CSR), what areas it covers, what is driving such interest, and how HRM might be involved in CSR in the context of the global context of business.

CHAPTER 7

IHRM, Culture and Knowledge Flows in International Alliances, Joint Ventures, Mergers and Acquisitions

Paul Iles

LEARNING OUTCOMES

By the end of the chapter, you should be able to:

- Understand the nature of international mergers and acquisitions, joint ventures and alliances and the different approaches adopted to them by IEs, with particular reference to organisational and national culture.

- Understand the impact of country of origin, host country, people and cultural issues on successful international mergers and acquisitions, alliances and joint ventures.

- Discuss the IHRM implications of international acquisitions and mergers, joint ventures and alliances at different stages.

- Appreciate IHRM's role in implementing effective alliances, joint ventures, and mergers and acquisitions.

- Critically analyse the role of IHRM in transferring and diffusing knowledge in multinational enterprises and in international joint ventures and alliances, and the factors affecting the transfer of IHRM knowledge across borders.

INTRODUCTION

In this chapter we are interested in how IHRM is evolving, with particular attention to the ways in which IHRM now 'goes beyond boundaries' in several senses, such as international mergers and acquisitions (IM&As) and joint ventures and alliances (IJVs) (Briscoe et al 2012; Schuler et al 2004; Pucik et al 2011). For example, the proportion of cross-border M&As increased from less than 30% in 2000 to nearly 50% in 2007 (Pucik et al 2011); globalisation has spurred unprecedented interest in IM&As, especially within Asia by Asian firms. Three-quarters of the foreign direct investment (FDI) into the UK has been via IM&As (Boxall and Purcell 2011).

IEs can 'internationalise' through several vehicles, such as starting up a foreign operation (for example greenfield site through FDI); they can export from the home country, perhaps through an agent in another country; and they can operate through some form of *alliance or combination*. Here we consider *international alliances* (where two or more firms enter into a formal or informal agreement without fusing); *international joint ventures* (where two or more 'parent' firms create a separate 'infant' entity); and *international mergers or acquisitions* (two or more separate firms fusing to become one entity). Many IEs have entered into a variety of strategic partnerships and alliances; though presenting significant challenges of coordination and integration, IEs increasingly use them to gain access to new global markets and resources, such as technology, skills and talents (for example BP–Amoco, Daimler–Chrysler, Tata–Jaguar–Land Rover, etc). Such resources may be too expensive, or take too long, to acquire solo, or be impossible to develop internally. In some countries, partnerships and alliances with locals may be the only, or best, way to enter a market, as was the case for many years in China.

We first look at IM&As before looking at alliances and joint ventures.

REFLECTIVE ACTIVITY 7.1

Look up the following websites on IM&As:

The Institute of Mergers, Acquisitions and Alliances at:

> http://www.imaa-institute.org/

> http://www.imaa-institute.org/ statistics-mergers-acquisitions.html

> http://www.imaa-institute.org/ publications-studies-mergers- acquisitions-alliances.html? PHPSESSID=6d6f1cafebb1fb754537b4 49c93e6451

Or Deloitte at:

> http://www.deloitte.com/view/ en_US/us/Services/additional-

services/merger-acquisition-services/ merger-acquisition-library/merger- acquisition-strategy/index.htm

And:

> http://www.deloitte.com/view/ en_US/us/Services/additional- services/merger-acquisition-services/ merger-acquisition-library/index.htm

1   Why do you think IEs are increasingly using IM&As?

2   What kinds of problems do they often encounter?

IHRM IN INTERNATIONAL MERGERS AND ACQUISITIONS

The acquisition of organisations, and the coming together of two or more organisations to form a new entity, often from different countries, is becoming increasingly common in a more global, competitive business landscape. In IM&As two companies agree to join their operations together to form a new company; in an international acquisition, one firm buys controlling or full interest in another, with the buyer determining how the combination will be managed (Briscoe et al 2012). Sometimes the acquired business continues as a separate entity, with little initial change to its HR practices and with only gradual changes in structures, processes and personnel (for example Asda and Walmart; see Taylor 2005). Other mergers may involve changes, including changes to HR practices, that may be much more dramatic and rapid.

Figure 7.1 shows the IM&A process.

Figure 7.1: International merger or acquisition

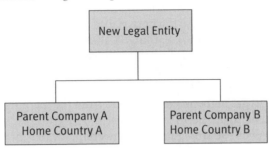

Many mergers and acquisitions, as well as alliances and joint ventures, 'fail', despite 'due diligence', in terms of not delivering on their initial objectives; this is often the result of neglect or misunderstanding of people and HR issues, giving a range of 'people problems' such as lower commitment, job insecurity, cultural conflict, stress and inertia due to narrowed focus (for example the Daimler–Chrysler merger).

HOW CAN HRM HELP IN MERGERS?

So, given the relative failure of many mergers, in part due to failing to take into account people issues and cultural differences between the parent organisations, what can HRM do to mitigate such problems and help ensure a smoother merger process? In many IM&As, people may feel uncertain, experiencing anger, fear, worry and upset. Rumour and gossip may be rife, with people speculating over redundancy, forced job changes or pay cuts; there may be widespread dissatisfaction among staff with communications, with people feeling 'we have been abandoned and no one cares enough to tell us what is going on. Why have we been sold and what is going to happen to us?' There may be a culture clash, with ways of doing things that are totally different. New recruits may not feel adequate measures have been taken to help them integrate or fit in.

The HR function needs to ask:

1   Have organisational and cultural differences – both national and corporate – been identified and addressed?

2   Is there a leadership group from both parties leading the change process?

3   Has the shared vision of the new organisation been created and communicated to all, with clearly defined goals, roles and responsibilities?

4   Have links been made between HR and business strategy?

5   Is there a plan to consolidate and integrate policies on HR issues?

In addition to issues of 'national culture', differences in 'organisational culture' are also an issue; though our main interest will be in 'national culture', we need to keep organisational cultural differences (and perhaps sectoral or professional cultural differences) in mind as well. The importance of 'regional' cultural differences in mergers is discussed in Case Study 7.1 with reference to Nigeria. Indeed, Pucik et al (2011) argue that the fear of national cultural differences upsetting IM&As may be exaggerated – cultural distance may have positive, as well as negative, effects on IM&A performance, perhaps because cultural differences sensitise managers to the importance of culture in IM&As and provide opportunities for mutual learning. A study of Finnish international acquisitions by Vaara et al (2012) found that organisational and national cultural differences had different effects in IM&As. Organisational cultural differences prompted 'social identity building', leading to 'us and them' thinking and antagonism or segregation between employees from the merging parties. The parties involved tend to develop a lack of trust and in-group versus out-group biases, especially given the ambiguous and uncertain futures they may face.

However, cultural differences can also contribute to learning and knowledge transfer; organisational cultural differences may often be positively associated with social conflict, but national cultural differences can actually lead to a decrease in conflict, perhaps because of complementarities and synergies (Vaara et al 2012). In addition, both organisational and national cultural differences may be associated not with dysfunction but with knowledge transfer. Are national cultural differences less of a problem in IM&As than often thought? Organisational cultural differences may present more challenges to successful IM&As, and national cultural differences may be an asset or resource rather than a problem for organisations.

Organisational development techniques, such as the future search conference (a planning meeting that is task-focused, bringing together people in one room or parallel rooms), can be used to facilitate post-merger integration (Weisbord 1987). It brings people with resources, expertise, formal authority and need together for mutual learning among stakeholders as a catalyst for voluntary action and follow-up and new forms of cooperation that can continue for months or years. Future search and related techniques can be used to try to create a new culture in an organisation formed from the merger of two parent organisations using individual and group work among representatives of both parent organisations to obtain large-group consensus on a 'common future' taking cultural and people issues into account.

We explore knowledge transfer in IM&As and IJVs at the end of this section.

Institutional factors (explored in Chapter 1) may also play a part; Rees and Edwards (2009) discuss how these may slow or modify the merger integration process, for example the need for works council approval in many EU countries. They point out that the orientation of a parent in a merger may affect the success of the IM&A – the *country of origin* effect. In addition, the way that HR issues are handled at local level may show a *host-country* effect. For example, the UK-based mobile phone company Vodafone – which has grown rapidly through IM&As – found considerable opposition when it acquired the German firm Mannesmann, as such activities are less acceptable in Germany. US, Japanese, French or German firms, for example, seem to handle HR issues very differently in IM&As; US firms often prefer formal and regular appraisals and a more forceful, 'hands-on' approach to integration, whereas Japanese firms often take a slower approach, and French firms tend to operate a system of formal qualifications for promotion and a 'glass ceiling' for non-French managers.

Around one-third of IM&As are dissolved within a few months or years (Briscoe et al 2012). Expectations need to be managed, information given, the 'vision' of the new company communicated, and new roles and contributions explained. A major issue is overestimation of the other party's capabilities, exaggeration of possible 'synergies' and cultural incompatibility; groups with very different norms and values, including very different legal and regulatory systems, accounting practices, and HR policies and practices, are expected to work together. Some kind of pre-merger *cultural analysis* of both parties may be useful to identify tension points, as well as HR-oriented *due diligence* (Taylor 2005).

DIFFERENT APPROACHES TO IM&AS

M&As practise different approaches from IM&As; some may use a *portfolio* approach, where managers in both companies maintain autonomy; others may require *assimilation* into one 'legitimate' culture. Some may try *blending*, mixing the best elements of both cultures; others try to *create a new culture* derived from all parties. Pucik et al (2011) suggest that the strategic logic of the merger, as well as the management of the integration process, affect IM&A outcomes. Mirvis and Marks (1992) refer to different kinds of post-merger outcome:

1   *preservation* – no cultural change in acquired company, retaining independence and autonomy and boundary protection

2   *absorption* – large change for acquired company, assimilating to acquirer

3   *transformation* – cultural change in both companies to 'break with the past'

4   *best of both* – selective combination of 'best' features of both parties to form a 'merger of equals'

5   *reverse merger* – acquired company dictates terms.

Another classification framework refers to three main integration approaches (Schwieger et al (1993); the higher the need for integration, the higher the degree of change required in organisational culture, identity and HR practices:

1   *Assimilation* – one party (voluntarily or forced) adopts the identity and practices of the other, replicating the dominant party's HR and other practices, as in 'absorption' above, perhaps leading to culture clash, hostility and resistance to change.

2   *Novation* – the combination develops new working practices, culture and identity through cultural integration ('best of both' above) or new and distinctive practices ('transformation' above).

3   *Structural integration* – units retain their own identities, as in 'preservation' above, though perhaps avoiding initial conflict, which may emerge later.

Case Study 7.1 shows these approaches in the Nigerian banking industry.

MERGERS AND ACQUISITIONS IN NIGERIAN BANKS

CASE STUDY 7.1

M&As are growing in Africa, especially in South Africa and the Nigerian banking sector. This is prompted by government regulation enforcing consolidation of the sector, but is an under-researched area. In Nigeria mergers involved merging 70 previously independent banks to create 19 new banks. As elsewhere, the human factor and HRM are critical to success. Such HRM issues as cultural due diligence (undertaking an assessment of the different cultures involved and their potential for clash or complementarity), pre-merger communication, management and employee due diligence (for example the different HR policies and practices and staff skills, competencies, age levels, demographics, experience, qualifications, etc) and future rewards all play a role in merger success.

Within the Nigerian banking sector, these measures led to large job losses and continued monitoring by the Central Bank of Nigeria. Banks anticipated acquiring other resources such as IT and talent, enhancing capability, achieving complementarity and widening their regional coverage within Nigeria. In many cases prior relationships, family connections and informal personal links facilitated the 'courtship' needed to 'find a partner', despite a general sense of urgency and time pressure due to the need to comply with the government directive; others adopted more formal joint seminars and use of consultants. *Regional* cultural differences were underestimated in many cases, especially between the Muslim north and the south, over issues such as dress code, age of bosses/subordinates, closing times for prayers and regional

origins of senior managers in the new merged bank.

Communications through seminars, emails, packs, training and the intranet played a key role in helping overcome resistance, enhance interaction and build understanding and integration. Some banks were much more 'open' and 'transparent' than others over issues such as what came next – some restricted information to top management only and some employees only got information from the local newspaper!

Nine banks followed an *assimilation* approach, where one or more of the combined firms adopted – voluntarily or by coercion – the identity, name, culture and policies of one partner. Four banks followed a *novation* approach, involving high levels of reorganisation and restructuring, often renaming themselves to symbolise 'combining the best of all parties'. Here HRM policies and practices played a particularly important role. Three followed a *structural integration* approach, where banks maintained high levels of autonomy, identity and separateness. This seemed particularly the case when merging banks came from both the north and south, so as to avoid culture clashes. These banks often made extensive use of training and induction to set out a common vision and build trust. Fear of job losses seemed to raise stress levels and also perceptions of regional difference, for example 'we're being marginalised'. Staff who were let go were often helped to find jobs elsewhere. HR themes emerging in successful mergers included quality of HRM due diligence, handling of regional cultural differences, extent and quality of communications and use of integration advisors.

(based on Gomes et al 2012)

Questions

1 What people problems are mentioned in this case?

2 How might you analyse these, for instance in terms of national

cultural dimensions such as collectivism or power distance and factors such as respect for age (Hofstede 2001)?

3 What other levels of culture are significant in the case?

4 What does the case indicate about the importance of HRM: pre-merger? post-merger?

WHAT IS NEEDED FROM HRM TO MAKE MERGERS SUCCESSFUL?

In answering the questions in Case Study 7.1, you might have cited such practices as:

- *an appropriate cultural assessment* to identify similarities and differences between the parties in terms of values, beliefs, attitudes and styles, as well as HR policies and practices
- *a human capital audit* of HR liabilities, policies, talents and skills, and selection of a management team
- *design of communication and integration strategies*, including inter-group cooperation through task forces or project groups containing employees from both organisations
- *retention of talent* as key employees often leave, especially in IM&As, for example Lenovo and IBM
- *top management commitment* to lead the new organisation into the future and create a new culture, perhaps with common policies and practices, including HR policies
- *the creation of a 'positive atmosphere'* and positive vision for the future of the company, involving people at all levels from both companies
- *managing the transition* through, for example, the provision of training and support for staff so that they can manage the change and acquire new skills, for example in implementing the new HR policies.

There are typically three stages involved in IM&As (Briscoe et al 2012; Pucik et al 2011):

1 *Pre-combination/initial planning stage* following the merger announcement: this involves initial screening and courtship, a *due diligence* review of the target, price-setting and negotiation, and contract agreement. HR issues include issues of corporate and national culture, executive styles, pending problems, succession plans, management capabilities, employee skill levels, language skills and specific HR issues, such as obligations, employment regulations, corporate cultures and HR practices.

2 *Agreement signing and planning/deal-closing stage*: this involves how to implement the deal, address differences and sign the agreement.

3   *Implementation/post-merger integration stage*: this involves integration of the parties, communication of the vision, new HR systems and management of resistance to change, given the feelings of insecurity, anxiety and concern often expressed by employees.

Though the HRM function is typically mostly involved in the third stage, it should be involved in all three stages. Specific HR areas of concern include staffing differences and tensions, such as practices and norms over strategy, time orientation, risk, power distribution, decision-making and consultation, information-sharing, hiring and firing staff, reward and compensation issues such as pay levels, pay scales and incentive plans, benefits differences (such as retirement, health and welfare programmes, and training and development programmes) as well as such issues as HR information systems, unions and employee involvement institutions and programmes.

In any IM&A there will need to be attention paid to (Taylor 2005: 22):

1   the design of the post-merger structure

2   harmonisation of the terms and conditions of employment

3   the management of redundancies

4   the merging of HR functions and processes – a danger here is that employees may perceive the 'unequal' adoption of policies and the subsuming of organisational identity, even in apparent 'mergers' rather than wholesale 'takeovers'

5   standardisation of HR processes and practices across the new organisation

6   ensuring that key talent is retained.

Appointing a dedicated 'integration manager' supported by transition teams selected from employees of both parties is often a useful way to make a successful post-merger transition. These often act as 'information gatekeepers' between the two sides, acting as a model for how the new organisation should act (Pucik et al 2011). Rapid implementation of the integration process is often most effective (Evans et al 2010).

One issue for EU-based organisations is the Transfer of Undertakings regulations (TUPE), over which legal advice should be taken. In principle they require a continuation of both individual terms and conditions of employment and collective agreements after a change of ownership, a ban on dismissal after ownership change unless there is an acceptable alternative economic, technical or organisational explanation, and a requirement for both transferor and transferee organisations to consult with staff representatives about planned changes at the earliest opportunity (Taylor 2005).

INTERNATIONAL ALLIANCES, JOINT VENTURES AND IHRM

International alliances can be seen as informal or formal partnerships not resulting in an independent legal entity; they may allow IEs to increase capabilities and enter new markets in relatively low-risk and low-cost ways. These alliances include outsourcing, information-sharing, consortia and joint marketing and research projects. As with IM&As, there are a number of design choices here (Briscoe et al 2012):

1   *operator model* – no dominant partner

2   *shared model* – organisation draws on culture and practices from both partners

3   *autonomous model* – new culture and structure is purposely developed.

International joint ventures (IJVs) are another form of international alliance or combination. Kanter (1989) distinguishes different types of combinations:

1   *pooled* (or cooperatives, usually research-based)

2   *alliances/joint ventures.*

Two broad categories of international combinations include *equity* combinations, such as international M&As (which we have just discussed) and international joint ventures; and those involving *no shared equity investment*, such as R&D consortia, co-production/co-marketing arrangements and long-term supply agreements in retail. 'Alliances' here refers to generic forms of cooperation, with equity joint ventures a special case cemented by ownership-sharing through equity holdings, a major vehicle used to enter new global markets. However, joint ventures, especially international joint ventures, often fail, associated with differences in culture, HRM practices and management style (Iles and Yolles 2002a, 2002b, 2003b).

Figure 7.2 shows these two types.

Figure 7.2: Types of alliances

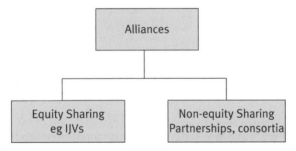

IJVs are legally defined and economically separate entities created by two or more parent firms that, unlike IM&As, continue to enjoy a separate existence, collectively invest financial and other (including human) resources, and have at least one firm headquartered outside the country of the joint venture. They are of a different nature to more formal mergers, acquisitions or intricate partnership agreements, being legally distinct organisations formed by two or more sponsoring partners originating in two or more countries; Figure 7.3 shows an example formed by two companies from two different countries.

Figure 7.3: International joint ventures

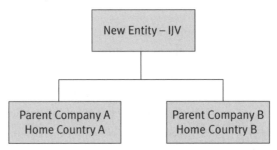

Joint ventures constitute entities with particularly complex sets of HRM practices owing to the high levels of interaction between employees of different corporate and national backgrounds – who may also be PCNs, HCNs or TCNs – from collaborating partners (see, for example, Dowling et al 1994; Schuler et al 1993). IJVs also need to use HRM and career management practices to reduce psychic distance and encourage identification with the joint venture; HRM therefore plays a significant role in affecting IJV success.

Particularly important issues are the 'integration' of firm and JV culture and practices, including:

1   Is the new firm to be an integrated entity drawing on the culture and practices of both firms, or is it an entirely new organisation?

2   How can it ensure the appropriate selection of IJV personnel?

3   How can it ensure the use of experienced PCNs?

4   Should it provide cross-cultural training (discussed in Chapter 4) for staff from both parents, as well as for staff newly recruited to the IJV?

5   Should it provide joint training for HCNs and PCNs?

6   How can it build a unique joint venture culture through HRM, taking elements of both host and home culture as well as new elements not found in either?

Clearly alliances involve sharing people and HRM practices. There will therefore need to be attention to HRM issues, especially orientation to the IJV and issues of corporate and national culture. IJVs provide significant opportunities for organisational learning, especially the transfer of culturally embedded knowledge if trust is developed and substantial non-contractual inputs invested (Fitzgerald 2000).

Employees working in alliances and partnerships will still be employees of the separate partners, and so potentially difficult to 'supervise', with other possible difficulties such as the different laws, claims and benefits experienced by different staff. IHRM issues needing clarification and attention include:

1   organisational structure and reporting relationships, especially in loose and fluid project structures

2   culture, both national and corporate

3   pre-alliance 'due diligence'

4   executive cross-cultural skills

5   succession plans

6   management capabilities and talent allocation

7   language skills

8   appropriate start-up and implementation teams.

Benefits are likely to be appropriated asymmetrically according to the organisational learning capacity of the partners (Pucik 1988). A vital part of such a learning infrastructure includes HRM policies supporting the protection of competitive advantage and influencing the IJV, especially the transfer and accumulation of knowledge, enabling parents to learn:

- more about each other,
- more from each other, and
- more from the alliance itself.

This learning can also be useful for other units and alliances. Some partners may emphasise learning, others may not; and 'the behaviours and styles of managers in organisations have a significant impact on the ability and willingness of a firm to learn' (Schuler 2001: 317). HRM policies and practices may support or inhibit knowledge flows, sharing and development; establishing mechanisms to enhance trust may benefit the relationship between alliance partners (Schuler 2001).

Schuler et al (2004) argue that four key stages are involved in an IJV:

1   *formation* – identifying the rationale for the IJV, its benefits, selecting a manager, finding potential partners, selecting the partner, building trust and managing conflict, and negotiating the arrangement

2   *development* – locating the IJV, establishing the appropriate structure, securing the IJV management team

3   *implementation* – establishing IJV vision, mission, values, culture and strategy; developing HRM policies and practices; dealing with issues; and staffing the IJV

4   *advancement* – learning between partners, transferring learning to parents, and transferring new knowledge to other locations.

We have emphasised the crucial roles played by organisational learning and knowledge transfer in successful IJVs. We next analyse this process in more detail, focusing on the role played by culture but also on other factors affecting the success of knowledge transfer.

KNOWLEDGE TRANSFER AND LEARNING IN INTERNATIONAL ALLIANCES

Knowledge management has emerged as an influential approach to understanding organisational practices, including HRM practices. Knowledge is often assumed to be a key economic resource, intangible asset and source of competitive advantage (Alvesson 1995, 2011; Davenport and Prusak 1998; Nonaka and Takeuchi 1995). From an HRM perspective, sharing and exchanging globally between organisational units (for example corporate HQ/affiliates; joint venture parties and actors) is often claimed to enhance organisational effectiveness (Argote et al 2003; Nonaka and Takeuchi 1995; Davenport and Prusak 1998). Organisational performance may be facilitated by knowledge creation, application and sharing behaviours internally embedded in an organisation's knowledge management system, such as routines and systems (Nonaka and Takeuchi 1995). While knowledge is embodied within individuals, it is also located collectively at the organisational level as employees engage with each other in work practices to develop collective pools of knowledge.

Polanyi (1966) distinguished tacit from explicit knowledge on the basis of its relative lack of formalisation and communicability; for Kostova (1996), tacit knowledge is located in individuals' cognitions and acquired through experience and reflection on behaviour, making it difficult to transfer to others. Tacit knowledge may be acquired by experience, observation and dialogue (Nonaka 1991, 1994). Explicit knowledge, in contrast, is codifiable, making it easier to share, distribute and transfer.

Knowledge-sharing is therefore often seen as an important dimension in knowledge management, but employees are often reluctant to share knowledge (Cabrera and Cabrera 2002). Nonaka and Takeuchi (1995) developed a knowledge-creating process model involving tacit and explicit knowledge; sharing knowledge with colleagues is seen as necessary for organisational learning, transforming individual learning processes into organisational learning processes.

Organisational and national culture may hinder or facilitate knowledge-sharing in international alliances, as well as power, self-interest and lack of skill, or sufficient incentives to do so. Organisations can exploit external sources of knowledge through different inter-organisational arrangements, including alliances and joint ventures, making 'knowledge transfer' an important process here (Argote et al 2003); in particular, the *absorptive capacity* of the organisation or its ability to identify, evaluate, integrate and apply new knowledge is critical (Cohen and Levinthal 1990). Knowledge transfer is influenced by levels of prior knowledge, knowledge similarities, social ties and networks, and combinative capabilities between the two or more alliance partners.

HRM policies and practices may support or inhibit knowledge flows, sharing and development; establishing mechanisms to enhance trust may benefit the relationship between alliance partners (Schuler 2001).

For Zander and Kogut (1994) there are four key domains or contexts involved in knowledge transfer: the *source* and *recipient contexts, the knowledge context* and *the situational context*. Source and recipient contexts include their experience, values, trust, motivation and the willingness of a source to transfer knowledge or sink to receive it (Cohen and Levinthal 1990). Structures, cultures and the ability to receive and apply new knowledge and the cultural and power differences between source and recipient are also key factors. In terms of the knowledge context, *tacit knowledge* is more ambiguous and difficult to transfer. The relational context includes such channel characteristics as proximity, ties and relationship quality (as in joint ventures), social interaction and communication, knowledge levels and cultural differences (Jackson 2001).

One question is what term best describes the 'knowledge transfer' process. Jankowicz (1999) uses metaphors of 'export sales' and 'new product development' to discuss knowledge transfer across cultural and linguistic boundaries. In the first case, the assumption is made that both parties share the same conceptual background and assumptions, whereas in the second case, the two parties are seen as co-equal collaborators. Every language encodes phenomena differently, so the meaning encoded by one party may be subtly different from that encoded by the other, as we shall see in our discussion of the different cultural meanings of 'talent' in Chapter 17.

This is particularly the case if translators or interpreters are used; one of the authors (Iles) was running a workshop for HR directors of steel companies in Inner Mongolia, China. I was asked about an organisational problem and replied that I saw it as a 'change management' issue. I wondered why the directors' body language became a lot more negative following the reply. When I asked the translator later, he said he had translated my reply as 'change the management' (that is, fire the guy who had asked the question) when what I actually meant by the phrase 'a change management problem' was that it was a 'managing change problem'!

Jankowicz (1999: 319) argues that instead of knowledge transfer, the term 'mutual knowledge creation' is preferable, as it refers to the negotiation of new understanding; Iles et al (2004) use the term *knowledge migration* instead, stressing the non-linear, multi-directional and emergent nature of knowledge flows between two or more 'world-views' in international joint ventures, alliances and partnerships (Czarniawska 1997; Czarniawska and Joerges 1996). As 'both information and knowledge are context-specific and relational in that they depend on the situation and are created dynamically in social interaction among people' (Nonaka and Takeuchi 1995: 256), knowledge is not a thing or commodity that can simply be handed over unchanged to another party.

A number of factors have been found to affect such knowledge migration: national and organisational cultures, a knowledge-sharing environment, information and communication technologies, and organisational structure. Knowledge migration may occur from a knowledge *source* (the knowledge base, often in the 'West', such as the corporate HQ of an international enterprise) to a knowledge *destination* or *sink*, often in the 'South' or 'East', such as an alliance or joint venture in China or the Middle East (Figure 7.4). The process may be facilitated by a 'knowledge intermediary' such as a consultant or academic, or by a project team, or by expatriates.

Figure 7.4: Knowledge migration in international JVs

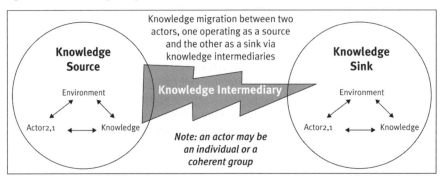

Parent-country system	Cultural distance	Host-country system
Parent-country culture	Motivation	Host culture
Parent-country HRM/D system	Willingness	Host HRM/D system
Learning orientation		Absorptive capacity

(adapted from Iles and Yolles 2002a, 2002b, 2003b)

The process of transfer or migration of HRM knowledge covers several stages, from 'identifying the knowledge to the actual process of transferring the knowledge to its final utilisation by the receiving unit' (Minbaeva et al 2003: 587). It is usually seen as a transfer from the headquarters (for example in the USA, UK or Japan) to the affiliate or alliance, though it could be 'reverse transfer' the other way, from affiliate to headquarters. A firm's HRM processes may constitute a significant source of competitive advantage over local firms, critical to successful operations; transferring such processes, and using HRM processes to help transfer other processes, is crucial to effectiveness. Grant et al (2000: 102 -129–) claim 'the movement of knowledge between different geographical locations is central' to adding value in international enterprises.

The role of expatriate managers and others in 'transferring' knowledge through training, coaching or mentoring has recently been emphasised (Minbaeva and Michailova 2004), including in collaborative alliances, perhaps facilitated by a 'knowledge intermediary' such as a consultant, academic or project team. The process has to span differing bases of knowledge and learning systems; expatriates are often knowledge brokers or gatekeepers (Lee and Juda 2004), given the job of transferring knowledge through training, coaching or mentoring, as in the Anglo-Chinese retail store studied by Gamble (2010). Their effectiveness depends on their willingness to do this and their ability to do this (which in turn depends, as Figure 7.4 shows, on the 'learning orientation' of the source and its strategic objectives). Motivation is considered to be a critical factor in knowledge transfer because without it the actual transfer could be compromised (Minbaeva et al 2003). Successful transfer is also affected by parent-country and host-country characteristics, such as national culture and institutional/business systems, including the HRM system, as well as by the cultural differences between source and sink. In addition, the learning capacity or 'absorptive capacity' of the sink affects how well transfer occurs.

The ability and willingness of local personnel to learn (Figure 7.4) will determine how well they acquire HRM knowledge; cultural differences and adaptability, language and communication, working relationships, and motivation and willingness affect the transfer process. Effective communication is vital for the transfer of knowledge, as in the case study of an alliance between Czech and British business schools (Iles and Yolles 2003b). Valuing different cultures, building relationships, listening and observing, coping with ambiguity, managing others, translating complex ideas, and taking action are all necessary, enhanced by HRM policies and practices such as training, assessment, performance management, and reward and compensation.

Knowledge-sharing is potentially connected with both global talent management and leadership development (Chapters 17 and 5). 'Careers' may be seen in terms of inflows, outflows and transformations of knowledge over sequences of work experiences as 'repositories of knowledge' (Bird 1994). Knowledge is created and transferred by shaping employees' work experiences and sharing them through experience-based learning. In international assignments, individuals move through new experiences characterised by variety, quality and affective intensity and a sequence of knowledge-creation modes (Nonaka 1991); global and cross-cultural experiences, encounters, challenges and decisions help develop new mental models and significant opportunities and material for tacit knowledge-creation and transformation, as well as tacit-to-tacit exchange, or 'socialisation' (Nonaka 1991). Opportunities are not always taken up, however; new knowledge gained by expatriates or inpatriates may not be valued and may be rejected in the repatriation phase. Here repatriate characteristics such as willingness, ability and motivation to transfer knowledge as well as organisational and contextual characteristics are likely to have similar effects on effective knowledge transfer.

Wang-Cowham (2007, 2011: 392) argues that talent development will be more effective if incorporated with a knowledge-sharing mechanism to facilitate workplace learning by engaging with participant social networks (Weir and Hutchings 2005), as knowledge is an active, situational and contextual concept. Knowledge-sharing is thus often linked to knowledge networks and communities of practice (Wenger 2000), encouraging knowledge production and flow. For Libeskind et al (1996: 438), networks 'warrant serious consideration as mechanisms for organising the transfer and integration of knowledge', such as within-team networks, inter-subsidiary networks and transfer networks.

Socialisation and knowledge transfer processes can be formal or informal, such as cross-functional projects, job rotation, matrix reporting structures, coaching and mentoring, training and development, professional associations and social events; all allow the sharing of tacit knowledge through social interaction, personal experience and a two-way exchange of knowledge and information. Coaching and job rotation can help develop collective competences and integrative skills

(Evans et al 2011). The multiplicity and quality of social networks and social interaction, management behaviour and HRM practices can all affect the quality of knowledge-sharing. Wang-Cowham (2011: 398–400) analysed how Chinese HRM managers acquired HRM knowledge; 'five aspects influencing their learning of HRM knowledge emerged: (1) on-the-job learning, (2) external degree studies, (3) overseas training and exposure, (4) learning desire and (5) social networks. Social networks were further divided into everyday, frequent and occasional networks.' These involved relationships both with Chinese co-workers and Western expatriates; as Wang-Cowham (2011: 404) points out, 'socialisation mechanisms can nurture an ideal environment for ideas testing, skills-practicing, knowledge and best practice-sharing'.

 REFLECTIVE ACTIVITY 7.2

Think about the times when you acquired, gained or shared knowledge from or with others.

1   What experiences were the most significant to you – formal (for example work, study) or informal (for example social events) situations?

2   What kinds of work environments do you prefer to work in, and how do you share your knowledge and experience with others?

3   What networks have proved particularly useful to you in knowledge acquisition and sharing?

In addition to concerns over whether 'knowledge' of Western HRM practices can be 'transferred' without problems, misunderstandings or new understandings in the way suggested, a further question arises as to whether it is appropriate to attempt to 'transfer' Western HRM practices to other contexts. Within joint ventures, one-way 'transplant' programmes are often less successful than more collaborative 'process-oriented' approaches that make use of local expertise as to what is needed and how it may be delivered in ways that suit local conditions and circumstances.

LEARNING SUMMARY

This chapter has discussed the role of IHRM in international mergers and acquisitions, joint ventures and alliances, distinguishing between equity and non-equity partnerships or combinations. Such combinations are of growing importance in developing new products, accessing new markets and securing new resources, including human resources and talent, but pose a number of challenges if they are to be successful. Issues of culture and people management are central to success at every stage, from planning the combination and selecting a partner to integration of the parties into a new company or alliance, but HRM is often ignored, making a contribution only at the integration stage. Here such issues as communication, training and development are key. The chapter discussed some of the HR issues involved and how their neglect may lead to problems for the combination, as well as examples where HRD and OD techniques such as future search may have a role to play in ensuring success.

The chapter also discussed the typical stages through which such combinations and partnerships pass, the different types of combination available to IEs, and the strategic advantages they offer. The impact of 'country of origin' effects was noted, as firms with different national origins typically approach such combinations and alliances differently. 'Host country' effects are also present; local culture, institutions and HR practices over such areas as employee representation, the role of trade unions and employment legislation all affect the course and success of any alliance or combination. Finally, the importance of, and challenges posed by, knowledge transfer or migration and organisational learning in alliances and combinations was also discussed, and factors affecting effective knowledge transfer identified.

PART 3

HRM IN DIFFERENT REGIONS

CHAPTER 8

HRM in North America and Western Europe: The Emergence of a 'Western' HRM Model?

Paul Iles

LEARNING OUTCOMES

By the end of the chapter, you should be able to:

- Analyse the emergence of the HRM paradigm in the USA.

- Critically analyse key differences in HRM approaches in the USA, the UK and western continental Europe.

- Identify the key assumptions behind such approaches and their links to cultural and institutional factors.

- Critically analyse the 'Germanic model' of HRM and approaches to vocational education and training to identify cultural and institutional factors that impact on these as well as recent transformations of this model.

INTRODUCTION

In Part 3 we explore patterns of and issues in HRM in different regions. We will use the culturalist and institutionalist perspectives introduced in Part 1 to explore these differences. We begin by exploring the emergence of the HR paradigm in the USA and western Europe, partly to understand developments here and partly to develop a paradigm of HRM with which to compare HRM models and systems in other regions, the subject of later chapters. Many HR initiatives have emerged first in this region; however, they have also been introduced in other regions through coercive, normative and mimetic isomorphism (Chapter 3), though not without some degree of local cultural and institutional adaptation (Chapters 1 and 2).

However, this is not to claim that all HRM initiatives have come from 'the West'; indeed, Japan has been a source of many, such as total quality management, kaizen, continuous improvement and quality circles, in addition to practices such as 'just in time' management, lean production and six sigma; these have been introduced, often in adapted form, by many Japanese MNCs (as well as consultancies) throughout the globe (Gamble 2010). Indeed, we shall pursue this issue in more detail in considering the adoption and adaptation of Japanese HRM models in China (Chapter 17) and we have already discussed this issue with respect to the establishment of a regional HQ by a leading Japanese car manufacturer (Chapter 3).

It is also the case that there is no one 'Western model' of HRM; we are primarily interested in this chapter in exploring some of the institutional and cultural differences between the US model and the continental western European model of HRM.

THE ORIGINS OF THE HRM PARADIGM IN THE USA

HRM as a term and way of thinking about managing people has been highly influential in both the USA and Europe over the last three decades, despite continuous criticism as to its lack of clarity and contested meaning. It first arose as a term in the USA in 1982 when Harvard University introduced an MBA course with this title, followed by a book (Beer et al 1984). This argued that HRM should be linked to business strategy, but also that workforce and trade union aspirations should also be recognised. HRM was defined in terms of its core policy areas: *employee influence*, *human resource flows*, *reward systems* and *work systems*. People, like other 'resources' such as finance and information, also needed to be managed 'strategically' – people were the last unmanaged organisational resource, but could be invested in, harvested, applied, deployed and removed for competitive advantage. The focus was clearly on the business success of the enterprise, and a *managerialist* conception of employment relations was adopted to ensure four Cs: *competence, commitment, congruence* and *cost-effectiveness*. This is often seen as an exemplar of 'soft' HRM, with an emphasis on *human* resource management, rooted in the 'human relations' movement; people's skills, creativity, knowledge and commitment need to be captured and utilised.

More *contingency-based* approaches also emerged at this time in the USA; the Michigan model (Fombrun et al 1984) also argued for the strategic importance of HRM, but claimed that there should be different approaches in different types of situation. As organisations vary in their environments, lifecycle stages, aims and structures, HRM policies and practices should also vary. Such *contingency-based* HR is also often associated with *strategic* HRM (SHRM); 'good practice' HRM has involved HR in becoming more 'strategic', linking it more closely to strategic management, the process by which organisations determine their objectives, decide on actions and suitable timescales, implement those actions and assess progress and results. HRM, in contrast to earlier models of 'personnel management' or 'personnel administration', is therefore often identified with a strategic approach, linking the management of people to the achievement of business objectives.

The Michigan Business School model is a less humanistic model than the Harvard model, as it considers people – not necessarily employees, given the rise in outsourcing and subcontracting work – as resources in the same way as other business resources; an exemplar of 'hard' HRM, emphasising the 'resource' aspects of human *resource* management. In this model, HRM is defined more in terms of a *cycle of activities*: acquiring/selecting individuals, maintaining and improving performance, motivating and rewarding them, and developing and training them, activities all focused on delivering employee performance in line with strategic objectives.

The rise of SHRM has also led to a concern with *external* or *vertical 'fit'* between corporate and HRM strategy and the need for *horizontal* or *internal integration*, greater connection or coherence of the various components or functions of an HRM strategy – recruitment, selection, training, etc – with each other. The need for all components of HRM to drive performance so as to achieve competitive advantage was also emphasised. Strategic integration involves developing HR policies that fit either the organisation's stage of development (lifecycle models) or its strategic orientation (Legge 1995). The fundamental strategic management problem is to keep the strategy, structure and HR dimensions of the organisation in alignment.

This interest in SHRM also led to an interest in 'devolution' (making line managers responsible for many HR practices such as recruitment and selection, appraisal and performance management, and training and development). The HRM function itself was charged with developing the strategic framework, setting and monitoring standards, and acting as consultants. Ulrich and Brockbank (2005) have updated Ulrich's (1997) original US work delineating four key roles – *employee champion, administrative expert, change agent* and *strategic partner* – to identify five key HR roles, namely *employee advocate, human capital developer, strategic partner, functional expert* and *HR leader*. Interestingly, the 'champion' role now includes not just 'advocacy', but 'human capital developer', focusing on tomorrow's needs, as well as today's requirements. Some practitioners regret that this focus on HR as a 'strategic business partner' has meant a shift away from HR's role as an employee-facing 'employee champion' or 'employee advocate', trying to ensure reciprocal value, respect, equity and fairness in the workplace.

GOING INSIDE THE BLACK BOX: HUMAN RESOURCES AND HUMAN CAPITAL MANAGEMENT IN CONTEXT

In the 1990s dominant models of strategy developed in the USA shifted from an external to an internal orientation, as embodied in the resource-based view (RBV) of the firm (Grant 1991; Barney 1991; Colbert 2004), reflecting the increasing importance given to 'intangible resources' in the strategy literature (Martin-Alcazar et al 2008) and the increased international activity of firms and the new organisational forms emerging in response to these pressures (Brewster 2007a, 2007b; Schuler et al 1993). HRM has responded by focusing on how such attributes as competences, skills, knowledge and human and intellectual capital could generate sustained competitive advantage (Wright et al 1994; Kamoche 1996).

In doing so, HRM has increasingly borrowed from and adapted theoretical concepts and models from other disciplines, leaving HRM exhibiting a multiplicity of theoretical approaches, methodologies, levels of analysis and research interests (Martin-Alcazar et al 2008). They usefully summarise much of the debate on HRM by arguing that there are currently four main perspectives on HRM: *universalistic*, *contingent*, *configurational* and *contextual perspectives*.

Firstly, *universalistic*, or *best practice*, models argue that 'high-commitment' models of HRM deliver enhanced organisational performance (Huselid 1995; Becker and Gerhardt 1996; Delaney and Huselid 1996). Many view the organisation as a 'black box'; research on 'unlocking the black box' (Purcell et al 2003) has focused on what 'bundles' of HR practices can impact on performance.

The major search for what's in the 'black box' has focused on what *bundles* of HR practices can make an impact; the favourite target has been the *high performance work system* (HPWS) and its associated work practices (Huselid 1995), also termed 'high commitment', 'high involvement' or 'high road' practices. HPWS is best seen as a system, rather than as individual components; for Pfeffer (1998), such practices revolve around employment security and stability; selective hiring of new personnel; self-managed teams and decentralisation; high compensation contingent on organisational performance; extensive training; reduced status distinctions; and extensive sharing of information. The list of HPWS practices alleged to play a key role in enhancing organisational performance (for example Arthur 1992, 1994; Delaney and Huselid 1996; Pauwe 2004), however, also includes personnel selection, performance appraisal, incentive compensation, job design, grievance procedures, information-sharing, attitude assessment, labour-management participation, intensive recruiting, intensive training and promotion criteria.

Many have taken the RBV (Grant 1991) as a way of testing and supporting the link between HPWS and company performance; some claim that such HR practices affect employee *attitudes* such as commitment and motivation, as well as enhance employee *competence*, and this provides the link to company performance as intervening variables in the HPWS–performance relationship. Most emphasis has been placed, however, on employee *motivation* (Delaney and Huselid 1996) or 'discretionary effort' (Appelbaum et al 2000); companies that provide employees with the opportunities to participate give them both the skills to participate and the incentives to participate, and 'discretionary effort' will then result and competitive performance improve. Effort above and beyond requirements is necessary, including the application of imagination, tacit knowledge and creativity and composed of three elements: motivation, skills and opportunities to participate. All of these are enhanced by HPWS, leading to discretionary effort, higher performance and higher levels of commitment, trust and communication.

Boxall et al (2011: 1507), drawing on labour process theory, argue that 'best practice', however, cannot be generalised; HRM can contain complex, subtle messages reflecting multiple goals and tensions, and not all target groups in the organisation are subject to the same HR system.

REFLECTIVE ACTIVITY 8.1

What are the aspects of high commitment/high performance models of HRM that differentiate them from traditional 'personnel management'?

Secondly, *contingent* perspectives, as we have seen, add intervening variables between HRM practice and outcome, usually strategy (Fombrun et al 1984), organisational context (Pfeffer 1998) or external environment (Boxall 1996), or 'organisational learning capability' (Camps and Luna-Arocas 2012).

Thirdly, the *configurational* perspective analyses the internal dynamics of the HRM system and how different elements can be combined synergistically in different patterns or 'bundles', representing different orientations to HRM (Delery and Doty 1996).

Finally, *contextual* perspectives emphasise the significance of the context, not merely as a contingent variable but as a framework for HRM decision-making that both influences and is influenced by the environment within which it is embedded (for example Brewster 2007a, 2007b; Caligiuri and Stroh 1995; Shen 2005). In particular, the international context and associated cultural, social, political and institutional influences are key (Schuler et al 1993; Sparrow 2007; Tarique and Schuler 2010). This is the approach taken in this book; HR practices need to be analysed in their social, political, institutional and cultural contexts.

These different perspectives are often associated with different methodologies; universalists tend to employ deductive tools to test hypotheses and relationships between variables; configurational theorists often apply structural equation modelling to identify HRM configurations. In contrast, contextual perspectives often employ inductive logic using observation, participant observation and interviews to build theory through the identification of key constructs and variables, and seek explanation through the establishment of relationships among constructs and theoretical rationales for any observed relationships.

This emphasis on the internal determinants of competitiveness – what's inside the black box! – in US HRM has shifted attention to *human capital* and its development to deliver organisational performance. Much research has claimed to measure and demonstrate the link between an organisation's HRM practices and its performance, showing that the often-used (and abused?) rhetoric that 'our people are our greatest asset' indeed has empirical validity. In part, this has been driven by the need of HR managers claiming to be 'business partners' or 'strategic partners' to 'prove' the value of HRM to senior executives in the 'language of business' – money – and help legitimise the HR function by showing that HRM can make a difference to the 'bottom line'.

REFLECTIVE ACTIVITY 8.2

1   Is 'the bottom line' the only legitimate or feasible goal for HRM?

2   What other goals in your view should HRM pursue?

Guest (1990: 377) notes: 'American multinationals have been to the forefront of HRM innovation in the UK (Purcell et al 1987) and the leading advocates are all American', claiming also that 'HRM is yet another manifestation of the American Dream and its popularity and attractiveness must be understood in this context'. HRM is embedded in 'a kind of rugged entrepreneurial individualism reflected in and reinforced by a strong organisational culture' (391) with an emphasis on individual self-improvement, opportunity and progress; as Chapter 2 noted, most studies of US culture emphasise its high individualism, high masculinity and short-term orientation, so perhaps we should not be surprised at this association of the HRM model with the USA.

Other cultures, as we have seen in Chapter 2, take more 'collectivist' and 'contextual' stances. In other chapters we offer critiques of these essentialist and individualist approaches; Chapter 15 explores more collectivist views of 'competence', while individualistic, exclusive and essentialist conceptions of 'talent' and 'talent management' are challenged in Chapter 17, conceptualising talent in more inclusive, collective and position-related ways. Chapter 5 discussed how 'leadership' too has been individualised in US approaches to refer to the attributes, competences and characteristics of leaders and leadership development to a form of human capital development. Leadership can, however, also be reconceptualised in more social, collective and relational ways, as in concepts of 'distributed leadership'; leadership development can be seen as involving the development of social capital. A more contextual, collective perspective is also evident in the treatment in Chapter 7 of knowledge transfer in joint ventures, rejecting 'commodity' views of knowledge transfer in favour of knowledge migration between different 'world-views'.

However, Guest (1990) also points out that even in the USA, HRM in practice was only evident in a few well-known, frequently cited cases, and that the 'reality' of managerial practice of HRM in organisations was more complex than the 'rhetoric' of the best-practice HRM paradigm would suggest.

However, many North American organisations have adopted, at least in rhetoric (Werner 2007), the following view of HRM:

1   HRM as a strategic business partner

2   a focus on HR systems rather than individual policies

3   attempts to show the short-term financial impact of these systems through metrics that capture the impact of HRM systems on financial measures and the return on investment (ROI) of HR policies.

REFLECTIVE ACTIVITY 8.3

1   To what extent do you think this model of HRM reflects specifically American cultural values?

2   To what extent do you think it is transferable to other regions?

3   To what extent does it describe the philosophy and practice of HRM in your own country?

EMERGING ISSUES FOR NORTH AMERICAN HRM

Werner (2007) identifies a number of leading issues in relation to HRM in the USA and Canada, including *globalisation, the new factory, technology-based training, sexual harassment, legal compliance* and *the changing family*; of course, such issues have emerged as important in other regions, including western Europe and the UK. Areas of increased importance for HRM include *ethics* (Chapter 6), *health and safety, competitive advantage and counterproductive leader behaviour* (Chapters 5 and 6), while emerging trends include *outsourcing, the cost of employee benefits, executive compensation* (Chapter 19) and *the role of HRM in dealing with both natural and man-made crises and disasters* such as floods, earthquakes and terrorist incidents; again, also true of other regions.

THE ARRIVAL OF HRM IN THE UK AND WESTERN EUROPE AND ITS IMPLICATIONS FOR THE HRM PROFESSION

We might expect HRM to be more welcome in the UK than in continental Europe from both 'culturalist' and 'institutionalist' perspectives (Chapters 1 and 2). The UK and USA share certain cultural similarities, both being within the 'low power distance/individualist' cluster (like the Netherlands and other Anglo-Saxon countries) but unlike France and other southern European countries (large power distance/individualism) or Germany and other northern/central European countries (more collectivist, low power distance).

However, HRM took several years to arrive in the UK, where the dominant labels for the function had been 'personnel' administration or management, and its introduction was not always uncontested. Some have resisted this change, emphasising the 'welfare'/mediating' role of a function standing between managers and workers (Torrington 1989). The HRM function in contrast was now clearly being asked to play a strategic role as a full member of the 'executive team' with an avowed mission to enhance organisational performance.

Guest (1987) distinguished traditional personnel management from HRM by virtue of the way in which the former (personnel) ignored, but the latter (HRM) embraced, strategy. HRM has an agenda addressing business-related issues. Guest (1987) sought to define HRM in terms of its objectives, influenced primarily by the 'softer', more employee-oriented conceptions of HRM embodied in the Harvard model – HRM was a *specific form* of people management, not merely a synonym or re-labelling of it. HRM was a *particular employee relations strategy* pursuing the strategic goals of '*high commitment, high quality, flexibility and strategic integration*' (Guest 1990: 378). Hendry and Pettigrew (1990) focused on harder, 'strategic' HRM and the use of planning, matching/strategic integration, and a philosophy that saw people as a strategic resource for competitive advantage. Storey (1989, 1992) attempted to integrate these approaches by identifying 15 core elements defining HRM and distinguishing it from personnel management, grouped into: *beliefs and assumptions*; *strategic aspects*; *line management*; and *key levers*.

As with the USA, HRM in the UK was often promoted as essential for improving the country's competitiveness, especially in the face of increased global competition. In recent years, increasing attention has been paid to issues of productivity, or workforce efficiency, driven by a concern that the UK's long-run trend rate of growth of labour productivity may have fallen. HRM is often held to have a major contribution to make; the CIPD in the UK (www.cipd.co.uk) has often highlighted the productivity gap between the UK and its major international competitors, arguing that improved people management could help bridge the gap. However, the personnel function had often become segmented into an unfavourably isolated department, unconnected with strategic management; for Purcell and Ahlstrand (1994), the authority of personnel departments was becoming increasingly ambiguous and uncertain, simply because 'corporate personnel departments have ill-defined boundaries and muddy roles' (113).

The HR profession thus had an enduring problem of *establishing credibility, enhancing image and gaining power* inside organisations; at the operational level, the HR function had been considered as a cost department, without direct contribution to the organisation. Was there no substantive difference between HRM and personnel management? For some, 'the rhetoric has outstripped the reality' (Blyton and Turnbull 1992: vii). Or was HRM 'a radically new approach to managing people, demarcated sharply from traditional personnel management' (Storey 1989: 4)?

When the term HRM had the prefix 'strategic' attached, comparisons between HRM and SHRM were also explored; did SHRM add new strategic components (Fombrun et al 1984)? Were many of the key messages of SHRM new, or just old elements repackaged (Salaman et al 1992)? Was the HRM label merely a modern, up-to-date term for 'managing people', promising greater material and status rewards for HRM managers and academics (for example seats on the board for directors, professorships for academics)? Or was it a *specific* form of managing people and employment focused on obtaining employee *commitment* (Guest 1987; Storey 1992)? Interestingly, the main UK professional body, the CIPD, terms its leading practitioner magazine *People Management*; but it described it in 1998 as 'the magazine for professionals in personnel, training and development' (representing its members from the IPD and ITD, which had merged in the 1980s). In 1994 it was 'the magazine for human resource professionals'; it now (2012) calls it 'the magazine of the Chartered Institute of Personnel and Development'.

This view that HRM was merely a generic label for 'managing people' was not, however, the dominant one, as most in the UK saw HRM as a specific, distinctive (and presumably superior) approach, seeing people as resources to be managed strategically; in the UK, it was often termed SHRM. Different HRM policies and practices could be designed, and be effective, depending on the firm's strategic orientation; there was no 'universal' model of 'best practices' that led to effectiveness or competitive advantage but a series of 'contingent' models depending on product–market strategy in particular (for example cost leadership, quality, innovation, focus, etc). HRM is now often seen in both the USA and UK as a key factor differentiating successful from unsuccessful organisations; an organisation is held to gain comparative advantage by using its people effectively, drawing on their expertise and ingenuity to meet its objectives.

The view of HRM in the UK for Storey (1992) has changed over the years, from being the 'handmaidens/regulators' operating in a reactive mode to issues to being viewed as 'change makers' putting managing people and employee relations on a new footing and emphasising the needs of the organisation; in practice, however, many HR managers still operate reactively and tactically in 'transactional' operational activities.

Other terminologies have been proposed to reflect this new strategic/business direction for HR; it is often called *business partnering* in the UK. Strategic partners saw themselves as more 'strategic-proactive', more involved and influential, more positive about others' perceptions of the function, and as spending more time on strategy and less on implementation, at least in their own eyes (Caldwell 2003). Francis and Keegan (2006) found that this advocate/champion role was disintegrating in almost all the organisations they surveyed: employee issues were often subordinated to business issues. One example of this is the increase in advertisements seeking 'business partners' in *People Management*'s *Guide to Recruitment Consultancies*: http://www.peoplemanagement.co.uk/pm/supplements/recruitmentconsultancies/

HR practitioners also increasingly talk about shifting responsibilities to line managers and freeing up HR to perform more 'strategic' tasks. The CIPD (2008) has[MS2] captured some of this shift in its 'HR Profession Map' and concept of the 'thinking performer': http://www.cipd.co.uk/about/profstands/thinkingperformer.htm

Some of these 'strategic initiatives' include *outsourcing, shared service centres and the use of IT to integrate HR activities*; again, these are not initiatives confined to the UK or USA (Caldwell and Storey 2007). Downsides of this shift away from 'employee champion' may, however, include a loss of trust and confidence among employees as well as truncated HR careers as a two-tier divide emerges between those doing administrative, transactional work and those doing strategic work, resulting in professional 'fragmentation' and damage to employee well-being (Wright 2008). Being an 'employee champion' may now no longer be seen as a viable career move for the ambitious HR professional. However, questions still remain over the scope and nature of the 'business partner' role, its integration with other HRM roles and the barriers to achieving greater uptake of the role (Caldwell 2003).

REFLECTIVE ACTIVITY 8.4

1   How would you describe the role of the HR function in your country?

2   Which term best describes it?

So HRM is claimed in the UK to play a key role in securing competitive advantage, especially when linked to *human capital management*, where human capital evaluation and reporting inform business decision-making and enable better judgements about growth potential and performance. Human capital, alongside social and organisational capital, is often seen as a key part of intellectual capital. A key issue is how to analyse, measure and evaluate the contribution of people practices to creating value, using *HR data* such as recruitment figures, employee turnover and retention data, appraisal data and the tracking of talent flows to measure the effectiveness of the HR function and the effectiveness of 'people processes'. The CIPD (2012) has a factsheet and other resources on this (http://www.cipd.co.uk/hr-resources/factsheets/human-capital.aspx); see also Wright and McMahan (2011).

There is still argument in the UK over whether universal or contingent practices are superior in delivering such competitive advantage. Purcell (1999) argues against claims that a universalistic model of best practice in HRM exists with general applicability as such models lack a conception of strategy; firms employing other models to the HPWS, such as cost minimisation, can also be successful, as Boxall et al (2011) have shown with respect to highly scripted 'customer service' in Australian cinemas. Several methodological problems dog this field: reliance on *single respondents* (usually HR directors) answering quick, simple survey questions and excluding *processes* from consideration (for example 'teamworking' and 'performance-related pay systems' refer to many different types of design, introduced in many different ways). *Crude output measures* (often self-reported subjective measurements of relative performance) are often used; some groups of workers – for example outsourced and contingent, rather than core – may be excluded from consideration; the *direction of causality* may be difficult to determine in most one-off, snapshot surveys (do high-performing firms adopt a greater number of high-quality HR practices?) and any performance improvements may be due to the change process in a kind of 'Hawthorne effect'.

In current terminology, this issue is now often approached through the concept of *engagement* (http://www.cipd.co.uk/hr-resources/factsheets/employee-engagement.aspx).

In order to make HPWS work effectively, line managers need to motivate, engage with and enable employees using coaching, mentoring and other facilitative techniques (CIPD 2012). Pass (2005) argues that HPWS studies have failed to explain what is inside the black box from employee perspectives: 'relationships, respect and recognition' are key, highlighting the role of leadership (Kinnie et al 2005). However, line managers may lack the skills, time or incentive to be effective in this role; the 'business partner' model not only raises issues for HR practitioners, but also for line managers and the kinds of support they can expect and require from HR.

This focus on the role of the *line manager* in maintaining respect, recognition and positive relationships is especially pertinent when the 'devolution' of HRM to line managers is associated with HR seeking to be a business partner. Front-line managers have a vital mediating role to play in delivering HR policies and performance; relationships with staff are crucial in delivering high-performance HR practices through 'leader–member exchanges', making the role of leadership central. Purcell et al (2003) showed that front-line managers had great influence on employee attitudes, both to their jobs and to their employers, as well as on satisfaction with HR practices. The roles of first-line supervisors have been broadened, raising questions of role overload and conflict; line managers may not be performing these roles particularly well, resulting in gaps between espoused HR policies and practice as managers may not reflect top management value statements.

Hutchinson and Purcell (2007) see the 'causal chain' between HRM and organisational performance in terms of five linkages:

1   intended policies to actual practices

2   actual practices to experienced practices

3   experienced practices to employee reactions

4   employee reactions to employee outcomes

5   employee outcomes to unit-level outcomes.

The combined effect of leadership behaviour and satisfying perceived HR practices had a greater impact than either by itself, again highlighting the crucial role of leadership and leadership development to the effectiveness of HRM (Chapter 5).

HRM IN CONTINENTAL WESTERN EUROPE

As Europe consists of 47 countries with a population of around 732 million (Briscoe et al 2012), it is difficult to give a general picture of the state of HRM, as there are many strong institutional, national and regional differences. Here we focus on the European Union (EU), in particular western Europe; Chapter 9 discusses HRM in Russia and eastern Europe.

In general, continental European models of national HRM differ from the Anglo-American model in several ways discussed by institutionalist theorists (Chapter 1). From a *national business systems perspective* (Lane 1992), there are crucial differences between the UK and Germany in particular over the role of the state, the financial system, the network of business associations, the system of employee relations and the education and training systems. The UK is closer to the US on much of these issues – or at least, mid-Atlantic! For Whitley (1999), Germany (and some other European countries, as well as Japan) are *collaborative*, characterised by interlocking institutions encouraging cooperative behaviour, leading to *cooperative hierarchies* and corporatist/interventionist approaches to HRM. Owners and managers share more authority with employees and partners, and skilled manual workers are typically integrated into the organisation as core members. In contrast, both the UK and USA are *arms' length* systems characterised by flexible entry and exit within an institutionalised formal system. Competitive capital markets are accompanied by the state acting as regulator and training is seen as a matter for individual firm investment, not coordinated collaboration between the state, employers and unions. We discussed this issue in relation to national HRD in Chapter 1 in terms of distinctions between 'interventionism' and 'voluntarism' in VET. Here we look at a 'Germanic' system, in this case Austria (Stewart et al 2008).

 ADULT LEARNING AND SKILLS IN AUSTRIA

CASE STUDY 8.1

The main focus here has been on raising learning demand among employers and individuals through flexible provision and financial incentives. Supply and demand for adult learning are felt to be aligned effectively, and the OECD has observed that the adult education system in Austria provides for vast amounts of training for workers who want to upgrade their skills, with unemployment well below OECD and EU averages.

However, the lack of a coherent national policy on lifelong learning is seen to be a weakness in the system; the major political focus on other parts of the education system (pre-school and secondary school) has meant that adult skills training and lifelong learning are receiving less attention, with tensions between the two parties in the coalition government meaning that there is difficulty in achieving consensus.

Key features of the VET system include the lack of a single agency responsible for policy in adult education; the Ministry of Education, Science and Culture is responsible for schools, colleges and 'Fachhochschulen'

(higher-level vocational and technical colleges), open to adult learners to varying extents. Other training for adults is offered through the Public Employment Service, run by the Ministry of Economics and Labour. The nine regions have considerable autonomy in developing and funding adult learning policy. In addition, the main social partners, such as the Chamber of Labour and Economic Chamber, are also influential in the design and delivery of adult learning at local, regional and national levels. The system is therefore characterised by a high level of social partner involvement. The Labour and Economic Chambers play an important role in delivery of training, including trade union representatives, and the system is seen as particularly effective in aligning skills and learning supply and demand. Local and regional stakeholders are all actively engaged in designing and delivering provision, and high levels of regional devolution means that policies can be developed to meet specific regional needs. There are, however, concerns that the substantial variations in policy and funding, both between and within the nine regions, mean that it is difficult to discern a coherent national policy.

The Government subsidises adult learning and vocational training delivered through schools, colleges and Fachhochschulen – which means that course fees are generally low or waived. However, a very small proportion of the total education budget in Austria is spent on adult learning; both individuals and employers are expected to contribute. A number of reforms have opened up opportunities through more flexible programmes, increasing the base of highly skilled adults and widening participation in learning among more disadvantaged groups. Encouraging adults to attend academic secondary schools and undertake lengthy and demanding programmes requires flexibility of provision, as multiple entry and exit points are offered, including progression to universities or Fachhochsculen. Improving adult skills that better fits adult learners' needs is delivered through intensive apprenticeship programmes involving both college and work-based learning, offering an equivalent qualification to traditional longer apprenticeship programmes. Part-time vocational training courses are also offered in vocational colleges and Fachhochschulen.

Several recent initiatives aim to facilitate choice and overcome financial barriers to participation, such as creating demand among employers through federal tax incentives for employer training and demand among key groups of workers; the Employment Service offers grants to subsidise 66% of training costs for women and older employees. Individual learning vouchers are offered by most regions, but the amount and conditions vary. Individuals are also offered 'training leave' – absence from their employers for 3 to 12 months in order to take part in training, receiving a modest stipend from the Employment Service.

(Source: Johnson et al 2008)

Questions

1   How does this VET system compare with the one in your country?

2   Would you characterise it as interventionist or voluntarist?

3   To what extent does it illustrate a collaborative/cooperative national business system seeking to involve the 'social partners', rather than an arms' length/competitive one?

THE US AND EUROPEAN/GERMAN MODELS OF HRM

Other differences between the US and 'European' (especially German) model (Muller 1999; Brewster 1995, 2007a, 2007b) emerge in such areas as:

- *extent of interdependence*: impersonality, specialisation, differentiation of authority vary
- *restricted firm autonomy*: regulations are crucial. For example, HR staff often come from a legal 'labour law' background in Germany but a social science background in the UK or USA
- *dialogue between social partners*, for example unions, government and employers is more extensive, as Case Study 8.1 shows
- *corporate social responsibility* and employee protection are key issues (Chapter 6)

- *employee participation* is widespread, perhaps institutionalised in worker representatives on company boards as part of 'co-determination' arrangements (Chapter 20)
- enterprises are more likely to be *multilingual and multicultural* in Europe
- *informal systems*, for example in appraisal, are more common than in the USA
- *a longer timescale* of decision-making and accountability is likely compared with the USA ('long-term orientation', Chapter 2)
- greater *'collectivism'* in orientation than the 'individualist' USA (Chapter 2).

Other differences include:

- *the role of state*: social market versus market economy, with a more interventionist state (Chapter 1)
- *the role/importance of vocational training* (Case Study 8.1; Chapter 1)
- *more formal relationships*, including use of titles (for example 'Herr Doktor Professor'), not first names, more emphasis on rules, regulations, procedures and committees
- *the relationship with banks* is more cooperative and less antagonistic than in the USA or the UK (Chapter 1)
- *negative view of growth through mergers and acquisitions*, especially hostile foreign takeovers (Chapter 7)
- *higher status given to technical competence* and the engineering function; for example the importance of 'technik' to organisations, as represented by the slogan used by the car-maker Audi since the 1980s of 'Vorsprung durch technik' or advancement through technology
- *role/importance of 'industrial unions'*, not craft unions
- *industry-wide pay bargaining*
- *relative lack of career mobility* across companies and functions.

US researchers have tended to adopt 'universalistic' models of HRM, while European researchers tend to favour more 'contextual' models (Martin-Alcazar et al 2008). Brewster (1995, 2007b) argues that the US model has been characterised by 'organisational autonomy', whereas in continental Europe organisations have been much less autonomous, being constrained in HRM choices at a national level by ownership patterns and at the HRM level by trade union involvement, bargaining patterns, consultative arrangements and the labour market. Employment is more regulated, educational certification more formalised, and the industrial relations (IR) system more quasi-legal. Other regulations at both national and EU levels include health and safety, working time, pay, rights to trade union representation, requirements for consultation and co-determination. In Germany, many companies are owned largely by a tight network of banks, giving less pressure to generate short-term profits and disincentives to drive competitors out of business. European countries tend to be more centralised in their bargaining arrangements, with multi-employer negotiations and national industry pay bargaining. There is greater use of the internal labour market and investment in skills training, and more developed systems of vocational training outside the organisation, as well as greater public expenditure on labour market programmes such as retraining and job transition support, job-creation schemes and programmes to facilitate the movement of young people and the long-term unemployed (Case Study 8.1). In contrast to the UK emphasis on 'competitive flexibility', many continental European organisations practise 'constructive flexibility', combining adaptability with social protection.

Muller (1999) argues that there has been a change towards a more positive appreciation of the German rather than US HRM model, with some 'convergence' or 'hybridisation': HRM has been incorporated into the German paradigm, while its unitarist values have been rejected. German labour market institutions have not prevented the introduction of 'modern' US-style HRM techniques, but in an adapted form.

There is continuing debate as to whether the European and US models are 'converging' as neo-institutionalist models would suggest (Chapter 1) or remain divergent, as indicated by culturalist and institutionalist models (Chapter 1). For example, both Sweden (Chapter 1) and Austria (Case Study 8.1) have moved to more market-oriented, demand-led national HRD models, though Austria retains a greater consensual commitment to 'social partnership'. Though the Germanic HRM model has shown clear contrasts with the US or UK HRM model, recently a more 'flexible' labour market model of 'dual flexibility' has developed. This involves expanding flexible or 'atypical' jobs and increasing flexibility in standardised employment through wage moderation and working-time flexibility (Eichhorst 2012; Eichhorst and Marx 2010). Most continental European labour markets and welfare states have undergone major transformations in their employment models, moving from low employment and limited labour market inequality to higher employment and greater inequality. For Eichhorst (2012: 1) Germany 'exhibits growing employment figures and growing shares of low pay and non-standard work. Changes in labour market institutions such as unemployment benefits, active labour market policies and employment protection play a major role, but changes in industrial relations at the sectoral level and individual firms' staffing practices are equally important in explaining actual labour market outcomes.' Reform of employment protection and increasing or decreasing unemployment benefit generosity, both mostly addressing those workers at the margins of the labour market, are contributing to a growing *dualisation* of the employment system; yet the status of 'insiders' has been much less affected by legislative changes. Growing reliance on internal flexibility for the skilled core workforce and increasing use of non-standard types of employment in less specifically skilled occupations reinforce this 'dualisation'.

Standardised full-time jobs still predominate, with minimum income and dismissal protection and labour standards. A system of short-time work is often used; a firm in financial difficulties can apply to the employment agency for approval of a package to reduce working hours and variable pay in proportion while refraining from layoffs. Workers are then reimbursed by the employment agency for 60–70% of their lost pay. Employee bargaining power has also declined in Germany since reunification with the East in 1990, reflected in declines in union membership and coverage, increasingly decentralised wage bargaining and union concessions such as the use of working-time accounts, partly stimulated by the emergence of eastern Europe as a competing location for manufacturing production (Burda and Hunt 2011).

In Part 4 we explore these institutional and cultural differences between western Europe and the USA in more detail, especially in Chapter 18 on performance management and Chapter 20 on employee relations.

LEARNING SUMMARY

HRM, as distinct from personnel administration or personnel management, was first introduced in the USA in the 1980s, reflecting an 'American' model of people management of individualism, results orientation, a 'managerialist' orientation prioritising links with corporate strategy, and the autonomy of managers and enterprises to devise their own HR systems. There is little legal or institutional regulation of, or union influence on, the employment relationship, beyond certain minimum rights, except in the areas of equal employment opportunity and affirmative action legislation and the ability of employees to seek legal redress against alleged unfair, illegal or discriminatory decisions.

This model was first exported into the UK (unsurprisingly perhaps given close historical, cultural and language links), but not without contestation or adaptation. However, in both countries the rhetoric – if not the reality in practice – was an HRM function that aspired to be a 'strategic business partner'. In continental Europe, and especially Germany, the situation was rather different; cultural and institutional factors impacted on HRM, especially the different legal environments and the greater role played by regulations and trade unions as 'social partners'. These differences manifest themselves in many areas of HRM; we focused on approaches to VET, noting differences within Europe, for example the greater role of social partnership in Germanic countries. We ended by discussing recent changes to the German model in the direction of greater flexibility and precariousness for non-core employees in a process of 'dualisation' of the labour market.

CHAPTER 9

HRM in Russia and Central and Eastern Europe

Paul Iles

LEARNING OUTCOMES

By the end of the chapter, you should be able to:

- Analyse the main trends in HRM in the countries of central and eastern Europe and Russia after the transition from communism to a more market-oriented economy.

- Evaluate some of the cultural and policy differences between these countries.

- Discuss the impact of national culture and institutions on HRM policy and practice in the region, identifying cultural differences.

- Critically evaluate approaches to HRD and management development in the region and their relationship to national culture.

- Critically analyse changing approaches to HRM in Russia, with particular reference to culture, training and development, and recruitment and selection.

INTRODUCTION

Since 1989, the fall of the Berlin Wall and the collapse of communism in the USSR and central and eastern Europe (including countries of central and eastern Europe (CCEE), and former Soviet Republics (FSRs), as well as Russia) there has been considerable interest in management, HRM and HRD in the region. Recent studies include books by Domsch and Lidokhover (2007) on Russia and Morley et al (2009) on central and eastern Europe. Ardichvili and Kuchinke (2002: 114) however note that large-scale surveys of HR practice, such as the CRANET surveys often drawn on by Morley et al (2009) comparing HR practices in both eastern and western Europe, may not 'take into account the political realities of conducting social science research in countries with long authoritarian histories which present the likelihood of further response bias'.

Though often seen in terms of a shared Soviet communist past, for some countries, for example the Baltic states, this had been quite recent, but in others (for example Russia), more extensive. In addition, the region is very diverse culturally, economically and historically; there are major differences in religion, with some central European countries such as Poland, Hungary and the Czech Republic looking to the Catholic West, others such as Bulgaria, Russia and Serbia to an Orthodox East, and others such as Azerbaijan, Uzbekistan and parts of the Balkans to an Islamic central Asia. The Czech Republic was also much more industrialised and richer than other countries further east. Some countries – for example Bulgaria, the Baltic states of Latvia, Lithuania and Estonia, Hungary, Poland, Romania and Slovenia – are now also members of the EU and subject to EU influences on their HRM systems; others are as yet not EU members, or indeed wish to be so.

Despite this diversity, a common discourse of *'market fundamentalism'* and *'transition'* came to dominate 'Western' perspectives on this region (Henderson and Whitley, 1995) as official policy and rhetoric, supported by the IMF and the European Bank for Reconstruction and Development, favoured *privatisation and free-market restructuring* to ease the transition from a planned economy under communism to a free market under capitalism. From 1990 and the fall of the Berlin Wall and the end of the old Soviet Union there have been significant flows of FDI to the region. In Chapter 14 we look at the very different path of transition from a planned economy taken by China, which has received even more FDI.

Despite considerable differences between countries in terms of levels of reform and economic development, there appear to have been similar deep, widespread changes across the region's organisations and managerial markets. These include rises in salary and benefit levels, narrowing of some skill gaps, moves towards more sophisticated methods of recruitment and selection, and shifts to more 'Western' management practices, including HRM practices. However, severe shortages of qualified managers have appeared across the region, with tight managerial labour markets, and foreign and joint venture firms have appeared to rely disproportionately on expatriate managers, with insufficient emphasis on the management development of local resources.

We first discuss HRM in the CCEE, but most of our attention will be on HRM in Russia as one of the emerging BRIC countries (O'Neill 2011). We cannot of course cover the whole region, but will also focus on the Czech Republic and Bulgaria. First we look at the institutional and cultural contexts of HRM in the region (Chapters 1 and 2).

THE INSTITUTIONAL AND CULTURAL CONTEXTS OF HRM IN THE CCEE

After the collapse of the centrally controlled state planning system in the 1990s and accession of some countries to the EU, there have been studies of the transfer of best practices by Western MNCs, often in joint ventures (discussed in Chapter 7) and the emergence of more 'strategic' HRM and Western models of HRM in such areas as recruitment and selection, compensation and performance management – again, issues we also pursue in Chapter 14 with respect to China. These have been adopted variably within the CCEE, leading to diversity of HRM and 'hybrid' practices often mixing Western and indigenous approaches, as in

Africa and Latin America (Chapters 11 and 12). We consider this in more depth when we discuss individual countries.

As Woldu and Budhwar (2011: 1365) point out, 'one of the most crucial challenges international businesses face is the lack of understanding of the cultural background in emerging countries'; this is especially true in this region, in part as Hofstede (1984) did not include them in his original studies of national cultural differences. Kolman et al (2003) compared the Czech Republic, Hungary, Poland, Slovakia and the Netherlands, finding not only major cultural differences between the CCEE and the Netherlands, but also within the CCEE themselves, with Slovakia showing an extreme position on four of the five dimensions of Hofstede (1984). Differences in terms of power distance were small (Slovakia the largest, Poland the smallest, all larger than western Europe), and only Slovakia scored markedly more highly on collectivism than the Netherlands. The Czech Republic here emerged as the most individualistic of the CCEE countries. This reinforces the point about the heterogeneity of this region.

Woldu and Budhwar (2011) focus on gender-based cultural differences in CCEE and FSR countries; gender inequality greatly increased in the late 1980s alongside economic restructuring, despite communist ideology – not realised in practice – about gender equality. Though communist rhetoric urged gender equality, in practice most jobs performed by women were lower-status, and lower-paying, than those performed by men. More recently, professional women have begun moving into more challenging jobs. Using a large-scale survey, Woldu and Budhwar (2011) found that countries within the CCEE – the Czech Republic, former East Germany (FEG), Poland – were more similar to each other culturally than to those in the FSR – Georgia, Uzbekistan – and vice versa. The CCEE and FSR countries were not culturally homogeneous. The Russian cultural value system appeared to lie between the two, while Poland and the Czech Republic seemed closer to FEG than to each other. The CCEE countries manifested higher risk tolerance and weaker 'subjugation' values, and seemed to be drifting culturally 'West' compared with the FSR countries. Females generally indicated higher acceptance – perhaps realistic in the circumstances – for unequal distributions of power, but no significant gender differences were found for Georgia, and the highest gender-based differences were found for FEG. More cultural variation was found among women than among men. In Poland, for example, the business press since the transition has offered positive images of successful 'modern' enterprises, often Western, contrasted with old, failed enterprises (always Polish) and a strongly gendered, idealised and Americanised image of management (Kostera 1995, 2000).

Thus within the CCEE, Russia and FSR, cross-cultural issues cannot be described in terms of simplified dichotomies between 'East' (ie the CCEE) and 'West'. A study of leadership styles and cultural values among managers and subordinates in the USA, Germany and four countries of the former Soviet Union confirms this; significant differences were found not only between the 'Western' and 'Eastern' groups of countries but also within them (Ardichvili and Kuchinke 2002). The former Soviet countries differed in showing much lower levels of power distance, higher levels of masculinity and much longer planning horizons.

Grouping countries based on cultural, geographical or religious proximity can be equally problematic; Kazakhstan and the Kyrgyz Republic were here more closely aligned with Russia or Georgia than with each other on all four socio-cultural dimensions employed in the study, suggesting that HRM and HRD initiatives should be tailored to each country's specificity, rather than assuming cultural homogeneity.

Moral crusades promoted by Western political and financial institutions, trainers and consultants have often adopted an unreflexive 'knowledge transfer' view (Chapter 7) as HRM or management development 'missionaries' with unproblematic assumptions about HRM or management learning. They have often neglected or disparaged the cultural and institutional heritages of the countries in which they work, such as strengths in economics and mathematics (for example Kostera 1995, 2000; Jankowicz 1994; Henderson and Whitley 1995; Voros and Schermerhorn 1993). Host partner trainees or students may 'comply' in class with Western models but reject such ideas privately as inappropriate (for example Kostera 1995, 2000). Enterprise managers may subscribe in principle to the need for technological, financial and structural restructuring, but may not see the need for managerial restructuring (for example Kelemen and Lightfoot 1999). Holden and Cooper (1994) found Russian construction managers had a tendency to learned helplessness, a preference for authoritative exposition and a lack of a common managerial vocabulary. This often led Western trainers to develop a directive, 'modelling' approach to training. Such an approach may not best facilitate transfer of meaning, self-directed learning or long-term application and transfer of learning in the host country.

Bedward et al (2003) in contrast made use of the 'travel of ideas' concepts first developed by Czarniawska and Joerges (1996) in a discussion of management ideas and models used by Warsaw City Council, Poland (Czarniawska 1997). Receiving organisations could flexibly amend material in the light of their own experience and needs, avoiding the 'cultural dominance' implicit in much discussion of 'knowledge transfer' models and allowing the negotiation of new meanings and alternative perspectives among participants in a 'process'-oriented rather than 'transplant'-oriented approach (Gilbert and Gorlenko 1999).

 REFLECTIVE ACTIVITY 9.1

1   How useful do you think such cultural comparisons are, given rapid change in the region?

2   What are their implications for IHRM in the region?

We next introduce a brief discussion of HRM in the Czech Republic and Bulgaria before turning our attention to Russia.

HRM IN THE CZECH REPUBLIC

Before the Second World War, the Czech Republic was one of the most prosperous, developed regions in Europe; communism imposed centralised decision-making and personnel management became more administrative until the 1989 revolution. Since then the role and visibility of HRM has increased, with the emergence of independent trade unions followed by declines in membership. HR activity in areas such as recruitment has become more shared with line managers and outsourced to agencies; formal appraisal and variable and performance-based pay systems have grown in popularity, though getting top management support for HRM remains a challenge (Morley et al 2009; Koubek 2009). The country separated from Slovakia in 1993 and joined the EU in 2004.

Czech VET and national HRD systems have also undergone transformation (Johnson et al 2008). There is a very high level of youth participation in post-compulsory education; official estimates of the rate vary, but all put it at above 90% (and as high as 96%), well above the EU average. Participation was at high levels during the communist era and has remained at high levels since then, owing to the long history of support for the value of education in Czech society.

However, the wider education system in the Czech Republic is undergoing change, which is centrally designed and driven but relying on local implementation to better align the VET system with labour market needs, particularly those of foreign-owned businesses locating in the Czech Republic, and to increase the supply of skilled workers. The Czech economy currently relies heavily on immigrant labour. Several reforms have been introduced in recent years, modelled on lessons learned and policies adopted in other EU member states, particularly the UK. These reforms have been designed and implemented mainly through EU funding; there is little political will to commit state funds to education, with a relatively low proportion of GDP allocated to the education budget. EU funding is finite, so one of the critical factors is the extent to which the country is prepared to sustain funding for the reforms when the EU investment comes to an end. It has not yet made consistent use of financial incentives to encourage participation of either individuals or employers in training, although there is some evidence of incentives being offered to employers in regions with high levels of unemployment, and support for large foreign companies. Other measures designed to stimulate demand have had a limited impact to date, even when subsidised training is offered; the central government funded retraining courses for unemployed people looking for work, or seeking to change jobs, but take-up of these courses has been very low, with only around 10% of the target groups participating.

HRM IN BULGARIA

Bulgaria joined the EU in 2007; this catalysed reform, with Morley et al (2008: 15) pointing out that its 'transition process has been marked by a desire to establish a competitive, knowledge-based economy'. Vatchkova (2009) points to significant inward investment and the establishment of a 2002 Labour Code regulating industrial relations (IR) and providing for tripartite cooperation. Unionisation is high compared the other CCEE, but trade union influence and recognition have been declining. HR has become more 'strategic' and shared between the HR department and line managers, with increases in flexible working and recognition of the importance of HRD alongside difficulties in funding it, leaving it in many cases to individual initiative. However, to increase human capital and the skill base, a National Social Network for Vocational Training and an EU-supported HRD Operational Programme have been launched to facilitate integration into the EU. Its Corruption Perceptions Index rates it at 86, much lower than Russia and similar to Brazil, China and India (but much higher than the Czech Republic at 57). Case Study 9.1 illustrates some of the factors that may inhibit HRM change in Bulgaria.

CASE STUDY 9.1

TRANSFORMATIONAL CHANGE IN BULGARIAN NATIONAL RADIO (BNR)

In 2002 one of the authors (Iles) led a workshop with the University of Sofia and 15 participants from Bulgarian National Radio (BNR) from both the centre and two regional radio stations. BNR was a well-established, formerly state-run media organisation now facing a much more competitive environment as the Bulgarian economy entered a period of reform and transition and new private radio stations were established.

Participants identified a number of issues facing BNR. Their supervising body, NCRT, had no clear functions, but potentially could act as a buffer against institutional pressures. Legal constraints minimised the role of sponsorship and advertising, and state subsidies were limited, preventing technological investment and upgrading. There were inadequate communications between national and regional radio stations, especially the lack of an integrated computer network with free access by all levels of staff.

Important issues included:

- the transformation of BNR from a state-run to a public institution in a more competitive media environment and market economy

- Bulgaria's desire for access to the EU

- the need to align BNR with European industry standards

- the need to raise industry standards and consumer rights to European levels

- the need to preserve Bulgarian national identity and to respect ethnic and religious diversity.

Threats included restricted freedom of speech, self-censorship by journalists, state pressures on journalists and a lack of adequate legal protection. The Bulgarian media industry was developing rapidly, but in a sporadic and uncontrolled way, with different radio stations seeking different target audiences. BNR was lacking in modern structures and technologies, but could grasp opportunities by building on the depth and breadth of its national and regional programmes. It had a well-established and positive image, giving staff a sense of pride in its legacy and a wish to build on the high prestige it enjoyed with the public and the trust and respect in which it was held. Its high degree of professionalism, creativity and teamwork were also highly valued.

However, a number of more negative or worrying feelings also emerged, which included:

- difficult vertical and horizontal communications

- non-transparent decision-making

- poor remuneration

- feelings of insecurity

- pressures of routine work and an inadequate, outdated technical infrastructure

- insufficient motivation

- subjectivity in appraisals and reward

- shortages of resources

- high workloads

- work pressures.

Groups also identified a lack of incentives for professional development and the bypassing of accepted recruitment procedures through appointments to key positions of under-qualified staff as troubling, as well as bureaucratic pressures and interference in programming.

The following year, another workshop was held involving staff from BNR. One outcome from the first session was that a new structural element had been introduced into BNR, facilitated by a single individual within BNR who had participated in the earlier workshop. At an earlier stage of his career, he had been a very senior figure within BNR and was highly respected by many members of staff. Together with members of the first workshop, a team of BNR staff established a Knowledge Coordination and Change Unit, the function of which was to track knowledge processes in the organisation, and seek new opportunities.

Question

1 What does this case tell us about the importance of culture and institutional legacies in changing HRM and HRD policies and practices in this region?

HRM IN RUSSIA

When O'Neill (2011) at Goldman Sachs coined the term 'BRIC' countries in 2001 he was trying to describe where he thought world growth and economic power was going to come from in coming decades, highlighting Brazil, Russia, India and China. Over the next several years, investors have moved into Russia as its resource economy (for example oil, gas) has thrived in an era of fast-rising oil prices. However, doubts have been expressed as to whether Russia belongs in that 'club', despite Moscow having the largest number of billionaires in the world in a few short decades. The other countries have seen large increases in population with huge numbers of young, educated workers desperate for jobs, while Russia's population has gone into decline after the end of the Cold War, as did much of its industrial base, consisting of old and inefficient industries from the Soviet era. However, commodity producers are still doing well, as Russia is now the largest oil exporter in the world and the second largest exporter of natural gas; its petrochemical and steel industries have also prospered. The Russian Government relies on oil and gas sales for 40% of its tax revenues. It also has a huge, underdeveloped land mass, massive mineral resources and some world-class industries, such as nuclear power, defence and space technology. In 2007,

Goldman Sachs was still arguing that Russian GDP would overhaul all European countries by 2030 and Japan by 2038 (Wilson and Stupnytska 2007).

RUSSIAN INSTITUTIONAL CONTEXT

However, unlike China, the country's infrastructure is crumbling and, as with many oil-producing countries, corruption is rife, which acts as a further brake on economic growth and development. Some commentators are arguing in favour of Indonesia replacing Russia or, at the least, for Indonesia to join the other four to form BRIICs. Judah et al (2011: 9) argue that the 2008 global financial crisis has 'shattered Russia's dream of being a BRIC that is on a par with China, India and Brazil', citing the return of the authoritarian Putin as president, its governance crisis, weak institutions, personalisation of power and corruption and over-reliance on oil as eroding these dreams (in 2009 its GDP fell by nearly 9%, faster than any other G-20 state). Its global competiveness index ranks it at 66, as does its Human Development Index (Ardichvili et al 2012). Its life expectancy ranks it at 135 and its corruption perception at 143, alongside Nigeria and Togo, considerably higher than China at 75, Brazil at 73 or India at 95 (http:// cpi.transparency.org/cpi2011/results/).

Despite these reservations, Russia's size, resource endowments and large population are likely to ensure it remains a global player, making understanding its HRM system imperative. Few books, however, have explored HRM in Russia, often treating it as one part of a general analysis of eastern Europe (for example Morley et al 2009). However, the size, multi-ethnic population, fast-growing economy and increasing collaborations with foreign companies demand a deeper, more complex analysis of business in Russia and especially of HRM (Domsch and Lidokhover 2007).

Morley et al (2009) and Gurkov and Zelanova (2009) argue that Russia is set apart from other CCEE countries by 'Russian exceptionalism' – such features as the use of forced labour and a longer period of communist rule. The transition from communism since 1989 has been accompanied by wild fluctuations in economic growth, such as abrupt falls in the 1990s, rapid improvements between 2004 and 2007, and sharp drops between 2008 and 2009, mainly due to Russia's dependency on world demand for oil and gas.

National politics has continued to influence HRM, especially the impact of President/Prime Minister Putin's recent authoritarian and nationalistic policies. May and Ledgerwood (2007) argue that national policies after Putin's appointment as president have affected HRM. Russian companies became committed to reform between 2000 and 2003, but after his re-election 'the rules changed'. Concerns over renewed authoritarianism have led to greater capital flight, heightened by the reversals of privatisations such as the arrest of Khodorkovsky (CEO of a private oil company, now nationalised) in the 'Yukos affair'. In many cases this has caused firms to delay introducing new strategic plans or HRM initiatives and to refocus on networking with state officials – a process known as enhancing 'blat' in Russian.

This importance of 'networking' has some similarities with 'guanxi' in China (Chapter 14; see Hutchings and Michailova 2004). 'Blatters', people who can cultivate and use political connections to government to advantage, are once again becoming important, often former 'Red Directors' from the Soviet years. This raises problems for HRM over issues such as trust (for example blatters are often open to corruption and lack of accountability, often leading to 'parallel organisations' acting off the record to hold them in check), performance appraisal, and recruitment and selection (for example back-door appointments of people on the basis of who they know, not job competence).

RUSSIAN CULTURAL CONTEXT

As we have seen, Russian cultural values seem to lie mid-way between the CCEE and FSR countries (Woldu and Budhwar 2011). A GLOBE study (Chapter 2) involving a multi-country survey including the views of 450 Russian managers in the mid-1990s found Russian managers at the time displaying values originating in the Soviet or pre-Soviet era. These included a short-range orientation, low uncertainty avoidance, high power distance, a low performance orientation, in-group collectivism and a low humane orientation – a position of 'creative survival'. However, in looking to the future they saw many of these values as inappropriate to a market-oriented economy (Grachev and Bobina 2006). Ambrozheichik (2011) reviews a number of Russian studies to argue that Russian culture may be characterised by low to medium individualism, medium to high power distance, medium masculinity, high uncertainty avoidance, medium long-term orientation and fairly high paternalism (contradicting Grachev and Bobina 2006 on uncertainty avoidance).

Muratbekova-Touron (2011) has more recently compared perceptions of cultural differences between France and Russia through a qualitative study exploring the perceptions of French managers living in Russia and those of Russian managers living in France. Key differences (though with some asymmetry and differences of emphasis between the two groups) included:

- *hierarchy*: Russian managers were perceived to show a more centralised, authoritarian management style
- *time*: Russian managers were perceived to be more short term in orientation
- *affectivity*: Russian managers were perceived to be warmer, more hospitable and more spontaneous
- *human nature*: Russian managers were perceived to adopt a more 'theory X' view of employees, seeking to control and supervise them from a lack of trust
- *particularism*: Russian managers were perceived to be more social than task-oriented, more particularistic and more relationship-oriented
- *high-context communication*: Russian managers were perceived to be more secretive, with lower flows of information
- *space*: Russian managers were perceived to be more diffuse, mixing professional and private life
- *femininity*: Russian managers were perceived to be more masculine, ambitious and competitive.

The most symmetrical perceptions were over hierarchy and particularism; the most asymmetrical perceptions were over masculinity/femininity.

CHALLENGES FOR HRM IN RUSSIA

Challenges for HRM include seeking out the best expertise, committing significant resources to HRM, managing the 'talent flight' of in-demand staff, overcoming the lack of evaluation of HR activities, addressing the lack of specific skills, managing a dependence on powerful owners to get things done, and widening the common focus on large companies towards SMEs (Morley et al 2009; Gurkov and Zelanova 2009). Trade unions are relatively weak, restricted by the Labour Code of 2002, and there is a high level of state involvement in HRM. Unemployment is thought to be considerably higher than official figures suggest. As HR under communism was divided between the Communist Party, union, personnel, and the salary and engineering departments, there was no clear view of strategic HRM and how it could support the organisation (Morley et al 2009). This remains an issue, and HR's main role has been in recruitment and selection and performance-related pay, with stock-related rewards for many managers. Professional education and training, especially for managers, has expanded, however, and the growth of the energy and defence sectors means HRD is likely to grow in importance as specialist skills shortages emerge.

Russian HRM practices, based on a comparison of 2009 surveys with a 2008 CRANET survey (Gurkov and Zelanova 2012), currently exhibit low formalisation of performance assessment, great diversity in payment arrangements, and high flexibility of working and contractual arrangements; these arrangements have helped companies to successfully adapt to recessionary conditions without massive lay-offs arising from the world financial crisis. This crisis, beginning in 2008, led to sharp drops in prices for major Russian exports (for example oil, gas, metals) and a decline in industrial production of over 10%. Unemployment in 2008–9 rose only modestly, however, much less than predicted, partly due to the use of 'partial employment' measures (for example part-time work, unpaid holidays) and 'voluntary redundancies'.

Russian employees have extremely limited opportunities for collective bargaining and pay arrangements determined by national or regional agreements – less than in Bulgaria. Many forms of 'flexible working' are present, such as annualised hours, shift work and compressed working weeks, as well as fixed-term contracts and temporary/casual employment and part-time work. Teleworking is also quite common, as is variable take-home pay and benefits and tolerance of wage arrears and other disturbances to payments. Federal law nominally sets a minimum wage, but many workers in agriculture, social services and health and education in particular receive wages below this level. Maternity leave, paternity leave, paid leave to care for sick children and education holidays are legally obligatory, but not always used by companies. Additional healthcare schemes are more often used than in Bulgarian companies, with benefits rising with seniority in most cases. For large companies, often subsidiaries of MNCs, the situation may be more positive, with greater use of formalised performance assessment and promotion criteria and greater presence of trade unions.

HRD in Russia

In terms of national HRD, Ardichvili et al (2012) argue that in terms of present human capital capacity, Russia is ahead of India and China, but is likely to fall behind in the coming decade. It has high levels of primary school enrolment, but hundreds of thousands of homeless children who lack access to school are not included in official figures. Though education is one of the Government's top priority areas, with reforms aimed at ending regional disparities, assuring quality and monitoring exclusions of children, vocational education and training was badly affected by the end of central planning and the close ties of professional training colleges with state-owned enterprises, guaranteeing apprenticeships and job placements. This began to change in the late 1990s as EU-funded projects helped the country refocus on marketable skills, service industry skills and regional responsibility.

The main factors holding Russian human capital development back were *imbalances in the educational system* (inadequate government support leading to growth in private colleges; a lack of prestige for many health/education roles); social *stratification* (imbalances in access to healthcare, benefits and consumer credit alongside regional and social inequality); and a *shrinking workforce pool* (a decline in population from 148 to 142 million from 1991 to 2009; and a massive outflow of skilled workers in the 1990s). Though present Human Development indices are relatively high, educational underfunding and a failure to reform a system geared to extraction and manufacturing industries and the development of a 'neo-market' model of low government intervention and planning in HRD are likely to lead to a relative decline with respect to China, India and even Brazil.

One example of training decline in an industry previously under strong state regulation in Soviet times is shipbuilding (Ejova and Olimpieva 2007). It experienced severe shocks as a result of the 1990s transitions to a capitalist market economy, despite once being seen as a high-tech and high-skill occupation and a strategic branch of the military industrial complex (VPK), with a culture of patriotism, discipline and hierarchical authority in an industry geared to export, mainly to other 'socialist' countries. Training and retraining staff had always been a priority, initially within a planned economy based on educational-level gradation and close ties with technical training colleges and other institutions, funded or part-funded by enterprise budgets. The emphasis was on practical work at the enterprise and obligatory work for three years post-graduation. A mix of day and evening classes was used, with only gradual professional specialisation; training enjoyed relatively large budgets, modern training rooms and technology, and highly paid teachers and lecturers.

This system came under a series of challenges in the 1990s, with privatisation of some shipyards and a lack of orders and working capital, resulting in wages being delayed, mass redundancies and the transfer of training responsibilities to municipal ownership or privatisation. Enterprises themselves were now entirely responsible for enterprise training and retraining, and began to win new orders from the Chinese and Indian navies and for Arctic and northern navigation. There was a sharp drop in the inflow of young workers and an ageing workforce as the attraction of workers receiving housing in the city had been removed. Work specialisms lost prestige and the number of specialist/technical schools sharply declined, with a high level of staff mobility.

Some enterprises, such as the Admiralty Shipyards, managed to develop policies aimed at continuous professional development, within an educational centre that is now an independent, modern, well-equipped structure. Other enterprises are in a more precarious position, with unmotivated workers only interested in pay. New players have entered the field, such as consultants, new educational centres and non-commercial partnerships, such as the 'Protei' research and educational centre, serving not only the local shipbuilding enterprises but a wider range of regional and international clients. Cooperation with foreign partners has also become more common, especially with German and Finnish partners.

A strict hierarchy and complex bureaucracy often inhibit in-company training; companies find it difficult to decide training aims and the problems they wish training and development to address, partly due to the relatively low status of HRM within many Russian companies (Solitskaya and Andreeva 2007).

Ardichvili and Gasparishvili (2001: 58) argue that HRD issues and processes developed for established legal and organisational frameworks in the West are unlikely to apply in a radical, unstable and volatile environment (for example delivering credit and loan training), and that HRD needs to be explored in relation 'to specific socio-political, organisational and cultural frameworks'. Within the Russian banking sector, HRD was seen as part of 'personnel management', rather than a function in its own right, and there was a stronger emphasis on recruitment and selection than on training and development, though there was growing interest in learning technologies in medium-sized banks and in internal training centres generally. A turbulent political and economic environment was seen as a major barrier to the development of HRD, alongside a lack of practical experience in trainers.

Employee resourcing in Russia

Recent economic, social and political changes have greatly altered Russia's labour market, fragmenting it both by region and size, as the most dynamic companies are not the largest (often most bureaucratic and hierarchical) companies (Yakubovich and Kozina 2007). Many Russian companies are still state-owned, with recent re-nationalisation of companies considered strategically significant, especially in the oil and gas sectors. Moscow and its region have become more detached from the rest of the country in terms of wealth, so that several labour markets and salary levels now exist in parallel, often independently, according to industry, size, geography, ownership and legality of reward structure. Many firms pay nominal salaries with unofficial payments on top.

Russian cultural values, especially particularism and power distance, also affect employee resourcing policies and practices. Recruitment channels operating in the Russian labour market consist of the internal labour market (the candidates first considered for most vacancies), the external labour market and the *extended internal labour market*, or the social networks of the firm's current workers (Yakubovich and Kozina 2007).

These recruitment pools deliver different costs and benefits to the firm. In the Russian context, former employees often maintain contact, and may return after employment elsewhere, and firms prefer to recruit from the extended internal labour market rather than the external one. Deriving from the Soviet era, and perhaps deeper Russian cultural traditions, personal, particularistic relationships influence paternalistic recruitment practices, and 'loyalty' to the boss is a major selection criterion. New managers often swiftly replace many employees with recruits of their choice. This contrasts with the meritocratic criteria often regarded in the West as 'good practice'. Recruitment is often highly centralised in the hands of the CEO, with informal criteria dominating; the HR function is often reduced to administering paperwork.

More foreigners are now employed in Russian companies, and there is also now reverse migration to increasingly attractive smaller towns with better infrastructure in the north. Mobile young professionals, however, often still move to Moscow or regional capitals without their families, who may join them later. Western firms often reject employees over 35 as unable to integrate into Western management practices. Salaries paid to top executives in Russian companies far exceed those paid by Western ones, with wage inflation, turnover and poaching being much in evidence. Few recruitment consultancies are genuine 'search' firms, except for some foreign brands, which have only gradually returned after the 1998 crisis. Print media play a major role in recruiting blue-collar and junior executive staff, while job boards on the Internet are also very popular, for example 'job.ru' and 'headhunter.ru' or, for professionals, 'e-xecutive.ru', which also provides articles and information (Loos 2007). Case Study 9.2 gives an example of employment in one Russian company.

CASE STUDY 9.2

EMPLOYMENT IN A MEDIUM-SIZED MOSCOW IT COMPANY

This company is a 'new economy' firm founded in 1997 as a privately held enterprise by four shareholders, including the current CEO. As a closed joint-stock company, it is not obliged to publish annual reports. Its leaders are 'business intellectuals' with technical or economics degrees and a high degree of team spirit and product knowledge. As the company grew, so did confusion over power and authority, as the original leaders were perceived to lack leadership and organisation-building skills by new entrants from other social groups (for

example ex-state-owned company managers). Greater formalisation of business processes was introduced, not always successfully, by 2003, though the company did become the market leader in its segment. An HR policy was introduced in 2002 focusing on higher professional standards and capabilities and a better work environment, with more effective training and development, knowledge management, job descriptions and reward systems. However, such goals proved difficult to achieve, and some top managers, including a number from abroad, were hired and then dismissed.

Various management 'clusters' attempted to gain influence over other clusters, resulting in overt conflict, insults and withholding of information, only resolved by the CEO moving staff into other departments. Failing to meet deadlines resulted in 'blame games', involving first finding/sacking the 'culprit', then furious extra work so as to emerge as 'heroes'. Informal networks proved more reliable than official meetings or emails as sources of information. Monthly salaries were paid in US dollars, with bonuses after successful project completion in a relatively random manner. The HR department was liquidated in 2004; it was not taken seriously as a strategic partner, mainly organising parties, holidays and visa support. Western

management concepts, for example customer focus and internal communications, were used but practised very differently; 'performance assessment' meant scolding staff in public or dismissing people on an apparent whim, with managers often going back to local Russian management models, accompanied by frequent dismissals. Knowing when a 'crisis/ emergency' mode was coming seemed a core management skill in order to stop people relaxing!

(Source: Loos 2007)

Question

1   How might you analyse what occurred in this company in terms of Russian business culture and HRM practices?

LEARNING SUMMARY

HRM practices in Russia and central and eastern Europe have been undergoing a transition from the collapse of communism in 1989 and the economic shocks of the early 1990s – with mass lay-offs, privatisation and redundancies in many countries – and more recently the global financial crisis beginning in 2008. However, this experience has been uneven across the CCEE and FSR, with some countries moving more quickly than others to a market model and towards Western HRM practices. In terms of culture, the countries of the region are not homogeneous; they differ, for example, in terms of religious background, experience of industrialisation and experience of communism. Though the region as a whole has been seen as showing collectivism, masculinity, uncertainty avoidance, a short-term orientation and high power distance, in part due to the Soviet legacy and in part due to pre-Soviet rural/authoritarian influences, some countries, for example Poland and the Czech Republic, appear to be 'moving West' culturally while others, for example Uzbekistan, are much less so, with Russia in between. The chapter explored the HR situation in more detail in the Czech Republic and Bulgaria, highlighting both change and continuity.

Russia in particular seems characterised by high power distance and particularism, which has affected HRM practice in significant ways (for example recruiting from personal networks, using 'blat', demanding loyalty, operating a culture of secrecy and restricted information flow). Russia is often seen as an emerging economy – one of the BRICs – and some of its industries around Moscow and St Petersburg have made significant changes in areas such as training; but it remains dependent on oil and gas to a significant extent, and its lack of attention to education and human capital development, as well as its shrinking labour pool, may cause it to fall behind rivals such as India, Brazil and China.

INTERNET RESOURCES

Federal State Statistics Service (ROSSTAT): http://www.gks.ru

Russian Union of Industrialists and Entrepreneurs (RSPP): http://www.rspp.biz

Russia Expoonline: http://russiaexpoonline.com/en/associations

CHAPTER 10

HRM in the Middle East and North Africa

Paul Iles and Niki Kyriakidou

LEARNING OUTCOMES

By the end of this chapter, you should be able to:

- Discuss the rising economic significance of the Middle East/North Africa (MENA) and the need to analyse its patterns of HRM.

- Have a good understanding of the management of HR in MENA, including the public sector.

- Identify similarities and differences from the managerial and HRM models that prevail in the West.

- Analyse the influence of culture and Islam on HRM, and in particular the significance of 'wasta', or connections/networks, in affecting HRM practices.

- Explore public sector HRM in the region, with particular reference to the challenges of corruption, integrity and nepotism.

INTRODUCTION

Management and HRM in the Middle East and North Africa (MENA), especially in the Arab world, has received relatively little attention in the literature. HRM is greatly influenced by culture, Islam, national and global politics, and the role of 'wasta', or connections (Tlaiss and Kauser 2011; Weir and Hutchings 2005, 2009; Hutchings and Weir 2006b; Cunningham and Sarayrah 1993, 1994). There is a clear neglect of Arab cases and examples in textbooks of 'management', 'HRM' and 'international business' (Weir 2000a, 2003). However, in recent years there has been increasing interest in the HRM systems in the Middle East (for example Budhwar and Mellahi 2006; Özbilgin and Healy 2003; Özbilgin and Syed 2010; Iles et al 2013; Sultan et al 2011, 2012; Metcalfe and Mnoumi 2011).

The region is undergoing significant transformation with the 'Arab Spring', making predictions of future development difficult, especially given continuing tensions between Israel, Iran and the Palestinians and the continuing re-integration of Turkey into the region and perhaps away from Europe (Turkey is not considered here). Geographically, the focus of this chapter is primarily on the 'Levant' of Syria, Lebanon, Palestine, Israel and Jordan, and the Arab heartland of Iraq, Saudi Arabia and the Gulf States of the Cooperation Council (GCC) for the Arab States of the Gulf. North African states are also included, as well as Iran. Sub-Saharan Africa is the focus of Chapter 11.

The region is characterised by extremes of wealth and poverty, instability and continuity, and high levels of illiteracy coinciding with high levels of educational achievement. The countries are very diverse in terms of religion – for example Sunni and Shia Islam, various Muslim sects such as Alawite and Druze, Christianity in many Eastern and Western versions, and Judaism (Dalrymple 1998). They are also diverse in language – for example Arabic, Kurdish, Turkish, Farsi and Hebrew, as well as many minority languages such as Berber or Tamazight in North Africa or Tamaseq/Tamashek, a Toureg language of the Sahara region. Further, there is a significant economic divide: while some, especially in the Gulf, are oil-rich and rely heavily on migrant labour, others lacking in oil often depend on traditional markets, plus remittances from expatriate labour (often to oil-rich Gulf regions).

Arabs and Persians have a long tradition of trade, even with distant parts of the world, which has coloured the way they do business (Weir 2000a, 2000b, 2003). Arabic traders also facilitated the flow of knowledge from the classical world, India and China to 'the West' (Hourani 1991), especially in preserving and developing Greek and Roman 'classical' texts lost to the West in the Dark Ages. Arabs in Sicily and Spain, for example, made significant contributions to Western mathematics and medicine (for example 'Arabic' numerals, algebra, algorithms) and Chinese inventions such as the compass, paper and printing, and gunpowder were probably transmitted to the West via Arab intermediaries.

After a discussion of the rising economic significance of MENA and the need to analyse its patterns of HRM, the chapter analyses the influence of culture and Islam on HRM, and in particular the significance of *wasta*, or connections/ networks, in affecting HRM practices. It then focuses on public sector HRM in the region, with particular reference to the challenges of corruption, integrity and nepotism. The final section presents a Libyan case study and concludes with an analysis of the challenges facing HRM in the region.

THE SIGNIFICANCE OF MENA FOR HRM AND THE CONTEXT OF HRM

The Arab world in particular is an area of increasing economic significance (Weir and Hutchings 2005; Hutchings and Weir 2006b), not only for Western economic interests but also because it comprises a large proportion of the world's Islamic people, who account for 20% of the world's believers (Weir 2003). In addition, regions and city-states such as Dubai, Abu Dhabi and Oman, media companies such as al-Jazeera, and airlines such as Emirates and Qatar Airways have become key international players and highly successful in a globally competitive market, doing well in melding 'the appropriate elements of contemporary HRM as practiced in leading-edge Western organisations to a management matrix that conforms to local customs and expectations' (Weir 2003: 80), an example of 'hybridisation', also discussed in Chapters 11 and 12.

REFLECTIVE ACTIVITY 10.1

DID YOU KNOW?

1   Dubai has evolved from a trading enclave to become the leading Middle East business/leisure centre, aiming to become a hybrid East/West economic, social and religious model that may act as a catalyst for change, though significant differences exist between management in MENA and that in Western societies (Tang and Ibrahim 1998).

2   Bahrain also has a national aspiration, seeking to be the financial capital and 'Switzerland of the Middle East', using good education and healthcare systems, world-class transportation and telecommunication infrastructures, and a qualified and highly competitive labour force.

However, many other Middle East (ME) countries have not experienced the economic growth of other 'developing' countries in Asia, Africa or Latin America; Abed (2003) points to underdeveloped financial markets, trade restrictiveness and inappropriate exchange regimes combined with slow political reforms and dominant public sectors as inhibiting growth. Other factors cited include growing unemployment, lack of integration into the global economy, over-dominance of the oil sector, and the lack or weakness of privatisation programmes. The situation in this region is of course rapidly changing, with the 'Arab Spring' and uprisings against military, dictatorial and authoritarian regimes ongoing, with successful regime changes (at the time of writing) in Libya, Tunisia, Egypt and elsewhere. This makes predictions over the direction of this region quite hazardous (Zorob 2012).

Bourne and Özbilgin (2008) see careers in MENA, and by extension HRM in general, as intertwined with *international and national politics, legal, cultural, social and economic dynamics,* and *gender and ethnicity.* Common themes include *the impact of Western higher education,* which facilitates graduate careers and the transfer of 'Western' HRM knowledge; *migration,* both inward, as to oil-rich countries in the process of modernisation, and outward, as in the export from poorer countries of skilled workers and professionals to the West and to the oil-rich countries. *Foreign investment* into the region is also significant, with expatriate managers often employed in key roles in multinational companies. Strongly *gendered career development* and persistent inequalities, with a frequent lack of support for women's career achievement, are also pervasive themes, alongside economic nationalism (Metcalfe 2006; Hutchings et al 2010) Despite improvements in some countries, women's economic and political participation remains low in the Arab region, in particular in the Gulf countries, with numerous legal, institutional and cultural constraints preventing Arab women's full participation (Kauser and Tleiss 2011; Metcalfe 2011a, 2011b). Of course, these issues are not unique to this region; for example we discuss the role of migration and foreign investment in Chapter 11 on Africa as well.

Nationalisation or 'localisation' programmes designed to encourage and support the employment of nationals in preference to expatriates have become a key feature of HRM throughout the Middle East (for example Oman, Saudi Arabia and the United Arab Emirates), but with little academic research (Rees et al 2007). A case study of Emiratisation demonstrates complexities over design, management commitment, evaluation, resistance to change and the role of expatriates in implementing such programmes. Harry (2007) discusses issues of employment creation and localisation in the states of the GCC and the factors underlying the issues, such as rapid demographic changes, fluctuating oil prices, wealth inequality, inadequate education systems and ineffective government policies. The private sector has been focused on maximising short-term gain, creating long-term problems. Governments have attempted to reduce dependence on foreign labour rather than creating a productive indigenous workforce and worthwhile jobs for their citizens.

'Saudisation', the replacement of expatriates by Saudi nationals (there are other similar programmes such as Omanisation, which vary in areas such as target sector and target/quota employment levels and enforcement, inspection, compensation and approval regimes) is intended to protect local employees against global economic forces, but the absence of career development programmes may lead to a preoccupation with litigation, rather than full utilisation of the local workforce, as is often the case with diversity/equal opportunity legislation in the West (Mashood et al 2010). Local preferences for public sector employment as a career destination, associated with an arts/humanities education and perceived attractiveness in terms of salary and working conditions, social/political controls on women's employment, legal controls on the careers of immigrant workers and negative stereotypes of local workers' productivity, expense and motivation combine to restrict the available local labour force. The banking sector is often where most success has been achieved. Many MENA organisations, especially in the GCC countries, employ large numbers of experienced, skilled expatriate managers and professionals in key positions, often from the West or from the Indian sub-continent, with few legal protections, while reserving strategic decisions to senior family members (see Case Study 10.1).

CASE STUDY 10.1

SAUDISATION OF THE INDUSTRIAL SECTOR BOOSTED

Based on AHMED HASSAN

Published: Apr 16, 2012 02:16 Updated: Apr 18, 2012 01:15

JEDDAH: Arrangements are currently under way to set up the first vocational training institute in the industrial city of Jeddah as part of the Kingdom's plan to accelerate Saudisation of the industrial sector and make available a trained Saudi technical workforce as part of the Kingdom's 9th development plan.

It aims to apply advanced technology in industrial training.

The fifth Industrial forum is also to be held there on May 26, supported by the Council of Saudi Chambers of Commerce and Industry, the Ministry of Labor, King Abdullah University of Science and Technology, Saudi banks and export development funds to highlight challenges facing industrial investment, solutions, application of the latest advances in the field of industrial projects, and the transfer of technology.

Source: Hassan 2012

Questions

1   Why do such nationalisation efforts often fail to reach their targets?

2   What steps would help make them more successful?

THE INFLUENCE OF CULTURE AND RELIGION ON HRM IN THE MIDDLE EAST

The question of 'suitable' practices and policies in different environments has given attention to the influence of culture on management, as we saw in Chapter 2. HRM in particular is associated with social issues and activities. Major differentiating factors between countries are contextual, and there is growing support for country-based elements having a significant impact on international HRM. Such factors include: the economic, political, legal and historical environments and the socio-cultural characteristics of the workforce and society. The impact of culture in the public sector may be even more prominent, as globalisation may speed up the diffusion of business practices to the private sector.

Alongside these elements, particularly the institutional elements discussed in Chapter 1 in terms of 'national business systems', culture has generated most interest in the field of comparative HRM because of the belief that culture is at the base of people's behaviour (Hofstede 2001). Many aspects of HRM seem affected by differences in national culture; we discussed this issue extensively in Part 2 in relation to areas such as learning, ethics, leadership, and mergers and acquisitions. Indeed, the very expression 'human resource' is derived from a cultural framework in which humans are considered to be instruments of production like financial, technical or physical resources, a specifically Western perspective. This is typical of Israel, which bases much of its HRM, including in the public sector, on such a Western philosophy (Baruch 2001; Lawrence 1990). Harel and Tzafrir (2001/2002) found similarities and differences here in applying HRM between the public and private sectors; while public firms emphasised selection and grievance procedures, private firms focused on employee growth and motivation. Nevertheless, their results suggested that the public sector was moving closer to the private sector by adopting a 'high performance work system'.

Whereas Israel has benefited from a number of studies in the area of management, including HRM, research into Arab management, organisation and HRM has only emerged recently, and contains contradictory views about what type of management, and what type of HRM, is found in Arab business organisations. Some have suggested that there is no 'Arab' management theory; Ali (1993), however, argues that Arab management thinking is not yet advanced because of 'cultural discontinuity' stemming from the sudden processes of industrialisation. More recent commentators, such as Weir (2003), argue that 'Arab management' constitutes a fourth management paradigm alongside the Anglo-American (free-market), the European (corporatist, social market) and the Japanese (others might include the Korean family-based 'chaebol' or the Chinese family firm/network as paradigms, Chapter 1). We discuss in other chapters similar concepts being developed as 'indigenous' HRM models, like 'ubuntu' in Africa, Confucianism in China and 'karma capitalism' in India. For Weir, HRD (and we would add HRM) 'is normally seen as a simplistic concept, derived from the first paradigm' (2003: 69). As an example, he gives the notion of 'being hired' as anathema in many Arab practices. For Weir (2003: 81), 'the goals of HRM as conceived in typical organisations in the West have emerged from a specific historical development, formation and experience … these goals … may well be attainable by other means, more empathetic to the traditions and cultures of the Arab Middle East and its economies'.

This division into different paradigms is a simplistic, even crude classification, but nonetheless a useful one; the Arab paradigm is seen as characterised by *familial businesses, autocratic but consultative ownership, a focus on interpersonal relationships within an ethical framework, and a universalistic, networked culture.* However, Mellahi and Budhwar (2006: 296) argue from their review that 'perhaps the strongest conclusion is that there is no such thing as a "Middle Eastern HRM model", that is, a specific HRM model with distinct Middle Eastern characteristics'; organisations use a whole mosaic of different policies and practices, developed in different historical contexts. Some countries in North Africa, such as Algeria, Tunisia and Morocco, are more influenced by European, especially French, practices than the GCC countries, due to their extensive history of French colonisation, which tended to be more 'direct' and 'assimilationist' than the British equivalent, and these are also less likely to show persistent gender equalities. While unions and the right to strike are legally allowed in many North African countries, as well as in Israel, this is not the case in most GCC countries.

Mellahi and Budwhar (2006) argue that a key theme in the ME is the impact of national culture on HRM, work values and management practices in which Islamic values and Arab traditions play a key role. Tayeb (1997) has discussed the 'Islamic Revival' in Asia with respect to Iran, Malaysia and six Middle Eastern Arab countries, drawing on Muna (1980). Her central assertion (Tayeb 1997: 353) is that 'in a predominantly Muslim country, Islam, through national culture, influences organisations. HRM is a significant aspect of organisations which is most likely to be subject to cultural influences.' Many countries in the region have attempted to institute, or re-institute, Islamic ways of organising, such as interest-free Islamic banks. The Koran, as the divinely recited words of Allah, and to a lesser extent the traditions and sayings ascribed to the Prophet, the Hadith, and the life of the Prophet Mohammed himself, constitute the most important source of guidance to believers. Islam, as an all-encompassing creed, is often seen as governing all areas of life, including business life and government activity. Individual enterprise and reward are advocated, and employers urged to pay reasonable wages and manage employees appropriately.

REFLECTIVE ACTIVITY 10.2

STOP AND REFLECT
Can you identify any factors impacting on HRM within Arab organisations?

Latifi (1997), in her study of Iranian managers, identified the following Islamic work-related characteristics: equality before Allah; individual responsibility within a framework of cooperation; treating subordinates kindly, as siblings; and encouraging consultation at all levels. Muna (1980) argued that Arab Middle Eastern countries are characterised by consultative decision-making styles in rhetoric, as influenced by Islamic values of 'shura' or consultation, but in practice decisions are not made jointly, and are not delegated down the hierarchy. Subordinates are seen as viewing joint decision-making as an indication of weakness, and do not have expectations for participation in decision-making. For some managers, consultation is used to manage conflicts, persuade potential allies and 'save face', as well as gather information. Arab executives generally dislike committees or group meetings, preferring one-to-one consultation in a personalised and informal way.

Managers preferred face-to-face communication and were frequently seen in the roles of mentor, coach, teacher or adviser.

Yousef (1997, 1998) found that consultative styles of leadership were the most common and effective in non-Western, culturally mixed environments, but participative styles of management were more likely among younger and more highly educated managers. Sherif (1975) points to the importance of such values as trust, sincerity, responsibility, discipline, diligence, moderation and diligence, while Kabasakal and Bodur (2002) identified an 'Arab cluster', which was group-oriented, hierarchical, masculine and low on future orientation (Hofstede 2001).

Aycan et al (2007) examined the influence of cultural orientations on employee preferences of human resource management (HRM) policies and practices in Oman. There were a number of differences among Omani employees regarding value orientations related to age, education and work experience, cautioning us against assuming cultural homogeneity. A strong orientation towards mastery, harmony, thinking and doing, and a weak orientation towards hierarchy, collectivism, subjugation and human nature as evil was found, with relationships between value orientations and preferences for particular HRM policies and practices. Group-oriented HRM practices were preferred by those scoring highly on collectivism and being orientations, and lowly on thinking and doing orientations. Hierarchy-oriented HRM practices were preferred by those scoring high on hierarchy, subjugation and human nature as bad orientations, and those scoring low on thinking and mastery orientations. A preference for loose and informal HRM practices was positively associated with being, and negatively associated with thinking, doing and harmony orientations.

Yousef (2000, 2001) has used a 46-item scale developed by Ali (1988) to measure the 'Islamic work ethic' (IWE). Based on the Koran, it consists of items on such issues as cooperation, creative work, laziness and hard work. Yousef (2000) found that the IWE influenced United Arab Emirates (UAE) employee attitudes towards organisational change and organisational commitment; affective commitment mediated the influences of the IWE towards change. Yousef (2001) and Rokhman (2010) found that IWE directly affected both organisational commitment and job satisfaction (but not turnover) and moderated the relationship between these two variables. Support for the IWE differed across age, education level, work experience, national culture, organisation type and type of ownership. Arab expatriates showed stronger support than UAE nationals or Asian expatriates, and those who worked in government organisations showed stronger support than those who worked in private organisations.

MENA, in particular the Arab world, scores relatively highly on the power/distance index (Hofstede 2001). Power and status (and perceived skills) are linked to seniority, and power is reflective of the attainment of family, friends, charisma and the ability to use force (Weir 2000a, 2000b). More recent studies reveal that the Arab world scores in the middle of the individualism index, but comprises group-based societies in which people have a high need for affiliation, and reputation is important. The Arab world is regarded as moderately masculine, demonstrating strong sex role distinctions, and the role of women is clearly identified as lying within the family domain.

In Arab countries women's participation and companies managed and/or owned by women is the lowest in the world (World Bank 2007, 2011). Unemployment is particularly high among women, though women outnumber men in many university programmes across the Arab region (Metcalfe and Mutlaq 2011). Though Islamic law guarantees women's rights to own property and keep control of wealth brought into marriage, banks in many Arab countries often require women looking for finance to have their husbands or brothers also sign for loans. Strict gender segregation in some countries also makes female employment highly expensive. This has been challenged both by secular and Islamic feminists, who often point to powerful role models for women in business such as Khadija, the first wife of the Prophet, to challenge such negative social attitudes. See Case Study 10.2 for the example of Bahrain (undertaken before the current 'Arab Spring').

CASE STUDY 10.2

GENDER AND HUMAN RESOURCE MANAGEMENT IN BAHRAIN

The case study tried to assess how Islamic values have affected women's work experiences in Bahrain, and how Islam shapes gender and HRM policies based on 53 survey responses and 27 semi-structured interviews from female professionals participating in career development workshops. Women's employment has grown in importance in the Middle East, and governments are attempting to design national development strategies within an Islamic framework to support women's advancement in the public sphere. Women experience career and development constraints due to *equal* but *different* gender roles, and gender or equality issues are largely absent from HRM policies, including women's management training.

Source: Metcalfe (2007).

The extended family system is often the major feature of the household. The Arab household used to consist of a married couple, their married and unmarried children, and some other relatives such as parents, unmarried sisters and brothers. However, more recently this form of household has started to diminish in urban areas, such as Abu Dhabi and Dubai, because of the limited size of modernised houses and apartments, and the tendency of younger generations to have their own homes and independent life. Nevertheless, individual social identity and loyalty continue to be oriented to the largely extended family, and people coordinate their personal interests to those of the grand family (Suliman 2006). By the late 1980s, social relationships and values had tended to change in the UAE. The relationships between male and female members of society started to take a more open form, and younger people have tended to adopt new values, attitudes and customs that are different and sometimes contradictory to those adopted by the older generations. Though often hierarchical and respecting of authority, with family permeating business as well as social life, more individualised work values have emerged in several MENA countries, such as Morocco and Algeria (Mellahi and Budwhar 2006).

We also note in other chapters the growth of individualistic values, especially among younger generations, in parts of Africa, China and India. Many factors have led to this change, such as increased physical and social mobility and development of education. Crucially, globalisation has led to more interaction between the world's different cultures through satellite channels, the Internet and other advanced communication means, including Arab-owned channels like the Qatar-owned Al-Jazeera, as well as social media such as Twitter and Facebook, or in China Weibo. Elsaid and Elsaid (2012) in comparing Egypt with the GLOBE study (Chapter 2) found Egyptian managers to score lower on assertiveness, uncertainty avoidance and gender egalitarianism, but be most interested in reducing the power distance and increasing the future orientation of their societies.

REFLECTIVE ACTIVITY 10.3

What do you think the consequences of these cultural values might be on HRM and HRD policies and practice?

THE ROLE OF NETWORKS IN HRM IN THE ARAB MIDDLE EAST

One of the greatest challenges to managers and researchers in the Arab world has been in understanding the social networks, or *wasta*, that pervade business activities in the Arab world. However, 'while considerable attention has been devoted to analyzing China's guanxi, the Arab World's wasta has not been adequately researched nor has there been any substantive literature examining the similarities and differences between interpersonal connections in the two regions' (Hutchings and Weir 2006b). The business culture of the region is based on strong family networks or *wasta* connections underpinned by Islamic ethics and values; political boundaries and philosophies are claimed as comparatively surface phenomena compared with the deeper infrastructures of belief, family, kin and obligation (Weir 2003). In a similar way, networking is crucial in the Israeli environment, though other non-family-based networks, such as contacts from university or military service, apply. In North Africa, the phenomenon may be more commonly referred to as *piston* (Mellahi and Budwhar 2006).

For Mohamed and Mohamad (2011), *wasta* is an Arabic word that refers to the intervention of a patron in favour of a client in an attempt to obtain privileges or resources from a third party. It is often used to obtain employment, causing unequal opportunity; however, those using *wasta* in obtaining employment may be perceived as less competent and moral than those who do not. Egyptians discounted the competency and morality of employees using *wasta* to obtain jobs; those from lower socio-economic groups evaluated *wasta* users more positively than more affluent subjects, perhaps lacking other resources or social capital.

Conducting business in the Arab world often involves establishing a relationship first, building connections, and only then coming to the intended business at later meetings. *Wasta* involves a social network of interpersonal connections rooted in family and kinship ties and the exercise of power, influence and information-sharing through social and political/business networks. *Wasta* is intrinsic to the operation of many valuable social processes and is central to the transmission of knowledge and the creation of opportunity. In Tunisia, for example, recruitment is often carried out through 'word of mouth' in informal networks. As Yahiaouni and Zoubir (2006: 238) here point out, 'the wasta phenomenon remains prevalent to this day', though they also point out that it may also promote positive working conditions alongside the denial of equal opportunities, as do Branine and Analoui (2006) in respect of Jordan.

REFLECTIVE ACTIVITY 10.4

Taking Hosftede and Trompenaars' cultural dimensions into consideration as well as the *wasta* concept, try to identify and critically analyse the difficulties a management development scheme in MENA might encounter in practice in terms of definitions of the core skills of individual jobs.

Loewe et al (2007) claim:

> In Jordan, favouritism is referred to as 'wasta', which means 'connection'. Many businesspeople in Jordan rely on wasta rather than on their legal rights or their ability to compete. For them, having and using wasta is vital for attaining their individual ends; it is a social norm with positive rather than negative connotations in large areas of Arab societies. Resorting to it is individually rational, but collectively harmful. (2007: 17)

See Case Study 10.3 for an example of *wasta*.

VITAMIN W

CASE STUDY 10.3

Development, far from banishing *wasta*, has created new opportunities for it to adapt and flourish. The expansion of the Jordanian civil service enabled senior officials to fill new posts with employees from their extended family or region. Governments were preoccupied with building a state, leading to the growth of *wasta* and nepotism.

However, there is widespread dislike of *wasta*; a survey among Jordanians in 2000 found 86% agreed that it is a form of corruption and 87% thought it should be eliminated. However, 90% said they expected to use *wasta* at least 'sometimes' in the future and 42% thought their need for it was likely to increase, while only 13% thought their need would decrease.

Source: Whitaker 2009

Questions

1   What are the advantages of *wasta* for HRM?

2   What are the disadvantages for HRM?

3   How does it compare with 'Western' practices such as mentoring, networking and the use of school/family connections?

Is *wasta* still relevant to HRM in MENA (Weir and Hutchings 2009)? Tlaiss and Kauser (2011) found that *wasta* was frequently used in fostering the career progression of individuals in the Middle Eastern region, comparable with networking and mentoring, long familiar in Western HRM. On balance *wasta* was found to remain traditionally important in its influence in the career advancement of individuals and business life and social life; it was unlikely to diminish in the near future, despite the perception within the region that it constitutes an unfair practice. *Wasta* displayed similarities and differences with networking and mentoring, but knowledge on how *wasta* currently operates is limited, precluding reliable conclusions.

Weir and Hutchings (2005; Hutchings and Weir 2006b) argue that 'wasta requires a supportive framework of generally honourable dealing to be effective; a framework that comes in the form of Islam'. The formalities of social, family and political life are strictly preserved, even in managerial settings. It is impossible to undertake any kind of meeting in an Arab organisation without the ubiquitous coffee or tea rituals associated with the 'diwan' (Weir 2003). The family in the Arab world is the primary *wasta* channel. Although originally based upon family loyalty, *wasta* relationships have expanded to encompass the broader community of friends and acquaintances. *Wasta*-based recruitment and allocation of benefits reinforce family ties, thereby connecting the individual to the economy and government. Moreover, where a close family member appears at the office of even quite a senior manager, it is regarded as improper for the demands of organisational hierarchy to take precedence over the obligations due to family (Sulieman 1984).

Weir (2003) notes that the exchange of gifts in the Arab world should not necessarily be construed as an attempt to influence the judgement of a recipient but may be interpreted merely as a mark of respect, signifying reciprocal acceptance of status and marking the initiation or honouring of an agreed bond. However, Arabs themselves are increasingly concerned that favours are being interpreted as an attempt to change the behaviour of the recipient; *wasta* continues to make it difficult for those legitimately attempting to pursue issues within regulations (Cunningham and Sarayrah 1993). *Wasta/piston* often influences recruitment, selection, compensation and promotion in public sector organisations, in particular in the ME, as we saw in Chapter 6 on ethics in HRM and will discuss below.

HRM ISSUES AND PRACTICES IN MENA

Budhwar and Mellahi (2006) have developed a framework for analysing ME HRM, which recognises its social, cultural, institutional and political diversity and stage of economic development. We introduced it, alongside other frameworks such as Shen et al (2005), in Chapter 3. It emphasises:

- *national* factors (for example culture, institutions, sectors, business environment)
- *contingent* variables (for example organisational size, age, ownership, lifecycle stage)
- *organisational* strategies (for example generic strategies, HR policies).

Budhwar and Mellahi particularly emphasise the influence of national cultural and institutional factors. MENA management faces an ever-increasing challenge to keep up with management in developed countries due to globalisation; the introduction of MNE operations can result in the 'transfer' of best practices in HRM, as in Israel (Tzafrir et al 2006).

One example is provided by recruitment and selection. Namazie (2003) has explored the transferability of HRM practices in joint ventures based in Iran, finding that ownership and control of critical resources, the compatibility of national culture, socio-cultural differences, mutual trust and respect between partners and the compatibility of management styles were important factors. Less bureaucracy, and more flexibility, was seen in private sector Iranian companies as compared with public sector ones:

> the private sector is more flexible and change oriented ... there is a stronger drive for performance based procedures ... the private Iranian companies were more flexible to listen to their foreign partners' suggestions and apply them. (Namazie 2003: 363)

Generally, personnel policies and practices were left to the Iranian partner, especially issues relating to labour legislation. This was true of recruitment and selection, but 'due to factors such as nepotism and family relationships, many of the foreign partners became heavily involved in the recruitment and selection procedure' (Namazie 2003: 364), often using recruitment agencies to identify talent outside their partners' sphere. Since performance appraisals are not common in Iran, such systems were also often introduced by the foreign partner. Reward and compensation tended to be mutually negotiated. Though Iranian partners recognised the value of training, it was not usually linked to career development. Namazie and Frame (2007) have examined a number of features influencing the development of HRM in Iran, with particular reference to national factors and organisational strategies.

In the Arab world in particular, selection is often highly subjective, depending on personal contacts, nepotism, regionalism and family name, and it is common to employ friends or family members of existing employees. Kinship, locale, ethnicity, religion and wealth render some people more privileged than others in obtaining employment, university admission or equal treatment under the law (Hutchings and Weir 2006b). Concepts of motivation, incentives and leadership have quite different connotations in the Arab world. Motivational techniques used elsewhere may not work, such as promoting an employee away from the local area, and leaders will often be those who have age, rather than qualifications, as the basis of seniority.

Performance appraisals may need to be given to a group as a whole, but disciplinary action carried out in private so as not to cause loss of face/reputation to an individual and their group. As it is difficult within Arab culture to say 'no' face to face, successful managers are those who have developed the capability to give negative messages while maintaining strong interpersonal support. Worker satisfaction, and hence performance, is likely to be increased when recognition is given to the tacit communication styles used in these nations, and efforts made to use less direct communication strategies (Hutchings and Weir 2006b).

Abu-Doleh and Weir (2007) explored the attitudes of human resource managers working in the Jordanian private and public organisations towards performance appraisal and to how performance appraisal systems were implemented. Performance appraisal systems had a moderate impact, greater in the private sector, on promotion, retention/termination, lay-offs, identifying individual training needs, transfers and assignments. Appraisals were conducted once a year and managers were primarily responsible for conducting appraisals.

As may perhaps be expected, the case of HRM in Israel is different, as Israeli organisations tend to follow the US model of 'professional HRM' (see Baruch 2001; Tzafrir et al 2006). Issues such as equal employment opportunities have major relevance, and the legal system follows the UK legislation model (Tzafrir et al 2006).

HRM IN THE PUBLIC SECTOR IN THE MIDDLE EAST

As Kamoche (1997: 268) points out, 'the management of public corporations is a complex activity which entails the balancing of different and often contradictory objectives. These range from the provision of services and/or products at an acceptable cost to the achievement of political targets of economic development'. Government activities are typically highly personnel-intensive, so we might expect HRM to be central in improving the quality of government services. Indeed, in many GCC countries such as Qatar, training and development programmes are far more extensive in the public sector (Abdalla 2006) and performance appraisal is more common, though usually conducted in a centralised, top–down, subjective and confidential way. The public sector often gives priority in recruitment to locals, whereas the private sector often employs expatriates; public organisations tend to use written procedures, clear rules, job analyses and structured training programmes.

In Saudi Arabia and Kuwait, wages in the public sector tend to exceed those in the private sector, and such jobs are often perceived by locals as a 'right', with locals reluctant to take up private sector employment (Mellahi 2006; Ali and Al-Kazemi 2006). However, in much of the ME, multinational firms tend to apply more 'strategic' HRM, often with better pay and training, though with greater pressures on performance (Mellahi and Budhwar 2006). Large private sector firms tend to have higher pay, though lower job security, than many MENA public sector organisations. Privatisation has often been used to reduce government expenditures and to turn around unprofitable state-owned businesses, as in Algeria, Egypt, Jordan and Tunisia (Mellahi and Budhwar 2006). Job security in the public sector has been reduced, with greater unemployment and the decline of trade union influence and collective bargaining. Governments in many MENA countries have taken a less 'centralist' stand over HRM, allowing organisations a freer hand in developing appropriate HRM policies, especially in the private sector. However, local employees and job-seekers are becoming more concerned about the shrinking of the public sector, while many governments such as the UAE are concerned about tendencies to avoid employment in the private sector and have tried to introduce training, entrepreneurship and career guidance programmes (Suliman 2006).

It is still difficult to fire staff in the public sector in much of the ME; 'public sector organisations in Saudi Arabia, for example, must cross several legal hurdles before they are allowed to fire an employee' (Mellahi and Budhwar 2006: 294).

HRM systems are often outdated and ineffective, with low salaries, inability to dismiss poor performers, an absence of performance standards, no reward for performance, inability to attract talented people, promotion based on seniority or patronage, ineffective leadership and under-employment.

Jordan has created a Ministry of Administrative Development, with two ministries, Public Sector Reform and Government Performance, located in the prime minister's office (USAID 2005) to reform public sector HRM. However, reform efforts in the Ministry of Health, for example, are hampered by such factors as limited budgets for salaries and HR, the need for annual budget negotiations, a shortage of trained HR professionals in Jordan, a lack of an integrated set of goals as part of a long-term strategy, the failure of salary and benefits to follow the civil service job classification system, very small merit increases (*jedara*), a lack of career ladders for most professional staff such as nursing, non-transparent promotion criteria, few formal orientation programmes, and no assessment of training needs in line with ministerial priorities (USAID 2005).

Low public sector compensation, except in the Gulf States, has also often failed to attract or retain high-calibre staff, and bureaucratic restrictions on career advancement and seniority in promotion have failed to promote professionalism in HRM. The strong role of primary social organisations, such as the family and the tribe, and the relatively weak institutionalisation of many Arab societies may also lead to high tolerance for corruption in HRM, and most countries lack ethics regimes and integrity provisions to control discretion and prevent conflicts of interest (we discussed this in Chapter 6). In some countries, such as Egypt, there are regulations, but these are rarely enforced, as are regulations over declaring and verifying the assets of public officials.

In Kuwait, the legislature, in Jordan, the executive, and in Egypt, an administrative agency have taken some initiatives, but corruption remains a political challenge. Some countries, for example Tunisia, Yemen and Dubai, have reformed and modernised their civil services, but in many others the public sector pay structure encourages bribery and petty corruption, especially in agencies, such as the police, dealing directly with the public. Tunisia has introduced 'The Supervising Citizen' initiative to involve citizens in assessing public services, while Jordan has brought in more transparency in recruitment through online announcement of vacancies. Dubai has introduced more flexibility and an incentive structure in a more competitive framework, but the ethical dimensions of HR practices have not often been directly addressed. More recently and in collaboration with the Ministry of Finance and Industry and Harvard University, the UAE Government launched a programme entitled: Creating a High Performance Government: Public Sector Innovation. The programme provided executive training for senior government officials with the aim of enhancing their leadership and management skills, including managing people (Suliman 2006).

We explored the implications of this for ethics in HRM in the public sector in the ME in more detail in Chapter 7 on ethics and CSR (Ashour 2004). The role of politics in HRM in the public sector in many ME countries is shown by Al-Arkoubi and McCourt (2004) in their study of HRM in the Moroccan civil service. Stagnation in HRM is attributed to the French administrative heritage, which encourages civil servants to see themselves as technical experts rather than managers and the Civil Service Ministry (CSM) to see its function as ensuring that decisions conform with laws and regulations. Unfamiliarity with Western/Anglo-Saxon HRM models is also a factor, but a major issue is the source of real power in the Moroccan system, the Palace. The King plays a strong religious/patronage role within the democratic system, and political actors are reluctant to take bold initiatives. Focusing change efforts on management is therefore misplaced, as fundamental political action harnessing Palace authority is required. In Morocco, there was little evidence of strategic HRM-style strategic integration in the civil service, with no HR strategy and no link between HR activities and a strategic plan, or of HR practices to each other (horizontal and vertical integration). Promotion took a long time, requiring approval from the Ministry, from CSM, and from Finance. Delegation to lower-level staff was inhibited by high power distance and high pay/education differentials, while performance appraisal reports, which did not need to be discussed with subjects, had to go to both CSM and Finance.

HRM in the ME therefore faces a number of challenges (Suliman 2006) – many shared with other regions, including the West – such as:

- becoming an equal business partner
- increasing management awareness of the key role that HRM can potentially play
- achieving a strong professional identity
- meeting labour market demands
- ensuring that nationalisation/'Arabisation' is not imposed in a top–down way
- addressing leadership inaction, a lack of capability to manage change, inertia and a belief in traditional ways of doing things.

Despite moves to greater 'individualism' in some countries, there is a need to move away from relational HRM approaches based on *wasta* or *piston* towards competence and merit-based approaches to HRM, based on equal employment opportunity (for example Ashour 2004; Suliman 2006). This, as we saw in the Eritrean and Moroccan cases, requires political will, now being supplied by some GCC states, for example Tunisia and Jordan. As MENA transforms and modernises, HR practices may take on a more Western flavour or a 'hybrid' blend of Eastern and Western practice.

LEARNING SUMMARY

The Middle East and Arab world is an area of increasing economic significance not only for Western economic interests but also because it comprises a large proportion of the world's Islamic people, who account for 20% of the world's believers. As we have seen, HRM in the ME is greatly influenced by culture, Islam and the role of *wasta*, as well as by national and global politics. It is important to comprehend the *wasta* and associated dimensions of family and favours as well as the insider/outsider dichotomies that are core to these interpersonal connections.

In much public sector HRM in particular, conflicts of interest – where public sector employees are influenced by personal considerations and *wasta* – are widespread. Favouritism and relaxing merit and competence criteria in a partisan way, letting liking, obedience and exchange of favours influence performance ratings, salary recommendations and training places; using nepotism to obtain favours and benefits for family, relatives and partners in such areas as appointment, promotion, transfer, discipline, reward, sanctions and delegation are common. However, such practices are increasingly challenged on both performance/efficiency and equity/fairness grounds by those within the region themselves. In order to combat and avoid such conflicts of interest, the final section of this chapter discussed the main HR challenges facing public sector HRM in the region. As MENA transforms and modernises, HR practices may take on a more Western flavour or a 'hybrid' blend of local (for example Islamic) and Western practices, as in Africa, Latin America and Asia.

CHAPTER 11

HRM in Sub-Saharan Africa

Paul Iles

LEARNING OUTCOMES

By the end of this chapter, you should be able to:

- Appreciate the great ethnic, political, religious, linguistic and historical diversity of sub-Saharan Africa and its implications for HRM.

- Critically identify common HRM issues shared by most countries in sub-Saharan Africa.

- Critically evaluate the impact of structural adjustment programmes, globalisation and liberalisation on HRM in Africa.

- Critically evaluate the impact of Asian, especially Chinese, investment in Africa.

- Critically evaluate HRM issues in Africa, with particular reference to Nigeria, South Africa and Mauritius.

INTRODUCTION

In this chapter we explore (inevitably, selectively) some of the great ethnic, political, religious, linguistic and historical diversity of sub-Saharan Africa and its implications for HRM with the aim of critically identifying some common HRM issues shared by most countries in sub-Saharan Africa (given its religious, historical, cultural and linguistic links with the Arab Middle East, we have explored HRM issues in North Africa in Chapter 10). In particular, we first analyse the economic, historical and institutional and cultural context of sub-Saharan Africa and critically evaluate the impact of structural adjustment programmes, globalisation and liberalisation on HRM in Africa. In this context we explore the role of MNCs and foreign investment in Africa, and critically evaluate the recent but rapidly growing impact of Asian, especially Chinese, investment. We then discuss HRM issues with particular reference to Nigeria, South Africa and Mauritius.

HISTORICAL AND ECONOMIC CONTEXT

Pre-colonial Africa was in extensive contact with the rest of the 'old world' of Europe and Asia; see maps of Africa at:

www.un.org/Depts/Cartographic/map/profile/africa.pdf

www.worldatlas.com/webimage/countrys/af.htm

www.worldatlas.com/webimage/countrys/africa/africaa.htm

Our focus here is on sub-Saharan Africa, which witnessed the rise of great empires and states before the arrival of European colonialism. From the nineteenth century various European powers began extensive colonisation, and the French and British in particular have left their mark in the form of educational, political and legal institutions, culture, continuing influence and language.

Africa shows some unique features – though ones partially shared by much of Latin America (Chapter 12) – in terms of its specific institutional environment, including *economic and political uncertainty and instability, poor infrastructure, corruption* and *weak governance*, as well as *great religious and cultural diversity* (Kamoche et al 2004). Diversity exists across many dimensions – ethnic, historical, political, linguistic and religious. Within specific countries, there is also often great diversity, since European countries carved up Africa by drawing straight lines on a map, cutting across existing tribal and ethnic affiliations while grouping diverse ethno-cultural communities together within emerging nation-states (Meredith 2005). Countries also vary greatly in their stage of economic development, but in most countries, the peasantry remains important, and the informal sector has become increasingly so, as in Latin America. There are also vast differences in HRM practice between so-called 'failed states' such as Somalia – currently emerging from a destructive civil war – and stable multi-party democracies with growing economies such as Botswana (Brewster and Wood 2007). As *The Economist* (2011) has noted, 'six of the ten fastest growing countries in the world in 2000–2010 were African'.

Africa generally has a higher growth rate than Brazil of over 4% per annum, though infrastructural, skills capacity and other problems remain (Horwitz 2012); Horwitz points out that 38 out of 50 top-ranked African companies are South African.

INSTITUTIONAL AND CULTURAL CONTEXT OF HRM

Much research has been on development, trade, aid and political economy issues in Africa (given ongoing concerns with poverty, economic development, post-colonial administration and the role of the state, for example – see Dowden 2009). Less work has been done on HRM issues, but see Kamoche et al (2004); Budhwar and Debrah (2001); Wood and Brewster (2007), and a recent special issue of the *International Journal of HRM* in 2012. As Kamoche et al (2012: 2825) point out, 'the number of publications addressing management, organisational and entrepreneurial issues grows exponentially every year'. A number of African academics have begun to question the Western 'aid' paradigm of development, which has 'traditionally treated Africa as a receptacle for foreign aid, technology, knowledge, expatriates and financial resources' (Kamoche et al 2012: 2826), stressing access to capital and appropriate trade and governance policies and casting doubt on the ability of foreign aid and loans to provide a sustainable basis for poverty alleviation and development. The recent rise of a different paradigm, of foreign investment represented by Chinese involvement in Africa, has led to calls for a move to an 'Afro-Asian nexus' based on 'cross-vergence' and two-way knowledge flows (Horwitz 2012; Horwitz et al 2002; see Chapter 7).

Kamoche et al (2004: xv) point to factors affecting African development, such as 'the harsh global economic realities which directly impact Africa, economic mismanagement, political ineptitude and corruption. In spite of impressive advances in education and training, Africa is experiencing a serious brain drain…' (driven by civil wars, lack of employment opportunities and declining opportunities for personal and professional growth, as well as demoralisation and debilitation of the civil service through ongoing downsizing, outsourcing, and universal vilification as corrupt – Brewster and Wood 2007). However, 'there is no denying that Africa is now generating enviable success stories across a wide range of sectors' (Kamoche et al 2012: 2827); growth rates in many African countries have been impressive (for example Botswana, Mauritius), with both Nigeria and South Africa poised to emerge as among the leading global economies (O'Neill 2011).

Foreign MNCs play major roles in *human capital development* and investments *in leadership capital* and *knowledge diffusion*, but only if they act with *corporate social responsibility* (Chapter 6), *sensitivity to local cultures* (Chapter 2) and in *partnership with stakeholders*, avoiding 'the inappropriate use of foreign concepts, a reliance on particularistic practices driven by local institutional and legislative regimes and nepotistic considerations, lack of transparency in often highly politicised decision making, and a concern with procedural and transactional HRM rather than strategic issues' (Kamoche et al 2004: xvl).

Many of these issues of course arise in other contexts and regions also, as in Latin America (Chapter 12). As elsewhere, managers in Africa need to understand the particular contextual circumstances and challenges they face, creating particular difficulties for HRM managers, as Case Study 11.1 shows.

CASE STUDY 11.1

RECRUITMENT AND SELECTION DATABASE SYSTEM IN THE PUBLIC SERVICE COMMISSION OF KENYA

Adapted from Wachira 2010

For Kamoche et al (2004), Kenya has failed to reach its potential (for example recent crime and terrorism problems and Somali pirates have harmed its tourist industry). Graft, corruption and mismanagement are widespread – Kenya ranked 154th in Transparency International's Index of corruption perceptions:

http://cpi.transparency.org/cpi2011/results

Favouritism in recruitment and promotion, government interference in appointments, crime and insecurity have frequently damaged the Kenyan economy, while economic liberalisation has led to factory closures and job losses, with worsening poverty and declines in morale accompanied by an HIV/AIDS pandemic. Kamoche et al

(2004) argue that HR reforms are needed, especially in the public sector, to counter out-migration in skilled human resources and the inhibitors of hierarchical authority and political interference that have blocked the effective deployment of human resources. Some reforms have been undertaken in recent years; Wachira (2010) discusses progress in professionalising HRM in the Kenyan public service, where daily HR activities were primarily transactional and operational and HR staff had problems in relationships with other departments (see Chapter 8).

Established in 1954, the Public Service Commission of Kenya – an independent constitutional body involved in the appointment of people to hold or act in offices in the public service and in local authorities and exercise disciplinary control – had used a paper-based system to process job applications. In 2007 a recruitment and selection database system was launched to allow online job applications, benchmarked against successful systems in India, Malaysia and Singapore to enable job search, application and submission online and accessibility to commission jobs 24/7, as well as personalised application status tracking, registration

of biodata, and feedback to applicants via website, mobile/SMS, email, post and telephone. Integration of manual paper-based information, delivered by hand, courier or post, was also facilitated.

Efficiency and effectiveness, transparency, accountability and speed, especially on lead time, and personalised feedback were enhanced. Challenges included infrastructure costs, low connectivity/slow bandwidth, computer literacy of users and specialists, lack of involvement/ proactivity of HR staff, lack of integration with organisation-wide IT systems, resistance to change and a limited IT culture among Africans (there are only 3.5 million Kenyan Internet users, with daily computer use only rising from 2% in the 1970s to 5% in 2009).

Questions

1   What challenges does this case illustrate about practising HRM and introducing HRM reform in a Kenyan context?

2   How would you evaluate such an initiative and seek to deal with the challenges identified?

SPECIFIC HRM ISSUES AND CHALLENGES IN AFRICA

A number of common themes in African HRM will be discussed. These include:

- the effects of recent liberalisation, privatisation and adjustment programmes and trade union responses
- the impact of multinational companies and foreign investment
- the increasing impact of Asian, especially Chinese, investment
- the importance of governance and corporate social responsibility
- the significance of hybridisation in HR practice
- the development of indigenous HR models
- the importance and role of the informal economy
- the development of indigenous HRM concepts, such as 'ubuntu'
- the impact of HIV and AIDS
- the challenge of diversity.

THE EFFECTS OF RECENT LIBERALISATION, PRIVATISATION AND ADJUSTMENT PROGRAMMES

Some African countries, such as Zambia and Ghana, have undertaken extensive *privatisation* of state-owned enterprises (SOEs), reshaping HRM; in Zambia, many former SOEs have been bought by South African companies, bringing in their own HRM practices. The World Bank and the IMF *structural adjustment programs* (SAPs), inspired by the 'Washington Consensus', as in Latin America (Chapter 12), have opened up African markets to foreign competition, while many foreign markets have been closed to African products. Plant closures and unemployment have exacerbated wars in countries such as the Democratic Republic of Congo. Brewster and Wood (2007: 4) argue:

In reality, many tropical African states fail to fulfil these basic functions: some, such as the case of Somalia, fail to meet the basic prerequisites of a state at all. Nonetheless, most African states retain at least some functions of government, and, formally speaking at least, are engaged in the business of promoting social progress, even if their actual track record is patchy.

Kamoche et al (2004) identify this as one of the major issues in HRM in Africa; market-led reforms leading to economic liberalisation and privatisation programmes have attempted to reduce fiscal burdens, develop the private sector, broaden local ownership and increase productivity. For Brewster and Wood (2007: 2) the imposition of structural adjustment programmes (SAPs) – needed loan financing in return for neo-liberal reforms centring on radical reductions in the role of the state, marketed as mechanisms for economic recovery – in Africa in the 1980s proved devastating for the continent ... [resulting in] increasing debt, poor macro-economic performance, the collapse of education and health care systems, and an inability to meet the basic social needs of the bulk of the population.

Growing resistance to SAPs has led to the IMF replacing them with Poverty Reduction Strategy Papers (PRSPs), supposedly better-tailored policies, focused on the needs of individual countries, and incorporating local issues and concerns, but often representing little in the way of improvement (Zack-Williams and Mohan 2005); debt relief remains contingent on further privatisation and the elimination of blockages on private investment. Privatisation has led to massive job losses, deteriorating conditions of employment and trade union resistance, but also to new issues for HRM and employment relations in Africa.

Kamoche et al (2004) argue there is a need to examine organisational and HRM responses to such processes, involving changing labour markets, changing psychological contracts and changing HRM strategies for attracting, retaining and motivating talent. Amankwah-Amoah and Debrah (2011) discuss the rising importance of talent management in the liberalised African airline industry following privatisation, with airline closures and the entry of new carriers (for example from the Middle East) all increasing employees' inter-firm mobility. The migration of professionals and knowledge workers from Africa, or between African countries, has increased, with competition for skilled personnel available and moves towards labour market flexibility, subcontracting and outsourcing, often resulting in a growing casualisation of labour.

THE IMPACT OF MULTINATIONAL COMPANIES AND FOREIGN INVESTMENT

Strategic HRM in Africa has often been limited to foreign MNCs and some South African MNCs such as SAB Miller and de Beers. As we saw in Chapter 3, foreign-owned MNCs often develop 'ethnocentric' HR practices oriented to their country of origin (for example major German motor manufacturers have successfully transferred advanced production paradigms in South Africa – Brewster and Wood 2007). Secondly, some IEs may follow 'polycentric' strategies, employing HR practices of the 'host' country of operation, perhaps taking advantages of local institutional shortcomings to suppress labour organisation and/or pay low wages. Thirdly, IEs may adopt a mixed or 'hybrid' model, reserving most senior positions for expatriates and consigning local employees to relatively low-paid positions. Many local firms are run more like extended families along patriarchal lines, accessing both capital and labour via personal networks (Brewster and Wood 2007).

A legacy of paternalism from both pre-colonial (for example kings or tribal chiefs) and colonial epochs (for example many colonial employers treated employees not as adults but as children) has led to the persistence of Taylorist (and pre-Taylorist) work systems, characterised by authoritarianism, fixed divisions of labour, limited and informal training (also a product of weak local training institutions), and low levels of participation and involvement (Brewster and Wood 2007: 6). Some local firms are increasingly linked to global commodity chains to upgrade their practices, but labour standards continue to receive a low priority compared with cost or quality (Mellahi and Wood 2002).

THE INCREASING IMPACT OF ASIAN INVESTMENT

A theme of growing importance concerns the impact of Chinese (and to some extent Indian and other Asian) multinational investment in Africa (Dowden 2009; Corkin et al 2008). China has overtaken Western countries as the largest investor in Africa; for Broadman (2007: 1),

China and India's newfound interest in trade and investment with Africa … presents a significant opportunity for growth and integration of the Sub-Saharan continent into the global economy. … In contemporary times, Chinese trade and investment with Africa actually dates back several decades, with most of the early investments made in infrastructure sectors, such as railways, at the start of Africa's post-colonial era. … Today's scale and pace of China and India's trade and investment flows with Africa, however, are wholly unprecedented.

Dowden (2009: 485) points out that China had traded with Africa for centuries until the 1430s, and then again under Mao from the 1960s in such projects as the Tanzam Railway; China's 'impact on Africa … is the biggest global geopolitical shift of the early twenty-first century', alongside growing investment from other Asian countries such as Japan, South Korea, India, Malaysia and Indonesia. China's trade had increased around 20 times in 15 years, making China Africa's biggest trading partner, with around 1 million Chinese workers in Africa, ranging from businesspeople and managers to labourers and entrepreneurs. The Centre for Chinese Studies at the University of Stellenbosch, South Africa publishes extensively on this, including a regular 'China Monitor' (see www.sun.ac.za/ccs).

Kamoche et al (2012: 2826) also point out: 'The last decade has witnessed a substantial amount of investment by Indian, Malaysian and Singaporean corporations in Africa, but by far the most significant has been the unprecedented engagement with China....' This has brought a number of benefits to Africa, such as opportunities to diversify trading partnerships and enhancing the value of many African resources and commodities. China's engagement includes foreign direct investment (FDI) and aid projects, accompanied by state financing – often in the form of subsidised (soft) loans and hard infrastructure projects, such as a north–south road in Mozambique, housing in Angola, and railways, stadia and government buildings and the redevelopment of mines in Zambia.

While bringing much-needed additional investment, trade and development, this process also generates new challenges, as Chinese firms are also engaging in market-seeking behaviour, as in South Africa's telecommunications sector. China's industry can out-compete domestic African industries, especially light industry, across the region when investments are subsidised and/or institutionally supported by the Chinese state, inhibiting the upgrading of Africa's position in global production chains. This double-edged sword is also true of Latin America, where Brazil has benefited from Chinese commodity demand and Mexico has seen China as a low-cost competitor for its own industry (Chapter 12).

Kamoche et al (2012) point to the lopsided nature of much of this engagement, and the need for African partners to position themselves as equal partners with respect to employment practices and employee rights. Chinese management and HR practices in Africa have also often been highlighted, with strikes and other forms of industrial unrest, but little is known about the impact on the employment conditions of African workers. Given weaknesses in the institutional and financial capabilities of many African states and the resultant large scope of autonomy assumed by MNCs, it is unlikely that Asian MNCs will voluntarily adopt high levels of labour standards without tangible benefits, particularly smaller MNCs from emerging economies, as they often slip through the net of international pressure groups focused on large Western MNCs and are unlikely to receive pressure in their home country to observe labour standards overseas, as Akorsu and Cooke (2011) found in Ghana. Environmental and governance issues may not be high on their list of priorities. We explored this issue in Chapter 7 on corporate social responsibility and ethics.

It is useful to note here that several African states come out relatively well on measures of corruption according to Transparency International (www.transparency.org/; www.transparency.org/country/). Botswana, for example, ranks in 2011 at 32, similar to Spain and Portugal and ahead of Italy at number 69; Cape Verde is 41, Mauritius 46, Seychelles 50 and Namibia 57, higher than most of eastern and central Europe. Other countries such as Kenya and Nigeria score more highly.

THE IMPORTANCE OF GOVERNANCE AND CORPORATE SOCIAL RESPONSIBILITY

As with Latin America, the issue of how MNEs address corporate governance and CSR issues within HRM has become increasingly important. Eritrea, for example, a small country located in north-east Africa, has sought to bring about public service reform, including of the civil and police services, given problems such as nepotism and political interference (Teclemichael Tessema and Soeters 2006). In 2011 Eritrea ranked 134th in Transparency International's Corruption Perceptions Index (www.transparency.org).

Between 1995 and 1997, after liberation from Ethiopia, the Eritrean Government introduced civil service reforms to streamline the civil service, set up the Eritrean Institute of Management, introduced a new salary scale, and launched the Eritrean HRD project. In promotion, merit and seniority were not seen as the main criteria; other influences, such as political considerations, were more significant. Ex-fighter civil servants were given special privileges in recruitment and selection, placement, promotion, training and compensation, politicising the civil service and eroding values of objectivity, rectitude, impartiality and neutrality, and reducing the link between performance and reward. Budget constraints affected the ability to pay employees comparably with private sector and international NGO levels, affecting recruitment and retention.

As Teclemichael Tessema and Soeters (2006: 99) point out, 'In an environment where there are no promising economic and political factors (peace and stability as well as good governance), it is unlikely that a higher impact of HR practices on employee performance will be achieved.'

REFLECTIVE ACTIVITY 11.1

Look up your country's corruption score and Transparency Index at:

www.transparency.org/research/cpi/overview/

1   What are the likely impacts on HRM in your own country?

2   How do you assess the methodology employed in this evaluation?

THE SIGNIFICANCE OF HYBRIDISATION IN HRM

The issue of hybridisation of HRM practices was introduced in Chapter 3, where we discussed the approach taken by neo-institutional theories to the spread or diffusion of HRM practices by IEs. Many of these, like culturalist or national business systems approaches, presented somewhat determinist arguments, leaving little scope for human agency at the firm or individual levels or adaptation to shifting local labour markets. As Kamoche et al (2012: 2825) point out, 'while researchers previously lamented the inappropriateness of Western management practices, more recent research suggests various forms of hybridisation', or a blend of transplanted, diffused or transferred practices and local or indigenous practices, as has been found in Latin America (Chapter 12), which stresses the frequent hybrid and pragmatic approaches often found (for example the Grupo San Nicholas case); Chapters 1 and 3 discussed the similar behaviour of Japanese retail stores in China (Gamble 2010).

HR managers may be influenced both by global, convergent factors such as technology and local, divergent factors such as nepotism, bribery and corruption practices, sometimes referred to as 'cross-vergence' as opposed to convergence or divergence (Horwitz 2012: 2943): 'yet within a country and national cultural context, variation between MNC and local firm propensity to adopt HRM occurs' over such issues as outsourcing and use of expatriates. Managers may adopt different cultural influences and draw on both local (for example paternalism) as well as Western (for example merit pay) practices. We discuss some of these issues in relation to the next theme, the development of indigenous African HRM concepts.

HYBRIDISATION AND THE DEVELOPMENT OF INDIGENOUS AFRICAN HRM CONCEPTS

Recent attempts by those promoting an 'African renaissance' to develop an 'African management paradigm' have focused around the more 'collectivist' culture of Africa, especially in southern Africa. Mozal, a multinational aluminium company in Mozambique owned by BHP Billiton – a UK company in partnership with Japanese, South African and Mozambican partners – shows a typical pattern, very similar to Kenya, of high levels of power distance, collectivism, uncertainty avoidance and femininity among the workforce (Sartorius et al 2011). However, these dimensions differed across employee levels, indicating cultural diversity and hybridisation. The workforce generally adhered to a 'collective-humanism' concept, similar to much of Latin America (Chapter 12), emphasising interpersonal relationships, dignity, respect for age and authority, caring, compassion and community (Kamoche et al 2004). For example, workers were often unhappy with their 'operator' job titles and lack of involvement of the company in family health and welfare issues.

These values have been formalised in the concept of '*ubuntu*', a communal 'I exist because of others' or 'I am who I am through others' concept, contrasted with Western individualism (Mbigi and Maree 1995). *Ubuntu* tries to capture the complex relationships between people and the idea of caring for others, with a focus on interdependence, humaneness and group decision-making, using *indaba* – debate in groups in Zulu – for TQM teams. This orientation to internal stakeholders, balancing stakeholder interests, sense of belonging, interrelatedness, collective solidarity and consultation and participation is similar to the 'humanism' and 'person-centred' focus found in Latin American HRM (Chapter 12). This may shape corporate governance and CSR in Africa (Kamoche et al 2012); at present, MNEs may fail to implement CSR and governance initiatives in part because of weaker regulatory and employment relations environments. With increasing Asian investment, this issue may become more urgent.

 HRM AND CULTURE IN TWO TANZANIAN BANKS

CASE STUDY 11.2

However, such concepts as *ubuntu* may be over-idealised or romanticised by proponents of an 'African renaissance'; Horwitz (2012: 2942) points out 'the African notion of "ubuntu" is not widespread in parts of modern Africa'; it may resonate with older, but not younger, workers (Horwitz 2012). In leadership development programmes in Namibia, one of the authors (Iles) was struck by the frustration of some younger, better-educated women with the way leadership positions in many community-based organisations, such as game conservation, were often automatically occupied by older, less-educated male authority figures.

Kamoche and Newenham-Kahindi (2012) compared the US-based Citibank and the South African-based Standard Bank in Tanzania. The first attempted to inculcate a distinctly American culture, such as rewarding individual effort and success; the second presented itself as officially supporting 'African' values, often family-based, such as 'ubuntu' and 'indaba'. Some 'American' features in Citibank, such as rapid promotion of younger employees and performance-related pay, were welcomed; others, such as an emphasis

on fitness and sport, were not, compromising the dignity of adult workers and many women especially, and job insecurity was less welcome. In Standard Bank, job security was valued, but not the denial of promotion to younger workers; these values were 'more acceptable to the older generation, and in particular men who derived from them stable career prospects, but were not always welcomed by women and younger workers ... to a section of its labour force, these values were just as alien as the American ones imposed by Citibank. This argument warns of the risk of assuming cultural homogeneity across the African continent' (Kamoche and Newenham-Kahindi (2012: 2867)). What one group of employees found as encouraging stability and job security, another found oppressive, with greater inter-generational tensions than in Citibank.

Question

What do you see as the advantages and disadvantages of an MNC 'imposing' its cultural values and HRM practices in foreign affiliates?

THE IMPORTANCE AND ROLE OF THE INFORMAL ECONOMY

The informal sector based on small enterprises is an important part of economic life and a significant dimension of economic activity. As with Latin America (Chapter 12), there is a dispute between 'marginalists' and 'structuralists'. Modernising marginalists take a negative view, seeing unregulated economic activity as often related to social inequality and poverty; informal activity may therefore represent a survival strategy of last resort, weakening regulatory machinery and state benefits. Increased tax shortfalls may force people to turn to the informal sector for survival. Structuralists in contrast see it as a source of entrepreneurial energy, a local dynamic resource and a potential catalyst of job creation and economic growth.

Debrah (2007) studied the informal sector in Ghana, one of the first African countries to implement SAPs and with a well-developed informal sector (employing around 80% of the working population) in traditional crafts, street and market vending and manual occupations, and an active 'interventionist' VET programme called STEP (Skills Training and Employment Programme) to help the unemployed develop marketable skills. This was primarily aimed at entry into the informal sector, refocusing VET away from just the formal sector towards providing indigenous vocational skills and agriculture – an essentially 'structuralist' view.

Ghanaian trades unions were sceptical over the ability of the informal sector to absorb significant numbers of the unemployed, seeing it as short-term expediency in the absence of a welfare programme. Debrah (2007: 1080) generally supports this sceptical 'marginalist' view: 'the informal sector is the result of the state's inability to expand the employment capacity of the formal sector'. STEP trainees pointed to a lack of a coherent informal sector employment policy; many had experienced business failures and aspired to join the formal sector, and criticised the courses for inadequate preparation, in addition to a lack of funding and capital for self-employment and the requirements to loan only to cooperative projects.

However, Debrah (2007) also argues that an informal sector employment strategy has a potentially positive contribution to make if linked to other employment and training programmes coherently, taking into account macroeconomic, social, political and cultural factors such as literacy, education, skills training, population growth, migration, school attendance and child labour issues.

Jackson (2012a: 2901), from a 'culturalist' position, takes a more positive view, seeing the informal economy as 'closer to local communities, and more appropriate to developments in Africa' as it emanates from local communities and reflects and supports cultural identities, especially women's activities. Claiming that Africans feel 'they are stepping out of their culture when they go to work each morning' in Western-style work organisations (ibid: 2901), he argues that 'it is also the very nature of strong family and community bonds and networks that provide leverage for success in entrepreneurial activity within the informal economy'. The informal economy is important to African development as a parallel set of institutions resisting and even challenging state predatory rule with its suppression of individual initiative (most brutally shown in Zimbabwe by the 2005 Operation Murambatsvina, or 'clear out the trash', which attempted to break up the informal sector and clear the streets of 'illegal' traders and vendors).

There has been a growth of informal economy national networks in Zambia and Zimbabwe (http://www.wiego.org/instututional-members/aziea.php) and international alliances such as Streetnet International (http://streetnet.org.za). Jackson (2012a: 2906) sees the sector as more attuned to African daily realities: 'when organisations in the informal sector become more aligned with the formal sector they in some respects begin to lose their "authentic" localism and indigenous basis and even legitimism'. There are both tensions between the two sectors as well as connections and alliances between them.

So rather than shrinking as a marginal activity, the proportion of informal jobs may even be increasing, as a large proportion of the population is being forced to turn to the informal sector for survival: 'a case can be made that the typical employment relationship in Africa is in the informal sector' (Brewster and Wood 2007: 7). This makes attempts at union organisation very difficult, as we discuss in Chapter 20.

THE CHALLENGES OF DIVERSITY

A third theme identified by Kamoche et al (2004) is diversity management; particularistic practices have predominated, often based on ethnic, gender and other non-job-related criteria. Many African countries have diverse ethno-cultural communities (Kamoche et al 2004; Horwitz 2012). South Africa has the most extensive employment equity legislation; the post-apartheid Constitution (1996) and the Employment Equity Act (1998) have sought to develop more representative workforces and increase the proportion of historically excluded groups. The 1998 Act was amended in 2003 to include measures of 'black empowerment' through a broad-based Black Economic Empowerment Act (BEE) (Horwitz 2012). This aims to enhance African share ownership and set targets in a range of sectors to redress access to formerly denied managerial, professional and economic opportunities. Employers are required to remove unfair discrimination practices and submit reports indicating progress on these objectives, as well as consult with trade unions.

Diversity is also an issue in other African countries, and often associated with discriminatory practices. In Chapter 7, we discussed regional/religious cultural clashes between merging banks in Nigeria. Mauritius, a small island ex-colony of the UK in the Indian Ocean, has often been ranked as among Africa's top countries for economic freedom, ease of doing business and good governance. As an ex-colony of the Netherlands, France and latterly Britain, it retains a small but economically still important Francophone community from the sugar plantocracy alongside large numbers of people drawn as slaves from Africa (Creoles). Though the largest group is Hindu, there are substantial Muslim, Confucian, Buddhist and Christian communities, and a complex linguistic picture. English is the 'official' language of government, business and education, but French is the primary language of the media, while a French/African-based Creole is also widely used. Many Mauritians also speak an Asian language at home.

Despite relative harmony between the various groups, these are primarily endogamous, and ethnicity remains an issue in Mauritian politics, with occasional ethnic riots and tensions and a belief that ethnic-based nepotism is widespread, mostly favouring the dominant population group; since independence (in 1968), all prime ministers have been drawn from the Hindu majority, though one from the Francophone minority has recently been elected prime minister. The official ideology is similar to India, deploring 'communalism' or appeals to sectional 'ethnic' interests. The civil service is officially committed to a merit-based, bureaucratic system, though there is the belief that ethnic-based nepotism, client-based patronage and political favouritism are pervasive, with many features persisting from the colonial era (McCourt and Ramgutty-Wong 2003). There appeared to be a lack of transparency in recruitment and selection, an absence of clear criteria, and a lack of scrutiny of selection and a perception that ethnic and political patronage were still prevalent, alluded to in the phrase 'Mauritian specificities'.

Ethnically based and clientilistic/patronage politics means that any devolution of responsibility in HR to line managers may result in their discretionary powers being abused to favour their own ethnic group. The Public Service Commission in Mauritius may act positively to contain or reduce nepotism and patronage; line managers may not currently have the skills or training to operate in a devolved system.

THE IMPACT AND MANAGEMENT OF HIV/AIDS

Another theme in Africa is the impact of the HIV/AIDS pandemic and the need for appropriate policies, especially as the greatest impact is on the younger, most productive part of the workforce. Here Botswana, South Africa and Uganda have made the most progress. In southern Africa, there has been a proliferation of workplace policies and programmes, often oriented towards awareness, education, prevention and safeguards against discrimination, but a frequent gap exists between rhetoric and reality, with South Africa having the most developed and extensive legislation. Few private sector companies in Malawi have begun to respond fully to the crisis, though death and sickness absence started to have an increasing impact through the 1990s. Malawi has, however, developed a high-level National Aids Coalition, with impressive successes in antiretroviral therapy (Bakuwa and Mamman 2012).

Finally, we focus on two African countries, South Africa and Nigeria, as the largest economies in Africa and most likely to emerge among the leading global economies (O'Neill 2011) as members of the BRICS (South Africa) or 'Next 11' (Nigeria).

HRM IN SOUTH AFRICA

South Africa successfully entered into democracy in 1994 after the ending of a white-dominated apartheid regime characterised by protectionism, closed markets and state-owned enterprises as well as preferential treatment of white workers and political exclusion of Africans (Wood and Mellahi 2001). From the 1970s increasing resistance and international pressures led to economic and other sanctions and disinvestment. Since the 1994 election of the ANC government, it has moved steadily towards a neo-liberal market-oriented policy, rapidly phasing out tariff barriers and experimenting with more flexible working, alongside a continuing commitment to trade unionism and collective bargaining. While workers enjoy strong, effectively enforced protection by advanced labour legislation, unions have faced wholesale job losses and problems in reaching out to the informal sector (Wood and Dibben 2007). We will discuss this further in Chapter 20.

Horwitz et al (2004) highlight high unemployment, the HIV/AIDS pandemic and a young workforce lacking in education and skills (partly a legacy of education under apartheid) as key issues, though equity legislation has caused a more professional approach to recruitment and selection, with trends towards performance-related and skill-based pay systems. An African middle class has emerged alongside rising income inequalities, and South African annual trade with Africa has increased fivefold, with the country now the biggest foreign direct investor in the continent. This growth has not always been uncontested, with local accusations of racism and authoritarian management, and there is growing competition between Chinese, Indian and South African MNCs in many parts of Africa (Corkin et al 2008).

A relatively sound financial system and dynamic economy led to South Africa becoming a member of the BRICS group in 2011 (O'Neill 2011), and South African multinationals have also begun to invest in other regions, including China, where they claimed their experience of transformation and multi-cultural sensitivity gives them an advantage, as well as proximity between collective, relationship-based African *ubuntu* and Chinese *guanxi* (Horwitz 2012). South African multinationals include Nando's International (food franchise), Sasol (petro-chemicals), MTN International (telecoms) and SAB Miller (brewing), successfully expanding both in Africa and globally (Wocke 2007; Wocke and Klein 2007). These have adopted diverse HRM strategies, emphasising either global integration or local responsiveness (Chapter 3), and show different levels of adaptation to local culture and use of expatriates to transfer HR practices. Sasol shows high convergence; Nando's demonstrates low convergence or cross-vergence, with limited formalised HR partly due to its recent expansion and partly its franchise-based business model. SAB Miller, with operations in most regions, uses a core group of expatriates to transfer its culture to acquired companies. MTN has largely been active in Africa, and its HRM function plays a key role in standardised performance and talent management and human capital development, using expatriates and technicians seconded from South Africa (often leading to clashes with local employees and customers).

HRM IN NIGERIA

Nigeria, despite a reputation for corruption and mismanagement by the country's elite – with a corruption index among the highest in the world of 2.6 in 2010 (http://www.guardian.co.uk/news/datablog/2010/oct/26/corruption-index-2010-transparency-international; www.transparency.org) and ranked 143rd by Transparency International – is now seen by Goldman Sachs (O'Neill 2011) and others as among the next 11 rapidly emerging economies (N-11) after the BRICS. Nigeria's economy could by 2050 become one of the largest in the world, outstripping those of France, Canada and others (http://www.goldmansachs.com/our-thinking/global-economic-outlook/the-growth-map/index.html; http://www.vanguardngr.com/2010/12/nigeria-may-be-africas-1st-bric-member).

Nigeria is the most populous country and second largest economy in Africa after South Africa, but displays widespread poverty and dependence on oil export earnings and widespread perceptions of environmentally and socially dubious activities by oil companies in the Niger delta (Chapter 7). Though it has abundant labour, talent is scarce (Fajana et al 2011). Most organisations are highly unionised, especially in the public sector; until 2005 the Government promoted compulsory membership. The colonial legacy and the influence of oil on the state in general and industrial relations in particular are important factors.

With the oil boom of the 1970s and tendency to import from abroad, de-industrialisation occurred in the 1980s and 1990s, with a decline in employment in the sector. Ovadje and Ankomah (2001) argue that return to democratic rule in 1999 and active policies of liberalisation and privatisation made Nigeria attractive to FDI. The current Nigerian Government (Ituma et al 2011) has embarked on widespread economic reforms, privatising many state-owned enterprises, offsetting foreign debt and diversifying the productive base. This has resulted in greater FDI and growth in such sectors as IT, telecoms, banking, gas and oil, accompanied by a high inflation rate, economic insecurity, high unemployment and a lack of a national social welfare system.

Nigerians put strong emphasis on educational attainment, especially passing exams and gaining degrees, with employers paying for foreign-obtained credentials in particular. However, since 1985, the education system has been in some decline due to under-funding, deteriorating facilities, strikes by both students and lecturers, and a 'brain drain' of academics. There are serious skills shortages in many sectors.

Local values include respect for age, importance of the family (for example emphasis on burial allowances, compassionate leave, wedding allowances, family healthcare benefits, managerial commitment to caring and attending family/social functions and fulfilment of family obligations), a dislike of direct face-to-face criticism and a tendency to recruit/trust people from one's family/ethnic group. Nigeria is broadly collectivist, with acceptance of hierarchy, deference to authority, status differentials, respect for age and priority given to male careers; the extended family, with its strong ties and obligations, acts as a 'social insurance'. High power distance is confirmed by the GLOBE study of House et al (2004), where Nigeria ranked second out of 62 countries studied. Individuals, especially men, tend to define 'career success' in terms of financial stability – in part to provide welfare support to others – and as achieving social standing, visible status and career advancement (Ituma et al 2011).

There have been recent trends towards contracting out services, greater female participation in the private sector and in management, and greater use of IT in HRM. IT companies tend to have flatter structures and are more informal and knowledge-driven than other Nigerian firms (Ovadje and Ankomah 2001).

LEARNING SUMMARY

Africa is a continent of great ethnic, political, religious, linguistic and historical diversity. Here we focused on sub-Saharan Africa and sought to identify common HRM issues shared by most countries in the region. The chapter critically evaluated the impact of structural adjustment programmes, globalisation and liberalisation initiatives on HRM in Africa, especially their impact on unemployment, employee conditions of work and mobility.

Another issue is the increasing impact of Chinese and Indian investment in Africa, often involving soft loans and infrastructure development – for example roads, railways, sports stadia, hospitals – being built in return for access to oil and other raw materials to fuel Chinese growth. Concerns are expressed over the deleterious impact of Chinese competition on African industries, as well as over Chinese management practices and lack of attention to transparency and governance issues, but little research has been done on these.

The chapter went on to discuss a range of HRM issues, including those in Nigeria and South Africa, the continuing importance of particularism and the development of collectivist managerial concepts such as *ubuntu*. One issue raised was the potential for both South Africa and Nigeria to continue to grow and realise their potential to rank among the global economic powers in the coming decades. To achieve their potential, effective HRM is likely to be a key lever; as Brewster and Wood (2007: 1) argue, 'The way that people are managed, their role in such management and the relationships between people and their representatives and their employers will be crucial factors in Africa's development.'

CHAPTER 12

HRM in Latin America

Paul Iles

LEARNING OUTCOMES

By the end of this chapter, you should be able to:

- Critically analyse the institutional context in which HRM operates in Latin America, such as the role of government intervention, political instability, liberalisation, privatisation, structural market reforms and foreign investment.

- Critically analyse the cultural context of Latin American business life and its implications for HRM, while recognising that Latin America is not homogeneous.

- Identify key HRM issues facing Latin American organisations, such as the transitional role of trade unions, family-oriented values, a person-centred view of HRM and the rise of the formal economy.

- Critically analyse the importance of pragmatism, humanism, hybridism and stakeholder management to Latin American HRM, especially in relation to CSR.

- Critically evaluate the role of HRM in Brazil and Mexico, especially in terms of their aspirations to be major global 'growth economies', with particular reference to CSR.

INTRODUCTION

In this chapter we focus specifically on *the institutional and cultural contexts* of HRM (Chapters 1 and 2) and *specific HRM issues and challenges* for Latin America in general before focusing on the two largest economies and most populous countries, Mexico (sometimes considered geographically part of North America) and Brazil, both forecast to be among the top global economies within the coming decades (O'Neill 2011). Following the framework outlined in Chapter 1 and its discussion of institutionalist/national business systems approaches, we first review the institutional and historical context in which HRM operates in Latin America, such as the role of government intervention, political instability and volatility, the recent rise of liberalisation, privatisation, 'structural reforms' and market reforms, and foreign investment. Following the analysis presented in Chapter 2, we then critically analyse the cultural context of Latin American business life and its implications for HRM, while recognising that Latin America is not homogeneous, that different subcultures exist and that all cultures are dynamic and changing.

We then attempt to identify some key HRM issues facing Latin American organisations, such as the transitional role of trade unions, family-oriented values, a person-centred view of HRM and the rise of the formal economy, before critically analysing the importance of factors such as pragmatism, humanism, hybridism and stakeholder management to Latin American HRM, especially in relation to CSR (Chapter 7). The analysis of transferring HRM and changes in HRM practice presented in Chapter 1 is particularly useful in exploring hybridisation of HR policy and practice. We end with a critical evaluation of the role of HRM in Brazil and Mexico, especially in terms of their aspirations to be major global 'growth economies', again with particular reference to CSR.

INSTITUTIONAL CONTEXT OF HRM

HISTORICAL AND ECONOMIC CONTEXT

This region witnessed the rise of great indigenous empires, such as the Toltec, Maya and Aztec in Central America and the Inca in South America, but became subject to European colonial rule from the late fifteenth century. Spain and Portugal remained the major colonial powers in Latin America until the liberation wars of the nineteenth century, with some involvement by France, the Dutch and Britain, especially in the Caribbean and in Belize and Guyana/Guiana/Surinam. You can find maps of the region at:

- www.maps.com/map.aspx?pid=9089
- www.worldatlas.com/webimage/countrys/camerica.htm
- www.infoplease.com/atlas/southamerica.html/

Latin America and the Caribbean have a total population of around 600 million, with a median age considerably lower than Europe, Asia and North America owing to high birth rates and very young populations (Briscoe et al 2012). Latin American economies have continued to grow in recent years, with significant foreign investment as their economies have opened up and undergone democratic transformation. In 2005, among the Forbes 500 Top International Firms, 12 were from Brazil and Mexico, while there were 38 Latin American companies among the Forbes Top 2000 World Firms (Elvira and Davila 2005).

Davila and Elvira (2009) point out the crucial strategic role played by *foreign investors* in Latin America, despite its position as a low-cost manufacturer being undermined by Asia in recent years, especially China. MNCs have been withdrawing or reducing operations in a variety of sectors such as telecoms, banking, power, water, retail and oil, partly from concerns over government intervention, such as in Argentina and Venezuela. Investments in oil and gas are focused on Venezuela, Argentina and the Andean countries, in minerals in the southern cone, and in goods and services in Mexico and Brazil. Manufacturing third-tier suppliers are mostly found in Mexico and the Caribbean.

Latin America has attempted to respond by attracting FDI into value-added industries and through Latin American firms (*translatinas*) themselves internationalising, increasing inter- regional FDI and making increasing investments in Asia, Europe and North America (for example the Mexican concrete producer CEMEX, the mineral company CVRD of Brazil, the auto parts company Alfa of Mexico, the Mexican telecoms company TELMEX, the Chilean wine company Concha and Toro, the Peruvian soft drinks company Grupo Kola Real, the Venezuelan state-owned oil company PDVSA).

INSTITUTIONAL CONTEXT

Latin America has historically been characterised *by a high concentration of wealth, high government intervention* in regulating the economy, *extreme volatility, abrupt changes* from closed to open economies, and large investments in *low value-added industries.* Casanova (2005) emphasises the impact of the 'Washington Consensus' policies of the 1990s, emphasising market-oriented reforms, liberalisation of FDI and trade, labour-market reforms to encourage 'flexibility' through more temporary and part-time contracts and easier terminations, and the large-scale privatisation of state-owned enterprises (as in Africa, Chapter 11). This process began in Chile after the military coup against President Allende in the 1970s, but has spread through 'structural reforms' to most of the region, though with variations (for example Ecuador and Nicaragua have shown little privatisation as compared with Argentina and Peru). Such IMF/ World Bank 'structural reform' processes have affected many industrial sectors, such as mining, telecoms, banking, energy, oil and gas, and infrastructure, with variable results.

Political stability and democratisation have developed as authoritarian and military governments have been replaced, facilitating economic stability and foreign investment and strengthening trade and investment links, such as the formation of NAFTA between Mexico, the USA and Canada, Mercosur (the southern common market of the 'southern cone' countries) and agreements with the European Union. While the USA has remained the largest foreign investor, Spanish investments in banking (for example Santander, Banco Bilbao Vizcaya), telecoms (for example Telefonica) and oil (Repsol) have grown dramatically (though Argentina nationalised Repsol in 2012), while Asian investment has also risen in recent years. Japanese companies have become major investors in *maquilas*, or in-bound assembly plants, in Mexico and Brazil, while Chinese investment has grown dramatically in the last few years. China has become a major competitor in low value-added sectors (for example shoes, toys, textiles) especially to Mexico, while its search for new international partners and markets and especially its search for stable sources of raw materials has conversely led to opportunities for Brazil, with major Chinese investments in forestry, food processing, transportation and light industry as well as high technology areas such as aerospace, defence and steel. Indeed, China was the largest foreign investor in Brazil in 2010, though the relationship is not without tensions (http:// www.economist.com/node/21542780).

Under the recently democratically re-elected government of Chávez, Venezuela has in recent years sought to challenge such neoliberal policies (for example Gott 2012), following the example of Simón Bolívar, the South American 'liberator' from Venezuela, one of South America's greatest generals. Cuba and other Caribbean and Central American countries often receive cheap Venezuelan oil, and Venezuela has fought against the policies of privatisation and renationalised many industries, including oil and gas (privatised during the 1990s), encouraging Argentina to default on its debt, reorganise its economy and renationalise its oil industry.

CULTURAL CONTEXT

Most Latin American countries following Hofstede (2001) show *high power distance* – lower in Chile, Argentina, Costa Rica and Uruguay; *collectivism* – lower in Argentina, Brazil, Uruguay and Mexico; *uncertainty avoidance* and *masculinity* – more dispersed, with Chile and Costa Rica scoring much lower than Venezuela or Mexico. However, this 'myth of cultural homogeneity' is now under attack, as significant cultural differences exist between countries such as Argentina and Chile (traditional and hierarchical in organisational structure) compared with Brazil and Colombia (flatter structures and greater 'modernity' – Friedrich et al 2006). The countries also differ in respect of growth, income per capita, population and employment rate; while Brazil may be the largest, Chile has a higher GDP per capita, and Brazil has higher urban unemployment than Chile, Peru and El Salvador, as well as higher illiteracy rates than many other countries (Carlier et al 2012).

These cultural characteristics are often associated in research with centralised, pyramidal organisations, group loyalty, discrimination against women and bureaucratic, risk-averse and controlling organisations. For Elvira and Davila (2005), power distance and collectivism need to be understood in connection with the central importance of *respect for authority* and *social relationships*. With regard to authority, they argue that this has often been associated with *benevolent paternalism*: bosses have a personal obligation to protect and safeguard the needs of employees in a hierarchical, but 'family-oriented'/'fraternal' climate. Elvira and Davila (2005) trace this to the 'hacienda'/large landowner or leadership style of the 'patron' or owner-boss (in Brazil, *fazendas*) transposed into a modern setting, encouraging dependency, avoidance of conflict or confrontation in public, social distance, valuing of job titles as status symbols and community support. Collectivism is manifested in the importance of personal contact and communication, cordial and affective relationships, interpersonal trust and in-group loyalty, often accompanied by displays of popular religiosity in the workplace.

These cultural dimensions appear to affect many HR practices; staffing and promotion practices, for instance, have generally been based on personality traits, family links (such as hiring family members and close relatives), personal connections of education, geography and social class, and physical characteristics (gender, age, class, race, appearance). Family considerations also influence reward and recognition schemes and such common initiatives as holiday/visiting/

picnics, as well as status symbols, job titles, loyalty ceremonies and practices emphasising seniority. In performance management, group and seniority recognition is also often stressed.

SPECIFIC HRM ISSUES IN LATIN AMERICA

Briscoe et al (2012) stress three key HRM issues for Latin America, linked to the importance of authority and collectivism but also to the changing economic and institutional context discussed above:

1   family-oriented work values

2   person-centred views of HRM

3   emergence of the informal economy.

FAMILY-ORIENTED AND PERSON-CENTRED WORK VALUES

Latin America has shown a strongly collectivist, paternalist attitude towards work, leading to family-like organisations, where supervisors act as 'father figures'. Organisations are also characterised by hierarchy, status and social distance, with confrontation by subordinates discouraged. There is a strong emphasis on symbolic benefits such as job titles and levels to reflect social status.

However, the traditional 'nuclear family' no longer constitutes a majority of Latin American homes (Carlier et al 2012). Both flexible and part-time working are uncommon in Chile, Brazil, Colombia and Peru, but common in El Salvador; there were, however, greater similarities in maternity leave offerings beyond the requirements of national regulations. Flexible vacation schedules and efforts to reinstate staff after long leaves of absence were less developed in Latin America than in Spain. Despite high awareness of work–family policies, more informal practices seemed to be the norm, perhaps reflecting more 'personalised' HRM, especially in SMEs. For many Latin Americans, there are expectations that firms will often provide for social, as well as economic, needs by promoting a climate of teamwork, community and cohesion. HRM's role is often to play the role of employee advocate. However, recent challenges such as globalisation and privatisation have led to changes as HRM becomes more performance-driven and psychological and social contracts are renegotiated.

EMERGENCE OF THE INFORMAL ECONOMY

In much of Latin America, as in Africa as we saw in Chapter 11, the *informal economy* (one not monitored or regulated by the state) is becoming more important, in particular the growth of self-employment. The informal economy comprises family and micro-enterprises or 'informal self-owned enterprises that may employ family workers and one or more employees on an occasional or continuous basis' (Debrah 2007: 1064). It has been estimated to involve nearly 60% of the non-agricultural population, with serious implications for recruitment and trade union organisation. Estimates by the IMF in 2008 of its size varied from less than 15% of GDP for the Bahamas to over 70% for Paraguay (www.imf.org/external/pubs/ft/wp/2008/wp08102.pdf).

Peru, for example, has distinct geographical and cultural regions (the more traditional indigenous Andean cultures of the highlands and the more prosperous coastal Hispanic-mestizo, or mixed regions), resulting in a 'dual economy'. Informal organisations are more family-based, social networks, with other informal organisations important; informal credit and barter systems may be used (Sully de Luque and Arbaiza 2005).

The main debates on the informal economy have been between 'marginalists' and 'structuralists' (Debrah 2007). In Latin America, the second group include the ILO, the World Bank and the Chilean-based PREALC (see http://lcms.eur.nl/iss/PREALCwp22OCR.pdf).

These view the informal economy as a tool for alleviating poverty; it is an alternative, dynamic economy, a reservoir of indigenous local entrepreneurial dynamism outside the regulatory framework with the potential to generate growth and employment. The first group (mostly 'modernising' Marxists and neo-liberals) see it as peripheral to economic development, often growing due to state inadequacies and the lack of employee protection; its low wages, technology and productivity only offer 'survival' to employees. Progressive state intervention and regulation are needed, especially as many may be 'dependent' workers or linked to the formal sector through outsourcing or commission. These contend that it is a transitory stage on the way to modern capitalism; however, the informal economy has increased, not disappeared, especially during times of recession and transition, and is perhaps a 'new path' to development.

OTHER ISSUES IN LATIN AMERICAN HRM

However, there are other important HR issues in Latin America; Elvira and Davila (2005) add the relationships between HRM practices and the political, economic, social and environmental forces in Latin America, lessons from successful global practices, the role of HRM in business strategy, and the links between HRM and economic development. For Davila and Elvira (2009), HRM in Latin America is focused on *pragmatism* (doing what is possible in environmental complexity and violent unstable environments in which many companies function) and *humanism* (concern with both people and economic perspectives). The unique context companies operate in, such as 'economic and political instability, the role of the enterprise as a social institution, and the value of the individual within the society' (Davila and Elvira 2009: 8), needs to be considered.

Key issues involving these dimensions include the importance of *stakeholder management* – for example in land ownership disputes between MNCs and indigenous people, where sharing of control and ownership rights and privileges with employees are often high on the agenda.

Cultural hybridism is another important concept, which we began to discuss in Chapter 1 in terms of the 'transfer' and diffusion of HRM practices. Hybridisation is a process, not an outcome, leading to contested but negotiable responses in organisations. Rather than wholesale diffusion of home-country practices or wholesale adaptation to local practices, these might include the evolution of hybrid HRM configurations, mixing local indigenous and global or Western/Japanese practices. As we discussed, Gamble (2010) showed this to be the case with Japanese retail MNCs in China, showing neither total global standardisation nor local adaptation but complex, dynamic and pragmatic mixes and blends of practices. As we saw in Chapter 11, this is also true of IHRM in Africa.

Davila and Elvira (2009: 3) argue that many Latin American IEs have developed a *hybrid* HRM model combining 'Human Resource Management practices responsive to global competition and traditional Latin American practices derived from cultural work values', challenging traditional 'universal' HRM models as only offering partial explanations in a region where 'multiple contextual elements challenge the use of a single theoretical view' (Davila and Elvira 2009: 182). One example of a pragmatic approach to HRM – selecting what works – is shown by Case Study 12.1.

 GRUPO SAN NICHOLAS, EL SALVADOR

CASE STUDY 12.1

This company was ranked 'best employer in Central America' in 2005 and 'Best medium-sized employer in Latin America' in 2006. El Salvador, like many Latin American countries, illustrates the importance of close family and small group relationships, acceptance of power distance and low tolerance of uncertainty in much of Latin America, alongside poverty, violence and instability. This has influenced the leadership style of the CEO, who adopted 'contingent' practices that put people at the centre of strategy, such as 'benevolent paternalism', emphasising personal dignity and loyalty. This was shown in visits and assistance after a major

earthquake, and specific employee benefits such as discounts, educational family scholarships, free medical examinations and group reading sessions, alongside such 'universal' practices enhancing communication and intrinsic motivation.

(adapted from Leguizamon et al 2009)

Question

What Latin American cultural and institutional factors have been important in this case, and how does it illustrate some of the specific HRM themes and issues discussed above?

Latin America shows the greatest *wage inequality* of any region, with many unskilled workers earning around the minimum wage; it is a region of *high political instability*, with frequent military coups, dictatorships and suppression of trade unions; and businesses have to deal with a range of inherited *social conflicts* and *complex stakeholder situations* (as we see below). In addition, terrorism, child labour, discrimination on the basis of race, class and gender, informal work and corruption remain major features, impacting negatively on foreign investment.

As a result, the Anglo-Saxon HRM model is difficult to apply in its original North American or European form, even assuming this was appropriate and desirable

(Perez Arrau et al 2012). However, in Chile progress has been made in institutionalising HRM in companies and universities; Chile has higher average incomes, more stability, less corruption and a more positive climate for HRM than many other Latin American countries. However, many workers – as elsewhere in Latin America – have 'precarious' jobs in unstable, often unsafe, and informal work contexts, lacking health insurance and/or pensions, working long hours and with minimal union protection. Gender discrimination and sexual harassment are also issues, as is a sense of fatalism and a lack of interpersonal trust (even lower than in many other Latin American countries). HRM in practice has often resembled a 'hard' model, poorly managed and within operated a hybrid system. Some cooperatives have also added modern HRM practices; see Case Study 12.2.

 HACIENDA GAVILANES, COLOMBIA

CASE STUDY 12.2

Hacienda Gavilanes (HG) began as a sugar cane farm located in an area of high paramilitary activity, but now has five business units also involved in pig- and cattle-raising, cold storage and guava plantation. In the 1990s, low margins forced it to restructure its hiring and incentives policy, encouraging the formation of a labour cooperative, Cofudeco, which not only improved employee working conditions but also profits and security. HG became a client of the cooperative, negotiating rewards for task completion and creating incentives for quality improvements. Workers can attend courses, literacy programmes and train others, and can access credit as the cooperative guarantees personal loans. Workers are also given

considerable discretion in performing tasks, in contrast to the widespread feudal arrangements elsewhere in the region. Confudeco has also begun acquiring work tools and machines. HG is now not only sustainable, but it is the only farm that does not need armed guards.

(based on Andonova et al 2009)

Questions

1   In what ways does this case show evidence of hybridisation, pragmatism and corporate social responsibility?

2   Do you see any downsides to organisations subcontracting to workers' cooperatives?

STAKEHOLDER MANAGEMENT, CORPORATE SOCIAL RESPONSIBILITY AND ETHICS IN LATIN AMERICAN HRM

An issue for companies operating in Latin America is the role of ethics and corporate social responsibility, discussed in more detail in Chapter 7, as IEs often face a different set of ethical beliefs, values and attitudes than those present in their own societies. Herrera and Erdener (2009) argue that Latin American understandings of ethics are rooted in particularist traditions regarding personal relationships that prioritise in-group goals, with HR acting as advocate for the employee; to what degree can Western ethical theories and models apply here?

The importance of *stakeholder management*, where HRM systems are designed to satisfy key stakeholders' demands and the degree of legitimacy, power or urgency of such demands affects organisational objectives, is shown in particular by land ownership disputes between MNCs and indigenous people, often silent or 'silenced' stakeholders. Colombia provides an example of an unstable, violent and conflict-ridden environment, with many legal and illegal armed actors (troops, guerrillas, paramilitaries, drug traffickers). In the 1990s it underwent downsizing and privatisation of state agencies against a background of high levels of inequality and poverty. Andonova et al (2009), as we saw in Case Study 12.2, argue that close employment relations and CSR are of strategic importance in such contexts for gaining a 'license to operate', with social legitimacy obtained through sharing economic interests, control rights and ownership-related privileges. These can enhance 'psychological closeness' with employees. Examples such as Indupalma (an African palm tree business subcontracting with cooperatives) and Hocol (an oil company which created a foundation to develop micro-enterprise and education programmes) show the importance of CSR in keeping third-party involvement in conflicts (such as armed actors) at bay.

This point is reinforced by the example of CMSA, a Colombian natural resource/ mining company now belonging to BHP Billiton (Jiminez and Davila 2009), which supports three non-profit educational, health and quality of life foundations for its employees. Three stakeholder management principles were found to be important: accepting inherent contradictions between economic and social imperatives, including employees' rights of association and worker–employer parity committees; implementing management systems to foster the integration of HRM, organisational culture and the institutional context; and the participation of senior managers, increasingly Colombians rather than expatriates, in HRM policy and practice.

HRM IN MEXICO AND BRAZIL

In this section we have selected Mexico and Brazil for further analysis because they have the largest populations and biggest GDPs in Latin America and are both forecast to be in the top five global largest economies by 2050 (O'Neill 2011). However, they have reacted to the economic rise of China and its increasing involvement in Latin America in different ways; Brazil has become China's most important partner in its commodity boom, while Mexico sees China as a threat to its own low-cost industrial position (http:// globalpublicsquare.blogs.cnn.com/2012/06/24/mexico-on-the-rise/).

Brazil is often classified as one of the 'BRICS' (Brazil, Russia, India, China and South Africa), countries deemed to be at a similar stage of 'emerging' or newly advanced economic development and estimated to overtake G7 economies by 2027 (O'Neill 2011). The continental size, large population (nearly 200 million), linguistic unity and cultural diversity of Brazil, with the largest GDP in Latin America, mark it out, as do its vast reserves of natural resources and a rapidly growing, cash-rich middle class. Its economy has boomed since 2005 on the back of a strong growth in services, accounting for about two-thirds of the economy. Britain and Italy have already (2012) been deposed by Brazil as the sixth/seventh largest economies in the world, behind the US, China, Japan, Germany and France (O'Neill 2011). By 2010 Brazil had overtaken Italy to become the seventh largest economy in the world, with a GDP of $2.1 trillion (£1.3 trillion).

Brazil's stable political situation and recent moves towards full democracy have also provided foreign investors with reassurance that the status quo is unlikely to be overturned by popular revolutions or military dictatorships, which characterised it throughout the twentieth century until civilian control in 1985. It also has respectable corporate governance, a sustainable supply of well-educated people and a convenient geographic location to service both Europe and the USA. The development of the financial centre, São Paulo, with over 20 million people and a huge output of students, is also a key asset.

However, the Brazilian economy has more recently been set for a slowdown, with industrial production contracting as domestic manufacturers struggle with rising interest rates, a strong currency and a weakening global economy, revising its 2012 growth forecasts. Brazil is therefore showing recent signs that its post-2008 economic rebound is slowing down, raising questions about its ability to generate persistently strong growth.

Mexico is often regarded as comparable, but was excluded initially as being already more developed and a member of the OECD. The term 'Next 11' (N-11) includes Mexico and (South) Korea, as well as other growth economies such as Indonesia, Turkey and Nigeria (O'Neill 2011). N-11 countries show high rates of population growth, a growing pool of potential consumers and rising disposable incomes, and have typically begun to export heavy manufactured or refined products. In 2006, Mexico had the highest sum of private final consumption expenditure among the N-11. Mexican growth fell in 2006 due to the Mexican economy's close links to the US economy, which experienced decelerating growth in 2007 owing to a growing credit crisis, particularly in the housing sector. In 2006 Mexico sent 86% of its exports to the USA. Some projections place Mexico as the world's fifth largest economy in 2050, compared with its current position narrowly missing the top 10, behind China, the US, India and Brazil, but ahead of Russia (O'Neill 2011). Shifts in global commodity prices affect all such producers; falling commodity prices and shrinking capital inflows may act as brakes on future growth, but high oil prices benefit Mexico. Domestic political events such as ongoing political instability associated with drug wars and killings may restrict growth prospects. Such violence, while it holds potential to damage tourism revenues, has had little impact thus far in dampening investor enthusiasm, and Mexico's market is showing considerable resilience

HRM IN BRAZIL: HISTORICAL AND INSTITUTIONAL CONTEXT

Brazil began to industrialise in the late nineteenth century, but industry in this period was small, highly concentrated and characterised by the production of simple consumer goods, such as textiles (Hanley 2010). Not until the 1930s did the state attempt to stimulate industrial development directly, and not until the 1950s did the sector move towards heavy industry. This contrasts in 'national business system' terms (Chapter 1) with economies such as Japan and South

Korea, where the state was much more heavily involved. Brazilian industrialisation was held back by a small urban population, a large African slave population unable to own property, a state either neglectful of, or hostile to, industrial development, and inadequate transport networks. In institutionalist terms, this perhaps resembles a *particularistic ideal type* (Whitley 1999), where firms lack trust in formal institutions, there is a weak or predatory state and weak collective intermediaries and norms governing transactions and *opportunistic hierarchies*; the control exercised by the owner is typically direct and personal, as we have seen, and coordination is highly personal and non-routinised. Firms mostly exercised paternalistic authority relationships, perhaps based on the *fazenda* system.

The coffee boom, development of railways and new institutions, such as the use of limited-liability joint-stock corporations for business formation, were also crucial to industrial development; Brazil 'represented one of the few instances in which a primary export product boom generated the successful and lasting transformation of an agricultural economy' (Hanley 2010: 51- 270. This draws our attention to a feature cited in institutionalist, but not in culturalist, accounts; the critical role played by institutions, in this case the financial institution of the limited-liability joint-stock corporation.

However, Brazil lacks, especially when compared with China, a comprehensive national HRD strategy (Chapter 1). Instead of an 'interventionist' policy, it shows more 'voluntarism', with less coordination between various agencies and constituencies than China, or indeed South Korea (Ardichvili et al 2012). Its composite Human Development Index has been growing steadily, standing at 54th place in the World Bank ratings in 2010, ahead of India and similar to China (see http://hdr.undp.org/en/statistics/hdi/). It is trying to transform itself into a knowledge-based economy through the development of free state-sponsored education and a parallel private education alongside PLANFOR, a 1995 National Plan for Vocational Education aimed at enhancing employability and lifelong learning. Levels of investment in education are growing alongside a federal scheme to bolster family income provided children attend school, suggesting a more 'interventionist' policy. It also created five new universities between 2003 and 2006, giving subsidies to universities to expand offerings, especially in technology, though demand outstrips supply. However, poverty, illiteracy and continued discrimination against those of African descent continue to hold Brazil back; it is following a more 'neo-market' model of HRD, with lower levels of government intervention and planning.

HRM PRACTICES IN BRAZIL

Mergers and acquisitions, labour relations, multiple stakeholders, outsourcing, talent management and work–life balance are key issues in Brazilian HRM. Workplace culture in Brazil, as in much of Latin America, is characterised by high power distance, ambiguity, personal relations, conflict avoidance, harmony, paternalism, loyalty, fear of erring and trust centred on the leader. A major challenge, as elsewhere, is how to turn HR into a strategic partner (Tanure 2005). Interestingly, there appears to be a demand for 'soft HRM' in Brazil, related to the rise of Brazilian managerial gurus (of whom Ricardo Semler is most globally famous – Cooke et al 2012) and perhaps related to the importance of 'humanism', which we discussed earlier. The dominant discourse and rhetoric stresses empowerment, commitment, knowledge management and employability (not always present in reality); perhaps the cultural values of power concentration, affectivity, flexibility and personal relationships also favour loyalty to charismatic 'soft HRM' gurus.

CSR is another key theme for HRM in Brazil, as it is for Colombia, where *multiple stakeholder management* is again necessary. Osland et al (2009) show the importance of *multiple stakeholder management* in the case of Aracruz Celulose S.A, an award-winning Brazilian firm involved in producing leached eucalyptus pulp in paper manufacture. Despite policies focusing on environmental and social concerns and sustainability, the company was targeted by critics for creating a monoculture of eucalyptus trees and using harmful chemicals. In addition, the neighbouring indigenous population in the Espirito Santo region was engaged in property disputes involving legal battles, squatters and NGOs.

Land and property are contested arenas in Latin America, with unclear titles, lack of government and legal support, and frequent seizures, expropriation and land grabs by the rich, the poor and governments alike. Brazil has around 4 million landless families, represented by the MST or Landless Workers Movement, raising worker expectations and enjoying a degree of moral legitimacy and government support. Situational stakeholder management is clearly necessary in this environment and culture of high power distance; HR is more likely than most to have training and skills in problem-solving, but is often not regarded as a strategic partner in such situations, as elsewhere.

HRM IN MEXICO: HISTORICAL, INSTITUTIONAL AND CULTURAL CONTEXT

After the Mexican revolution in the early twentieth century, a new constitution with improved labour legislation was passed in 1917, seen by some employers as excessively paternalistic and protective and creating difficulties in dismissing poor employees. These laws are currently under debate (see http://www.usatoday.com/story/news/world/2012/11/14/mexico-labor/1704479/).

One-party rule by the PRI and extensive corruption were also issues, while the 1960s and 1970s showed impressive growth of 7% or more in GDP, but with subsequent slow-downs and crises. Most Mexican businesses are small, but others are transnational (for example Bimbo, a bread company, Cemex, a cement firm, and Corona beer), and foreign MNCs are present, especially from the USA (Arias-Galicia 2005).

Regional differences exist between the more tropical south and the more industrialised desert north, especially Monterrey, more influenced by the USA. In terms of Hofstede (2001), Mexicans, like many Latin Americans, tend to be collectivist, with group loyalty and family ties of great importance, show high power distance, with an emphasis on titles and hierarchies, are high on uncertainty avoidance, with a preference for clear rules, formalism and bureaucracy, and tend to be masculine, with a focus on self-assertion, material goods and money. However, as we saw in Chapter 2, values are changing, especially among younger people.

Many Mexican firms have now become MNCs, often through mergers and acquisitions. Comex, a Mexican paint manufacturer, started in 1954 and established its own paint stores as concessions; it remains a family-owned and managed business with over 3,000 stores in Central and North America and is Mexico's number one paint retailer (number four in the region and number 12 globally). It began to expand through acquisitions, starting with a US-based company and going on to purchase major brands and stores in the US, Canada and Central America (Briscoe et al 2012: 109).

Performance management has become of greater concern to Mexican companies as companies become more performance-oriented. Performance appraisal not only shows the role of Mexican cultural values (for example paternalism, social interaction, avoidance of confrontation) and institutional factors (for example labour laws) but also the way e-HR may be used not to impose a Western or global practice but to develop a hybrid practice building on collectivist values. In general, appraisal has rarely been used as an incentive for individual performance in Mexico, and managers tend to overrate performance (Davila and Elvira 2007). During the economic downturns and downsizing of the 1980s and 1990s, firms that linked rewards to performance evaluation suppressed the level of rewards and used performance appraisal (PA) to downsize, leading employees to develop negative perceptions of PA. Cultural values such as benevolent paternalism have generated employee dependency and suppressed conflict, while the importance given to social relationships has required intense communication and face-to-face interaction. This has led to PA being used for employee expression (for example to express career aspirations) rather than compensation.

Mexican labour laws require firms to distribute a percentage of yearly profits to employees; this is variable, depending on profitability, so profit-sharing has become an institutionalised link between pay and performance. The cost of employee dismissal also encourages inaccurate performance evaluations. Some firms, in the absence of stable state resourcing, have developed social initiatives such as the beverage conglomerate FEMSA, offering medical, home loan, savings, food coupons, sports and cultural facilities to employees, families and relatives. Social networks within and outside organisations are important in many companies.

E-HR may provide opportunities for 360-degree feedback to avoid confrontational interviews, but is held back by limited IT skills and training. Mexican firms have implemented modern PA practices through imported methods and tools. Individual merit-based PA often threatens the Mexican working culture of collectivism and group loyalty.

LEARNING SUMMARY

This chapter began by analysing the institutional context in which HRM operates in Latin America, such as the historically significant role of government intervention in the economy and workplace. Political instability and volatility – often accompanied by violence in the form of military dictatorships and authoritarian rule, revolutions, terrorism and criminal violence often linked to the drug trade – have also characterised much of Latin America. European colonialism has also influenced culture and business life in Latin America, encouraging paternalism and dependency.

The region has witnessed a recent rise of liberalisation, privatisation, 'structural reforms' and market reforms in the 1980s and 1990s, often inspired by the IMF, the World Bank and the 'Washington Consensus', as in Africa, with recent exceptions such as Venezuela and Argentina (which have renationalised many industries).

The chapter also discussed the cultural context; Latin American business life shows cultural values such as collectivism, particularism, paternalism, respect for authority, the importance of social relationships, uncertainty avoidance and high power distance, which all have implications for HRM, while recognising that Latin America is not culturally homogeneous. In particular these values seem linked to authoritarian leadership, paternalism, dependency, loyalty, the importance of social, especially in-group, relationships, and the difficulties in introducing more individualistic merit-based practices in areas such as appraisal and recruitment and selection.

The chapter also identified a number of key HRM issues facing Latin American organisations, such as the importance of family-oriented values, a person-centred view of HRM, the rise of the formal economy, the relationships between HRM and the social context, and the links between HRM and economic development. Latin American HRM models display pragmatism, humanism, hybridism and stakeholder management, especially in relation to corporate social responsibility.

The chapter concluded with a closer examination of HRM in Brazil and Mexico, especially in terms of their aspirations to be major global 'growth economies', whether in the form of the BRICS (Brazil) or Next-11 (Mexico). It discussed the historical and social context of both countries, recent reforms and challenges in both countries to sustainable growth (for example violence in Mexico, discrimination and poor education levels in Brazil, and dependence on commodity prices in both).

CHAPTER 13

HRM in India

Crystal Zhang, Shakiya Nisa and Paul Iles

LEARNING OUTCOMES

By the end of this chapter, you should be able to:

- Analyse the external context driving the Indian HRM system.

- Evaluate the internal context of the Indian HRM system theoretically, empirically and methodologically, including both institutional and cultural factors.

- Critically analyse HR issues in India, especially in the IT and BPO sectors.

- Examine the emergence of Indian HR associations and professionals.

- Critically analyse some of the challenges facing HRM in India, such as engagement, commitment, retention and performance management.

INTRODUCTION

There is enough in the world for everybody's need, but not enough for anybody's greed. (Mohandas Gandhi)

This chapter explores HRM issues in India, the other 'rising star' of Asia alongside China as part of the BRICS (O'Neill 2011). We discuss the role of engagement, retention and commitment at a time of labour market difficulties for many organisations; the role of performance management and intrinsic rewards; and the attempt to develop more 'indigenous' models of management and leadership, such as 'karma capitalism'. We also examine specific issues holding back India's impressive investments in education, training and human capital development, such as low literacy levels, unequal access to education, gender imbalances and structural imbalances in the relationships between the education and skill formation system and the needs of the economy.

From its colonial past, India has sprung forward with a competitive advantage over China: English-speaking citizens who power the large outsourcing industry, with clients all over the Western world. India is a land full of great cultural heritage, with mathematical and artistic 'golden ages' in the fourth century in the north (Guptas) and ninth century in the south (Cholas), so perhaps it is not surprising that HRM can be traced back in its history. The *Bhagavad Gita*, a 500–200 BC Sanskrit text, describes a conversation between Lord Krishna and Prince Arjuna, teaching him the basics of self-management, anger management, stress management, conflict management, transformational leadership, motivation, goal-setting and many other aspects which are now essential parts of any HRM curriculum (Hee 2007). The above quotation from Gandhi illustrates how Western-style capitalism has been imported to India, but drawing on its rich and ancient history, Indian management is adopting a hybrid *karma capitalism* instead (Roka 2006; Engardio and McGregor 2006). In Latin America (Chapter 12), Africa (Chapter 11) and China (Chapter 14), hybrid systems of HRM have also emerged. Rather than the wholesale importation, diffusion and transfer of Western models (as might be suggested by neo-institutionalist theory, Chapter 1) or complete adaptation to local models, as might be suggested by national business systems models (Chapter 1), pragmatic, hybrid models have often emerged.

We look at the factors affecting Indian HRM, its evolution and its role in the economic growth of India, drawing examples primarily from research in the information technology/business processing outsourcing (IT-BPO) and high-tech sectors. As with other regions, we first explore the historical, economic and cultural contexts in which HRM operates in India.

THE EXTERNAL CONTEXT OF INDIAN HRM

India is often known as a country of festivals, a land of vibrant cultures and traditions, the world's largest democracy and the second most populous country (Chary 2009). There is great ethnic, linguistic and religious diversity in India within its 35 states. It is also the world's hub for business process outsourcing (BPO) (Sinha 2012) and a member of the emerging economies forming the BRICS countries, together with Brazil, Russia, China and South Africa (Chatterjee 2007; O'Neill 2011). This is in part thanks to economic reforms initiated in 1991, helping India become an emerging superpower (Budhwar and Varma 2011). India now has the third largest economy by purchasing power parity, having overtaken Japan (Banerji and Shah 2012), alongside persistent poverty and inequality.

This economic growth could be traced back to the 1991 Balance of Payments (BOP) crisis, which forced India to procure a $1.8 billion IMF loan (Cerra and Saxena 2002). The IMF bailout wounded pride and launched market-oriented economic reforms. According to a McKinsey report on India (Ablett et al 2007), the growing middle class, with money to spend, is a new phenomenon in India. In the past, Indians who had money would save their resources rather than spend. Now, with many choices and brands brought to the market in recent years and new employment opportunities, many Indians enjoy spending. India may become the world's fifth largest consumer market by 2025, with 583 million middle-class citizens (Ablett et al 2007).

Like much of Africa and Latin America (Chapters 11 and 12), the Indian economy after the BOP crisis was forced to adopt a structural adjustment programme at the beginning of 1991, initiating the opening-up of an otherwise closed economy (Som 2008). Liberalisation created a hypercompetitive environment with an influx of foreign capital and foreign MNCs, and an end to restrictive licensing systems and controls on mergers, acquisitions and joint ventures; Indian organisations adopted innovative changes in their HRM practices to enhance corporate performance. Alongside downsizing, deskilling, reskilling, multiskilling and the use of high-involvement work systems, innovative recruitment and compensation practices such as selective staffing, recruitment of professionals from the external labour market rather than internally or through word of mouth as before, and incentive- and competence-based rather than seniority pay were introduced. These all had a positive significant relationship with firm performance; recruitment, the role of the HR department in designing, evaluating and implementing change, and compensation practices in particular were all significantly changing within Indian firms.

In line with this newfound status is the need to develop Indian HRM to be fit for Indian business and able to react to changes in the external environment (that is, outside the organisation). Indeed, HRM is about developing, implementing and evaluating appropriate HR strategies, policies and practices to react to the external context, such as the social, cultural, economic and political factors present in the external environment (Farnham 2010).

THE SOCIAL AND ECONOMIC CONTEXT

The latest population census of India puts its population at 1.2 billion, about a sixth of the total world population (Census of India 2011). It is home to more than 2,000 ethnic groups, grouped into four major religious affiliations: Hindu (83%), Muslim (11%), Christian (2%), Sikh (1.9%), other (1.8%) (Census of India 2001). India has experienced several communal conflicts starting from its independence in 1947, but widespread riots and destruction have not destabilised it. Hooker (2008) proposes that this resilience comes from the role of the family and extended family, which emphasises relationships, mutual obligation and trust.

From the Hindu majority has come the *caste system*, which categorises communities into defined social groups or castes. Its four main groups are the Brahmins (priests and teachers), Kshatriya (rulers and warriors), Vaishya (merchants and managers), Shudra (artisans and workers), and untouchables/ Dalits (those outside the caste hierarchy – Chatterjee 2007). This division, along the lines of distinct labour categories, has created social inequalities owing to the correlation between caste hierarchy and economic prosperity and associated status differences in Indian society. However, this system is not as rigid as it used to be and it is possible to obtain higher office through meritocracy, for example the election of an untouchable/Dalit to the Indian presidency in 1997 (Burns 1997). As India's economy grows, the emerging professional middle class is challenging the caste system.

India has a significant traditional industry sector (its textile industries were world-leading until the British arrival and competition from powered textile mills and protectionism – Frank 1998) and strengths in pharmaceuticals, IT, BPO and automobiles. Tata is headquartered in Mumbai, with interests in steel and insurance as well as tea and other sectors; it recently acquired the British brands Jaguar and Land Rover and is one of the top five carmakers (http://www.tata.com/aboutus/sub_index.aspx?sectid=8hOk5Qq3EfQ).

In particular, India has fast-growing high-technology sectors in areas such as biotechnology, IT and software development, as well as leading outsourcing industries with technology transfer to developing countries (Ardichvili et al 2012) and growing investment in Africa (Chapter 11). The BPO sector directly employs 2.54 million workers in India and accounts for 6.4% of gross domestic product, the National Association of Software and Services Companies (NASSCOM) estimates (http://technology.inquirer.net/2126/santanders-indian-call-centers-to-return-to-uk).

US and other foreign firms have been drawn by India's large, educated and cheaper English-speaking workforce to allocate a wide range of jobs, such as answering client calls, train timetable enquiries and IT support. India has now been replaced as the call centre capital of the world by the Philippines as salaries have been increasing and land and infrastructure costs have increased. Ram (2010) claims that to modernise after its crisis, the US financial and healthcare industries need help from India's IT outsourcers; offshore resources can add speed and cost-effectiveness to the process, reverse-engineering existing code to validate the requirements of a legacy system. Without access to a global talent pool, major reforms will never be initiated; the issue is not on-site (for example US, UK) professionals losing out to programmers from India, but all benefiting from collaboration.

The BPO industry, and call centres in particular, has been initiated primarily to reduce costs while simultaneously providing high-quality service. However, these twin objectives of reducing costs per customer transaction and simultaneously encouraging employees to be quality-oriented are fundamentally contradictory, with serious repercussions. Spanish-owned Santander UK is returning its Indian call centres to Britain following a high number of complaints from customers (2011), as is New Call Telecom (http://technology.inquirer.net/2126/santanders-indian-call-centers-to-return-to-uk).

In one Indian call centre, the imbalance between efficiency and customer service was the primary reason for its closure, alongside a lack of resources, poor leadership and weak HR systems (D'Cruz and Noronha 2012). HR practices followed by the management during the process of closure were not 'socially responsible' (Chapter 6); the decision was not communicated in advance to the employees, and they were also deprived of their salaries and incentives for the last few months that they worked with the organisation.

However, given a buoyant economy, most employees were able to find jobs almost immediately in well-established organisations with higher salaries. The job search criteria used by participants emphasised non-economic criteria, of significance with respect to high labour turnover rates witnessed in the IT-enabled business services BPO industry. We explore turnover in this and other sectors in a later section; see Case Study 13.1.

 ATTRITION RATES IN INFOSYS

CASE STUDY 13.1

(adapted from Mishra 2012)

Infosys Technologies, India's second-largest IT services company, has had a lot of discontent among employees, expressing their unhappiness on the company's intranet portal and bulletin boards, over wages. Management is talking with employees over salary freeze rumours. BPO employees had already been assured of a rise, but not IT employees, which may increase attrition rates at the company. Attrition in the BPO industry is over 34%; Infosys's current attrition rate is marginally above its preferred rate. The company has also given promotions to around 10% of its total workforce, with salary rises. Most other Indian software companies were expected to follow the same path; in recent months the company has won many new contracts, with improvement in the demand for technology services by clients.

Questions

1 What does this case tell us about retention and attrition in the IT and BPO industries in India?

2 What specific issues are raised by the case?

THE CULTURAL CONTEXT

India, as a society, has a long history, with many languages, religions, traditions, subcultures and customs. In the light of its complexity, it is important to analyse its culture before introducing its HRM system. Hofstede (2001) identified five main dimensions of national cultural values (Chapter 2), though India is a very diverse country. Of particular note is that India scores 77, relatively highly, on the power distance dimension, and 48, moderately, on the individualism dimension. Its high scores for power distance indicate an appreciation for hierarchy and a top–down structure in society and organisation, with acceptance of unequal relationships between power-holders and those less privileged. Indian leaders tend to show paternalistic (or maternalistic, for example Indira Gandhi, termed 'Mataj' or 'Great Mother of India') styles, employing rewards in exchange for loyalty from their subordinates. Obedience from subordinates is usually expected from both leaders and peers; communication is often unidirectional, from the top, and directive in style. Saini and Budhwar (2004) argue that British rule strengthened the hierarchical, elitist tendencies of Indian organisations by promoting feudal lords and introducing the highly elitist model of bureaucracy embodied in the Indian civil service.

India's individualism score indicates collectivist traits, though not as pronounced as many Latin American or other Asian countries; individuals in India are highly influenced by their family, extended family, neighbours, work peers and other wider social networks. Acceptance by in-group members contains significant meaning for individuals in India, such as promotion opportunities.

India scores relatively highly (56) on the masculinity dimension and moderately (40) on the uncertainty avoidance dimension (similar to the USA and Canada, but lower than France). A high score on the masculinity dimension indicates that India is an achievement- and power-driven society; the display of success and power is proof of one's position in society, and visible signs of success in the workplace are often seen as essential to establish that position. Caring for others and quality of life, on the other hand, is downplayed; for example, the MBA degree is popular in Indian culture because of the status and prestige it brings as a mark of becoming a successful businessperson.

Trompenaars (1993) classifies India as a 'family culture', with a person-oriented, vertical, collectivist and hierarchical culture that tends to be power- and performance-oriented. As might therefore be expected, Chandra (2012) found that gender socialisation played a major role in perceptions of work–life balance. While American multinationals focused on flexible working practices, the focus for Indian companies was on employee welfare programmes. American and European companies ranked higher than the Indian companies in paying more attention to this issue.

India scores medium to low in terms of UAI, or preferences for avoiding uncertainty. Tolerance for unexpected events is quite high, and rules are not as important as in some Western countries or Japan. One can invent a solution to 'bypass the system'; thus adjustment and adaptation is an important aspect of Indian culture. On the long-term orientation dimension, India scores highly (61); Indian society shows a pragmatic, future-oriented perspective rather than a short-term point of view. Indian culture has a relatively high tolerance for different ideas, views, practices, philosophies, religions and beliefs; it is widely accepted in Indian society that there might be 'many truths'.

THE POLITICAL AND LEGAL CONTEXT

India has the world's largest democracy, a multi-party system with two main categories, that is, national party and state-level parties. According to Chhibber and Kollman (2004), India has five national parties and 48 state parties. The vast diversity originating from culture, religion and castes generates competing political influences, which influence government policies and in turn impacts on the business environment.

There is a large state presence in employee relations through a series of laws and institutions supporting collective bargaining and employee rights, with extensive use of complex legal means and interventions, such as the Industrial Disputes Act and Indian Labor Conference, though employers often evade these through unfair labour practices, and unionisation rates have slipped to below 10% of the total working population (Saini and Budhwar 2004). Ratnam and Verma (2011: 349) claim 'India has too many laws offering too little protection to too few who are mainly engaged in the formal/organised sector that accounts for barely 7% of the labour force'. They recommend having fewer, but better enforced, laws, among other changes; we refer to this further in Chapter 20. We discussed the importance of the informal sector, and difficulties in organising it, in Africa (Chapter 11) and Latin America (Chapter 12). Unions have also had little impact on MNCs operating in India.

A comprehensive legal framework for businesses in India on taxation policy has made it attractive for foreign direct investment and corporate governance. India's federal employment laws also have a major impact on the context for HRM. HR plays a significant role in enforcing employment-related laws in India. Affirmative action has been implemented, based on the caste system; for example, federal jobs and admissions to college are strongly influenced by quotas for specific castes. Indeed, the state government can set aside up to 75% of jobs for different castes, in part to get increased political support from the public (Heitzman and Worden 1995).

 REFLECTIVE ACTIVITY 13.1

Given the incredible variety of cultures and ethnic groups existing in India, how is it possible to manage such a diverse workforce?

THE EMERGENCE OF INDIAN HR ASSOCIATIONS AND PROFESSIONALS

The Indian HR association has been in existence for the last 60 years; in the 1920s, welfare concerns were expressed in companies such as Tata that helped shape some of the key developments in the HR profession. For example, Tata Steel appointed the first welfare officer in 1923 (Mahapatro 2010). Important changes in legislation emerged; in the 1940s the Industrial Disputes Act 1947 was passed, and the Factories Act 1948. In the 1950s, the Indian HR function was professionalised, and the 1960s saw the shift in the HR function moving towards facilitating organisational efficiency (Budhwar and Varma 2011). In the 1940s and early 1950s, two professional HR associations were established to acknowledge the importance of HR: the Indian Institute of Personnel Management (IIPM) and the National Institute of Labour Management (NIPM). In 1980, these two associations merged to form the National Institute of Personnel Management (NIPM), the only group in India engaged in the advancement of HR, industrial relations and labour welfare. Organisations in the 1990s were encouraged to be more cost-effective, with the help of technological advancements. HR became more involved in organisational dynamics programmes, and HRD networks started being formed. Furthermore, HR managers began to have a significant impact at board level, and an HR audit was set up. In the 2000s, there has been a significant shift in HRM, with an increase in the BPO sector. Interestingly, Saini and Budhwar (2004) have pointed out that the term 'HRM' has often been avoided in Indian organisations in favour of 'HRD'.

Jain et al (2012) examined innovative practices adopted by Indian and foreign high-tech firms operating in India, and Indian HRM managers' perceptions of 'ideal' practices. There were differences between foreign firms' perceptions of innovations in HRM and their Indian counterparts, such as greater emphasis on parent–subsidiary alignments in foreign MNCs, the balance between parent and subsidiary, and standardisation of HRM practices (Chapter 3). Indian MNCs were more focused on managing performance from within and innovative culture-building practices. Foreign MNCs also tended to be more cost- and performance-conscious than Indian MNCs.

Budhwar and Varma (2011) have outlined the evolution process of the Indian HRM function (see Table 13.1).

Table 13.1: Evolution of the Indian HRM function

Period	Development status	Outlook	Emphasis	Status
1920s–1930s (British rule)	Emerging	Pragmatic	Statutory, welfare, paternalism	Critical
1940s–1960s (independence and self-reliance)	Establishing	Technological/legalistic	Introduction of HRM techniques	Administrative
1970s–1980s (import substitution, licence system)	Improving/bureaucratic	Professional, legalistic, formal, impersonal	Regulatory conformance, compliance, standards	Managerial
1990s (liberalisation)	Promising	Philosophical	Human development, productivity through people	Executive
2000s (emergence as BRIC)	Rationalisation and formalisation	Strategic change agent	Organisational performance/development	Strategic and change partner

(adapted from Budhwar and Varma 2011)

THE INTERNAL CONTEXT OF INDIAN HRM

The external pressures on Indian organisations, such as the 1991 economic reforms that opened the Indian market to international companies, have triggered changes from HR being reactive, prescriptive and administrative personnel management to a more proactive, descriptive and executive HRM. We shall see how the 'open door' policies in 1979 in China similarly opened the country up for foreign investment, while ownership reforms such as privatisation and enterprise reforms such as marketisation similarly led to the emergence of a more strategic HRM (Chapter 14). HR practitioners were now seen at board level, prescribing operational and strategic changes for the organisation (Budhwar and

Sparrow 1997). Chatterjee (2007) outlines the following key HRM practices in Indian organisations:

- **Job description:** formal job descriptions used mostly in the public sector. Generally job descriptions not fully used in the private sector.
- **Recruitment:** mainly conducted from the formal labour market. Recruitment fairs from higher education campuses are organised in management and engineering. Recruitment agencies and the Internet also widely used.
- **Compensation:** job security and life-time employment generally expected in the public sector. Indian staff appreciate healthcare, housing and schooling for children as part of the benefits package.
- **Training and development:** not very popular in Indian organisations, although younger staff value training programmes. HRD is underdeveloped in most organisations.
- **Performance appraisal:** not formally covered in most cases; however, appraisal does take place informally.
- **Promotion and reward:** available in most organisations; seniority systems generally apply in the public sector, and use of merit and performance-based pay is limited.
- **Career planning:** generally limited in scope; however, progression available in the public sector, but limited in the private sector.
- **Gender equity:** proactive court rulings for equality; a number of reservation systems have been put into place by government.
- **Caste reservation system:** the central government has fixed 15% reservation for scheduled castes, 7.5% for 'scheduled tribes' and 27% for 'backward communities' such as Dalits. States vary in their reservation systems.

This raises issues of diversity management in Indian organisations. India has complex and restrictive laws here, though courts have also been active (Cooke 2011). Here, issues of caste discrimination and affirmative action for 'scheduled' castes and minorities have been significant, with protests over quotas in admission to universities, for example.

Haq (2012) has explored the managing diversity mindset in Indian public and private sector organisations, comparing attitudes, policies and practices in MNCs operating in India with those of public sector organisations regulated by the Indian affirmative action policy of 'reservation' for the scheduled castes, the scheduled tribes and other 'backward' classes. Although attempts are being made by the Government to extend reservation into the private sector, the current focus of voluntary managing diversity efforts in MNCs is exclusively on gender, while the reservations regulating public sector diversity are seen primarily in 'compliance', rather than 'business case', mode.

REFLECTIVE ACTIVITY 13.2

1   What do you think of the reservation system in India and its impact on HRM?

2   Is it similar to affirmative action programmes in the USA, or an obsolete system from British-ruled India?

There are many challenges currently facing HR management in India resulting from the changing nature of the business environment; India currently has a competitive advantage in the size of its workforce, with a younger, more English-fluent population than China. However, there are concerns regarding skills, available talent and workforce expectations of younger workers in the coming years. A lack of employment opportunities for young men, combined with a lack of female partners owing to gender imbalances, is a recipe for instability and social security dependence (as is also the case in China, Chapter 14). According to India's last completed census, among children aged six and under, there are only 914 girls counted for every 1,000 boys. Natural sex rates lead to a more even sex ratio at birth, suggesting abortion of female foetuses. While gender imbalances have stabilised in China, they are widening in India, and at their worst since 1947. Despite a ban on ultrasounds for the sole purpose of determining sex, imbalances are worst in richer provinces (http://www.freakonomics.com/2011/04/27/indias-worsening-gender-imbalance/; http://www.aljazeera.com/indepth/features/2011/10/201110415385524923.html).

The population boom in India means that there will be a larger workforce, which will require new jobs to be created to keep living standards from declining (Chatterjee 2007). A larger workforce does not necessarily equate to an equivalently skilled workforce, and a 2010 McKinsey/NASSCOM report (quoted in Budhwar and Varma 2011) predicted a shortfall of 150,000 IT engineers and 350,000 BPO staff over the next five years.

As we have seen, HRD is in general a poorly developed function in Indian enterprises. At the national level, Ardichvili et al (2012) argue that at present Brazil and Russia are ahead of China and India in terms of human capital, but unlike Brazil and Russia (Chapters 12 and 9), the Indian state has initiated impressive long-term national HRD programmes (Chapter 1) involving significant investment and targeted intervention in such areas as primary and secondary education, vocational education and training, and higher education aimed at developing a 'knowledge economy', especially in the science and technology areas.

In terms of the Human Development Index (HDI) (a composite statistic used to rank countries by level of human development, devised and launched by the Pakistani economist ul Haq, followed by the Indian economist Sen in 1990, http://en.wikipedia.org/wiki/Human_Development_Index), India's HDI has been growing annually to 0.612 in 2010, putting it among countries with 'medium levels of development'. It ranks behind the other BRICS in part owing to a low rating on the education component, as higher education has not been able to keep up with demand nor maintain quality. The Government now sees human capital as its main competitive advantage, pushing for educational reforms such as increased investment, increased number of institutions and expansion of vocational education and training (VET), a focus on quality and increased access to education supported by subsidies, with significant progress in terms of school enrolments, drop-out rates and gender equality, supported by subsidised meals and laws prohibiting child labour under 14. A science and technology policy has increased expenditure to 2% of GDP, though India still ranks only 110th among

145 countries on measures of the 'knowledge economy' (World Bank 2012). India and China lead Russia and Brazil in terms of scientific publications and research institution quality. India's national skills development policy aims to greatly increase numbers completing VET, with greater coordination between ministries, agencies and the private sector.

Ardichvili et al (2012) see the main factors holding India back as *stratification and poverty* (regional, caste and gender inequalities in particular); *levels of literacy* (regional disparities and primary education deficiencies in particular) and *structural imbalances* in VET (for example the failure of many graduates to find employment alongside talent shortages in new and emerging sectors). India, like China but unlike Russia and Brazil, has focused on high-technology and coordinated modernisation of all levels of its education system and VET system; Ardichvili et al (2012: 230) claim that 'in the near future China and India will overtake the economies of Russia and Brazil on most of the indices ... provided that they will maintain the momentum, created'.

REFLECTIVE ACTIVITY 13.3

1   In terms of our discussion of national HRD in Chapter 1, where would you place India?

2   Do you see it as following an *interventionist* 'developmental state'

model, or a neo-market *voluntarist* model in terms of VET and human capital development?

HRM IN INDIAN ORGANISATIONS

Foreign firms operating in India generally have a superior and more efficient HRM system than local firms; as a result, local firms in India benchmark against and emulate the HR practices of multinational corporations in an attempt to compete (Budhwar and Varma 2010). This in turn has spurred a rapid evolution of Indian HRM, contributing to India's attempt at global dominance in particular sectors such as IT-BPO. Indeed, Chatterjee (2007) notes that there has been a marked shift towards valuing HR in Indian organisations as they become increasingly strategy-driven. Budhwar and Khatri (2010), comparing British and Indian HR practices, found that, while Indian HRM systems are somewhat unstructured and less formal compared with Western countries, this gap is reducing rapidly. Nonetheless, it is important to acknowledge that Indian HRM is strongly influenced by social and political connection, caste, religion, economic power, labour legislation, trade unions and competition from foreign firms (Budhwar and Varma 2010).

There is also a significant paradigm shift occurring during the move from traditional personnel management to HRM. While personnel management used to deal primarily with recruitment and wages, HRM has more aspects to manage, such as meeting individual aspirations, stress at work and declining job security (Budhwar and Varma 2011). As such, HR departments in Indian organisations have to play a more strategic role and have tried to become strategic partners in the business. However, this has been misunderstood by Indian HR practitioners to some extent; for example, they define their role of strategic partner as being more high-tech and attempt to mechanise the HR process through technological advancement or increase the number of staff in the organisation, rather than trying to understand the needs of the business and enable the employees to operate at optimal levels (Budhwar and Varma 2010). However, there are positive signs that HR is improving organisational performance in India (Budhwar and Varma 2011; Som 2008; Jain et al 2012). Furthermore, the demographics of the Indian workforce are changing, with a multi-generational workforce consisting of younger, more-educated, tech-savvy employees having different aspirations, values and expectations of work, promotion, reward and benefits from older employees (also true in the Middle East, Africa and China – Chapters 10, 11 and 14 respectively). As organisations acknowledge this reality, their HR processes and policies have to adapt to and reflect the requirements for engaging every employee (Srinivasan 2012).

EMPLOYEE ENGAGEMENT AND COMMITMENT

In order to achieve employee engagement, it is often claimed that employees need to feel energised at work, believe in the organisational mission and vision, and work towards achieving this. Srivastava and Bhatnagar (2008) suggest that Indian employees feel engaged when they find personal meaning and motivation in their work, receive positive interpersonal support and function in an efficient work environment. Engagement is important in increasing psychological empowerment and releasing the innovative potential of the employees (Bhatnagar 2012). Psychological empowerment among managers in the pharmaceutical, heavy engineering, IT, electronics and aeronautics engineering industries affected work engagement and led to high innovation and lower turnover intention; it also strongly predicted work engagement and innovation. Work engagement was a strong mediator between psychological empowerment and innovation.

A majority of employees in India have confidence in their organisations, believe their organisations are managed effectively and feel that the products and services are of high quality (Business Standard 2008). As the Indian economy continues to grow, and organisations get larger and more international, employees may, however, feel lost and disconnected from their organisation (Budhwar and Varma 2011). Engagement requires attention to communication, supervisory relationships, empowerment and performance management (Srivastava and Bhatnagar 2008). This involves empowering employees through training and talent management (Chapter 19) (Paul and Anantharaman 2004). A Saxena survey found that 72% of Indian employees thought their current employer was helping to prepare them with the necessary skills for the future (Business Standard 2008). In part, organisations are wary of investing in training because of the risks of skilled and experienced employees being poached (Chatterjee 2007).

It is often assumed that an engaged workforce will eventually lead to employees being more committed to the organisation. Organisational commitment is often seen as a key component of organisational success, and HRM practices in organisations are considered as being effective tools for enhancing organisational commitment (Paul and Anantharaman 2004). In the Indian HRM context, this can be defined in terms of the recognition, empowerment, training and development, relationship and loyalty to the employer. Bhatanagar (2007) advocates a link between organisational commitment and strategic HRM roles within the Indian context. If employees feel that psychological empowerment (positive perceptions and attitudes towards their work) and a learning environment is created, this will lead to increased levels of commitment, and a virtuous circle created. The organisational culture also helps facilitate commitment within the workforce. Training employees to help develop their skills may also lead to better job satisfaction and commitment to the organisation. Paul and Anantharaman (2004) studied software engineers; here recognition, empowerment, competence development, salary and promotional opportunities had positive effects on organisational commitment.

Biswas and Varma (2012) found linkages among Indian executives between organisational commitment, organisational culture and in-role performance and intention to quit; *organisational citizenship behaviour* (OCB), where employees are often required to go beyond their in-role activities and take on extra-role activities to help the business run more smoothly, here mediated the relationship between culture and commitment, and performance and quit intentions. Individuals who demonstrate that they have OCB are often seen favourably, which has a positive impact on the individual's performance, leading to positive feedback. Indian managers should recognise and appreciate pro-social behaviours exhibited by team members, as these could lead to improved in-role performance and reduce chances of employee turnover.

Nambudiri (2012), in four pharmaceutical companies in India, found propensity to trust correlated significantly with affective and normative commitment, but not with continuance commitment. The relationship between propensity to trust and perceived trustworthiness of supervisor, peers and organisation was also significant, suggesting that propensity to trust had an impact on the commitment of employees and that organisations can 'manage' commitment through trust created by organisational practices and systems, including transparent and clearly communicated policies. These organisations are likely to have employees with higher levels of involvement in organisational activities.

EMPLOYEE RETENTION

Lifelong commitment to the organisation used to be the norm in the past, when jobs were scarce. However, market liberalisation of the 1990s and the rise of the BPO and IT sectors in India has led to an increased demand for skilled workers, for which there is a predicted shortfall in the coming years (Budhwar and Varma 2011). This has created a highly competitive labour market, especially in the BPO sector, where employee turnover rates can be very high (Budhwar and Varma 2011). Recruitment can be either of skilled and experienced workers from other competitors or of fresh graduates.

In the 'war for talent' (Chapter 19), employee poaching has become a more prevalent issue in India due to the IT sector's fast growth. In response, IT firms have developed strategies to poach efficient employees from their competitors, such as obtaining detailed information on staff at competitors (Silicon India 2011). They have also developed ways to prevent attrition from happening, such as introducing long notice periods and penalties (Sen 2010, http://news.techeye.net/business/ibm-accenture-capgemini-lock-up-employees-to-stop-attrition).

Major IT companies experiencing high attrition rates are asking employees to serve a three-month notice period, it being easier for employees to jump from one company to the other with a one-month notice period. However, this may discourage prospective candidates; placement consultancies and poachers will need to buy out the notice period and pay the notice period salary. It may even backfire on IT companies themselves as they are the biggest poachers.

Recruitment of graduates is a cheaper option, but involves training and development (Budhwar and Varma 2011). Structured training and development can help reduce attrition rates by increasing employee engagement and organisational commitment. For example, Tata Consultancy Service has a relationship with the Indian Institutes of Technology (IITs) to enhance its technical programmes, and Wipro uses job rotation and training camps to develop a well-rounded employee (Budhwar and Varma 2011). Tymon et al (2010) found that intrinsic rewards play a critical role in professional employee retention, satisfaction and career success, even in challenging labour environments such as the BPO industry, where annual attrition rates might reach 45%; such rewards included corporate social responsibility, pride in the organisation, manager support and performance management.

Bhatnagar (2007) proposes the following guidelines for better employee retention:

- identification of an engaged workforce passionate about continuous learning
- establishment of stronger psychological contracts based on relational rather than transactional needs
- creation of peers and mentors to care and nurture relationships, who take care of the emotional and involvement needs of employees
- treating employees as wealth co-creators and partners in the business, helping them create and fulfil new areas of business.

PERFORMANCE MANAGEMENT

As Sharma et al (2008) point out, the use of performance management systems, once under-emphasised, is increasing in Indian organisations, but performance management (Chapter 18) faces several challenges, such as appraisal transparency, linkages with rewards and a plethora of labour laws. There has been a shift from closed and confidential performance evaluations towards open dialogue and discussion, and towards more qualitative, development-oriented performance management incorporating peer evaluation, which is often web-based, especially in the IT sector. These shifts have been more common in the private sector, which has also seen more emphasis on performance-based and merit pay linked to performance evaluations. In BPO especially, evaluations are strongly data-driven, with little ratee involvement (perhaps reflecting the cultural dimension of high power distance). Performance management in local firms and the public sector in particular is affected by the hierarchical, power-oriented, top–down culture, with paternalistic managers leading employees to look for detailed guidance and complying with norms and regulations and risks of subjective, biased judgements.

LEADERSHIP

As India continues its economic growth and gains prominence in the global marketplace, it is important to better understand the characteristics of its business leaders. Palrecha et al (2011) found Indian leadership different from American-style leadership (Chapter 5); Indian socio-cultural traditions influenced leadership styles, with leaders more facilitators of social change than inventors of new organisational designs. Gutierrez et al (2012) compared Chinese, Indian and Western leadership; Indian CEOs showed greater consideration for the welfare of their nation in business decisions and were more ready to change or adapt new technologies, methods and business models to help India's poorer citizens. The Indian leaders displayed emotional maturity and inner strength, drawing on inner resources in difficult times, such as inconsistency in Indian business laws and the poor network infrastructure (an area where China is considerably ahead).

What these studies report is a particular style of Indian leadership and management, coined *karma capitalism* (Roka 2006; Engardio and McGregor 2006) – in essence, corporate social responsibility (Chapter 6) with Eastern philosophies, as captured in 'green is good' or 'doing well by doing good' In Chapter 5, we explored attempts by Turnbull (2012) to develop 'worldly leaders' rather than 'global leaders' by drawing on ancient Asian texts. As with concepts like *ubuntu* in Africa (Chapter 11) and Confucianism in China (Chapter 14), some Indian management scholars have proposed that ancient Vedic scriptures like the *Bhagavad Gita* are useful for a better understanding of leadership and managerial techniques (Hee 2007; Natesan et al 2009). Rather than studying the Chinese sage Sun-Tzu's *The Art of War*, the *Bhagavad Gita* is now on the reading list of top business schools (Engardio and McGregor 2006). Of course, a question here, as with similar initiatives elsewhere, is how much of this remains at the level of rhetoric, rather than reality; as we saw in the call-centre example, not all Indian leaders show CSR in practice (D'Cruz and Noronha 2012).

Another source of Indian leadership skills comes from Mohandas Gandhi, who led India to independence and indeed inspired other movements elsewhere, such as the US Civil Rights movement, the ANC in South Africa and CND in Europe. The important tenets espoused by Gandhi are as follows:

1   *satyagraha* (soul force): the sacrifice of self, and leading by example

2   *sarvodaya* (upliftment of all): serving the interests of all, including care of the earth, animals, forests, rivers and land

3   *swaraj* (self-government): self-transformation, self-discipline and self-restraint, and social transformation through small-scale, decentralised and participatory structures

4   *swadesi* (local economy): local production by all.

However, Budhwar and Varma (2011) indicate that there is a lack of leadership to sustain India's continued growth, with an increasing influx of expatriates to take up leadership roles in Indian companies and MNCs. The biggest challenge for Indian HR practitioners, as elsewhere, is thus to develop home-grown leaders with a global perspective and mindset.

 REFLECTIVE ACTIVITY 13.4

1   Do you think karma capitalism is sustainable?

2   Given the importance of India as a rising economy, can karma capitalism be exported to the West, or to other developing and emerging economies?

LEARNING SUMMARY

This chapter has briefly explored the evolution of HRM in India from the first welfare officer to its current, more strategic model. The 1991 Balance of Payments crisis and subsequent liberalisation are considered by many as the trigger for economic reforms leading to India's fast growth and membership of the BRICS, enabling India to overtake Japan's economy and establish itself in the knowledge economy through the IT sector. India has become the world's hub for business process outsourcing; the IT-BPO sector has played a significant role in transforming India's image from a slow-moving bureaucratic economy to a land of innovative entrepreneurs.

To continue this growth and to manage its 1.2 billion population, Indian HRM is attempting to adapt and draw on its great cultural history and diversity. In this project, we discussed the role of engagement, retention and commitment at a time of labour market difficulties for many organisations; the role of performance management and intrinsic rewards; the attempt to develop more 'indigenous' models of management and leadership such as 'karma capitalism'; and the specific problems holding back India's impressive investments in education, training and human capital development, such as low literacy levels, unequal access to education, gender imbalances and structural imbalances in the relationships between the education and skill formation system and the needs of the economy.

CHAPTER 14

HRM in China

Paul Iles and Xiaoxian Zhu

LEARNING OUTCOMES

By the end of this chapter, you should be able to:

- Identify and analyse approaches to HRM and its increasing importance in China.

- Discuss the moves in China towards a strategic HRM model and the development of hybrid models.

- Critically analyse the skills and talent challenges facing companies in China and the role of HRM in addressing these challenges.

- Critically analyse the characteristics of Chinese culture and the implications for HRM.

INTRODUCTION

This chapter explores HRM issues in this increasingly important country, noting the series of economic, ownership and enterprise reforms since the 'Open Door' policy began in 1979, which have accompanied moves away from a command and control, centralised 'iron rice bowl' model of HRM towards a more 'strategic' HRM model. It discusses the implications of Chinese cultural values for HRM and the skills and talent management challenges facing companies in China as they seek to upgrade their skills and technologies, and the role of HRM in addressing these.

CHANGING PATTERNS OF HRM IN CHINA AND THE HISTORICAL AND INSTITUTIONAL CONTEXT OF HRM

The People's Republic of China (PRC) has enjoyed nearly three decades of economic growth at an average of around 10% per annum over the years since Deng Xiao Ping launched the 'Open Door' and 'Four Modernisations' policies in 1978–9, slowing only recently as the global recession deepens (Warner 2008). By 2011, China had already built an economy the same size as the United States at purchasing power parity. China is estimated to match the USA by 2035 and double it by 2050, and has become the leading member of the unofficial BRICS group of rapidly emerging economies (O'Neill 2011). The RMB (Yuan) may match or replace the dollar as a reserve currency in the near future. Ardichvili et al (2012), however, point out that despite impressive growth, China's GDP by capita only puts it at 128th among 227 nations; its Human Development Index, growing rapidly to 0.772 in 2007, is still below Russia and Brazil but ahead of India. It also ranks 81 on the index of knowledge economy out of 145 countries.

Cooke (2012) and a special issue of the *International Journal of Human Resource Management* in 2012 (Warner 2012) discuss some key trends in HRM in China, primarily associated with the *downsizing and privatisation* of state-owned enterprises (SOEs), the introduction of *performance management systems* into the public sector, the growing strength of the *private sector* in the economy, the continuing *growth of FDI*, the participation of *migrant workers* into the urban economy and continuing *unemployment*. These changes have led to both a series of *labour regulations* and the growing *informalisation* of employment (Chapter 3), as also seen in Africa and Latin America (Chapters 11 and 12), and widespread questioning of *trade unions' ability* to protect Chinese workers (Chapter 20).

There are different *institutional actors* in dynamic interaction shaping the evolution of the Chinese HR and labour market system (Chapter 1); these include the state (both central and local), trade unions, employers and employer associations, employment agencies, non-profit organisations, and vocational and higher education institutions. There has been a shift from direct state 'control' to 'guidance' as SOEs become more autonomous and private sector actors more powerful; the state has been 'mobilising other institutional actors in more subtle and strategic ways to promote, with a level of success, certain HRM practices' (Cooke 2012: 8).

Before the 'Open Door' policy of 1979, China's model of HRM was associated with heavy state- owned industry in a command economy, with a centrally planned system of public ownership and limited autonomy granted to enterprises. The 'iron rice bowl' model of lifetime employment and lack of enterprise control over hiring and firing predominated. Government – dominated by the Chinese Communist Party (CCP) – was heavily involved in enterprise management, the provision of lifetime employment and welfare systems, and the central fixation of wages and salaries. In comparing Japan with China, Gamble (2010: 707) points out: until recently, one could draw parallels between employment regimes in these two countries; both shared an ideal of lifetime employment with extensive company welfare benefits, privileges available to those in large firms. Similarly, in both … hierarchies were compressed, with salaries linked partly to employees' needs rather than solely to their contribution to the firm. However, HRM practices in China's transitional have been accelerating away from this model. Labour has rapidly marketised with wide divergences in income at both the firm and the social level … where once a comparable Maoist model might be discerned, during the reform era it has become increasingly difficult to delineate a 'Chinese model'.

Since 1982 there have, however, been accelerating moves to a market-oriented system, involving *ownership reform* and a *modern enterprise* system. In 1986, employment contracts were introduced to increase labour flexibility, though over-staffing was still evident in many SOEs, as well as low labour turnover. 'Informal' recruiting and giving priority to children and relatives was still common, and managerial recruitment often solely internal. Interviews predominated over other methods of assessment, and political loyalty, harmonious relationships and good moral practice often figured as selection criteria. Employee dismissal, though made easier by the post-economic reform labour laws, remained rare, perhaps because of concerns over its negative impacts on welfare provision. Pay differences between professions and levels had historically been minimised, with pay determined primarily by seniority, nepotism and political orientation. Welfare benefits such as accommodation, meals, childcare and medical assistance have often been provided by the enterprise, as well as contributions to public pension and insurance funds (Lewis 2003).

There has also been a shift away from heavy industry towards services, light manufacturing and IT. Such HR activities as recruitment, selection and staffing have become significant with the growth of an external labour market and moves away from state-approved recruitment, allocation, transfer and dismissal (Zhu and Dowling 2001). Dramatic changes have taken place in China's enterprise structure and management, including the decentralisation of planning and decision-making processes, the introduction of responsibility systems enhancing individual accountability for performance, and the encouragement of international joint ventures (IJVs) and private independently owned enterprises (IOEs) and foreign-owned/invested enterprises (FIEs). The Chinese labour management system is currently in a state of transition (Warner 2002a, 2002b, 2004, 2008; Warner and Goodall 2009). Warner (2008: 774) argues:

> the 'narrative' of Chinese human resource management … may thus be seen as taking a recognisable path, from 'plan to market', from 'egalitarian to inegalitarian' and from 'status to contract', unintended consequences notwithstanding.

Zhu et al (2012: 3964) 'divide HRM in contemporary China into three categories: Paternalistic; Transactional; and Differentiated' (a mix of paternalistic and transactional HRM policies and practices). They argue that 'as China's economy has evolved from paternalistic socialism to market socialism in recent decades, Chinese HRM has responded, moving along the continuum from paternalistic to transactional HRM'; both paternalistic socialism and marketisation have left their mark on HRM, but paternalistic HRM, common in state-owned enterprises in the pre-reform era, has evolved towards either transactional or differentiated HRM, with a decline in the welfare benefits and employment security of workers, the former socialist 'masters of society'. Frear et al (2012) found that CEO exposure to HR ideology in China was related to whether the firm adopted Western-style HR practices; CEO embeddedness in the Chinese institutional environment was negatively related to Western-style HR adoption.

Given these changes in HRM in China, can we speak of a 'new paradigm' or 'paradigm shift' in HRM in China? Warner (2012: 3943) explores 'whether there is a dominant existing paradigm in play … we conclude that it would be premature as yet to say whether there is a "new paradigm" emerging in the field'. Warner (2004), Goodall and Warner (1997) and Rowley et al (2004) argue that HRM in China has been moving to *hybrid* models. In some companies, the old model of HRM may still predominate (many SOEs). In others, some aspects of the old model remain (many multinational companies (MNCs)). In others, pure Western HRM models may be found (rare, but growing; found in some IJVs or FIEs). This is illustrated in Figure 14.1.

This model still seems valid; what has changed is the proportion of organisations in each cell. There are widespread variations in the pace of change between localities and ownership forms; SOEs have been slower to implement change owing to historical legacies, organisational inertia and continued interference by central, regional and local government (Hassard et al 2002, 2004); many are still located in quadrants A or B in Figure 14.1.

The numbers of organisations in cells C and B have, however, greatly increased, while those in cell A have greatly declined. One example of a 'pure imported' approach is given by Gamble's (2000, 2003) analysis of the British store B&Q in Shenzen and Shanghai; here the HRM model was almost identical to the one used in the UK, and indeed was generally welcomed by Chinese employees as superior to the 'Chinese' models emphasised in the SOE retail stores they had worked in. Such 'British' features as rapid promotion, including of younger workers, performance-related pay, open communication and use of first names were all well received by employees; Chinese managers were less keen, however, in some cases preferring the old-style model of wearing a suit, sitting in the office and communicating in a top–down way.

Figure 14.1: Hybrid models of HRM in China

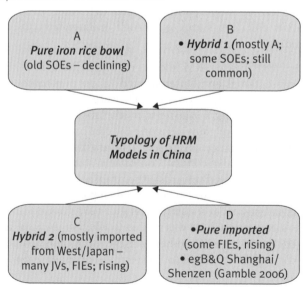

Source: Goodall and Warner 1997

We can see some 'hybrid' models of HRM in Case Study 14.1 on Japanese retail firms in China.

 JAPANESE RETAIL FIRMS IN CHINA

CASE STUDY 14.1

Gamble (2010) studied three Japanese retail MNCs in both Japan and China. In Japan, they engaged in many practices considered typical of 'Japanese' HRM, such as careful and lengthy recruitment with testing and interviews, the use of the internal labour market for managers, extensive on-the-job training, high levels of customer service (for example greeting and farewell ceremonies for customers, with bows and greetings), patriarchal management (older male supervisors of female staff), job security for regular employees, flat salary differentials and seniority-based pay increases (alongside a trend to increase performance-based pay, though with some differences in emphasis).

In China, however, many modifications were made; firms made greater use of expatriates than European or US ones, with extensive communication back to HQ in Japan (Chapter 3). Senior positions were all held by Japanese staff. Customer service was still emphasised, seen as an even stronger differentiation from local firms. At first, both Chinese customers and employees found the greetings 'strange' and alien, even 'too polite', stimulating some historical anti-Japanese feelings, and Chinese employees did not fully internalise it. In China, firms made many more rules and codified knowledge mostly implicit in Japan, not trusting Chinese workers to 'naturally' show good service, backed up with warnings and fines (though Chinese workers resisted bag searches, unlike Japanese ones). As in Japan, the firms tried to offer job security to regular employees, but staff showed 'less loyalty', often leaving for higher salaries and promotion. Firms, unlike Chinese ones, also relied on internal labour markets for promotion, but at a faster pace than in Japan, as 'promoting by cohort', the Japanese approach, invited other companies to poach staff.

Far fewer 'part-time' staff were used, perhaps because of lower Chinese wages, and 'patriarchal' management was less common. Many managers and supervisors in China were female, often judged as better workers. Unlike in Japan, where the norm is for women to leave full-time work on marriage or motherhood, women's full-time employment is promoted by nursery provision and grandparent proximity. Companies often found it hard to replicate parent-country graduate recruitment schemes, as staff left quickly, in some cases to Walmart. Pay systems and sanctions were more stressed in China, especially performance-related pay, partly due to lack of trade union opposition in China. Seniority pay was less common in China.

Questions

1   Where would you place these firms, according to Figure 14.1?

2   What 'orientation' do they show, according to our discussion of international orientations in Chapter 3?

3   To what extent do these cases show examples of 'hybrid' HRM practices?

4   To what extent are these transferred 'Japanese' practices? To what extent are they local 'Chinese' ones?

5   Do you expect any 'reverse diffusion' of practices back to Japan?

Table 14.1 shows some of these changes in HRM in China, adapted from Zhu and Dowling (2001).

Table 14.1: Changing paradigms of HRM in China

HRM practice	HRM in traditional SOE	HRM emerging model
Recruitment, selection and firing	Central government quota Education, examination, connections, interviews Firing difficult	More autonomy; internal and external labour market Education, examination, connections, testing, interviews Easier to fire
Appraisal, promotion	Slow promotion; seniority Political criteria, connections, character	Faster promotion Bureaucratic Technical criteria, connections
Training	Initial training Moral and political education	More extensive career training More job- and business-related training
Pay and benefits	Fixed pay rates Low differentials Fringe benefits	Performance-related pay Higher differentials Fewer fringe benefits
Communication	Secretive communication Few briefings Hierarchical relations	Extensive communication and briefings
Welfare provision	Extensive: housing, social, meals, travel	Declining
HR planning	Command and control from Beijing ministry	Market economy: more local

Since 2003 *state policy* has moved from solely efficiency-driven development to the pursuit of social justice, harmony and environmental protection (Cooke 2012), influencing less through administrative regulation and more through legislation, standard-setting, best-practice sharing and the promotion of best-practice HRM and CSR (Chapter 6). China is seeking to establish 'harmonious relations' at the enterprise level and raise skill levels in management, professional and craft skills through various regulations and initiatives, implemented via other institutional actors via mechanisms discussed in Chapter 1 with respect to institutional theory, that is, coercive, mimetic and normative isomorphism (we explore how this has been done in a later discussion of talent management in China, and in Chapter 17 on talent management). Examples include the 2005 requirement for firms to set up superannuation/pension schemes to combat worsening social security provision, promulgated as CSR and to attract talent.

We discuss trade unions in China in more detail in Chapter 20 on employee relations. *Employers' associations* are also less well established than elsewhere – again, only the China Enterprise Confederation (CEC) is recognised, also often acting on behalf of the state to implement policies. However, employers' lobbying power is rising outside the CEC through pressure groups, such as over the 2007 Labour Contract Law (Shen 2007).

Employment agencies are fairly new institutional actors – mostly funded by local government in response to large-scale downsizing of SOEs, migration of labour into cities and the growing numbers of unemployed students – and playing an increasingly important labour market role. *HR consultancy firms and outsourcing providers* are another increasingly influential emerging set of actors, often foreign-owned following the 2002 Regulation on Talent Market Management (Cooke 2012). These have, alongside MNCs, raised HR standards and HR competence levels, introducing many 'Western' practices such as assessment centres, 360-degree appraisal, performance management, coaching and mentoring, as well as legal services following the 2007 Labour Contract Law and 2008 Labour Disputes Mediation and Arbitration Law. To what extent, through 'mimetic isomorphism' (Chapter 1), will this result in the widespread adoption of strategic HRM in China?

THE EMERGENCE OF STRATEGIC HRM IN CHINA?

As we discussed in Chapter 3, 'globalisation' has already impacted on the labour market and employment experience in China and the Asia Pacific region as a whole. Warner et al (2002: 380) point out that 'while opportunities have been made more abundant for workers with highly prized skills, for the vast majority of employees the conditions of work have tilted towards increasing job insecurity, greater intensity and benefit erosion'; for Warner (2002b: 386), 'China's vast population and vast labour force … puts human resources high on the agenda as far as WTO entry is concerned.' Accession to the World Trade Organization (WTO) occurred in 2001 (Iles and Yolles 2006; Guo et al 2011).

We can therefore see that changes in HRM in Chinese enterprises cannot be understood without understanding the global context in which their enterprises have operated. Under the impact of such drivers as globalisation, marketisation, WTO entry and informatisation (Chapter 3), Chinese enterprises have undergone significant *economic* reforms (such as the 'Open Door' policy, which has led to significant foreign investment), *ownership* reforms (for example growth of private, independently owned companies, joint ventures, town and village enterprises (TVEs) and foreign-invested enterprises (FIEs)) and *enterprise* reforms (for example marketisation). These have led to pressures to introduce operational and managerial reforms, including HR reforms, as Figure 14.2 shows.

Figure 14.2: Changes in Chinese HRM

(adapted from Zhu and Dowling 2001, Figure 1.2)

Zhu and Nyland (2004) argue that many employers, especially in the private sector, have been evading their CSR and social protection responsibilities as the WTO 'seeks to shape the rules of the game' to facilitate globalisation (Warner 2002b: 368). This has been interpreted as subjecting the economy and society to market disciplines; the state is being compelled to adopt regulations to restrain employer avoidance of social protection responsibilities, such as age discrimination by the private sector (with a preference for employing younger, less experienced and perhaps more pliable labour, often young migrant women from the countryside).

THE CULTURAL CONTEXT

In an earlier discussion (Chapter 3) of the impacts of globalisation and ICT on enterprises in China and their effects on HRM in China, we argued that HRM in China needs to be sensitive to the cultural context (for example the continuing importance of *guanxi*, or connections, to career development). This was partly demonstrated in Case Study 14.1 (for example different attitudes to customer service, patriarchal management, lifetime employment). Chow (2004), in a comparison of HR practices in the PRC, Taiwan and Hong Kong, found the HR function in the PRC to be underdeveloped, reactive and operationally oriented; individualistic models may not be appropriate, but need to take the Chinese context into account. Older senior managers revealed that career development in

China showed the continuing importance of such cultural features as *guanxi* (connections), as well as a concern with status and 'face'. Older managers made frequent references to the importance of age, seniority, harmony, *guanxi* and 'face' to career progression. Face, meaning 'honour' or 'personal prestige', is considered important in Chinese society (Weir and Hutchings 2005), as in *'liu mianzi'*, to 'grant or lose face'. This may make direct criticism of people in appraisals difficult (http://en.wikipedia.org/wiki/Face_%28sociological_concept%29).

Hutchings and Weir (2006a, 2006b) and Hutchings and Michailova (2004) also emphasise the importance of *guanxi* to Chinese business culture. Often senior managers had been allocated to SOEs under the pre-reform 'Maoist' model, and had started their managerial careers late owing to the Cultural Revolution, having to give up time in political work and in being sent to the countryside to live with, learn from and work with the peasants. Such managers acknowledged their lack of management skills and training, and eagerly sought further education and training, as well as recognising the importance of *guanxi* to their career development (for example Communist Party membership giving privileged opportunities to set up new SOEs). In Taiwan, Wang et al (2012) found that *guanxi*, norms and trust positively influenced knowledge-sharing; *guanxi* and norms positively influence trust; trust mediates *guanxi* and knowledge-sharing; and trust partially mediates norms and knowledge-sharing, showing the continuing importance of *guanxi* (we noticed similarities to 'wasta' in Chapter 10 on the Middle East and North Africa).

However, this is a study of older, senior managers; we have already discussed cultural change in Chapter 2, pointing out the growth of more 'individualist' values in China among young people, who often seem less tolerant also of high power distance and such now-officially promoted 'Confucian' doctrines as 'harmony', which often served to encourage obedience and stifle dissent, similar to 'ubuntu' in Africa (Chapter 11). Confucius, a fifth-century BC Chinese sage, or 'kongzi' ('Master Kong') had been seen as the exemplar of feudal bureaucratic backwardness in the Maoist era, but is now held up as an ideal philosopher for promoting the 'harmonious society' idealised by the current government; see the Chinese cultural institutes known as 'Confucius Institutes' – http:// en.wikipedia.org/wiki/Confucius_Institute).

We noted in Chapter 2 the emphasis in studies of Chinese culture on collectivism, power distance, moderate masculinity, uncertainty avoidance and especially long-term orientation in studies drawn from Hofstede (2001), as well as some critiques of this approach. Fan (2002) developed a list of 71 values, running across eight categories: national traits, interpersonal relations, family/social orientation, work attitude, business philosophy, personal traits, time orientation and relationship with nature. Of particular interest are his six generic categories: respect; honour; synergy; allegiances; learning; and sensibility (Iles and Yolles 2006). Cooke (2012: 18) argues that 'societal culture remains a highly valid factor in explaining the enduring differences in Chinese HRM practices. ... While Chinese firms are beginning to embrace HRM practices originated in the West, these practices need to be adapted in order to be accepted by Chinese employees.'

REFLECTIVE ACTIVITY 14.1

What do you think the consequences of these Chinese cultural values might be on HR policies and practice?

NEW ISSUES FOR HRM IN CHINA: SKILLS AND TALENT CHALLENGES

HRM in China faces two new challenges: skills upgrading and talent management, both necessary to ensure its continued growth and development as a high-value, high-skilled and high-tech economy. We look at skills first, then talent.

SKILLS AND HUMAN CAPITAL CHALLENGES FOR CHINESE HRM

China's growth has been largely driven by fixed capital investment, infrastructure projects, capital accumulation and a large labour supply working for wage rates a fraction of those in the West. A pool of talented labour in engineering has allowed China to transform otherwise capital-intensive productions into labour-intensive processes. The huge source of cheap labour, the clustering of FDI and business in export and development zones and the towns and villages enterprises (TVE) networks has allowed the simplification of production processes into small steps, which lowers technical and capital barriers to entry (Shutt et al 2012).

With the immense rate of savings, this has culminated in an unbalanced economy substantially dependent on capital accumulation and exports, and which still lags behind in technology. Outgoing president Hu Jintao has argued that China suffers a serious lack of balance, coordination and sustainability of its development; we must accelerate strategic adjustment of the economic structure, scientific and technological progress and innovation and the building of a resource- consuming and environmentally friendly society. (http://english.gov.cn/, November 2011)

China's latest five-year plan (2011–15) aims to decrease the reliance on exports, increase domestic consumption and increase technological innovations. For this, higher skills are needed.

China is trying to use the current international financial crisis to accelerate rebalancing and restructuring the economy, reduce its export dependence, and rely more on domestic consumption, combining accelerated spending on existing projects with large new programmes. These include affordable housing, railways and other transport infrastructure investment, earthquake relief, healthcare, education, rural infrastructure and environmental projects.

Alongside the rebalancing of the economy, China is restructuring its business and management, including HRM. China's low-wage model has started to change into one that depends on higher pay and greater productivity. Already low technological content and low-end manufacturing are moving to other countries in the Asia region, such as Vietnam, Pakistan and Indonesia. China gradually has to compete in areas where the need is for higher value-added products, state-of-the-art facilities and highly skilled labour. The state intends to transform the economy from low-technology, low-end manufacturing to high-value-added, high-end technology production and to service development and cultural industries; this is to be achieved by combining investment in national skills and technology development and innovation. Strong collaboration between academic institutions and the private sector, and linking to international pools of knowledge, is a long-held policy, reinforced by the latest five-year plan (2011–15). Case Study 14.2 shows some issues in this area.

 ZH GROUP CO. LTD, XIAOSHAN HANGZHOU

CASE STUDY 14.2

The ZH Group, established in 1994, ranked in 2009 among the top 500 companies in China, with nearly 4,700 workers at the headquarters in Xiao Shan; there are around 5,700 workers in the whole group. Its main products are basic fabric materials; its customers are exporting factories and, with the international economic crisis, exports have decreased, reducing group sales.

ZH wants to develop as a technology- and capital-intensive company, away from being a low-skilled, labour-intensive one. The group is paying more attention to developing higher skills, needing chemical engineering and mechanical engineering skills, as well as finance and investment skills. It is not, however, satisfied with current educational provision, as many students from university are not suitable; education at university only helps acquire knowledge, not the ability to work, acquired through training in work positions. Graduates need instruction to become fully fledged workers; at university they do not learn how to do things that are only learned in the real world, such as the meaning of work and work goals. New workers have pre-work briefings to change their status from student to worker. For high-level positions, employees need to be trained for up to one year. The Ningbo factory in particular requires higher-level skills, often obtained from the wider petrochemical industry.

Most workers come from high school; in Ningbo, administrators are graduates and workers in the research department need to be postgraduates. Recruitment is carried out using school visits, the Internet and newspaper advertisements; for high-level workers, recruitment is carried out via Internet searches, as well poaching from competitors. ZH aims to retain talented workers through higher salaries and encourage younger workers to buy homes with low-interest loans, as it is hard to buy a home in China. The company tries to provide career development from within the company using internal labour markets, but 40% have now been recruited from outside the company.

(Source: Shutt et al 2012)

Questions

1   In what ways is this company like the retail companies in Case Study 14.1 in terms of recruitment, career development and the use of internal and external labour markets?

2   How satisfied is ZH with the skills supplied by graduates and their employability?

3   How would you enhance company satisfaction?

In some ways, this company is typical of many Chinese companies in thinking that its skill needs are not being met by university preparation of students for the labour market (Shutt et al 2012). This may be the case in other regions as well, of course.

Recognising its deficiencies in skill levels, China has put ambitious plans in place for human capital development, aimed at establishing a comprehensive VET system with defined occupational standards, certification and company incentives to train employees and collaborate with VET institutions (Ardichvili et al 2012). Here it aims to collaborate with German institutions and borrow their 'dual system' (Chapter 1). Its education system emphasises the development of science and technology, with quality assessment systems and recognition of the need to develop generalists with the capacity for innovation and independent thought. Regional disparities between the developed east coast and other areas, however, remain an issue, as does matching employee competences to business requirements (as we saw in Case Study 14.2).

For Ardichvili et al (2012), three structural problems in improving human capital development are *the quality of education* (more oriented to rote learning and examination-passing than skills, as we saw in Case Study 14.2, and with numerous private colleges of lower quality); *social stratification*, with growing inequality between high- and low-income groups and rural and urban citizens; and *the status of the VET system*, seen as a low-prestige 'last resort' for children who fail in academic education.

Other challenges not mentioned by Ardichvili et al (2012) are problems of pollution and environmental degradation (for example the dust storms that increasingly plague Beijing and other cities) and issues of failings in CSR, which we discussed with particular reference to China in Chapter 6, such as the role of Taylorist low-wage labour in supplying MNCs such as Apple and abuses of workers' rights. Bribery and corruption also remain issues; China ranks 75th out of 183 countries on Transparency International's Corruption Perceptions Index, similar to Brazil, Tunisia and Romania (http://cpi.transparency.org/cpi2011/results/).

However, Ardichvili et al (2012) expect China to overtake Russia and Brazil in terms of human capital development; it is already leading in such areas as numbers of patents granted, high-tech exports and share of scientific publications and 'in terms of the actual use of the potential and opportunities for future HC growth the BRICS can be arranged in this order: China, India, Brazil and Russia' (Ardichvili et al 2012: 229). This prediction is partly supported by the latest findings from the OECD's Program for International Student Assessment (PISA) study of 15-year-olds' academic achievement, where Shanghai students came top in reading, science and maths, overtaking the former leaders Finland and South Korea, with unpublished indications of similarly strong performance in other regions, including by children of migrant workers (see http://www.bbc.co.uk/news/business-17585201; http://www.oecd.org/unitedstates/presentationofthepisa2010results.htm).

TALENT MANAGEMENT CHALLENGES FOR HRM IN CHINA

There are, however, worries that a shortage of professional and managerial talent is holding back China's economic growth. As Cooke (2008a) has noted, there has also been little empirical research regarding talent and talent management (TM) (*rencai* and *rencai guanli*) in China. Does TM in China possess some features which are distinct from HRM? We discuss global TM in more detail in Chapter 18.

In addition to issues of recruitment, as shown in Case Study 14.2, an increasing talent loss/brain-drain crisis has become a very common and serious problem for many companies, as skilled staff leave for pay increases within a booming labour market; the attraction and retention of talented individuals has become a key strategic issue for many organisations. The Government has acknowledged the existence of a global market for talent, and that China must compete within that market, with an emphasis upon the development of human talent and technical skills, rather than the attraction of foreign capital and labour. To develop the policy of 'strengthening the country through human talent' (Government of People's Republic of China 2006), talent management has become increasingly seen as an important issue by business and political leaders. Going global has become a key objective for many large Chinese companies, but there are concerns that the shortage of managerial talent in particular could hold back China's economic growth, which, alongside the pressure of global competition, has helped fuel interest in TM.

In 2005, McKinsey claimed that over the next 10–15 years Chinese companies would need many more 'globally effective' leaders to realise their global ambitions than they currently possessed (reported in Wilson 2008). China possesses only a very limited pool of qualified employee talent in posts required by foreign-invested enterprises, and the demand for talent has created significant shortages in several functional areas within such enterprises across the country. As Buxton et al (2007: 1) observe:

> In the past, the MNCs' biggest challenge was with patent protection, but today, the single largest brake in China is the struggle to attract – and even more importantly, retain – an executive workforce that possesses the right skill sets to sustain the growth for the long term.

Other McKinsey research (Lane and Pollner 2008) has specifically addressed this issue of growing talent shortages in China and the imbalance between business opportunities and talent supply, of qualified managers and executives in particular. The growing need for talented managers is a major challenge to both multinationals and local businesses. Many Chinese executives reported that insufficient talent was a major barrier to expansion; continued growth increased demands for talent at a time when multinationals are increasingly competing with local firms for scarce talent in the same talent pool. In addition, there is often a mismatch between the graduates turned out by Chinese universities and the skills and attributes required by employers (Case Study 14.2). Those recruited often have high expectations, which if not met may lead to high turnover (Shutt et al 2012).

Chinese companies worried about a lack of managerial capabilities increasingly look abroad to recruit talent – the McKinsey survey found that many executives expected the future proportion of foreign managers at senior levels to increase. As a result, expatriates continue to fill many talent gaps, with increasing use of Asia-Pacific expatriates (for example Singapore), Chinese returning from study or work abroad, and foreign-born Chinese managers. Mercer, cited in Wilson (2008), found that most respondents in China claimed that their main challenge in staff recruitment was a lack of qualified candidates in the labour market.

Another key challenge was how to develop and retain existing staff, making the management and leadership development of local staff a priority. Many older leaders, coming up to retirement but still influential, were educated during the Cultural Revolution, and may lack the skills and experience in such areas as strategy, innovation, enterprise and empowerment, while younger leaders, despite high educational levels, may have received little management training and development. However, many companies in China lack the commitment to develop a comprehensive leadership development strategy, or the expertise to implement one (Chapter 5), confirmed by Qiao's (2008) study of leadership development in four multinational companies in China. Here, talent development could not keep pace with business development. Two local Chinese companies (Lenovo and BenQ) employed an 'exclusive-people' perspective on TM (Chapter 17), skewing their training budget to those identified as A+, or those in the talent pool outperforming their peers. Succession planning was often seen as not working well, owing to a shortage of talent ready to fill leadership positions, fast-changing and volatile markets, and the 'over-high' expectations of those identified as 'talented'. Short-term business goals also often conflicted with long-term talent development objectives. 'Talent readiness' was seen as a key issue by CEOs, line managers and high-potentials, but HR tended to use non-strategic measures such as turnover rates and internal fill-in rates as its success criteria, not 'talent-readiness' as a measure.

Other factors contribute to this interest in TM. China's families, under the influence of the 'one-child' policy (currently under review) are producing children significantly below the rate necessary to maintain the country's population; within the next decade, the working population in China, as in Japan and much of Europe, is forecast to begin to shrink (Jackson and Howe 2004). The projected supply of Chinese university graduates between 2003 and 2008 was estimated at 15.7 million; however, only about 1.2 million were judged to be suitable for employment in MNCs (as in Case Study 14.2).

Thus, TM is clearly of growing importance in China; what then is distinctive about TM here? For many companies TM promises new and rather different approaches to the management of the people resource in organisations; rather than a simple repackaging of old techniques and ideas with a new label, it offers a distinct approach to HRM. Iles et al (2010c) found that MNCs in Beijing saw continuity with HRM; both TM and HRM emphasised integration with business strategy, and both covered the same functional areas of recruitment, selection, training and development, and appraisal and reward management. However, there were also differences; HRM had a broader scope than TM, focusing on management functions. TM was more specific, focusing on the people involved, and particularly the attraction, retention and development of 'talents'.

Preece et al (2011) found that TM was not seen simply as a management fashion; the main driving forces were business development and pressing requirements for the attraction and retention of talent. 'Traditional' HRM was seen as lacking a systematic focus upon particular groups of people; TM helped address a deteriorating situation in the external talent market, and the attraction and retention of 'talents' was a key motivating factor. Pressure from corporate HQ in the West to adopt TM was an influence, but not Chinese governmental promulgation. Some interviewees claimed that their companies were more likely to be fashion-setters rather than followers, and consulting firms (often regarded as active management fashion-setters) were claimed not to play an important role. In the main, companies embraced TM because they thought it could address their need to attract, retain and motivate 'talented' people in an intensifying talent war and help provide targeted and tailored services and focus for different groups of employees, not least with respect to career development. Some did acknowledge, however, that TM brought enhanced corporate reputation and assistance in employer branding.

What attributes make organisations attractive to Chinese employees? Many of these are similar to Western organisations – pay, development opportunities, career development, etc – but some seem specifically related to Chinese cultural values. Hartmann et al (2010) found that Shanghai-based German MNCs focused on building organisational cultures, supporting the development of personal relationships, and developing team spirit and commitment through joint sports activities, welfare and donation programmes, and other group events, unlike their practice in Germany (that is, a 'host-country' effect, Chapter 3). Companies claimed that it was very important to build belongingness and pride to reduce employee turnover in China; emotional bonds with supervisors and co-workers are important determinants of organisational commitment, as are personal relationships and pleasant, healthy and harmonious working climates, perhaps promoted through informal social events such as picnics and even 'dating parties'.

One of the authors (Iles) observed this emphasis on a recent study visit to Alibaba in Hangzhou, the global leader in e-commerce for small businesses, the biggest IT company in China and second in the world as a business-to-business platform for online trading markets. In addition to establishing headquarters in Hong Kong and Hangzhou, Alibaba has set up three overseas branches and joint ventures in Silicon Valley in the US and London in the UK, and a dozen branches and offices in other areas in China. It is striving to create 'a close family atmosphere' with a 'positive, flexible and a results-oriented working environment' in a campus-like environment. Staff are mostly young, the average age of employees being only 27, and casual dress is the norm, with much emphasis on sports, clubs, societies, dancing and social events, and team-building events.

LEARNING SUMMARY

In this chapter we examined the growth in importance of HRM in China as the country seeks to rebalance its economy away from export industries operating under a low-skill, low-pay regime towards a more domestic consumption-focused, high-skill and knowledge-driven economy. We explored the changes in HRM strategy in Chinese companies away from the command and control, centralised 'iron rice bowl' model of the Maoist era towards a more 'strategic HRM' model giving companies greater autonomy over HRM decisions. It traced this evolution to the Open Door policy of 1979, when economic and ownership reforms as well as labour market reforms led to enterprise reforms giving a greater role to private enterprises, in addition to massive foreign investment in the form of FIEs and international joint ventures. We also discussed some of the barriers to HRM in China, such as the education system, its emphasis on examinations, its failure to develop employability skills, regional imbalances, increasing inequality, and challenges of pollution and CSR. Relationships between Chinese cultural values and HRM were also discussed, as well as the skills challenges facing HRM as China seeks to move away from a low-skill, low-wage economy towards a higher-skilled, higher-technology economy.

This transition has given greater importance to both skills and talent as high on the agendas of both political and business leaders. We noted how a shortage of talent – especially managerial and professional talent – of the right kind with appropriate knowledge, skills and other attributes such as motivation was holding back the efforts of Chinese IEs to internationalise, leading to the use of expatriates, especially from the Asia-Pacific area, returning Chinese resident in the West and Japan, and Chinese educated abroad (despite some concerns over the high expectations and salary demands of such staff).

The chapter noted that companies in China regarded TM not as a passing fashion but as a way of dealing with the real problems they faced in the 'talent war' to attract and retain talented staff. Most saw TM as different from HRM in offering a more differentiated, segmented approach to workforce management and development, and the chapter also discussed the apparently greater weight given to 'social value' in recruitment and retention in China, manifest in emphases on team sports, outings, dating activities, parties and relationship-building initiatives in Chinese employer branding activities. This might reflect the more 'collectivist' values displayed by Chinese employees and applicants, as we discussed in Chapter 2.

PART 4

INTERNATIONAL HRM POLICIES IN IES

CHAPTER 15

Employee Resourcing: Staffing, Recruitment and Selection in International Contexts

Paul Iles and Tingting Jiang

LEARNING OUTCOMES

At the end of this chapter, you should be able to:

- Critically analyse the process of composing an international staff.

- Appreciate the mix of staff and the advantages and disadvantages of employing different categories of staff.

- Understand the differences between international recruitment and selection and its importance to organisations and to competitive advantage in IEs.

- Define job analysis, person specifications, job descriptions and competency profiles and their role in recruitment and selection in IEs.

- Distinguish between recruitment and selection in IEs and appreciate the role of employer branding in IE recruitment.

- Discuss a number of selection methods and critically analyse their use in international organisations, including the evaluative standards that can be applied to them.

INTRODUCTION

This chapter discusses employee resourcing in a global context, with particular reference to issues of recruitment and selection in IEs. It explores the recruitment/selection of international staff in a global labour market, including (but not limited to) expatriates (Chapter 3). The overall process of resourcing an organisation is often termed 'staffing', especially in the USA; its purpose is to ensure that the organisation has qualified workers at all levels to meet its short- and long-term business objectives.

COMPOSING AN INTERNATIONAL STAFF

In recruiting and selecting staff, whether domestically or internationally, we need to answer the following questions:

1   How do we know what employee resources we need? (human resource planning, job analysis)

2   How do we get them interested in us? (recruitment, attraction and branding processes)

3   How do we choose the best person? (selection processes)

4   How do we remain legal, honest and respectful, acting ethically and with integrity? (discussed in Chapter 6)

5   How do we retain them once we get them? (discussed in Chapter 19)

6   How do we know we made the right decision? (evaluation and validation processes).

In IEs, the assignment cycle is often seen to involve three phases (Bonache and Brewster 2001):

- *pre-assignment*: recruitment and selection, briefing
- *assignment*: adjustment and performance
- *post-assignment*: repatriation or transfer.

Here we will only discuss the pre-assignment recruitment and selection stage; Chapter 16 addresses the later stages of adjustment, adaptation and repatriation.

HOW DO WE KNOW WHAT EMPLOYEE RESOURCES WE NEED?

Before we go about recruiting staff, we need to know what we want them *for* and what we want them to do. In analysing the internationalisation of Chinese firms, Deng (2012) draws particular importance to issues of organisational design and structure. Of particular interest are issues of expatriate management and multinational team management. What are the IE's *motives* for recruiting staff?

IEs may have several motives for recruiting or assigning staff; these motives in part relate to the advantages and disadvantages of employing different categories of international staff. As we saw in Chapter 3, these may be expatriates or parent-country nationals (PCNs), locals or host-country nationals (HCNs) or third-country nationals (TCNs).

Edstrom and Galbraith (1977) found three general assignment motives: *to fill positions/transfer knowledge*; *to develop managers*; and *to develop organisations* through creating information networks and socialising both expatriate and local managers into the corporate culture. Motives for international assignments (Reiche and Harzing 2011; Gamble 2010) include:

- to fill positions with qualified competent staff
- to alleviate problems caused by a lack of suitably qualified, competent locals
- to ensure corporate control/coordination and deliver bottom-line results

- to encourage transfer of knowledge, organisational development and enhancement of information networks, develop a common corporate culture, common policies and practices, increase coordination and control, and build greater corporate loyalty (for example Riusala and Suutari 2004; Bonache and Brewster 2001)
- to develop international staff to ensure global business objectives (Chapter 16)
- to facilitate management development by increasing global awareness, giving experience and ensuring career development for high-potential staff (Chapter 16).

These motives are not necessarily mutually exclusive – IEs may want staff to fulfil several motives simultaneously, say coordinating processes and delivering results while transferring knowledge to the local affiliate and staff and developing locals. Interestingly, German-language work on the issue (Reiche and Harzing 2011) more often stresses *direct control and coordination* by expatriates as a motive; could this be related to the relatively high German scores on uncertainty avoidance (65) (Chapter 2)?

Harzing (2001) has explored this further, distinguishing between:

- *bears* (focusing on surveillance/control)
- *bumble bees* (focusing on coordination and socialisation)
- *spiders* (focusing on developing informal communication networks).

These motives for international assignments (IAs) are related to the international orientation of the firm, especially its IHRM orientation, as saw in Chapter 3. There we discussed four common postures or orientations taken towards international HRM in IEs, each with major implications for IHRM, especially for composing an international staff: ethnocentric, polycentric, geocentric, and regiocentric.

Expatriates/PCNs (of course TCNs are 'expatriated' too, but here we will use the term to refer to PCNs) offer a range of advantages to IEs as part of an 'ethnocentric' strategy; they are more likely to show familiarity with headquarters and more likely to be able to successfully liaise with it, knowing the language and people involved. They probably have a known track record and competence profile, and may be trusted to exercise control over local affiliates on behalf of the corporate HQ. However, they also come with disadvantages: they are more likely to experience local adaptation and language problems, are expensive (not only high salaries, but travel, training, accommodation, transport, schooling and other costs), host countries may exercise localisation pressures on the company to recruit locals (Arabisation, indigenisation, Africanisation, etc – Chapter 10) and their family may find adjustment difficult.

This strategy is most commonly used in Japanese companies (perhaps also linked to high levels of uncertainty avoidance – Chapter 2) and in banks, perhaps due to control/trust issues; it is also more commonly used in developing regions such as Africa (Chapter 11), where staff with appropriate skills, education and experience may be harder to find (Reiche and Harzing 2011).

In contrast, locals or HCNs also offer many advantages, such as local familiarity, lower costs (probably lower salaries and no need to incur support costs). In offering locals opportunities, they may be seen as responding to local government pressures for indigenisation/localisation. However, the enterprise may harbour (not necessarily accurately) doubts about their ability to exercise control on behalf of the company and their ability to liaise and communicate with HQ, not knowing the people or even the language fluently. In addition, employing locals may be seen as denying international opportunities for their own PCNs, which may have been a strong brand offering in graduate recruitment.

Using TCNs also has its attractions, perhaps as a useful compromise between local and global; TCNs are often cosmopolitan 'career internationals' with extensive global experience. They are also likely to be cheaper than PCNs and may already have extensive host-country knowledge. However, there are disadvantages: there may be host-country sensitivity to employing certain national groups, and the host country may see this strategy as blocking local opportunities and preventing successful nationalisation or 'localisation'. TCNs are most commonly employed in European MNCs; PCNs are most likely to be the financial director, MD or CEO; locals the HR director and the bulk of the workforce (Reiche and Harzing 2011).

Factors affecting which choice to make include *parent-country/company* factors, such as high uncertainty avoidance countries of origin (Chapter 2). Here, as in Japan (score 92), PCNs may be viewed positively as exercising 'control', and seniority favoured, especially operating in culturally distant countries (Gamble 2010). There are also *industry* effects; financial services are more likely to use PCNs, presumably for control and trust reasons, while the advertising, electronics and food sectors are more likely to use HCNs, either for reasons of local responsiveness (food, advertising) or because the industry is global, such as electronics (Reiche and Harzing 2011). There are also *host-country effects*; PCNs are more likely to be used in countries with low education levels and cost of living. *Subsidiary* characteristics such as age, acquisition status and performance also affect choice; HCNs are more likely in older, more successful subsidiaries and in acquired subsidiaries.

Spider and *bumble bee* roles seem particularly important in polycentric subsidiaries with high levels of local responsiveness and in acquisitions rather than greenfield sites, where the subsidiary may operate quite independently of the HQ and where expatriate presence is generally lower (Reiche and Harzing 2011). Geocentric orientations emphasising control and standardisation tend to make more use of *bears*, especially expatriates. We explored the role of international assignments as knowledge managers/diffusers of knowledge in Chapter 7 (Bonache and Brewster 2001; Riusala and Suutari 2004; Wang-Cowham 2011).

For international assignments (IAs), it is therefore important to clarify the nature of the job, role or position intended to be filled and its link with the motives for assignment. Is it to:

- do a technical job?
- transfer knowledge?

- develop the individual?
- develop the organisation?

Answers to these questions will influence job analysis; what do we expect in terms of roles, duties, responsibilities and priorities from the international employee?

ISSUES AND PROBLEMS IN INTERNATIONAL ASSIGNMENTS

International assignees, especially expatriates, are likely to run into a series of problems on international assignments. Many of these can be alleviated by careful recruitment and selection; the role of training and development and performance and reward management, which can also address some of these issues, is explored further in later chapters. In order to mitigate these problems, a *person specification* will need to identify relevant skills, knowledge and other attributes necessary for success prior to departure.

Assessing intercultural competence

With many IAs, the stress has been on employee technical skills and experience and not on what is often termed intercultural competence. Chew (2004) found that the great majority of Australian respondents (HR managers) placed great importance on the technical competence of their expatriates, with fewer acknowledging personality traits, relational abilities and motivational state as highly important criteria. Family situation was moderately important, language skills somewhat unimportant and prior expatriate experience moderately unimportant, though this reduced the need for orientation. Technical expertise and domestic track record were by far the two most dominant selection criteria of these participating firms.

In Chapter 5 we discussed the 'cultural quotient' (CQ), 'a person's capability for successful adaptation to new cultural settings, i.e. for unfamiliar settings attributable to cultural context' (Earley and Ang 2003). Cross-cultural leaders needed to be successful in terms of cultural adaptability, emotional and cultural intelligence, and the ability to be global and local at the same time (Alon and Higgins 2005).

Intercultural competence has been found to be as important to success in IAs as technical ability; what skills, competences and experience are necessary for success in international assignments? Technical skills and experience, while necessary, may not be sufficient; interpersonal, communication and intercultural competence skills also seem necessary. Ronen (1989) identifies the following factors as necessary for successful expatriates:

- *job factors*: technical, managerial, administrative skills; acquaintance with headquarters
- *relational factors*: tolerance of ambiguity; behavioural flexibility; non-judgementalism; empathy/lack of ethnocentrism; interpersonal skills
- *motivational factors*: belief in the mission; perceived congruence with career path; interest in international work and the specific culture; a willingness to learn and change
- *family factors*

- *language factors.*

Mendenhall and Oddou (1985) argue that expatriate acculturation and adjustment involves four dimensions (which we discuss further in Chapter 16):

1   *self-orientation*: self-confidence, self-esteem

2   *others' orientation*: enhance effective interaction with HCNs

3   *perceptual*: understand others' behaviour, attributions

4   *cultural toughness*: the first three are even more important in culturally tough/distant countries.

Gertsen (1990) identified the following dimensions of 'intercultural competence' as important:

- *affective:* empathy; openness; flexibility; self- confidence; lack of ethnocentrism; tolerance of ambiguity
- *cognitive*: broad categorisation; culture knowledge
- *communicative*: express respect, empathy; listen; flexibility; language; non-verbal communication skills.

Here 'broad categorisation' refers to avoiding stereotypes, for example 'all English people are stiff-upper-lipped', and using broader categories more able to handle differences and contradictions.

❓ REFLECTIVE ACTIVITY 15.1

Look at the websites below for information on the OAI (Overseas Assignment Inventory), an online assessment tool that measures nine attributes and six context factors crucial for successful adaptation to another culture. It is provided for both the expatriate job candidate and his or her spouse or partner in many US companies:

> www.tuckerintl.com/

> www.tuckerintl.com/general/products/IntlAssessment1.html

www.performanceprograms.com/surveys/Overseas_Assignment_Inventory.html

www.performanceprograms.com/surveys/Overseas_Assisgnment_Inventory_Training.html

1   How useful do you think this is?

2   How does it relate to the analysis of Gertsen (1990) and Ronen (1989)?

Graf and Mertesacker (2009) suggest assessing intercultural competence as part of a training needs analysis on six measures; their model, based in part on Gertsen (1990) is presented in Figure 15.1. Questionnaire results were here correlated with observations of student behaviour in intercultural exercises. Measures included the Intercultural Sensitivity Inventory and other scales.

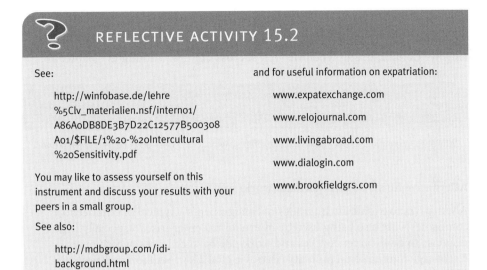

REFLECTIVE ACTIVITY 15.2

See:

http://winfobase.de/lehre
%5Clv_materialien.nsf/interno1/
A86A0DB8DE3B7D22C12577B500308
A01/$FILE/1%20-%20Intercultural
%20Sensitivity.pdf

You may like to assess yourself on this
instrument and discuss your results with your
peers in a small group.

See also:

http://mdbgroup.com/idi-
background.html

and for useful information on expatriation:

www.expatexchange.com

www.relojournal.com

www.livingabroad.com

www.dialogin.com

www.brookfieldgrs.com

Figure 15.1: Intercultural competence dimensions

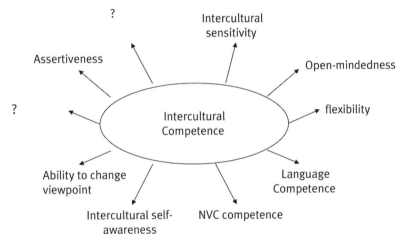

These dimensions are now often reflected in the concept of 'emotional
intelligence' (explored later and introduced in Chapter 5). Though emotional
intelligence, personality traits and interpersonal skills are very important for
international selection, as we have seen, in practice, most companies still often
use technical competence and knowledge of company systems as key criteria
(Reiche and Harzing 2011). Personal recommendations via an informal 'coffee-
machine system' are common (Harris and Brewster 1999). Here, in a closed/
informal system, candidates are not formally evaluated against a formal person
specification, but through an informal chat over coffee; the candidate pool is very
restricted and the organisation fails to behave strategically.

With respect to expatriates and other IAs, selection is often an informal process,
but it needs to be treated as formally as domestic selection. In addition, technical

skills and previous track record are often given priority, but interpersonal and communication skills and emotional intelligence are equally important. This is an issue we explore further when we look at cross-cultural training in Chapter 16.

REFLECTIVE ACTIVITY 15.3

Why does international selection in practice differ so widely from best-practice recommendations?

Alternative forms of international working

Alternatives to expatriate international assignments – typical of ethnocentric companies – are also being used by international enterprises, especially in response to dual-career couples and work–life balance issues, which may discourage international mobility (Petrovic et al 2000; Scullion and Brewster 2001; Mayrhofer and Scullion 2002). Desires to reduce expatriation costs and respond to localisation pressures from governments are also generating interest in alternatives to typical expatriation assignments, such as:

- *short-term assignments*, for example postings between 1 and 12 months unaccompanied by family; especially useful for problem-solving/skills transfer
- *international commuting*
- *frequent flying* or business trips for irregular specific tasks
- *home-based managers* focusing on different global markets, but with a global outlook
- *internationally mobile* managers, creating a cadre of 'career internationals'
- *rotating technical professionals*, for example oil rigs
- *self-initiated international assignments*
- *virtual assignments*, for example team distribution of international responsibilities through IT, email, social media, videoconferencing, etc (Morley et al 2003)
- *'inpatriation'*, that is, bringing subsidiary staff, whether TCNs or HCNs, to the headquarters to learn and apply parent company operations and culture, transfer knowledge, test suitability, socialise into company culture and build multicultural teams.

Inpatriates – transfers to HQ of subsidiary managers – may take on a lynchpin role, especially with regard to the transfer of tacit knowledge and developing a global mindset, but inpatriates may experience status differences and cultural adjustment challenges. Inpatriation is more likely to occur in geocentric companies (or, on a regional basis, in regiocentric companies, see Chapter 3; Reiche and Harzing 2011).

These roles all have implications for the type of HRM required and the skills that need to be developed. 'Virtual' assignments through international collaboration on projects through videoconferencing, email and telephone rather than physical travel are becoming more common, but face-to-face communication is often still necessary to build and maintain trust and clear up misunderstandings. The use of a greater variety of shorter assignments (troubleshooting, contractual assignments, rotational assignments, knowledge-transfer activities, training, personal development, short-term commuters, frequent flyers) is also increasing. Collings et al (2007) claim that the desire to create global core competency and cultural diversity of perspectives in the top team has driven these alternatives, as well as the desire to offer career opportunities to high-potential HCNs and TCNs and encourage bilateral knowledge transfer.

REFLECTIVE ACTIVITY 15.4

1   Will the development of modern ICT technologies make the traditional expatriate assignment disappear?

2   How do we get them interested in us: recruitment, attraction, and branding processes?

Having outlined some distinctive features of international recruitment and selection, we next look at the stages and processes involved , beginning with international recruitment.

INTERNATIONAL RECRUITMENT

The kinds of jobs offered by organisations clearly differ in terms of their skill and ability demands; this is as true of international assignments as domestic ones. The differences between people – in terms of their knowledge, skills, personality, motivation and other attributes – are therefore clearly relevant to these resourcing decisions, so recruitment and selection is clearly of great interest to IHRM theory, research and practice.

International recruitment is the process of attracting qualified candidates to apply for vacant positions within an international organisation. It depends upon factors such as brand/image of the organisation, salary, perks and potential growth avenues. An important component of the recruitment process is the *person specification* to attract potential candidates. This leads to the next task of staff *selection*, where decisions are made as to who will be chosen for the vacant position from candidates both interested in the position and qualified to fill it. First preference in IAs is often to promote or assign internally; when there are no qualified employees to fill the position, external recruitment channels needs to be activated.

See the CIPD's research and factsheets on this area (http://www.cipd.co.uk/binaries/5874%20RTM%20SR%20%28WEB%29.pdf).

Job analysis

Jobs have traditionally been seen as building blocks of an organisation; understanding and matching job requirements with qualified people is seen as necessary to achieve high-quality performance. Job analysis is carried out to design a *job description* and *person specification* so that people with the required specification are then attracted to the organisation. Job analysis indicates 'the psychological attributes required by an individual who may fill the job effectively' (Robertson and Smith 2001: 442). Applicants are then assessed in terms of how closely their profiles match or fit this specification, and candidates selected in terms of closeness of fit. The process is then evaluated in terms of whether this match was successful: were the people selected actually able to do the job effectively, as measured by some criterion of success?

However, jobs are now very dynamic and can change due to a variety of forces, especially international jobs, which will continually change and be redesigned as organisations struggle to remain competitive in global markets. There is no 'one best way' to do the job; the job is not static and unchanging (Iles 2007). Job analysis now seems increasingly problematic, given the instability of jobs, new technologies and new organisational forms (Lievens et al 2002). This, and the proactive shaping of jobs and roles by role occupants, has led to a focus less on 'jobs' and more on tasks and cross-functional skills (Hough and Oswald 2000) or *competencies*.

Knowledge in itself is rarely seen as sufficient to ensure satisfactory job performance, needing connection to skills. Both 'knowledge' and 'skill' are contested terms; for Felstead et al (2002) skill refers to competence to carry out tasks successfully. 'Competence' is also a contested term, blurring traditional psychometric distinctions between construct (predictor) and criterion (performance measure). Does it refer to *inputs* (for example abilities), *outputs* (for example job performance) or *processes* (for example behaviours)? Underlying the development of specific products, with their limited lifecycles, is the acquisition and development of *strategic skill pools*, *capabilities* and *core competencies* (Collis and Montgomery 1995; Hamel 1991); competence can therefore be seen at both individual and organisational levels (Prahalad and Hamel 1990). Once identified, HRM processes can then ensure that employees with the requisite skills and qualities are successfully assessed, placed, appraised, developed and rewarded against appropriate competency criteria.

The term *competence* is now often used to refer to an ability to perform within an occupational area to a *standard* required in employment; British in origin, it asks whether employee work *outputs* are meeting occupational standards as specified by performance criteria (Armstrong 2002). *Competency*, in contrast, refers to behaviour or process, and is American in origin; for Boyatzis (1982), it defines what characteristics or abilities enable staff to achieve effective or superior performance. The concept has proven resilient against academic attacks, both from within the psychometric community, suspicious of its status as a construct, and from the critical discourse community, who see it as describing people in essentialist, individualist ways, as attributes of individuals. The 'psychometric-objective' model (Newell and Shackleton 2000; Newell 2009) assumes that stable and objectively measurable individual differences between people are the main cause of differential job performance. French conceptions, in contrast, often add a third, more 'relational' dimension; in addition to 'savoir' (knowing what or knowledge) and 'savoir-faire' (know-how or skills), there is 'savoir-être', referring to social capital and social networks (Delamare et al 2005; Malloch et al 2007; Kleymann and Malloch 2012). This has received more emphasis with claims that the ability to form social networks and access knowledge from others will grow in importance as knowledge management becomes increasingly critical to organisational success (Newell 1999).

REFLECTIVE ACTIVITY 15.5

How might you analyse the job of an IHRM manager?

In the traditional model, methods are then designed to evaluate candidates' capabilities on these attributes or competencies, and validation procedures used to 'assess the extent to which the personnel selection methods provide valid predictors of job performance, or other criterion variables such as absenteeism or turnover' (Robertson and Smith 2001: 442).

Performance criteria are often selected by convenience, however, rather than through theoretical models or task analysis; as Robertson and Smith (2001: 442) note: 'the hegemony of supervisory ratings as a criterion has if anything been strengthened by the current emphasis on contextual and citizenship behaviours as an element of job performance'. Indeed, moves towards 'selecting for fit' (for example person–organisation, person–job, person–team) and emphasis on emotional intelligence and emotional labour (Chapter 5) have meant that the construct of 'job performance' has been considerably broadened (Viswesvaran and Ones 2000). Peer, subordinate or customer ratings may also now be used alongside supervisor judgements, as with 360-degree feedback or multi-rater assessment systems (Chapter 18). Figure 15.2 presents the stages involved in international recruitment and selection.

Figure 15.2: Stages of the international recruitment and selection process

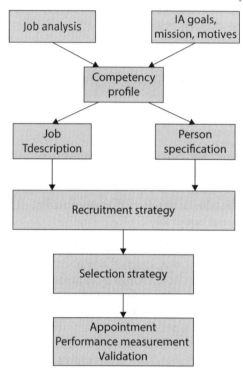

(adapted from Taylor 2005: 145)

Attracting candidates

In this section we explore how to attract the 'right' kinds of applicants to the IE, answering the question: *How do we get them interested in us?*

Note, however, that it should not be automatically assumed that the organisation needs to recruit a direct replacement for a vacancy. The necessity for the post should be reviewed, and whether the job should be redesigned or job-holders reallocated to other duties considered, as well as internal promotion of existing staff or further training and development to equip internal staff, such as HCNs or locals, to fill the position.

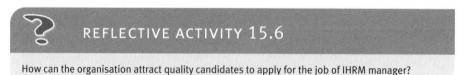

REFLECTIVE ACTIVITY 15.6

How can the organisation attract quality candidates to apply for the job of IHRM manager?

As we shall see in Chapter 17, there is a claim that the global 'war for talent' is making it increasingly difficult for many organisations to attract suitable candidates. Organisations need to attract as large a field of suitably experienced and skilled applicants as possible, while discouraging unsuitable ones.

Advertising, especially in the general or specialist print media, has traditionally been the main vehicle for attracting candidates, with some use of local radio (Cooper et al 2003).

For senior jobs, recruitment agencies and 'headhunters' (search and selection agencies) may be used to employ their personal contacts and databases to identify suitable candidates, many of whom may not be actively looking for other jobs. Agencies may hold large databases of job-seekers, as well as perhaps supplying interim managers and temporary staff. These may be taken on as permanent staff if their performance is judged satisfactory.

A widely used recruitment method is internal advertising (either before external advertising or simultaneously) to existing staff, whose knowledge, skills and experience are more likely to be known to the organisation. However, there may be times when the organisation feels it lacks internal candidates with sufficient experience or skill, or feels that it needs a 'fresh perspective' that 'new blood' may bring. Word of mouth is also often still used, using existing staff networks of relatives, friends and colleagues or ex-colleagues. However, there is the danger that such methods, by reaching a bounded population, limit diversity and perpetuate unfairness. This may result in the organisation falling foul of equality and anti-discrimination laws.

Most applicants in the UK submit an application form or CV/résumé. Application forms, if well designed, can make screening easier, especially if they ask candidates to show evidence of how they meet essential and desirable criteria or ask candidates to show how they possess specific required job competencies. Application forms, especially if well structured, also make it easier to compare candidates and enhance *reliability or consistency* (that is, the extent to which the use of an application form to sift candidates yields the same result under similar conditions).

There has been a major increase in the use of the *Internet* for recruitment, to solicit applications and screen employees. Job vacancies can be posted on the Internet or an intranet (for example advertised on a homepage) and the applicant may download application forms, applications may be tracked, CVs/résumés may be stored and candidates screened. A CIPD (2012) survey shows that large companies in the UK are more likely to use corporate websites (http://www.cipd.co.uk/hr-resources/survey-reports/resourcing-talent-planning-2012.aspx).

This may enhance the global reach of a company; the organisation may carry out these processes itself or contract it out to a recruitment service. Such an agency may maintain a searchable database of job vacancies and help applicants in career planning, CV-posting and job-matching, as well as maintain a pre-screened pool of applicants for assessment by the organisation. In addition, selection tests or biodata forms may be delivered online, with test processing carried out within the organisation or by an outside contractor. Online testing may be used to handle intensive screening (delivered in different languages). Rather than hand-score and hand-process application forms and psychometric tests, online personality and workplace values inventories and timed tests can be used, with feedback sent to applicants on their results along with careers advice (feedback may also be available by telephone). This frees management time, as well as helping to portray the company in a contemporary, modern light.

However, the Internet is mainly used for graduate recruitment or IT-related jobs; senior managers are much less likely to be recruited in this way, perhaps due to the demands for 'discretion' often emphasised at this level. Here, 'headhunters' are more likely to be used. We will discuss social media shortly.

Other emerging areas of interest in recruitment and selection have been the increasing importance of *employer branding*.

Recruitment and branding

There is growing interest in corporate/employer as well as product branding (Ahonen 2008). Employer branding (EB) describes how organisations market their offerings to potential and existing employees, communicate with them and maintain their loyalty by 'promoting, both within and outside the firm, a clear view of what makes a firm different and desirable as an employer' (Backhaus and Tikoo 2004: 502.

Ambler and Barrow (1996) first applied the concept of *brand* to HRM, viewing the employer as the brand and the employee as the consumer/customer. EB is 'the package of functional, economic and psychological benefits provided by employment, and identified with the employing company' (Ambler and Barrow 1996: 187). EB therefore provides both instrumental (economic) and symbolic (psychological) benefits to employees. For the CIPD (2009a) EB is 'a set of attributes and qualities – often intangible – that makes an organisation distinctive, promises a particular kind of employment experience, and appeals to those people who will thrive and perform best in its culture'. It thus involves efforts to communicate to existing and prospective staff that the organisation is a desirable place to work, so creating compelling, distinctive employee value propositions (EVPs).

Case Study 15.1 illustrates this with respect to a hospital in China.

CASE STUDY 15.1

EMPLOYER BRANDING AND EMPLOYEE VALUE PROPOSITION IN SRRS HOSPITAL, HANGZHOU, ZHEJIANG PROVINCE

On 3 May 1994 SRRS Hospital was established with funding by a Hong Kong-based entrepreneur and 50% funding from the Zhejiang provincial government. It is supported by the US hospital Loma Linda of Los Angeles, engaging in joint research. Its mission is to 'do our best to develop health,

both mental and physical health': a modern research hospital focusing on management, cooperation, teamwork and quality.

It has 1,350 beds, 2,700 staff, with 2 staff per bed; 960 nurses, 580 doctors, 380 technical/ancillary staff plus administration, IT, etc. The HR department was established in 1985, originally in another hospital, but it moved to this hospital in 1992. It has 94 staff, with 60 new graduates. Recruitment is no problem: new graduates come into various specialisms. Some posts are more problematic to fill, however; for example, surgeons. It recruits over 100 graduates per annum; 50% nurses, 30% doctors, 20% technicians; the rest are admin staff. All front-line services staff are graduates – a few support staff are college graduates. They tend not to employ foreign-educated students because they ask for higher salaries.

Offering to graduates

The hospital is part of Zhejiang University as a 'teaching hospital', and offers graduates:

- an educational hospital – widening their career opportunities

- an open management style – emphasising discussion

- a fulfilling career

- a set salary comparable with larger hospitals; cancer hospitals pay more, others according to size/scale

- the advantages of an educational/research centre

- high levels of training – after university, basic initial training is similar; English skills are advantageous

- they only employ two traditional Chinese medicine (TCM) doctors – there are two large TCM hospitals in the region.

Most graduates find jobs in the healthcare system – the key is their major in university; but often the right skills/characteristics are hard to find.

(adapted from Shutt et al 2012)

Questions

1   What is the employee value proposition (EVP) being offered here to graduates?

2   How might it differ for other staff, for example surgeons?

It is often claimed that EB can help an organisation compete effectively for talent (Jiang and Iles 2011). It can enhance employee engagement, recruitment and retention so that the organisation is perceived positively by existing, potential and former employees as a good place to work. For example, a company might seek to develop an EB which complements its customer brand proposition, devising credible, compelling and differentiated EVPs which describe what the organisation stands for and requires, a perspective linked to earlier work in HR on the 'psychological contract' and the 'employer of choice' agendas.

SELECTING INTERNATIONAL STAFF

Selection is used by organisations to try to answer the third question: How do we choose the best person?

SELECTION TECHNIQUES

There are a variety of assessment and selection techniques available if we wish to make judgements on the suitability of candidates. There is no one 'right technique' to be used in all circumstances, but there are 'evaluative criteria' or 'evaluative standards' against which we can assess the suitability of a technique. Evaluative standards refer to the standards by which the quality of a selection procedure is assessed, such as reliability, validity, interpretability and practicality (Cooper et al 2003).

Validity itself is a complex construct, composed of:

- *face validity*: does it feel valid to candidates? Though not a technical assessment of validity, this may affect candidate reactions to the test, and its acceptability
- *content validity*: the extent to which a measure represents all facets of a given construct
- *construct validity*: variables such as cognitive ability or personality traits are defined in theoretical terms; this is of major interest to psychometric researchers interested in consistent patterns of individual differences between people, usually assessed by tests
- *criterion-related validity*: this is probably the most important aspect of validity in practice, especially 'predictive validity', measuring the relationship between scores on a predictor (for example test, interview) and a criterion (usually job performance, often assessed in terms of supervisor appraisal, promotion, output, training success, turnover or tenure). There is a problem with these measures as proxies for 'real' job performance, however. A job-holder may do well at the job level, but poorly at the team level (for example refusing to collaborate) or the organisational level (for example not passing on information).

However, other evaluative standards are relevant, including the 'adverse impact' or discriminatory impact of selection methods; another is the acceptability to candidates, especially the role of fairness perceptions (Robertson et al 1991).

It is possible to classify selection techniques in terms of whether they seek to assess past, current or future behaviour (Table 15.1). Shortlisted candidates are usually assessed through interviews, perhaps supplemented by tests or work-sample methods. The logic of 'past' methods is that nothing predicts future behaviour as much as past behaviour; the logic of 'future' methods is that intentions are a useful guide to performance. 'Present' methods assess current levels of performance (Iles and Robertson 1989; Robertson and Iles 1988).

Table 15.1: Types of selection method

PAST (for example track record, experience)
Structured/criterion-related or behavioural interviews
References
Peer observation
Astrology
Biodata
PRESENT (for example current performance)
Graphology
Ability tests
Aptitude tests
Self-assessment
Personality inventories
Unstructured interviews
Work samples
Assessment centres
FUTURE (for example future intentions)
Situational interviews
Hypothetical interviews

Table 15.2 shows how well some techniques do when assessed against the criterion of predictive validity.

Table 15.2: Validity of predictors compared

Perfect prediction	1.0	
	0.9	
	0.8	
	0.7	
	0.6	◄──── Structured interviews
	0.5	⎧ Psychometric tests of ability
		⎨ Work samples
	0.4	⎩ Assessment centres
		◄──
		⎧ Biodata
		⎨ Psychometric tests of personality
	0.3	⎩ Unstructured interviews
	0.2	
	0.1	References (UK)
Random prediction	0.0	◄──── Graphology (France)
Astrology (India)		Astrology (India)

(adapted from Corbridge and Pilbeam 1998: 102)

Different countries use different selection techniques (Iles 1994, 2000). As Table 15.2 shows, such techniques as references – extensively used in the UK, but less so elsewhere – and graphology (extensively used in France and some other continental European countries) or astrology (used in India) do very poorly, while others, such as structured interviews, ability tests, work samples and assessment centres do very well. Biodata and personality tests do moderately well. The interview in particular has often received a 'bad press', typically viewed as lacking in reliability and validity as interviewers often gather different information on candidates, and their judgements are open to a number of biases. However, these factors, and the poor reliability and validity of interviews, are typically found in non-standardised, unstructured interviews, and more recent trends have been to standardise and structure the interview. The interview has increasingly been based on job-related competencies and the same topics are probed for in the same order (Cooper et al 2003).

Another area of growing interest is 'emotional intelligence' (explored in Chapter 5 on leadership), as the higher up the organisation, the more difference EI is seen to make to performance. Leaders who 'derail' often show deficiencies in emotional competencies such as interpersonal relationships, teamwork and dealing with change. It is also important to expatriates and to others on IAs; all the 'relational' factors deemed important by Ronen (1989) and Gertsen (1990) to expatriate success involve EI.

For Goleman (1996), the best managers are seen to make decisions based on a combination of self-management and relationship skills and an awareness of how their behaviour affects others in the organisation (though some authors argue that EI is not new, merely a relabelling of attributes that we already knew were important influences on behaviour and success). Clearly this interest in emotions is not just confined to work, but is part of a wider cultural trend. Emotional intelligence covers:

- self-awareness
- self-management
- social awareness
- relationship management.

REFLECTIVE ACTIVITY 15.7

Why do you think interest in EI has grown in recent years?

INTERNET TESTING AND SOCIAL MEDIA

As we saw in the discussion on changing recruitment practices, Internet recruitment and testing has grown in popularity in recent years; though a CIPD survey in 2006 found that only 5% of organisations in the UK were using it, mostly larger ones, many expected it to increase rapidly in the future. It is possible not just to recreate tests in computerised formats, but enhance value by adding audio and video: for example, presenting short videotaped interactions between customers and employees to candidates for their response. Virtual reality may enhance the 'realism' of multimedia testing even further. The CIPD (2012) recruitment survey (http://www.cipd.co.uk/hr-resources/survey-reports/ resourcing-talent-planning-2012.aspx) gives an example of Interserve, which used an online video interviewing tool with webcams; candidate, HR and recruiter did not all need to be available simultaneously – very useful for a pan-European company.

In addition, there are important developments in the use of social media and social networking sites – both proprietary, such as Facebook or Twitter (or Weibo in China), and organisationally based ones for recruitment and selection. These present new and unforeseen challenges and, to an extent, unknown threats and opportunities to organisations and to the HR function.

A significant example with implications for IHRM is the rise of professional networking sites such as LinkedIn (see their 'Apply Now' feature, http:// blog.linkedin.com/2011/07/24/apply-with-linkedin/), which have a direct and overt focus on individual career management and development, and so a direct and overt impact on employers' recruitment and selection strategies. The CIPD 2012 survey of recruitment practices in the UK found significant increases in the use of professional networking sites such as LinkedIn (from 14% in 2010 to 22% in 2012), though this was most popular in the private sector. The rise of social networking sites such as Facebook was less pronounced (from 3% to 8%).

Some organisations express concern over unrestricted use of such tools at work; others encourage their use. Some express concerns over 'off-duty' contact and its implications for their reputation. Pre-screening may happen through social media, as quick searches on candidates can reveal personal information on social media profiles; candidates can also research companies. Companies hope to find candidates that fit their culture, while job-seekers try to find companies that suit their personality or values. Younger, tech-savvy workers in particular may appreciate being found in locations where they spend much of their time.

However, recruiters can 'accidently' find things out about candidates – the person's 'cyber-reputation' or 'digital footprint' (www.yoname.com) – that they would be better off not knowing, such as health problems or pregnancy plans; without set processes in place, companies may be leaving themselves open to lawsuits. Companies need to ask: is such a practice getting valid information? Is it legal or potentially discriminatory? Is it worth it – what value does it add? Does it introduce biases based on, say, attractiveness as rated from photographs earlier in the selection process? Given that this is a new and developing field, the situation for screening (but not recruitment marketing, where it has a useful role to play, though it may be difficult to target the right audience, unlike more selective Internet boards) is likely to remain problematic; legal advice should be sought, as well as more research carried out!

 REFLECTIVE ACTIVITY 15.8

1   What do you see as the pros and cons of Internet testing as compared with traditional paper and pencil testing?

2   What is your view about the use of social media in recruitment and selection?

3   See the various guidelines developed by organisations, varying in tone and approach. What do you think such guidelines should contain?

http://www.cipd.co.uk/blogs/cipd_events/b/weblog/archive/2011/11/22/10-social-media-policy-amp-guidelines-documents.aspx

Other assessment techniques may play a role in international selection, especially *assessment centres* – not a place, but a process, where multiple candidates go through multiple activities, of which some at least are 'simulations' or 'samples' of the job applied for, such as presentations, role-plays or team exercises, observed by multiple assessors. Companies will sequence selection processes, using different techniques at different points in time; a large IE expecting to receive large numbers of applicants may initially ask them to fill in, perhaps online, a scored, competency-based application form or biodata bank. Candidates who score highly may then be invited to an assessment centre and/or structured, competency-based interview before being offered jobs. Interserve used its video interview to select graduates for an assessment centre.

LEARNING SUMMARY

The chapter began with a discussion of how to compose an international staff, exploring the different options available to IEs, the different motives for international assignment and the different types of international assignment available to companies, with their respective advantages and disadvantages.

It then went on to consider recruitment and selection; without effective recruitment (and an effective employer brand), the organisation will fail to attract sufficient people with the skills, knowledge, experience and motivation to fill available positions. Without an effective, valid way of selecting from applicants, the organisation will not be able to hire and place high-performers in the appropriate jobs. In developing an effective staffing strategy, organisations need to carry out an appropriate job analysis so that a suitable job description can be drawn up and a person specification or competency profile developed that enables the required skills, knowledge and other attributes to be described and communicated to potential applicants through recruitment channels.

Traditionally recruitment has been carried out through advertisements, but increasingly the Internet and social media sites are playing a growing important role, especially in graduate recruitment.

The chapter also discussed the evaluative standards by which we can judge the value of any selection procedure or system. These include the importance of reliability – does the instrument or test give consistent measurements? Another important criterion is validity, of which there are several different kinds, such as: face validity (does it feel valid to candidates?), construct validity (does it assess what it claims to assess?), content validity (does the selection instrument sample job content accurately?). However, the most important criterion is criterion-related validity: does performance on the test or procedure predict performance against some criterion? However, this is multi-faceted and it may not be possible to obtain one 'objective' criterion of performance. On this criterion, certain procedures such as structured interviews and assessment centres perform relatively well, with relatively high 'validity coefficients'.

CHAPTER 16

Cross-cultural Training and International HRD

Crystal Zhang and Paul Iles

LEARNING OUTCOMES

By the end of this chapter, you should be able to:

- Understand the nature of international HRD.

- Analyse the role and contribution of cross-cultural training and its importance.

- Understand various models of training and their complexity.

- Appreciate the factors to take into account in designing cross-cultural training programmes.

INTRODUCTION

In this chapter we look at international HRD, in particular cross-cultural training (CCT). Garavan and Carbery (2012) subdivide international HRD research in a similar fashion to this book: into an *international* trajectory, referring to HRD conducted in the context of the IE; a *comparative* trajectory, focused on 'national HRD' in different countries; and a *cross-cultural* trajectory, oriented towards analysing how national culture can influence HRD. We looked at aspects of comparative and national HRD in Chapter 1 and Chapter 8 while exploring 'institutionalist' explanations of national difference. In particular, we posited a distinction in skill formation and vocational education and training policies between those countries taking a broadly *voluntarist* approach to HRD (perhaps providing encouragement but leaving much provision to the market-related activities of individuals and firms, such as the USA and UK) and those pursuing a much more *interventionist* approach, where the state plays a much bigger role in regulation, policy and provision (for example Austria, South Korea, China). We noted some 'hybrid' systems and some recent swings from interventionism to market-oriented, demand-led voluntarism (for example Sweden). We also discussed the contributions of national HRD to economic development and human capital development in some of the BRICS countries, such as the role of national HRD in China as compared with Brazil, India and Russia (Ardichvili et al 2012). We also discussed in Chapter 4 the effects of culture on learning and training and development styles.

Here, however, we focus on the other two trajectories: international HRD, and in particular cross-cultural HRD, and cross-cultural training (CCT) at the enterprise level.

CULTURAL ADAPTATION, ACCULTURATION AND CCT

> If you were in Rome, live in the Roman way; if you are elsewhere, live as they do there. (Proverb)

Does this old proverb still hold true even now? Although globalisation has produced a hybrid Westernised culture in many parts of the world, localisation remains an important aspect of doing business. The award-winning adverts from the HSBC banking group with the tagline 'the world's local bank' echo the imperatives of understanding the customs and needs of the local community for conducting good business. The preceeding chapters in Parts 1 and 2 introduced the cultural diversities awaiting the cross-cultural traveller. In this chapter, we look at the adaptation and acculturation issues experienced when crossing cultures, leading to the experience of culture shock (Oberg 1960). One explanation for this culture shock would be that Hofstede's 'software of the mind' (Hofstede et al 2010) does not work in a different cultural setting, and requires a degree of 'reprogamming' to make it work. This 'reprogamming' often takes the form of cross-cultural training (CCT), offered to both individals (such as the often-quoted expatriates and foreign students) and organisations wishing to expand in or collaborate with foreign markets, perhaps through mergers or joint ventures (Chapter 7).

CULTURE SHOCK AND ACCULTURATION

The current trend for globalisation has led to increased encounters between cultures. For example, during Japan's growth years between the 1970s and the 1990s, there was a 700% increase in British business travellers to Japan (Ward et al 2001). Statistics from the Chinese Ministry of Human Resources and Social Security showed that nearly half a million expatriates were living legally in China, including many from African countries. However, there is evidence of a high cost of using expatriates who often 'fail', leaving early or underperforming; there are not just the direct costs of recruitment, travel, support and training, but indirect costs to relationships, reputation and brand. This is often caused by a failure to adjust on international assignments (Black et al 1991), leading to poor performance (Copeland and Griggs 1985). In the previous chapter on recruitment we discussed some of these issues. This adjustment, or acculturation, process has been the subject of academic research. In Chapter 15 we looked at the role of recruitment and selection in reducing or avoiding such problems; here we look at another strategy: training and development.

A major theory of acculturation – or adaptation and adjustment to a different culture – is provided by Oberg (1960), who first used the term 'culture shock' to refer to the long-term process of adapting to new cultural behaviours, including physical, biological and social changes. Culture shock is often experienced as a lack of direction, a feeling of not knowing what to do or how to do things in a new environment, and not knowing what is appropriate or inappropriate. This feeling of culture shock generally sets in after the first few weeks of coming to a new place.

REFLECTIVE ACTIVITY 16.1

1   When have you, as a student, traveller or worker, experienced 'culture shock'?

2   What 'symptoms' did it display?

3   How long did it last?

4   What did you do to address it?

Oberg (1960) discussed culture shock in terms of four phases of emotional reactions – associated with a U-curve – to cross-cultural journeys:

1   *the honeymoon*, with emphasis on the initial reactions of euphoria, enchantment, fascination and enthusiasm (for example 'it's warm, the people are friendly, I love my flat!')

2   *the crisis*, characterised by feelings of inadequacy, frustration, anxiety and anger ('it's not working – I can't make myself clear – I'm just not getting through to people')

3   *the recovery*, including crisis resolution and culture learning ('I found trying to learn the language/socialise with colleagues/network outside work really helpful – I'm finally communicating!')

4   *the adjustment*, reflecting enjoyment of, and functional competence in, the new environment ('I'm enjoying this – it's going really well – I've met some great people – I don't want to go back!')

Oberg's U-curve theory of acculturation was later expanded by Gullahorn and Gullahorn (1963) to include 'reverse culture shock', when the cross-cultural traveller returns back to the home culture. This re-entry stage can be considered as a second cycle of adjustment. For example, 'some of my newly acquired behaviours are not in use in the old home culture; my old boss has retired; my colleagues seem to have left or been sacked by those new foreign owners; my spouse and kids miss the lifestyle; no one seems to want to know about what I've learned overseas or how we can apply it here!'

REFLECTIVE ACTIVITY 16.2

Discuss in groups about your personal experience when facing a new and distant culture, or returning to an old one. How much do you agree with Oberg's culture shock theory?

Emphasis has also shifted from the description of negative psychological experience associated with stress (Oberg 1960; Gullahorn and Gullahorn 1963) to viewing acculturation as a learning experience (Brislin 1981; Ward et al 2001) and accounting for the various factors that influence its outcomes. For example, Brislin (2000) suggests the importance of skills in *cross-cultural contact*, including language and communication skills. Thus the foreigner's efforts to speak the language of the host country, even imperfectly, may be appreciated by the host nationals – though this has not always been found by the British in Paris, nor by foreigners in Britain! Such skill stimulates *interaction effectiveness* during the acculturation process. Since adaptation can be learned as a skill, Brislin suggests *cross-cultural training* (CCT) can help overcome adaptation difficulties and decrease the possibility of stress. Indeed, intercultural adaptation is a function of uncertainty reduction – the more we know about the unknown ahead, the less the culture shock, and the easier it is to cope (Gudykunst and Hammer 1988), and the experience of culture shock becomes a learning experience (Adler 1991).

Black et al (1991) provide a useful framework which integrates both acculturation and socialisation theories (for expatriates in particular) in the international business context, identifying three categories of *pre-departure* variables and two *post-arrival* variables.

The former includes *previous experience, pre-departure training* and *candidate selection* – already discussed in the previous chapter. The latter refers to *individual skills* (that is, self-efficacy, relation skills and perception skills) and *non-work factors* (that is, family adjustment and culture novelty). The socialisation framework is termed 'domestic adjustment', consisting of two stages: prior to entry and after entry.

Before entering the organisation, both individual factors (that is, accurate or realistic expectations) and organisational factors (that is, selection mechanisms and criteria – again, poor or missing!) are very important, since they result in *anticipatory adjustment*, which may be helped by a *realistic job preview* rather than an over-optimistic picture trying to 'sell' the asignment to the assignee.

After entry, three factors influence adjustment: *organisational socialisation factors* (that is, socialisation tactics), *job factors* (that is, role clarity, role discretion, role novelty and role conflict) and *organisational culture factors* (that is, organisational culture novelty and social support). These factors influence mode and degree of adjustment, as illustrated in Figure 16.1.

Figure 16.1: Adjustment to new culture

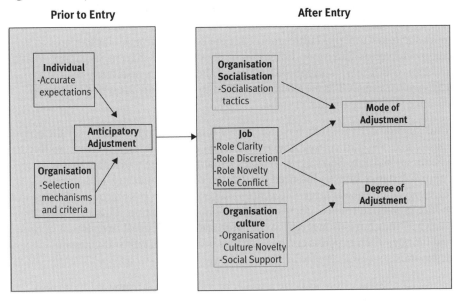

(Source: Black et al 1991)

According to Littrell and colleagues (2006: 356), *cross-cultural* training (CCT) can be defined as 'the educative processes used to improve intercultural learning via the development of the cognitive, affective, and behavioral competencies needed for successful interactions in diverse cultures'. *Culture-specific* training usually refers to 'information about a given culture and guidelines for interaction with members of that culture' (Brislin and Pedersen 1976: 6) or training that is 'specific to a particular culture' (Triandis 1977: 21). *Culture-general* training would thus be 'such topics as cultural awareness and sensitivity training that allow one to learn about himself (or herself) as preparation for interaction in *any culture*' (Brislin and Pedersen 1976: 6). Psychological adaptation, social adaptation and motivational orientation can be affected by a number of factors here (Ward et al 2001). In designing CCT, the following factors appear to be important: *culture distance*, *language*, *communication* and *individual variables* (such as interaction with host culture and personal learning style).

CULTURE DISTANCE

Culture/cultural distance refers to how similar two cultures are in terms of dimensions such as language, religion, etc. Though geographically close, Spain and Morocco are culturally distant; though physically distant, the UK and New Zealand are culturally close. Berry (1980) found that variations in stress and culture change patterns were dependent to some extent upon the cultural and psychological characteristics of the culture group, and the degree and nature of previous contact with culturally diverse groups. Groups experience lower stress when their culture is more similar to the second culture – for example a French expatriate working in Belgium – and has greater contact with the other cultural group, as compared with a French expatriate in Kenya. Ward and Kennedy (1999) showed that English cross-cultural travellers in Singapore experienced more socio-cultural difficulties than Chinese counterparts; Malaysian cross-cultural travellers had more difficulties in New Zealand than in Singapore. Waxin and Panaccio (2005) highlighted that cultural distance is negatively related to adjustment, and CCT is an effective method to reduce the presence of culture distance felt by expatriates in India.

Thus cultural distance may have an impact on acculturation; the closer the home culture is to the host culture, the less difficulty or stress is experienced, leading to a better adaptation. Berry (1997) suggests that this is due to the fact that greater cultural distance implies the need for greater 'culture shedding' and 'culture learning', and perhaps large differences trigger negative inter-group attitudes and induce greater culture conflict, leading to poorer adaptation. This also suggests that CCT may have its biggest pay-off, and justify the biggest investment of time and money, when experienced by assignees moving to a culturally distant destination.

In addition to the extent and the attitude of interaction, Furnham (2004) also suggests that the *quality of interaction* (for example quality of friendship) with the host culture is sometimes more important. This suggests another important variable in determining investment in CCT – if the assignee is going to spend a long time interacting with locals in a position where high-quality interaction is necessary (for example a three-year stint for a British expatriate as B&Q store manager in China – Gamble 2003), CCT is highly recommended. If the assignment is a one-week technical assignment with little time spent with locals, CCT may not be necessary, or may be quite brief.

Bochner et al (1977) suggest friendship networks for foreign students are helpful, including bonds with fellow compatriots, and formal and informal relationships with local students, other overseas students, teachers, university staff and government officials. These interactions form the basis of a 'social capital', commonly termed as '*guanxi*' in the Chinese context, but very important in any social setting. Communication interactions among members of intercultural groups can be eased with the use of social capital, the goodwill that has been built up between group members. If multinational group members expect that other group members will behave with respect and consideration toward them, they will be inclined to interpret a cultural *faux pas* as unintended, and the result of not knowing cultural differences in acceptable behaviour, rather than a calculated insult.

INTERACTION WITH HOST CULTURE NATIONALS AND ADAPTATION

A journey of a thousand miles begins with a single step. (Lao-Tsu)

Interaction with host culture nationals can usually be considered from three aspects: *attitude*, *extent* and *quality* (Ward et al 2001). Thus the success of CCT depends on the attitude of the cross-cultural traveller to the move, the perception of whether this is a short, temporary period or a long stay, and the quality of the interactions, as we suggested above.

The degree of voluntariness in migration motivation or expatriation, for example, is an important factor affecting the acculturation process. Richmond (1993) suggests that 'reactive' and 'proactive' form two extreme types of migrant; the former are motivated by factors experienced as constraining or exclusionary, and generally negative in character. The latter are motivated by factors that are experienced as facilitating or enabling, and generally positive in character. These contrasting factors have also been referred to as *push/pull* factors in the literature (Berry 1997). In a common scenario involving business meetings, success is dependent on whether each party is willing to make it work. A proactive attitude will result in a greater willingness to engage with the new culture and proactively seek opportunities to interact with the host culture. Ward et al (2001) also found that international students with more extensive interactions with host nationals, and who are more satisfied with these relationships, experience fewer socio-cultural adaptation problems (for example stress, homesickness) than others. The extent of interaction can result from friendship, education, accommodation, daily language used, cultural knowledge and effective communication (Hammer et al 1978; Brislin 1981).

LANGUAGE TRAINING

> If you talk to a man in a language he understands, that goes to his head. If you talk to him in his own language, that goes to his heart. (Nelson Mandela)

If culture is communication, the reverse is also true: communication is culture (Selmer 2006). Boyer (1990: B4) points out that people 'should become familiar with other languages and cultures so that (they) will be better able to live, with confidence, in an increasingly interdependent world'. Thus, to live in another culture without learning some of the host language is counterproductive to successful cultural adjustment. Some attempts at using the local language are necessary to demonstrate an interest in the people and/or culture. Language thus becomes the means that promotes the development of culture.

As a legacy of the British Empire and later US global dominance, English is normally regarded as an international language, playing an important part even in countries with few or no historical ties to the UK; it is learned as the principal foreign language in most schools in western Europe and Asia. However, according to the CIA World Fact Book, only 5.6% of the world's total population actually speaks English as a primary language. If we include people who speak English as a second or third language, the number barely makes up 20% of the world's population. However, with the emergence of China as an economic power, Mandarin is now regarded as a desirable second language to learn, especially in East Asia. This is supported by the increased numbers of Confucius Institutes (http://en.wikipedia.org/wiki/Confucius_Institute) set up by the Chinese Government in multiple locations around the world to promote Chinese language and culture.

Communication is crucial to management; but communication depends on a common language, a condition that seldom exists in many international business settings. We explored some of the issues involved in interpretation and translation in Chapter 7 on knowledge transfer in alliances. A study from Western expatriates in China found that the English language was mainly used at work (Selmer 2006) as English proficiency of Chinese is increasing, especially in larger first-tier cities like Beijing and Shanghai.

However, language cannot be seen as separate from its cultural context; subtleties of 'who to talk to, how to talk, when to talk, what to talk about' can be lost. Similarly, a conversation or business meeting conducted in a local language can easily lose its subtleties if one side (the Westerner) is not a native speaker. Indeed, Tannen (1981) argued that socio-cultural knowledge affects interpretation and fluency in a language but does not necessarily ensure accuracy in intercultural communication (Gass and Varonis 1991). Furthermore, a study of Canadian and Chinese university students showed that listeners in intercultural groups could retrieve only 50% of the information sent, versus 75% in intra-cultural situations (Li 1999), meaning that language ability alone was not enough for intercultural communication. Interestingly, a study on non-native Asian speakers of English found that they could speak more easily with other non-native speakers, regardless of their native culture or language, than with a native English speaker (Lee 2003).

REFLECTIVE ACTIVITY 16.3

1   Has this been your experience?   2   If so, why do you think this is the case?

Hence, we may argue that to interact competently, you need to know not only the language, but also the cultural rules of the other party. Language ability and proficiency in cultural rules together provide a capacity for effective communication activities. Taken separately, neither one is sufficient. These observations strongly suggest that language training should be combined with cultural training and preparation. Thus governmental language centres, such as the Confucius Institute, Cervantes Institute, l'Alliance Française and the British Council (www.britishcouncil.org) also provide programmes of cultural events to promote the advancement of the culture as well as the language. In a similar vein, newspapers report of staff at Indian call centres (non-native English speakers) getting crash courses in popular British culture (for example watching videos of British soaps and reading tabloid newspapers) and training about Britain's unfailingly changeable climate, the royal family and Premier League games (Hills 2011).

COST OF SCRAPPING FOREIGN LANGUAGES HITS HOME

CASE STUDY 16.1

British diplomats used to be admired worldwide for their foreign language skills, but new figures show that just one in 40 is fluent in the language of the country in which they have been posted. Most lack even a basic grasp sufficient for day-to-day exchanges.

The figures were uncovered by the Conservative MP Stephen Barclay, who sits on the UK's Public Accounts Select Committee, and MPs fear Britain could be losing lucrative trade deals as a result. They say the problem is in part the legacy of a decision by the Treasury when Gordon Brown was Chancellor to close the Foreign Office language school to save £1 million a year.

In India, whose government has declared France the preferred bidder over Britain to supply 126 fighter jets in a £7 billion deal, just one UK diplomat can speak Hindi. There is only one Arabic-speaking diplomat registered in each of the UK's embassies in the oil states of Oman, Qatar, Saudi Arabia and Yemen.

Figures show that 48 of Britain's 1,900 diplomats receive extra pay because they have an 'extensive' grip of a

language, meaning they are close to communicating like a native. Another 145 have an 'operational' grasp, meaning they can cope with day-to-day life in the country. Fifteen are recognised as having language 'confidence', defined as being able to read road signs and book a hotel room. But some 1,690 staff, or 90% of Britain's diplomatic service, have no recognised language abilities for the country to which they have been posted.

(Source: Holehouse 2012)

Questions

1   Do you think diplomats in the case study should have language training? Why?

2   What other forms of training and development would be useful?

3   When should this be given, and what form do you think it should take?

4   How might it be evaluated?

DESIGNING CROSS-CULTURAL TRAINING

Tung (1981) identifies five different training programmes, which are complementary to each other and dependent on the type of job and country of foreign assigment. The higher the culture distance, the more CCT is required. The different training modes are:

1   *Didactic training*, delivery of training via lectures, briefings or written materials. Practical information and facts about the host culture are given, such as living conditions and cultural differences, providing a framework for evaluating new situations and enhancing cognitive skills to enable assignees to understand the host culture (Littrell et al 2006).

2   *Culture assimilators*, one of the most popular methods of CCT, especially in the USA, using a series of scenarios or incidents that normally involve culture clash or misunderstandings to prepare people for interacting with a specific

culture. Trainees are normally given scenarios and choice of explanations of a problem; feedback is obtained on the appropriateness of the choice made.

3   *Language training*: this can range from basic greetings to fluency in the host language.

4   *Sensitivity training* focuses on teaching trainees that other cultures have different ways of doing things, preparing assignees to accept cultural differences and to improve the motivation for interactions with the host culture.

5   *Field experience* refers to learning on the job, involving assignments to the host culture directly or to a 'microculture' (such as a local Chinatown or Little Tokyo, if the host culture is China or Japan). While microcultures are not exactly similar to the host culture, the experience gained by the trainee is beneficial for understanding the host culture.

As CCT prepares the assignee for potential difficulties during the foreign assignment, it also forms a level of expectations about the job. The theory of *met expectations* proposes that the closer the individual's expectations to the reality encountered, the greater the adjustment will be (Wanous et al 1992). Caligiuri et al (2001) found that pre-departure training helped provided expatriates with the skills for acculturation, forming expectations of the assignment; the more realistic these were, the more likely the expectations would be met or exceeded, leading to easier adjustment. Furthermore, in the absence of complete information, assignees who spoke the language of the host culture expected the assignment to be easy, leading to potential problems when expectations did not match reality, as experienced by some American expatriates in the UK (Wall 1994). On the other hand, those who did not speak the language may expect a difficult assignment.

Others have put forward other models; Black and Mendenhall (2007) have developed a similar framework, but refer to three modes of training and development:

- *factual* – didactic training in the form of lectures or handouts
- *analytical* – provision of analytical theories and models
- *experiential* – providing direct interaction with other cultures, as in field trips, projects, multicultural action learning, role-plays and multicultural outdoor development.

They argue that these modes vary both in terms of *rigour* and the extent of *modelling processes* (experiential modes use far more modelling than factual ones). When to use which depends in part on the *degree of culture novelty* (going to a culturally distant country suggests more experiental methods be used as compared with a close one, where factual briefings may suffice) and the *degree of interaction* expected with locals (the more expected, the more justification there is for using experiential methods).

Gudykunst and Hammer (1983) present a typology of CCT processes that distinguishes them in terms of:

- *methods of delivery*, for example didactic (cognitive) vs experiential (emotional/behavioural)

- *content*, for example culture-general vs culture-specific
- *focus*: work-oriented only, or private-life oriented, or both
- *arena*: is it delivered in a classroom or training room, or at work, perhaps through on-the-job learning, coaching and mentoring, or in virtual environments through e-learning or virtual learning environments?

REFLECTIVE ACTIVITY 16.4

1   What are the advantages of each of these approaches, in your experience?

2   Remembering our discussion of learning styles in Chapter 4, which mode is likely to suit which style?

We can map these approaches using the axes 'open vs closed' and 'culture-general vs culture-specific (Figure 16.2). A 'closed-specific' approach might be a briefing or handout on a specific culture; an 'open-specific' approach might involve a bi-cultural action learning set or reading a novel or biography of a local's experiences; here no one can predict the emergent outcomes, or what different individuals make of them. A closed-general approach might involve a general cultural model being presented, for example Hofstede (2001); an 'open-general' approach might involve multicultural action learning sets, projects or outdoor training, or reading multiple biographies or novels.

Figure 16.2: Modes of CCT

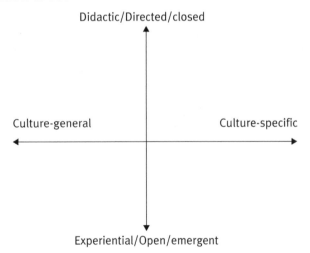

Mendenhall et al (2004) found lectures, presentations, culture assimilators and discussions to be the most frequently used methods; these were useful for knowledge transfer but less effective in changing behaviour and attitudes and enhancing adjustment and performance.

Pre-departure training, especially imparting basic information, has been found to positively affect the accuracy of prior expectations and subsequent adjustment

(Caligiuri et al 2001). Waxin and Panaccio (2005) found that CCT accelerated the adjustment of expatriates, but that this was moderated by prior international experience; CCT had its largest impact on those with little prior international experience. Cultural distance also moderated this effect; CCT tended to have most effect with greater cultural distance between home and host country. The type of CCT used also had an effect; experiential methods were generally more effective, especially if 'culture-specific'.

Examples of CCT include the use of dramas and other simulations in exploring decisions to invest in Mexico or China (Lewis 2005) and 'blended action learning', combining face-to-face action learning sets in five European partner countries and an e-learning platform called the 'Cultural Fluency Club'. These were used to develop cross-cultural skills and cultural awareness by sharing knowledge and experiences of SME leaders (Stewart 2008). Another example is the executive training programme (ETP) for European companies in Japan, mixing language training, seminars, company visits and in-house training in a hybrid blend of experiential and analytical methods in small groups (Lievens et al 2003).

In terms of content, Chien and McLean (2011) explored the Taiwan-specific intercultural training needs of US expatriates from the perspective of expats and locals: a 'culture-specific' approach. Relevant content included knowledge of Taiwan, relationship-building, interpersonal communication, business protocol, legal issues and living in Taiwan. US colleagues felt all items were needed more strongly than local colleagues.

Tung (1981) recommends a mixed training programme; first, pre-departure training would be offered, including didactic activities and culture assimilators. On arrival, training would switch to experiential learning. Finally, at the end of the assignment, didactic debriefings are offered to update the expatriate on the home organisation while he was on assignment.

Tarique and Caligiuri (2004) present a three-stage programme of CCT: *pre-departure*, involving online training needs analysis and briefing; *intial post-arrival*, using CCT with e-support and coaching; and *later post-arrival*, using more sophisticated CCT with e-support, such as CD-ROMs, DVDs, Internet/intranet-based training, multimedia and distance/blended learning.

Tarique and Caliguri (2004: 285) have also put forward some guidelines for designing effective CCT:

- *Identifying the type of global assignment* for which CCT is needed; is the position technical, functional, high-potential or strategic/executive?
- *Determining specific CCT needs*: what are the organisational context, the individual needs and level of the assignment?
- *Establishing goals and measures* to determine CCT effectiveness in the short and long term, such as cognitive, affective and behavioural changes necessary to enhance adjustment and success.
- *Developing and delivering CCT*: deciding the content, the methods, the sequencing and which models to use; the mix of didactic and experiential

methods; and whether delivered pre-departure, post-departure or both. Basic didactic information may be appropriate pre-departure, deeper experiential learning post-departure.

- *Evaluating the programme's success* against stated goals, for example adjustment might be measured by interviews, surveys and appraisal records balancing home- and host-culture data sources; CCT may be linked with other HR practices, especially recruitment, selection, reward, appraisal and career/talent management.
- *Considering the training needs of HCNs and TCNs*, not just PCNs, as we saw in joint ventures (Chapter 7).

Other issues include (Briscoe and Schuler 2004):

- Who delivers CCT? Corporate HQ? Regional HQ? Local affiliates? This is likely to be related to the international orientation of the firm.
- Should each subsidiary/JV develop its own CCT?
- Who takes responsibility? The company? The affiliate? The regional HQ? The individual?
- Should CCT be exported or employees brought to regional or centralised training centres?
- Should it be localised or integrated into a global programme?
- What are the effects of language differences? These may be especially potent if translators are used.

TRAINING NEEDS ANALYSIS IN CCT

Tung (1981) presents a comprehensive flowchart for the selection and training of expatriates, proposing that a local national HCN, not a PCN, is the most desirable person for filling the assignment if possible. However, when not possible, the training needs of the selected assignee should be assesed on several factors:

1 willingness to go on the international assignment

2 degree of interaction required with the host culture

3 differences between home and host culture

4 personal circumstances.

If there is much interaction with the host culture (sales or marketing), or if the cultural difference is very large (for example, UK and Japan), all types of CCT programme should be offered. For smaller assignments (troubleshooting equipment) or when there are relatively few cultural differences (for example Canada vs UK), didactic training may be sufficient. Personal circumstances should also be considered, such as marital status, gender, family and location of the assignment (cosmopolitan city or sleepy town?).

Mendenhall and Oddou (1985) expanded US expatriate training needs into seven different profiles, based on degrees of self-orientation (SO), others-orientation (OO) and perceptual orientation (PO); for each, different training is required. SO refers to the degree to which the assignee engages in activities that represent concern for self-preservation, self-enjoyment and mental hygiene. OO refers to the degree to which they express concern for and desire to interact with host nationals. Finally, PO refers to the degree to which the assignee understands the nature and reasoning behind the host national behaviour. The seven expatriate profiles are:

1   *Ideal expatriate*: high on SO, OO and PO, likely to successfully adjust to the host culture and only require repatriation training.

2   *Academic observer*: high on SO and PO, but low on OO, and not interacting well with the host culture. Suggestions are to increase interactions through language training and simulations.

3   *Well-intentioned missionary*: high on SO and OO but low on PO, misinterpreting situations and unaware of host culture and values. Suggestions are to increase cultural awareness and practise interpreting situations.

4   *Type A expatriate*: high on PO, but low on SO and OO, so good intercultural skills but stressed very easily. Suggestions are to give more culture assimilator training and role-plays.

5   *Introvert*: high on SO and PO, but low on OO; does not interact well and exhibits socially inappropriate behaviours. Suggestions are to improve language fluency and learn culturally appropriate behaviours through culture assimilator training.

6   *Ugly American* (sic!): high on SO but low on OO and PO; very high self-confidence but low interpersonal skills and exhibits socially inappropriate behaviours, requiring culture assimilator and sensitivity training.

7   *Dependent expatriate*: high OO but low SO and PO; good interpersonal skills but stressed easily and does not understand the host culture. Suggestions are to increase cultural awareness.

REPATRIATION TRAINING

Many employees may accept foreign assignments believing they will create career opportunities and advancement (Mendenhall et al 2002; Stahl et al 2002), perhaps drawn from popular press accounts and anecdotal evidence (Fisher 2005). However, the reality may be different; a study of 1,001 chief executives revealed that international experience, from longer and multiple assignments, instead often slowed career advancement (Hamori and Koyuncu 2011). Black et al (1991) found that only a few employees were promoted when they returned, and most companies did not give post-expatriation employment guarantees (Tung 1998). Up to 50% of returnees were no longer employed by their companies within two years of returning (Black 1989; Stroh et al 1998), often feeling that new skills and knowledge acquired were not valued by the company.

Given the costs of foreign assignments, it is in the organisation's interest to maximise its investment. Thus the final stage of CCT should focus on *repatriation training*, an often overlooked area, especially as it is often assumed that the return to the home country does not require any special adjustment. However, repatriation is often not easy, with many finding it frustrating and stressful (Mendenhall and Oddou 1985; Shen and Hall 2009) with reverse culture shock when returning to the home culture. Expatriates often seem to consider their assignment as an exile from the home office, where 'out of sight is out of mind' (Ramsey and Shaetti 1999), fearing that they are being sidelined from promotions. There is also the (rational) fear that their international experience is not valued (Bolino 2007). Furthermore, many expatriates consider their assignments as a 'sacrifice' for the company, for which they expect appreciation in the form of a promotion (Stahl et al 2002).

Thus repatriation training should include the following:

1   *Clear career development plans*, so that assignees understand the reasons for the assignment and the benefits for acceptance (Feldman and Thomas 1992). While this should not imply guarantees, it should provide motivation for successful completion of the assignment.

2   *Regular updates* with the home office, for example 'home' mentor (Feldman and Thomas 1992) or regular visits back to the home office (Guzzo et al 1994) to help assignees maintain their network of colleagues on return and increase awareness of internal career opportunities.

Although these are helpful for the repatriation success, they also require that the organisation is willing and able to use assignees' international experience and skills. Specifically, the organisation needs to have a global strategic posture (Kostova and Roth 2003). For example, the banking group HSBC has a dedicated programme for international managers. Furthermore, for smaller organisations, the top management team should also have extensive international experience, so that the value of expatriates' experience can be properly assessed and deployed (Reuber and Fischer 1997).

REFLECTIVE ACTIVITY 16.5

Visit the International Management Programme for HSBC in detail:

http://www.hsbc.com/1/2/careers/im/about

1   How useful do you think this is?

2   Based on the aforementioned theories, do you think HSBC's International Management Programme is effective?

QUALIFICATIONS FOR CCT TRAINERS

Effective trainers are important to a successful CCT programme (Eastwood and Renard 2008). Kohls (1984) suggested the following criteria for successful trainers:

1   experience of living abroad for at least two years

2   experience of culture shock personally

3   comprehensive knowledge of host country, including religion, politics, cultural values, accepted business practices

4   clear understanding of home culture, so as to distinguish home from host

5   positive attitude to cultural experience.

Furthermore, they should have sound knowledge of the acculturation process, be familiar with the literature on expatriate acculturation and have the ability for one-on-one training.

While these are general guidelines, it would also be important to consider the learning style of the expatriate's culture, as CCT in itself can also be subject to cultural differences. As we have seen in previous chapters, differences in learning styles can affect the training process; what works for one type of culture may not work for the other. For example, Sarkar-Barney (2004) found that experiential training programmes are very common in the United States, an individualistic and low power distance culture, but may not be suitable for collectivist cultures, which may prefer didactic training. Furthermore, the study found that interaction between trainers and trainee was also important, highlighting the importance of matching trainers to trainees and to having suitable trainers.

LEARNING SUMMARY

In this chapter, we covered the acculturation aspects of the cross-cultural traveller. The experience of culture shock should be viewed positively as a learning experience, and CCT programmes should help reduce the uncertainty about the unknown culture and improve adjustment to the host culture. We explored some design and implementation issues in CCT, such as when, where and how to deliver training and development, and open vs closed methods or factual vs analytical vs experiential learning, and what to include in terms of culture-general and culture-specific content. We also gave some company examples, and considered the final stage of expatriation, successful repatriation to the home culture, and proposed repatriation training to improve retention. Throughout, the use of multiple mentorships for pre-departure, expatriation and repatriation stages is a valued strategy for improving acculturation and successful outcomes (Mezias and Scandura 2005). International mentoring, while costly, has benefits that can easily outweigh the costs, helping give advice on adjustment and career advancement. Mentors may gain information on foreign assignments and a more global perspective without having to go abroad themselves, and both parties can benefit from the increased social capital.

As a final note, it is suggested that all CCT should be evaluated; training and development programmes are often costly, and the organisation expects a return on its investment (McNulty and Tharenou 2004). Psychometric and acculturation tests used during training needs analysis can be re-used throughout to assess the effectiveness of training. While there might be issues with the type of tests used (Cardon and Barlett 2006), such feedback may be valuable. As no two organisations are the same and no two foreign assignments the same, feedback can enable better and more effective training and development programmes to be tailored to particular needs.

QUESTIONS

1   Explain Oberg's culture shock theory and its implication for international human resource management/development practice.

2   Discuss how to employ Tung's theory to develop a CCT programme for sending an international manager to one of the BRICS countries.

3   Debate whether CCT for repatriation is a return on investment or a cost for an organisation.

CHAPTER 17

Global Talent Management

Paul Iles and Xiaoxian Zhu

LEARNING OUTCOMES

By the end of this chapter, you should be able to:

- Identify and analyse approaches to global talent management (GTM).

- Define and apply the concept of employer branding to GTM.

- Appreciate national and corporate differences in GTM policy and practice.

- Consider and analyse some key theoretical perspectives on GTM.

- Evaluate the implications of the above perspectives for international HRM.

INTRODUCTION TO TALENT MANAGEMENT

This chapter discusses talent management (TM) in a global context – global talent management (GTM) – with particular reference to issues of branding, recruitment and selection, development and retention. It explores comparative talent management practices and the management of international talent including (but not limited to) expatriates. It also discusses national and corporate differences in GTM policy and practice, as well as the application of the concept of employer branding to GTM.

WHAT IS DRIVING THIS INTEREST IN TM?

Talent management is a fairly new term and concept in IHRM; what is driving this interest, and why are IEs and researchers now interested in it? Talent management (TM) is a term in common use today, yet it did not appear until the late 1990s, when McKinsey & Company first referred to it in their report, and later, book, *The War for Talent* (Michaels et al 2001). TM was claimed to be critical to organisational success, giving a competitive edge through the identification, development and redeployment of talented employees. Interest in TM has been driven by a variety of factors:

- the shift from an industrial to a knowledge/information age
- the intensifying global demand for high-calibre talent, especially managerial and professional talent

- the growing propensity of employees to switch companies and careers and the rise of 'boundaryless' careers as people increasingly cross national, organisational and career boundaries
- work–life balance issues
- demographic changes, such as ageing populations in much of Europe and Japan, changes in the international division of labour, and increased population migration.

Figure 17.1 shows the impact of some of these changes.

Figure 17.1: Drivers of talent management

Technological change, changing business models, the 'knowledge economy' and the globalisation of markets have increased the demand for highly skilled people. Think of the English Premier League; until the 1980s most players were British, and foreign coaches and owners a rarity. Now it recruits players from everywhere in the world; many top managers are foreign; and increasingly this is also true of owners and investors. Meanwhile, workforce ageing and an inadequate supply of young talent in many European countries and Japan – and even China (Chapter 14) – have created a supply gap in many labour markets. This is less true of the UK and USA, given higher levels of immigration of younger workers. The creation, development and retention of a 'talented' workforce, which is more mobile and informed than ever before, has increasingly come to be the focus of IHRM strategies and attention.

So with such demographic shifts, many organisations across the globe have faced a major and potentially long-term struggle to fill job vacancies with appropriately skilled employees. Associated with these demographic shifts, the nature of the psychological contract has changed. Talent shortages have meant that the labour market has swung back towards the job-hunter's advantage (though it may swing back again in any recession).

The management of senior managers and 'high-potential' people who have been identified as strategic human resources has therefore been recognised as a key role for the corporate HR function, especially in the global firm (Scullion et al 2010; Scullion and Collings 2006, 2011). Martin and Hetrick (2006) argue that as the knowledge economy continues to develop, the value of 'outstanding talent' will continue to be recognised. International talent flows are increasing as economies become more 'knowledge-based' (de Cieri et al 2009).

TM is often projected to be the next core competency in HR domain expertise (Morton et al 2005 ; Sandler 2006). Can HR can add more value by effective TM? Boudreau and Ramstad (2005) contend that TM requires a new paradigm for HR, while Berger (2004) believes that TM will become the primary responsibility for HR departments; 'traditional' HR activities will be outsourced, transferred to employees through technology or delegated to line managers. The remaining in-house HR functions will focus upon talent matters, including the nurturing of an organisational climate which fosters and stimulates 'talented individuals' through tailored employment packages. Indeed, Bersin (2007: 15) claims that TM means that the HR professional has become the 'steward of the organisation's talent management process'.

WHAT ARE THE IMPLICATIONS OF THIS?

For many, TM raises many issues for management, organisations and HRM, as it challenges bureaucratic emphases on systems and structures (talent, it is argued, involves an organisation-wide change towards a TM 'mindset') and egalitarian models of HRM. TM presents a differentiated or segmented view of the workforce in which certain talents are more highly prized than others. 'Talent' is a relative term – the talented exist in relation to the 'un'- or 'less' talented (as we will see later, however, the 'inclusive' perspective takes a rather different view). This perspective on TM has often been inspired by marketing theory, especially by concepts of *employer branding* (Jiang and Iles 2011).

WHAT IS TALENT MANAGEMENT?

There has been much exhortation and prescription on TM, particularly from consultants (Duttagupta 2005), but less academic research (Boudreau and Ramstad 2005); Lewis and Heckman (2006: 139–40) claim that 'the terms in the debate are not clear and confuse outcomes with processes with decision alternatives' (a position already encountered, as we have seen in Chapter 15 on competence) and point out:

> given the number of consulting firms engaging in talent management and the growing numbers of articles and books on the topic, one might also believe 'talent management' to be a well-defined area of practice supported by extensive research and a core set of principles … [but] the terms in the debate … are not clear and confuse outcomes with processes with decision alternatives.

For the Society of HRM in the USA, TM involves:

integrated strategies or systems designed to increase workplace productivity by developing improved processes for attracting, developing, retaining and utilising people with the required skills and aptitude to meet current and future business needs. (Lockwood 2005: 1)

The CIPD (2009b: 2) defines TM as:

the systematic attraction, identification, development, engagement/ retention and deployment of those individuals with high potential who are of particular value to an organisation; [talent is defined as] those individuals who can make a difference to organisational performance, either through their immediate contribution or in the longer term by demonstrating the highest levels of potential.

A joint Chartered Institute of Management/Ashridge study (Blass 2009: 2) sees TM as 'the additional management, processes and opportunities that are made available to people in the organisation who are considered to be "talent"'; every organisation has a TM system, whether by default or design – all organisations manage talent in some way, whether implicitly or explicitly.

REFLECTIVE ACTIVITY 17.1

What do these definitions of TM have in common?

An important element in common in these definitions is that talent is seen as an attribute *of individuals*; it refers to individual potential, performance or ability to add value to organisations. Another common factor is that *talent is 'exclusive'*; only some employees have it! In fact, this argument had been made in HRM long before the term was widely used. Purcell (1999: 35–6) points out that for sustainable competitive advantage ... the firm must be able to have resources and utilise them in ways that are rare and cannot be copied, adding that it is the ability to identify a distinctive group of employees who, for whatever reason, constitute this intangible strength that is important ... in practice the resource view will nearly always involve the identification of a core group of employees, sometimes small in number. This will involve the development of distinctive policies and practices to maximise their performance ... and a simultaneous differentiation with non-core, peripheral workers who may not be employees of the firm.

Purcell did not use the term 'talent management' for these practices, nor 'talent' for this small core group, but does give the rationale for adopting the terms. Of course, we need to first discuss and define what we mean by 'talent' if we are to define what we mean by 'talent management'.

REFLECTIVE ACTIVITY 17.2

1 How do you define the term 'talent', as distinct from other terms used in HRM such as 'skill' or 'competence'?

2 What do you understand by the terms 'talent pool' and 'talent pipeline'?

3 How helpful do you find these metaphors?

WHAT IS 'TALENT'?

Many organisations prefer to formulate their own meaning of talent rather than accept a universal or prescribed definition. Tansley (2011: 266) notes that 'people are rarely precise about what they mean by the term "talent" in organisations and the implications of defining talent for talent management practice' or the rationale for using the term, as distinct from skill, knowledge or competence. Talent is often defined in terms of an amalgam of skills, knowledge, ability, competence and potential; we noted in Chapter 15 that this has also been true of competence. Thus, organisations tend to have different talent targets.

REFLECTIVE ACTIVITY 17.3

1 Do you have the term 'talent' in your own language? If so, what is implied by it?

2 What particular talents do you have, perhaps as distinctive 'signature strengths' you are known and recognised for?

3 How do you use them at work and in education?

4 How have you developed them?

Share your answers in a pair or small group if possible.

Tansley et al (2007) found talent definitions in organisations mainly focused on the individual, with great variations over how talent was defined; talented individuals were often grouped into different *talent pools*, or collectives of employees defined as talent, and therefore 'talent-managed' to form a *talent pipeline*; Figure 17.2 shows different 'talent pools', which may refer to organisational level or function (for example sales, technical, leadership talent in an IT company; clinical, managerial, service in a hospital).

Figure 17.2: Talent pools

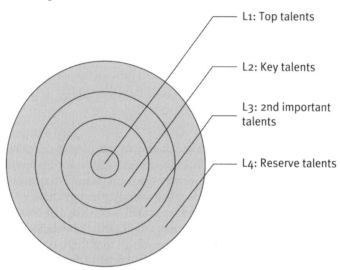

L1: Top talents

L2: Key talents

L3: 2nd important talents

L4: Reserve talents

While talent can be categorised as valuable, rare and hard-to-imitate, the specific prescriptions regarding 'talented employees' are unclear, and there is no universal definition of great talent. The definitions in use of talent will depend on an organisation's business strategy, the type of firm, the overall competitive environment, and so on, including culture. Therefore, it is often argued that definitions of talent should be tailored to individual organisations. As the CIPD (2007: 2) observes: 'TM requires HR professionals and their organisations to understand how they define talent, who they regard as "the talented" and what their typical background might be'.

A survey by Towers Perrin (2004) found that 87% of participants used a given definition of 'talent' consistently across their organisation; however, none of the 32 companies surveyed used the same definition, and definitions adopted depended on an organisation's business strategy, the type of firm, the overall competitive environment, and other factors (CIPD 2007). Accordingly, they recommend that definitions of talent be tailored to individual organisations, thus adopting a contingency approach (Towers Perrin 2004). Tulgan (2001) goes further, seeing little point in trying to define 'talent' because you 'know' who the valuable employees are; however, other commentators do feel that it is necessary and possible to define talent. Michaels et al (2001: xiii), for example, define talent very broadly as:

> A code for the most effective leaders and managers at all levels who can help a company fulfil its aspirations and drive its performance, managerial talent is some combination of a sharp strategic mind, leadership ability, emotional maturity, communications skills, the ability to attract and inspire other talented people, entrepreneurial instincts, functional skills, and the ability to deliver results.

For Williams (2000: 35), talented people are those who:

Regularly demonstrate exceptional ability and achievement either over a range of activities and situations, or within a specialised and narrow field of expertise; consistently indicate high competence in areas of activity that strongly suggest transferable, comparable ability in situations where they have yet to be tested and proved to be highly effective.

The dominant discourse in TM has been around the supposed global 'war for talent', where 'talent' refers to an 'exclusive' group of individuals showing high performance or high potential, able to add particular value to the organisation (Michaels et al 2001; Tansley et al 2007; Tansley 2009, 2011; Blass 2009; Beechler and Woodward 2009; Berger 2004).

We have seen, then, that defining talent has proved to be a challenging and problematic business for commentators – has this also been the case for talent management?

WHAT DOES TALENT MANAGEMENT INVOLVE?

As Ashton and Morton (2005: 30) have observed, '[Clearly] there isn't a single consistent or concise definition of TM'; Iles et al (2010c) identify three broad strands of thought regarding TM, often associated with a particular theoretical or disciplinary base (Lewis and Heckman 2006 present a related, but somewhat different, analysis).

TM is not essentially different from HRM

Both involve getting the right job at the right time and managing the supply, demand and flow of people through the organisation; TM involves a collection of typical HR activities such as recruitment, selection, training and appraisal. TM may then in this view just be a relabelling or rebranding exercise; replacing 'people' by 'talent' may enhance HR's credibility, status or 'fashionability' (as with earlier moves from 'personnel' to 'HRM'), but conceptualising TM in terms of the functions of traditional HRM seems to add little or nothing that is new to our understanding of how to manage talent strategically (Lewis and Heckman 2006). As Barlow (2006) has noted, TM could then in effect become a new label for HRM/D for many managers. We pursue this argument that TM is 'just the latest HRM fashion' a little later in this chapter, using neo-institutionalist theory that was first introduced in Chapter 1.

TM is integrated HRM with a selective focus

According to this view, TM may use the same tools as HRM, but the focus is on a relatively small segment of the workforce, defined as 'talented' by virtue of their current performance or future potential. TM thus covers a range of activities focused upon 'talented' individuals, with the key processes supportive of each other, focused upon selected, critically valuable employees. The key challenges are thus to attract, recruit, develop and retain such individuals (for example CIPD 2007; Iles 2007)), and TM consists of:

- *attracting* talent: branding, recruitment (Chapter 15)
- *retaining* talent: engagement, psychological contract (Chapter 19)

- *developing* talent: leadership development (Chapters 5 and 16)
- *transitioning* talent: assessment, deployment, promotion, succession, lateral movement, exit (Chapter 18).

Much of the theory adopting this perspective borrows concepts from *marketing* theory, such as *employer brand* and *workforce segmentation*, to focus on attracting and retaining key individuals (Tansley 2009; Martin and Hetrick 2006; Chapter 15).

TM is organisationally focused competence development through managing flows of talent through the organisation

The focus here is on talent *pipelines* rather than *pools*, and concepts are drawn from operational research and logistics theories; TM is akin to managing supply and demand and managing flows of people throughout the organisation (Cappelli 2008). This strand is more closely related to succession planning and human resource planning, and focuses primarily on talent continuity. TM is the strategic management of the flow of talented employees through a variety of roles and jobs in an organisation, often supported by software systems. TM programmes are designed to create talent pools that feed particular job classifications and focus on capturing and developing the individual skills, competencies and behaviours that make those jobs and employees successful in the future. The focus is more on developing an enterprise-wide, holistic 'talent mindset'. As Blass et al (2006: 1) note:

> TM is more than HRM, leadership development initiatives or succession planning. It is the collective approach to recruiting, retaining and developing talent within the organization for its future benefit, and extends beyond the domains listed above to include strategy, organizational culture and change management.

Case Study 17.1 shows how companies may adopt differing perspectives on what is 'talent' and what is 'talent management'.

 TALENT MANAGEMENT IN GRH

CASE STUDY 17.1

GRH employs over 900 staff, and the organisation has restaurants in London, the US and Europe as well as consultancies in Dubai and Tokyo. GR is co-chief executive (the other CEO is his father-in-law). He works closely with restaurant personnel and identifies creative talent in the workforce. The emphasis within the organisation is on developing talent rather than recruiting it in. As an example of this approach, the organisation frequently places a home-grown senior chef in charge of a new restaurant. As part of the training

for heading up a new restaurant, chefs are sent on a sabbatical to improve their cooking skills. These sabbaticals last between six and twelve months and usually involve working in prestigious restaurants outside the UK. Chefs are not required to return to the organisation at the end of the sabbatical but most do.

Source: adapted from CIPD (2007)

Questions

1 How would you characterise this approach to talent management?

2 To what extent does it display an 'integrated approach' to TM?

3 How effective is it at retaining talented individuals?

4 What other talent management initiatives might be considered?

DIFFERENT PERSPECTIVES ON TM

One question here is over the *theoretical and disciplinary base* of TM; what theories and disciplines have informed it? The TM literature has drawn upon a range of disciplines, including marketing (Tansley 2009), labour economics and operational research and supply chain theories (Cappelli 2008). Vaiman and Vance (2009) link TM to knowledge management: 'talented people' are seen as key agents in the creation, acquisition, transference and application of knowledge.

Blass (2009) identifies *process, cultural, competitive, developmental, HR planning* and *change management approaches* to TM. Various 'dimensions' concern the rationale for talent, the definition and entry point, how talent is managed, and the outcomes and benefits of TM. These dimensions include *the size of the talent pool, entry criteria, the breadth of the decision process, the permanency of the talent classification, whether recruitment is internal or external* and *the transparency of the talent system*. In terms of talent development, seven dimensions were identified: *the development path (accelerated or differentiated); the development focus (strengths or weaknesses); how much support is available ('sink or swim' or paternalistic); who influences the individuals' career; who they can talk to; the role of values;* and *tolerance of risk* in succession planning. In Case Study 3.1 in Chapter 3 a 'sink or swim' perspective was adopted, for example.

TM has also drawn on *employer branding*; just as product/service branding arguably leads customers to believe in a product or service and advocate purchase to others, so an employer brand encourages applicants to choose an organisation and advocate it to others, as well as giving existing employees reasons to stay and recommend the organisation to others. Different 'offers' or 'propositions' will therefore need to be targeted at different groups of employees and potential employees, just as different offers are made to different customer groupings (Case Study 15.1, Chapter 15).

These marketing-based definitions stress the need to segment not just 'people' (for example Boudreau and Ramstad 2005), but also 'positions' (for example Huselid et al 2005; Collings and Mellahi 2009). Drawing on Iles et al (2010c), we propose a framework identifying four types of talent management, based on the axes 'people vs position' and 'inclusive vs exclusive', to capture the contrasts in perspective between an *exclusive* (narrowly defined pool) versus an *inclusive* (widely defined pool) people focus, and a focus upon organisational *positions* (strategic or pivotal roles) as against the *people* themselves (focusing just on talented people, not on the roles they may occupy). Combining these contrasting perspectives results in the four-quadrant model captured in Figure 17.3.

Figure 17.3: Perspectives on talent management

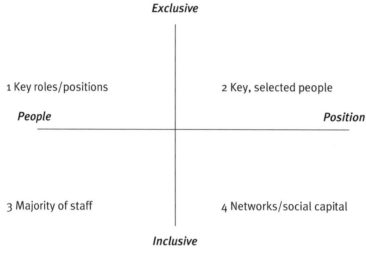

(based on Iles et al 2010c)

QUADRANT 1: EXCLUSIVE-PEOPLE

This TM perspective, perhaps the most common in practice if not in rhetoric, takes a relatively narrow view of talent as those people who have the capability to 'make a significant difference' to the current and future performance of the organisation. It takes the view that 'TM is integrated HRM with a selective focus'. An extensive range of the academic and practitioner literatures adopts this position; Berger (2004) talks about the 'superkeeper':

> Superkeepers are a very small group of individuals, who have demonstrated superior accomplishments, have inspired others to attain superior accomplishments, and who embody the core competencies and values of the organisation; their loss or absence severely retards organisation growth because of their disproportionately powerful impact on current and future organisation performance. (Berger 2004: 5)

On this view it is not possible for everyone in the organisation to be considered as a talent and managed accordingly – talented employees are fundamentally different in terms of their current and past performance and competence, as well as their potential, and should receive the bulk of the resources invested in such areas as training, development, leadership development and succession planning.

QUADRANT 2: EXCLUSIVE-POSITIONS

This perspective also takes a narrow/exclusive position, but on a different basis, going further in its focus on selectivity. For Huselid et al (2005), the talent-defining process is closely coupled with the identification of 'key positions' in the organisation; it makes little sense to 'top-grade' or recruit solely 'A players' across the enterprise, removing all 'C' players; the starting point of TM should be the identification of strategically critical jobs ('A positions') and only the people occupying those positions can be considered talents, receiving a disproportionate level of financial and managerial investment. Ideally a 'perfect match' of 'A players' and 'A positions' is expected to contribute to 'A performance'. Huselid et al (2005) argue that companies simply cannot afford to have 'A' players in all positions. A portfolio approach is recommended, placing the best employees in strategic positions, and good performers ('B players') in support positions; 'nonperforming' jobs and employees ('C players') that do not add value should be outsourced or eliminated.

This perspective also emphasises 'workforce differentiation' – talented 'players' should get disproportionate attention and investment according to the strategic importance of their position. Since marketing requires customer differentiation, doesn't talent management also require employee differentiation?

QUADRANT 3: INCLUSIVE-PEOPLE

In contrast to the above two exclusive perspectives on TM, this one takes an 'inclusive' stance, often from 'humanistic' considerations; potentially everyone in the organisation has 'talent' – the task is to manage all employees to deliver high performance. Everyone has a role to play and something to contribute; this inclusive 'whole workforce' approach to TM seems comparatively rare in practice (Clarke and Winkler 2006). Buckingham and Vosburgh (2001: 17–18) claim:

> The talent is inherent in each person. … HR's most basic challenge is to help one particular person increase his or her performance; to be successful in the future we must restore our focus on the unique talents of each individual employee, and on the right way to transform these talents into lasting performance.

Ashton and Morton (2005: 30) support this view, arguing that TM 'aspires to yield enhanced performance among all levels in the workforce, thus allowing everyone to reach his/her potential, no matter what that might be'.

QUADRANT 4: SOCIAL CAPITAL OR INCLUSIVE-POSITION PERSPECTIVE

This perspective views most TM writing as too dependent on an individualistic orientation, seeing talent essentially as a form of human capital, but neglecting the importance of context, social capital and organisational capital in relation to organisational performance. As we saw in Chapter 5, Iles and Preece (2006), following Day (2000), differentiate *leader* development (focused upon the individual, aimed at enhancing the human capital of leaders) from *leadership* development (focused upon collective/group actions aimed at enhancing social capital through developing bonds, bridges, trust and networks). In a similar vein, TM as usually defined over-stresses individual talents (attributes or characteristics of individuals), and downplays such factors as teams, cultures, divisions of labour, leadership and networks in giving talent direction and opportunity.

Organisational capital, in the form of routines and processes, can also be influential here, as shown by Groysberg et al's (2004) work. They found that when an organisation hired a 'star' from outside the organisation, the star's performance often plunged and he/she did not stay with the company for long. In addition, there was a sharp decline in the performance of the group the person worked with, and the company's market value fell. Organisations should therefore focus on growing talent internally and retaining stars who emerge; company-specific factors impact on the star's success, including resources and capabilities, systems and processes, leadership, internal networks, training and team membership.

Figure 17.4 shows an integrative framework for understanding TM (based on Iles et al 2010a; Preece et al 2011; Iles and Zhu 2012; Blass 2009). TM is driven by the increasing importance of knowledge, the global labour market, changing values and demographics and the use of IT. Its purpose is to attract and retain talent, ensure continuity of talent flows and develop organisational competence. Depending on the purpose selected, the organisation needs to choose a focus (Figure 17.4) and this will affect the dimensions of the talent pool used. The TM system will then employ specific TM practices.

Figure 17.4: TM framework

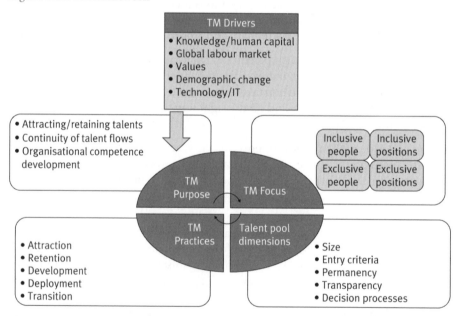

These different perspectives on TM and differences over how talent is to be defined and managed recur in discussions of global talent management, to which we next turn.

WHAT IS GLOBAL TALENT MANAGEMENT?

Interest in global talent management (GTM) has been driven by increasing recognition of the importance of global talent, by increasing global competition for talent (Beechler and Woodward 2009), and as a response to global talent shortages, which have constrained the implementation of global strategies. It has emerged as a critical element of strategic HRM in the MNE (Tarique and Schuler 2010), with increasing numbers of CEOs and corporate leaders spending time on it as a key priority, while often lacking the competence required to manage it effectively (Scullion and Collings 2011). GTM involves strategically integrating resourcing and development at the international level to proactively identify, develop and deploy high-performing and high-potential strategic employees on a global scale. For Farndale et al (2010), GTM refers to 'global organisational efforts to attract, select, develop, and retain talented staff as a key group of core employees'.

 REFLECTIVE ACTIVITY 17.4

In terms of the perspectives outlined in Figure 17.3, in which quadrant would you place these definitions of GTM?

Scullion and Collings (2006) have pointed out that GTM remains under-analysed as an identifiable area of theory, research and practice. 'Global' often implies a focus on standardisation across markets and centralised control from headquarters, with 'home' TM practices transferred to foreign affiliates, but there is considerable variation in GTM practice according to firm structure and strategy (Scullion and Starkey 2000; Farndale et al 2010) or national context (Hartmann et al 2010; Doh et al 2011; Iles et al 2010c; Preece et al 2011).

Scullion and Collings (2011: 4) define GTM in terms of 'strategic roles', moving the perspective to Quadrant 2 in Figure 17.3 and drawing attention to differences across national contexts to understand

the country/region specific contexts of talent management by providing comparative perspectives [and to examine the] global talent management strategies and practices in relation to the changing strategies of international business firms.

McKinsey have identified a number of global TM practices and challenges for international enterprises (http://www.mckinseyquarterly.com/ Why_multinationals_struggle_to_manage_talent_2140):

- global consistency of HR practices
- cultural diversity
- global leadership
- translating HR information into action
- relocating work to locations with talent
- shaping corporate agenda to include TM
- creating internal talent pools
- managing global assignments
- sourcing and recruiting global talent

- responding to changes in the global talent market.

Scullion and Collings (2006) have observed that TM approaches may vary across three distinctive HR forms of international firms: centralised, decentralised and transitional. Global firms wanting greater coordination and integration may prioritise greater central control over international manager/high-potential careers and mobility, while decentralised MNEs may pursue multi-domestic strategies with less coordination, centralisation or integration (Scullion and Starkey 2000, Farndale et al 2010). This may make the coordination of mobility across borders more problematic, as there may be greater tension between the short-term operational needs of the businesses and the long-term strategic plans of the company as a whole (Chapter 3). In addition, there is increasing recognition of 'the different nature of the challenges associated with the implementation of GTM strategies and policies in a variety of different contexts' (Scullion and Collings 2011: 4), such as different types of organisation where 'industry and organisational factors interact with institutional and cultural forces in shaping talent management in practice' (Scullion and Collings 2011: 4).

A major issue for GTM is how talent is defined, and who among the internal pool is defined as 'talented' for further development. This seems linked to national culture (Chapter 2). Holden and Tansley (2007) note that in Germany 'talent' is strongly related to specialised job knowledge, whereas in France it is associated with the precise and eloquent use of French. Kabwe (2011) comments that in Finnish, talent ('*lahjakkuus*' or '*kyky*') implies 'inborn' and 'domain-specific' attributes (for example mathematical or musical), which raises issues in companies committed to egalitarianism and low power distance. In a metal extractive MNE, the use of the term was avoided in favour of the more neutral term 'competence', yet the company in practice organised training and development programmes aimed at specific stratified talent pools or groupings – juniors, supervisory and senior managers. All this implies that GTM needs to be analysed in its specific socio-cultural context and, of particular interest here, the international orientation of the home country head office and the regional structure and mode of operation (see also Perlmutter 1969), as discussed in Chapter 3.

Mellahi and Collings (2010) identify several barriers to effective GTM in MNEs, such as a failure to promote talent from across the corporate network and blocking by corporate elites. Makela et al (2010) draw attention to factors influencing inclusion or exclusion in the talent pool in a Finnish MNE, such as cultural and institutional distance between the locations of decision-makers (Chapter 2) and the potential members of a talent pool; homophily between the individual and decision-makers; and the network position of the individual. McDonnell et al (2010 discuss some of the key challenges in the identification and evaluation of global talent, focusing on leadership and the tools that might be employed to achieve a balanced approach between internal and external labour markets.

Figure 17.5 shows some of the factors affecting Global TM.

Figure 17.5: Global TM

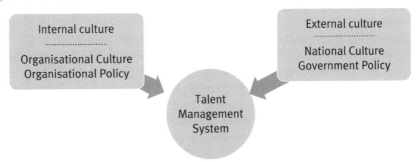

These points are drawn together by Evans et al (2011) in their discussion of the TM policies of the IE. Increasingly the 'multinational model of internal selection' is used; local affiliates recruit, select and develop professionals for functional jobs, and individuals from within these are then identified as high-potential 'talents' through nominations, assessment centres and performance reviews. There are a number of challenges and dilemmas here, many related to the overall *international orientation of the firm*, first discussed in Chapter 3:

- *When to identify potential* – early or late? Japanese companies may do this after graduation, expecting staff so identified to stay with them; Western and Chinese firms may fear poaching by competitors.
- *How much transparency* should there be about the decision? Egalitarian Nordic countries may be reluctant to make such decisions public, and fear possible demotivation of overlooked staff; American firms may worry more over the frustrations of high-potentials over lack of early recognition, while other firms may encourage self-nomination.
- *Who should be accountable*? Should the process be managed by the corporate or regional HQ, or the local country or business? If high-potentials are not 'corporate property', the local business may not pay enough attention to early career development. As Evans et al (2011: 211) comment:

> If the skill requirements at one level of responsibility are different from those at the next level of leadership, there are good arguments for suggesting that the process of identification and development of high-potential individuals should be managed by the corporation or region, not by the business or country. … Therein lies a major challenge for many multinational corporations … how to get the local company to pay attention to leadership development at early career stages. In a tightly run, cost-conscious local operation, there may not be much room for high-potential people with advanced degrees and high expectations but no hands-on experience. Furthermore, operationally oriented local HR managers may be ill-equipped to cope with the challenges of recruiting, developing and retaining such individuals. … An additional obstacle for leadership identification in multinationals is the natural tendency of subsidiary managers to act in their own interests and hide their best people (Mellahi and Collings 2010). The more one

praises an indispensable individual, the more likely it is that the person will be moved elsewhere in the name of corporate leadership development.

- *How to avoid bias in global talent reviews*: this is usually carried out with reference to some matrix, such as performance vs potential or fit with values or expectations to encourage open dialogue. Most interest is shown in those people assessed to be in the high-potential and performance boxes. However, this process may be biased against local 'distant' managers or HCNs lacking close relationships with corporate or regional HQ, damaging perceptions of justice. Senior executives therefore need to get to know local talent.

- *Going beyond identification*: in many companies there is emphasis on talent *assessment* rather than *development*. Evans et al (2011: 218–19) argue:

> Building co-ordination capabilities in a multinational firm requires 'unnatural acts' that will only occur if there is senior management intervention. If a company is to get out of its dependence on home-country expatriates in key positions, talented locals need experience in challenging line positions at the headquarters that will provide them with the matrix perspectives, the global mindset and the social networks to equip them for senior leadership positions in the regions. Yet these positions are precisely those that high-potential home-country nationals are jockeying to obtain. Without strong top-down leadership, probably from the highest levels, the path to transnational 'global *and* local' organisational development will be inevitably slow.

A common dilemma for IEs lies in optimising both short-term performance and long-term development of talents; for Evans et al (2011) these dilemmas include:

- *Balancing demand-driven and learning-driven assignments*: there are trade-offs between demands for 'immediate performance' (choosing experienced performers, perhaps locals) and 'learning and development' (choosing high-potentials) in assignments; though 'learning-driven' assignments are often accepted for expatriates, companies are less used to finding development roles for locals.

- *Focusing on 'A' positions as well as 'A' players*: 'Leadership development should therefore ensure that future leaders acquire experience in domains regarded as key capabilities ... development discussions should not focus excessively on individuals – the so-called A-players – without considering the A-positions ... that are critical to a firm's competitive advantage, as well as for the development of skills future leaders will need' (Evans et al 2011: 214). Problems arise when, as often is the case, the local business unit engages in succession planning in its own interest, while the region or corporate level maintains a talent pool of high-potential managers. This is essentially the view expressed in Quadrant 2 of Figure 17.3 (Huselid et al 2005).

- *Achieving the right amount of mobility*: job rotation or managed mobility and living and working overseas is seen as critical for developing global competencies, especially new challenges outside an area of expertise or 'comfort zone', requiring 'integrative skills'. However, too much mobility may compromise the ability to manage change, especially execution; it should be complemented by cross-boundary/function project assignment.

- *Succession planning versus talent pools*: 'succession planning may be viable in slower-moving, predictable work environments, but in many firms it is complemented by talent-pool management' (Huselid et al 2005: 216). Typically, local business units engage in succession planning, regions or corporate HQs engage in maintaining a talent pool to compete with the local designated successor.

Other researchers have drawn attention to GTM in its national, cultural and institutional context. Vaiman and Holden (2011) note the continuing absence of sufficient talent to operate businesses in a market economy in much of central and eastern Europe, despite the presence of high levels of skill and education in the region; here, TM may be interpreted by young graduates as offering opportunities to move abroad. Ali (2011) has drawn attention to how political instability in the Middle East has impacted human capital development, again encouraging talent emigration rather than talent retention.

In China, acute talent shortages and a series of institutional, cultural and sectoral challenges such as globalisation, the international migration of local talent and an ageing workforce threaten future supply; high turnover and 'poaching' have become issues, with less attention given to development, including leadership development (Cooke 2011c; Hartmann et al 2010). Hartmann et al (2010) found that German IEs in Shanghai had introduced more 'relational' activities to build 'team spirit' than back home in Germany, such as greater use of staff parties, events, social activities and sports events; this may reflect the greater importance given to these aspects of TM in more 'collectivist' countries such as China, as we saw in Chapter 2. Iles et al (2010a) in Beijing found only one of the four Western IEs they studied had adopted an 'inclusive-people' orientation (Quadrant 3 in Figure 17.3); most adopted an 'exclusive-people' view (Quadrant 1). However, the three consultancies they studied saw TM more in 'positional' terms, relating to Quadrants 2 and 4.

HRM and talent management (TM) in regional structures, as we noted in our discussion of regiocentric orientations in Chapter 3, is even more under-researched – we know little about how MNEs develop, promulgate, introduce and adapt TM to fit local/country/regional contexts.

THE GLOBAL DIFFUSION OF TALENT MANAGEMENT: IS IT A FAD OR FASHION?

Why has TM so quickly diffused globally? Many practices commonly associated with TM (such as assessment centres, succession planning and 360-degree appraisal) were developed as long ago as the 1950s (Cappelli 2008): is TM simply a repackaging of old ideas with a fresh name (Adamsky 2003)? Duttagupta (2005: 2) claims:

TM is a lot more than yet another HR process; the talent mindset is not just another HR fad. In the broadest possible terms, TM is the strategic management of the flow of talent through an organisation.

But is TM just a passing fad or fashion? One approach is to use print media indicators and bibliometrics – the number of publications on a concept in the course of time reflects interest in the topic. Journal article counts using the key words 'talent management' as a proxy for the development in popularity/fashion of the phenomenon were used by Iles et al (2010c) to reveal a notable increase in the number of articles relating to TM over this period. Does this show aspects of a fashion – though one yet to peak?

However, the Chinese companies studied by Preece et al (2011) denied they had 'followed fashion' in adopting TM, and the three consultancies all denied they were 'fashion-setters', or had adopted TM from pressures of 'mimetic isomorphism' (Chapter 1). All claimed TM had been adopted for solely technical, rational reasons – to address the challenges posed by the fierce 'war for talent' experienced in China. All denied it had been adopted for status or career or reputational reasons; however, these companies did concede they may be 'fashion-setters' for other, smaller, local companies in China. There was little evidence of normative isomorphism – there was no strong central professional body such as the CIPD in China – but they did concede some evidence of 'coercive isomorphism', partly from the state wishing to 'upgrade' China into a talent-driven economy, but more from corporate HQs in the USA, UK and Canada. These had developed corporate TM programmes and were keen to 'roll them out' to all their foreign affiliates, including their Chinese ones.

LEARNING SUMMARY

This chapter has analysed the concept of global talent management (GTM), beginning with a discussion of why TM has risen in popularity and how TM is defined, identifying three main perspectives in the literature. The chapter then explored different perspectives on TM – exclusive-people, exclusive-position, inclusive-people and inclusive-position – and the increasing influence of marketing theory on both HRM and GTM, in particular the concept of 'employee branding' and its impact on models of workforce segmentation and employee value propositions.

It then discussed GTM in particular, exploring how GTM varies with MNE strategy, cultural values and country of origin. The issue of whether GTM was merely the latest fashion or fad in HRM was then considered, and neo-institutional theory used to raise issues connected with the global diffusion of GTM and the implications of this debate for HRM practitioners.

CHAPTER 18

Managing the Performance of International Staff

Paul Iles

LEARNING OUTCOMES

By the end of this chapter, you should be able to:

- Appreciate changing perspectives on the importance and role of performance management (PM) in contemporary IEs.

- Understand the nature and purpose of performance management and performance appraisal in IEs, including the impact of cultural values on PM design, implementation and evaluation, and the characteristics of a successful PM system.

- Outline the stages involved in designing a performance management system in IEs.

- Identify and address the major challenges to PM in IEs and evaluate the implementation of performance management systems in IEs.

- Evaluate the contribution of 360-degree/multi-rater, multi-source feedback in PM in IEs.

INTRODUCTION

This chapter discusses performance management in a global context, with particular reference to issues of comparative appraisal practices and the management of the performance of international staff (including, but not limited to, expatriates). In recent years there has been increasing stress on organisational performance and competitiveness in IEs. This has meant a shift away from contracts of employment to contracts for *performance*, and a variety of HR initiatives have been attempted to maximise the contribution of individuals to organisational success. Effective PM in British hospitals helped clarify roles, identify training needs and made staff feel valued, leading to improved patient care and reductions in patient mortality (West et al 2002). Though it is difficult to obtain a single unambiguous 'objective' measure of performance (should we measure profitability, productivity or HR outcomes, such as wastage and turnover?), individual and team PM has come to be seen as an important strategy for enhancing individual, team and organisational effectiveness.

In this chapter, we focus on one key aspect of PM, *performance appraisal.* We do not discuss performance-related or merit pay in this chapter, but do so in Chapter 19 on reward management; Chapter 16 discussed the role of training and development in maintaining and improving performance.

PERFORMANCE APPRAISAL AND PERFORMANCE MANAGEMENT

Briscoe et al (2012: 344) define international PM as 'a designed, implemented and evaluated intervention of an MNE for the purpose of managing the performance of a global workforce so that performance (at the individual, team, and organisational level) contributes to the attainment of strategic global objectives and results in overall MNE desired performance'.

Once employees have been assigned to a role, the IE will need to evaluate how they are doing and how to maintain and improve their performance. PM has traditionally been seen in terms of performance appraisal – perhaps holding a meeting between an employee and a line manager to review performance over the year, with much emphasis on completing the relevant appraisal form. PM has, however, evolved away from this 'appraisal' model; it is now often seen as involving a framework of goals, objectives and standards. Setting goals, measuring goal achievement, giving feedback on performance and providing recognition and reward for high performance in order to add value to the organisation and enhance both current and future job performance are all part of PM. A comprehensive system of PM will incorporate the appraisal of performance alongside other initiatives, such as coaching, counselling, and performance-related pay. It may include:

1 *performance agreement*: defining objectives, identifying development needs

2 *performance monitoring*: reviewing performance

3 *performance reinforcement*: recognising and rewarding performance

4 *performance enhancement*: coaching, counselling, training and development.

Figure 18.1 shows how a PM system may be expected to operate; but does it do this in practice?

Figure 18.1: A performance management model

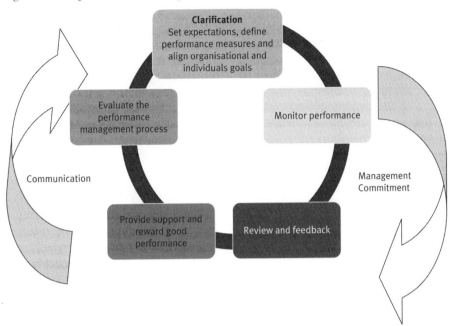

In this chapter, we focus on the first two steps, that is, performance appraisal (PA) leading to performance agreement, leading to performance planning and performance evaluation. We also explore why PM has often not met the expectations set for it, leading to attempts to employ more varied feedback (for example so-called 360-degree appraisal) and broader performance measures (for example behaviours and values, not just goals and objectives).

One example of a PA system in a south-east Asian government department (civil service) is shown in Figure 18.2. Here the system is designed as a systematic annual process, which is cyclical and contains specific periodic reviews. The process effectively begins with annual departmental planning; departmental activities, programmes, projects and strategies are decided with reference to organisational policy. From these, work plans for specified departments or work units are set, and the head of a department or unit is then held accountable for allocating work tasks and responsibilities so that the plans are implemented. This leads to the determination of work targets for employees after agreement between the employee and the manager over these targets. Note that in this department the system involves determination of salary as well as review of performance; reward management is the subject of Chapter 19.

Figure 18.2: Performance appraisal in a south-east Asian government department

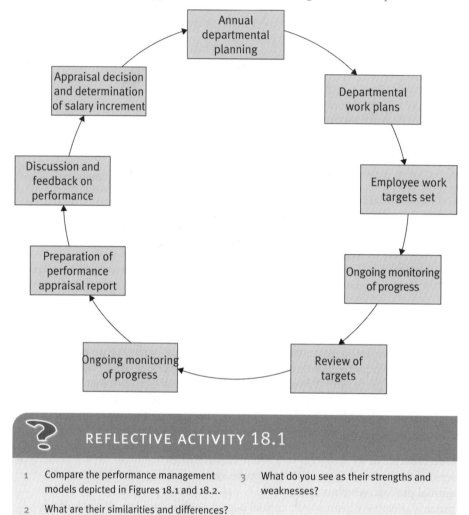

PERFORMANCE APPRAISAL DEFINED

PA remains the cornerstone of PM, referring to the use of formal, systematic procedures for assessing employee job performance on a regular basis. At a minimum, it involves an interview between employee and manager and completion of an appraisal form on which performance is recorded. More effective systems involve regular feedback on performance and the involvement of colleagues and other stakeholders in reviewing and enhancing performance. Appraisal systems attempt to formalise judgements and assessments of employees through observing, reviewing and discussing current performance in a job for the purpose of adding value.

An organisation's PA system is often seen as a key mechanism for aligning the efforts of individuals with the aims and goals of the organisation and for identifying and rewarding those who best exemplify, model and contribute to organisational goals. As Redman and Snape (1992: 32) succinctly put it: 'what gets measured gets done'. Unfortunately, however, there is considerable evidence of problems with the implementation of PA and high levels of dissatisfaction with PM (Fletcher 1997a, 1997b).

REFLECTIVE ACTIVITY 18.2

In contemporary organisations, including IEs, some see PA as only about form-filling, promising much, but delivering little; others see it as involving a searching discussion of objectives and results that sets new challenges and opens up new options; others as something they are stuck with, or have never heard of.

1 Which of the above views best characterises your organisation, or an organisation with which you are familiar?

2 For what purposes does your selected organisation use PA?

THE IMPORTANCE OF PM IN IHRM

PM has played a critical role in many models of HRM (discussed in Chapter 8); Fombrun et al (1984) see the goal of HRM as driving 'performance', as defined by corporate strategy. Appraisal plays a crucial role in rewarding and incentivising higher performance and informing the IE of employee training and development needs. Much has therefore been claimed for PM as the cornerstone of strategic HRM. Sophisticated PM systems can generate useful information on performance for HR to make informed placement, promotion, career development, training and development, reward and other decisions. PA can also inform the wider IE corporate strategy process, helping organisations answer such questions as:

- What should be our strategic focus? What are our core competences? (Chapter 15)
- Should we diversify?
- Should we make acquisitions/mergers, perhaps to acquire new skills and competences? (Chapter 7)

If a pharmaceutical company, for example, found its strengths were in R&D rather than in marketing, should it focus on gaining competitive advantage through innovation, or try to develop or acquire, perhaps through recruitment or acquisition/merger, more competence in marketing? Appraisal information may also help specify and define what needs to be done to what level to implement a strategy successfully, or help identify necessary changes in skill mix to implement long-term strategic plans by answering such questions as:

- What do managers/staff need to do differently to make necessary strategic changes?

- How can we align our HR capabilities with our strategic business goals?
- What training and development is necessary to help an IE realise its strategic goals? (Chapter 16)

PA also promises to help organisations facilitate cultural change if staff are appraised against a set of organisational core competencies, framed in behavioural terms, helping:

1   Define what is meant by 'strategy implementation' at the level of individual objectives and behaviour, making explicit what constitutes effective behaviour and helping communicate a shared vision of organisational purpose, values and expectations.

2   Sustain and enhance effective performance by clarifying what constitutes high performance and how employees need to achieve it, and enhancing motivation and commitment by recognising high performance.

3   Make accurate HRM decisions, especially placement, promotion, reward and training and development decisions.

PM: ROLES AND REALITIES

In most organisations, PM has two main purposes: *evaluation* and *development*. Evaluation goals include feedback to employees on where they stand, providing valid data for HR decisions, identifying 'talent' (Chapter 17) and helping management make separation and retention decisions. Development goals include helping managers improve performance, developing commitment, motivating employees through recognition, diagnosing problems, and identifying individual training and development needs (Briscoe et al 2012).

However, in spite of these claims and much rhetoric, the situation in reality in many IEs is far less clear:

> of all the activities in HRM, performance appraisal is arguably the most contentious and least popular among those who are involved. Managers do not appear to like doing it, employees see no point in it, and personnel and human resource managers as guardians of the organisation's appraisal policy and procedures have to stand by and watch their work fall into disrepute. (Bratton and Gold 1999: 214)

This point is reinforced by Grint (1993: 64): 'Rarely in the history of business can such a system have promised so much and delivered so little.'

So PA remains contentious and unpopular; muddle and confusion still surrounds its theory and practice. Does a PM perspective offer 'the potential to reverse past trends, so that it is viewed less of a threat and a waste of time and more as the source of continuous dialogue between organisational members' (Bratton and Gold 1999: 214)?

PA seems inherently linked to management control; for Barlow (1989: 500), 'institutionally elaborated systems of management appraisal and development are significant rhetorics in the apparatus of bureaucratic control'. We will explore this shortly after reviewing some issues in international PM (Varma et al 2008).

MANAGING PERFORMANCE IN INTERNATIONAL ASSIGNMENTS

In IEs, as in other organisations, the recommendation is for PM to be linked to corporate strategy and vision so performance goals can be set. However, there are a number of additional problems and issues for PM here compared with domestic PM:

1 *Cultural differences*: some collectivistic cultures (Chapter 2) may prefer team rather than individual appraisal, and may be uncomfortable with direct face-to-face feedback or criticism; some high power distance cultures may be uncomfortable with feedback from direct reports. Cultural differences in terms of attitudes to extrinsic rewards, group performance, specific formal appraisal methods, employee involvement, the role of off-job behaviours and attitudes to respect may all pose challenges to PM (Part 3).

2 *Observability*: in IEs, much behaviour is unobservable by headquarters; how much involvement should local subsidiary managers have (Chapter 3)?

3 *Conflicts of loyalty* between the HQ and subsidiary may exist; should IEs foster *dual allegiance*? Black and Gregersen (1991) found four types of expatriates, distinguished in terms of their allegiance to the local subsidiary or parent: the *hired gun*, showing little loyalty to either; the *heart at home*, still committed to the parent; the *going native*, more loyal to the locals; and the *dual citizen*, loyal to both the local subsidiary and the corporate HQ.

4 *Is it motivating to link performance and reward?* How easy is this in complex environments, where staff may work in multiple legal/employment contexts, such as in a joint venture (Chapter 7)? Or in different cultures (Chapter 2)?

5 *What mix of organisational and individual performance criteria should be used?* IAs may involve multiple goals, as we saw in Chapter 15 – filling a position, delivering results, developing the individual for a bigger role, transferring technology, and mentoring and developing locals, for example.

6 *How should incomparable data be taken into account?* For example, volatile environments, the separation of the IE from employees by time and distance, the variable maturity and goals of different markets, the difference between multi-domestic and global industries, the mix of short- and long-term measures involved in performance?

7 *Additional dimensions may be introduced*, such as the need for employees to act as envoys/diplomats, family circumstances, the importance of interpersonal skills, cultural and language differences (Chapters 2, 15 and 16).

8 *Need to balance global consistency and local conditions*, requiring local variations in PA. Should PM be a single, standardised practice throughout the organisation, or should divergent systems be used to reflect local conditions?

9 *Who conducts PA*, and how? The corporate HQ? The local affiliate? The regional HQ? See Chapter 3; conflicts may exist between these levels over evaluations of performance.

10 *What performance data* should be used? Objective? Subjective? Achievement of goals and targets? Competence profiles (Chapter 15)?

11 *Who counts as 'international'?* Are not all employees in IEs 'international'? Should not all 'think global' even if never leaving their desk in the corporate HQ? See Chapter 15 for different types of IAs.

We can use the 'international orientations' framework of Perlmutter (1969), introduced in Chapter 3, to analyse this further; ethnocentric IEs, for example, are likely to use a parent-country PM system designed and implemented by corporate HQ. This is likely to secure standardisation, integration and economy of scale goals, but miss out on achieving cultural responsiveness goals. Polycentric companies may use locally responsive PM systems that take cultural, institutional and market conditions into account; but it may then be difficult to compare performance across different countries for talent management, leadership development or succession planning purposes. Regiocentric IEs may use regionally standardised processes, allowing comparisons across the region and facilitating intra-regional mobility; but they may fail to allow standardisation or comparison between regions, creating 'regional silos' (Chapter 3).

Most attention in IPM has been given to issues of *culture*; for example, collectivist cultures (Chapter 2) may prefer PM focusing on broad targets, group-oriented appraisal, harmonious relationships, saving face and 'connections' such as *guanxi* (Chapter 14) or *wasta* (Chapter 10). They may dislike direct feedback and confrontation and avoid conflict, focusing on loyalty and hierarchical judgements. Cultural differences over power distance, uncertainty avoidance and femininity also seem associated with differences in PM systems, such as the role of formal regulations and negotiations between manager and employee over PM goals, criteria and processes.

There are noticeable 'country of origin' effects in PM, as the next section shows; in addition to 'culture' effects (Chapter 2), there are also 'institutional' effects (Chapter 1).

PM AND NATIONAL DIFFERENCES

Power distance and collectivism in particular seem to affect how PM operates. The Chinese PA system, though organisations are increasingly adopting PM, is often much less formal than many, with significant consideration given to issues of moral behaviour, 'face' and '*guanxi*', especially in the public sector (Cooke 2008b; Chapter 14). Lack of strategic HRM and appreciation of PM, seeing appraisal as a formality, and subjectivity in appraisal all remain challenges.

Appraisal has rarely been used as an incentive for individual performance in Mexico (Chapter 12) and managers tend to overrate performance (Davila and Elvira 2008). During the economic downturns and downsizing of the 1980s and 1990s, firms linking rewards to performance evaluation suppressed the level of rewards and used PA to downsize, leading employees to develop negative perceptions of PA. Cultural values such as *benevolent paternalism* have generated employee dependency and suppressed conflict. The importance given to social relationships has required intense communication and face-to-face interaction, leading to PA being used for employee expression (for example to express career aspirations) rather than compensation. The costs of employee dismissals also encourage inaccurate performance evaluations. E-HR may provide opportunities for 360-degree feedback to avoid confrontational interviews, but is held back by limited IT skills and training.

Some Mexican firms have implemented modern PA practices through imported methods and tools, yet 'the effectiveness of these practices is determined by the country's economy, work culture and organisational structures, all of which affect the purpose and acceptance of PA systems' (Davila and Elvira 2008: 123). Individual merit-based PA often threatens the Mexican working culture of collectivism and group loyalty where employees 'associate assessment with a threat to personal or private interests ... rather than as a potential source for individual or collective development ... some supervisors treat the process as a superficial artefact or an informal task to complete at the last minute, quickly and carelessly' (Davila and Elvira 2008: 126). More appropriate seems the linking of PA to career plans, training and promotion, not just financial rewards, and using PA for more collective purposes, such as enhancing sub-group rather than individual performance.

India (Chapter 13) also shows the influence of culture on PM; but as in Mexico, recent years have seen changes. Sharma et al (2008) point out that the use of PM systems, once under-emphasised, is increasing, but faces several challenges, such as *transparency, linkages with rewards* and, as in Mexico, the influence of a plethora of *labour laws*. There have been shifts from closed and confidential performance evaluations towards open dialogue and discussion. In addition, more qualitative, development-oriented PM incorporating peer evaluation (and often web-based) is now more common, especially in IT and the private sector more generally. More emphasis on performance-based and merit pay linked to performance evaluations is found here, and, in BPO especially, evaluations are strongly data-driven, with little ratee involvement, perhaps reflecting the cultural dimension of high power distance. PM in local firms and the public sector in particular is more affected by the hierarchical, power-oriented, top–down culture; paternalistic managers lead employees to look for detailed guidance and compliance with norms and regulations, risking subjective, biased judgements.

In more individualistic cultures, performance and its link with reward are more often emphasised. Though Pulakos et al (2008) argue that there is no overall 'US model' of PM, there are common trends and factors linked to a national culture of *individualism, capitalism* and *democracy* (Chapter 8). Most Americans expect evaluation on the basis of individual contribution and a competitive, rewards-based element in PM. They also expect a transparent, fair process with employee input, reinforced by a legal system that protects employees from discriminatory practice. PM is primarily used to make HR decisions (pay, promotion, bonuses, etc) rather than for development, unlike many other countries. There is a focus on results, with goals 'cascaded' down to every level, despite issues over the use of objectives; in practice, behavioural assessments are also used. There is also increasing use of automated HR information systems, including the facilitation of 360-degree feedback (to be discussed shortly), and a legal environment that allows appeals and challenges by employees.

Within the UK, there has been less emphasis on a precise overall rating in recent years, perhaps because of perceived 'demotivating' effects (Bach 2005). Many UK organisations use PA to identify training needs, but only a minority use it to make reward decisions, unlike the USA. PA now covers an increasing proportion of the workforce, not just managers, sales staff and professionals, often connected to harmonisation of terms and conditions. PA has also been extended to many public services, such as universities in the 1980s and schools in the 1990s. However, company directors have tended to be excluded from appraisal, though recent concerns with corporate governance have put this issue higher up the agenda (Chapter 6).

Sparrow (2008) points out that, consistent with our discussion of 'voluntarism' as characterising the UK national business system in Chapter 1, historically few employment interactions in the UK have had the force of law, but that this has been changing as UK law harmonises with EU law (Chapter 8). There is a 'floor of rights' over unfair dismissal, redundancy, equal opportunities, maternity leave, data protection and health and safety; structural support for collective bargaining; and restrictions around lawful action. Attention in PM systems has shifted from top–down 'objectives' in the 1980s to a more competence-based, development agenda in the 1990s (Chapter 16), followed by concerns with such issues as values, person–organisation fit, mutuality and engagement. In the 2000s, a concern with strategic imperatives and coherence between PM systems and other agendas such as talent management (Chapter 17) has become apparent.

Key factors impacting on PM in the UK include the role of specific cultural values such as low uncertainty avoidance and low power distance (Chapter 2), facilitating joint problem-solving and psychological contracting. Key challenges for a now mature mechanism used in virtually all UK organisations include work–life balance, employee diversity and age discrimination legislation. In general, PM historically has moved through the 4Cs identified as HR goals by the Harvard model (Chapter 8), progressing from cost-effectiveness to competence to commitment to coherence. There is a greater concern with user acceptability and political context in the UK, whereas the US has focused more on fairness and accuracy.

Barzantny and Festing (2008) discuss how IEs in particular have introduced apparently 'American' ideas (Chapter 8) such as the use of value/competency statements (Chapter 15) into PM systems in France and Germany. While large French or German companies may use similar measures to US companies, country-specific dimensions can be identified, especially over PM *processes* and how PM is carried out. The prevailing American unitarist concept of PM clashes with more pluralistic orientations in Europe, as well as with its more collectivist and social welfare traditions. Here, as we saw in Chapter 8, trade unions may be seen as social partners; limited organisational autonomy and different patterns of ownership and control also exercise influence.

France has maintained more hierarchical and conflict-intensive governance than Germany; in France social factors, social class, a broad general education, technical knowledge and educational selection for the prestigious 'Grande Ecole' system play a greater role in career systems, in contrast to the more northern 'egalitarian' tradition of Germany. Legal expertise is important in both countries, but more so in Germany – French labour laws allow some flexibility in assessing performance, within a merit-based, non-discriminatory framework. France is a 'moderately regulated' country in contrast to a 'highly regulated' German system with complex labour laws, contractual agreements with unions and co-determination.

Participation, consultation and information rights for workers in Germany mean that works councils need to approve PM system changes, with a larger range of explicit legal and institutional factors affecting PM, such as traditions of collective bargaining, co-determination and vocational training (Chapter 8). These have led to greater employee input and consensus-building, a long-term career focus and an emphasis on specialised technical knowledge and expertise or 'technik'. Alongside day-to-day informality, there are explicitly formalised roles, standards and criteria, regulated by co-determination; performance-based pay (Chapter 19) has been much slower to gain acceptance, given the emphasis on long-term goals and development. Lower power distance is associated with employee input into objectives, openness and informal dialogue between superior and subordinate; higher uncertainty avoidance is associated with a highly regulated work environment and formalised rules on PM. Feedback may include open confrontation, and a long-term orientation is associated with long-term employment relations, seniority and relative lack of career mobility outside the firm. This gives much German PM a strong 'developmental' role, but a more modest role in performance-related pay, except in MNCs; greater internationalisation has led, however, more recently to the adoption of more 'Anglo-Saxon' PM practices, often transferred from German foreign subsidiaries in a process of 'reverse diffusion' (Chapters 1 and 8).

Many French firms use centralised, non-transparent PM procedures, but larger firms are generally more open to a wider range of PM criteria and practices. French firms are required to invest by law a percentage of their annual payroll on training (an interventionist system of national HRD, Chapter 1) and are also often positive about high-technology, with CEOs often being from engineering backgrounds rather than accountancy or law, as in the UK or USA. France is a fairly high power distance, high uncertainty avoidance, high individualism and moderately masculine country (Hofstede 2001; Chapter 2) that also values quality of life and work–life balance. These values seem associated with a more 'elite' system in education and management, with greater pay inequality, a less open, less transparent PA process and a lack of trust or information-sharing, often leading to perceptions of unfairness in PM by employees.

In comparison, Nordic firms are more decentralised, with PM based on a broader range of hard and soft criteria in a 'balanced scorecard' approach using financial, customer, internal and development criteria, with considerable employee input into goal-setting (Dowling et al 2008).

This comparison shows the influence of 'distal' factors such as culture and institutions on PM system design and implementation, as well as the role of corporate strategy (Murphy and DeNisi 2008). These 'country of origin' effects come into play in international mergers and acquisitions (Chapter 9), as Case Study 18.1 shows.

 PM IN ASTRAZENECA

CASE STUDY 18.1

AstraZeneca was formed in 1999 by the merger of Astra AB of Sweden and Zeneca plc of the UK (from the old ICI), employing around 60,000 staff worldwide. The company sought to harmonise HR practices across the R&D group (10,000 employees) after the merger. Practices ranged from the very prescriptive/formal in the USA to the very open/informal in Sweden. As a matrix organisation involving project and functional teams working in parallel, it wished to focus on *team performance*: the Management of Individual and Team Performance (MITP) project was intended to deliver cultural change. Consultation with line managers and employees was extensive, to ensure commitment and acceptance as a line manager-owned initiative. This involved focus groups, interviews, questionnaires and union consultation, with an emphasis on personal benefits, and benchmarking against best practice elsewhere. The focus was on planning, delivering and reviewing individual performance, as well as team performance management. An implementation plan was developed, tailored to country, cultural and site needs, with awareness and skill training sessions built in, and the initiative was globally 'branded', with a dedicated MITP intranet site for resources, feedback, updates and performance planning/performance review document exchanges.

The PM process is intended to be continuous, with individuals proposing performance plans and targets in line with business objectives, as well as necessary key behaviours/skills, performance measures and development needs. Performance delivery is monitored and supported through preview coaching, interim reviews and updates, and review coaching; performance is reviewed through both downwards feedback from bosses and from other sources, such as key internal customers (including unsolicited feedback). This focuses on leadership capabilities, R&D, shared values, team behaviours and customer service, backed up with evidence. The forms are returned to the individual, not to HR or the line manager. Employees write the electronically supported performance review document to ensure ownership, with encouragement to record wider achievements, not just meeting narrow targets. The draft document is discussed at a meeting with the line manager, and employees edit the agreed form, with the line manager adding a summary. Senior managers ('grandparents') review the forms for consistency.

These reviews 'inform' rather than 'determine' annual pay awards, with staff grouped into three categories. Pay decisions are reviewed for consistency at annual meetings. In addition, a performance bonus scheme operates if the company as a whole, as well as a function such as R&D, meets its targets, multiplied by a factor representing individual performance. Given the difficulties in deciding who makes up a 'team' in a pharmaceutical environment, team performance is assessed in terms of the individual's contribution to team performance. The individual, the line manager and the project manager are each allocated specific roles and responsibilities: for example, the project leader is responsible for giving feedback and recognising team contribution, the line manager has overall accountability for overall performance review and reward decisions.

(Source: IDS 2003)

Questions

1   What are the main features of PM in this company?

2   What do you see as the strengths of the scheme?

3   What do you see as issues that might need to be addressed?

4   What does it say about the impact of national differences on PM?

TRENDS AND ISSUES IN PM

In PM, a wider range of output measures have become used; for example, the 'balanced scorecard' used in many companies (Kaplan and Norton 1996) focuses not just on financial measures, but also on customer service, internal business processes, and innovation and learning measures, including in local government (McAdam and Walker 2003). The various stakeholders of an organisation will have different views about which potential measures of performance are important; the use of the 'balanced scorecard' assists in the translation of strategic objectives into tangible operational improvements at service level through greater staff involvement and acceptance. Figure 18.3 shows a balanced scorecard attempting to measure and manage performance with reference to financial targets, customer relationships, employee management and development, and longer-term business development.

Figure 18.3: Balanced scorecard in PM

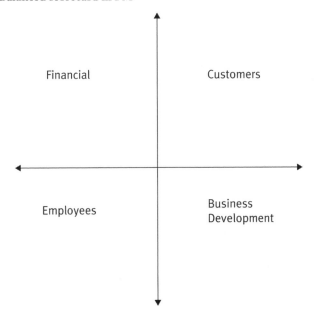

There has also been a shift towards using *input* as well as *output* measures, that is, measures of the *how* as well as the *what* of job performance. Linked to this has been a shift away from job-related to person-related criteria; such attributes as 'emotional intelligence' have become more sought after, especially in customer service jobs (Bach 2005).

A further trend has been to encourage employees to become more responsible for assessing their own performance, with greater reliance put on responding to feedback, self-assessment and commenting on one's own performance. In addition, the time focus of PM has shifted away from current performance (the focus of 'management by objectives') to recent past performance (the focus of performance-related pay) and to future performance (the focus of development efforts and concerns over competencies). HR departments have also begun to make more use of appraisal information to evaluate the effectiveness of other HR areas such as recruitment and selection, equal opportunity/diversity and training. Appraisers are key determinants of appraisal effectiveness, so training of appraisers and appraisees is likely to have a significant impact in this regard, improving both satisfaction with and the effectiveness of PM systems.

As Fletcher (1997a: 149) points out, knowledge workers in particular value autonomy and independence, self-discipline, adherence to specialised standards and ethics; they possess specialised knowledge skills, and are often answerable to governing professional bodies. All of these features conflict with the hierarchical authority, direction, administrative rules and procedures, organisationally defined goals and standards, and emphasis on organisational position and organisation loyalty characteristic of much conventional appraisal (Simmons et al 2005). In trying to do many different things, appraisal may try to do too much, become over-complex, and fail to do any of these things well.

The inherent tension between appraisal as judgement and appraiser as judge and as facilitating development or counsellor has been a theme since the classic studies of Meyer et al (1965) in GE, highlighting the ways criticism had negative effects but praise little effect on performance. Making career and salary decisions in appraisal impacted negatively on performance improvement. Two main approaches to PM can be identified: developmental or judgemental (evaluation). Developmental approaches are concerned with motivating an employee and agreeing aims and objectives; judgemental approaches with providing evaluations and assessments of past performance. This frequently involves deciding on levels of pay or reward for employees. Difficulties occur, however, when these two approaches to appraisal are confused (Armstrong and Baron 2005; Fletcher 1997a, 1997b).

Much of the orthodoxy on appraisal focuses on a developmental approach, generally preferred by appraisees. However, many organisations confuse this by linking pay awards to PA outcomes, and hence confound developmental and judgemental approaches.

There are a number of possible conflicts between different organisational stakeholders over these purposes. The organisation may be trying to use PM for both development and reward purposes; these two functions may come into conflict. Individuals may be trying both to gain accurate information on where they stand and can realistically go in the organisation, but also trying to present themselves in a possibly 'unrealistic' light in order to gain monetary and other rewards. Often the appraiser is acting both as a 'judge' and as a 'counsellor'. Figure 18.4 shows that each party may perceive the benefits of the process differently, while Figure 18.5 shows how parties' perceptions of PM may differ.

Figure 18.4: Perceived benefits of PM

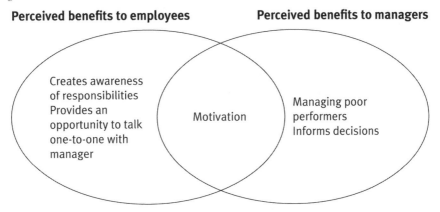

Figure 18.5: Perceptions of PM

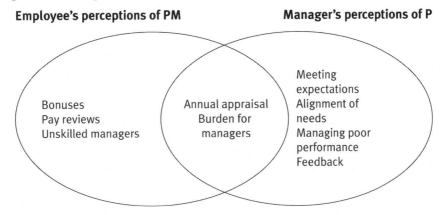

In different organisations, there will be different mixes of 'evaluation' and 'development'. If the focus is on past performance and results (the 'what'), heavily reliant on documentation and manager-led, the outcome is likely to be defensiveness, resistance and at best compliance on the part of the appraisee. If the focus is on future growth, on skills (the 'how') and is part of a shared dialogue between manager and employee, the outcome is more likely to be energy, commitment and enthusiasm on behalf of the appraisee.

What kind of appraisal balance is adopted is likely to be related to the culture and structure of the organisation and the national cultures of the home and host countries in the context of IEs. Hierarchical, authoritarian organisations and cultures may not welcome subordinate or peer feedback, for example, while in matrix organisations appraisees may not be committed to the appraisal process if the colleagues they work closely with on particular projects are not involved.

Employees also often appear to receive significantly higher ratings from appraisers of their own racial or ethnic group (for example Cox and Nkomo 1986). Performance rating is a social process – employees typically work in groups; much of their work is not observed; evaluators have different, mixed motives for evaluating performance; rating decisions are embedded in a social context; rating processes are subjective; and social processes enter into all phases of the rating. For example, supervisors seem to prefer to award positive ratings and show upward bias, giving more positive ratings than 'true' performance would merit. This may be because they perceive negative events to follow from negative ratings, such as employee resentment, deteriorating working relationships, appeals, grievances, and legal and industrial action.

There are other potential conflicts within PA, such as:

- the balance between the process and the people
- the balance between input (skills, competencies, behaviours) or output measures (for example financial, customer, learning or internal business measures) and the question of which measures to use. In many jobs there are few tangible, quantifiable objective measures of performance, and in many sectors, such as health or education, those measures are politically contentious. In other jobs, discretion may be limited. The pursuit of some, easily quantifiable, measures may be at the expense of other, less quantifiable but equally or more important, ones
- the balance between individual and team performance
- the balance between assessment and development ('you can't grow a cow by weighing it').

 REFLECTIVE ACTIVITY 18.4

What are some of the problems encountered with reviewing performance against objectives?

Figure 18.6 shows some of the limitations of PM.

Figure 18.6: Perceived limitations of PM

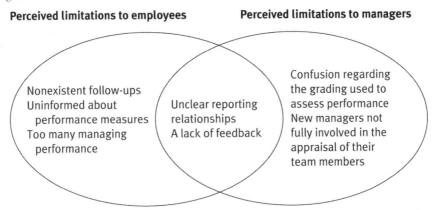

Perceived limitations to employees   **Perceived limitations to managers**

Nonexistent follow-ups
Uninformed about
  performance measures
Too many managing
performance

Unclear reporting
relationships
A lack of feedback

Confusion regarding
the grading used to
assess performance
New managers not
fully involved in the
appraisal of their
team members

IS 360 DEGREE APPRAISAL THE PANACEA?

For some organisations, there is increasing interest in so-called '360-degree' or 'multi-source, multi-rater' appraisal systems to overcome some of the limitations and problems inherent in traditional top–down appraisal systems. Fletcher and Baldry (1999), in their review of multi-source multi-rater (MSMR) assessment systems, point out that whether such systems are oriented to development or are part of ongoing performance appraisal has considerable implications for their structure and likely outcomes. Figure 18.7 shows one possible scheme.

Figure 18.7: 360-degree appraisal and feedback

In the USA, MSMR systems seem often to be related to appraisal and reward, but this appears as yet less true of the UK, where the emphasis has been on development. Such systems appear to have spread rapidly across both the private and public sectors in the UK, with a growing prescriptive literature on how to implement such systems alongside little empirical basis or research guidance. In part, the move away from traditional top–down assessments seems related to changes towards flatter and more fluid structures, autonomous work units and wider supervisory spans of control. This appears to legitimise the involvement of subordinates and peers in appraisal, since such employees observe more and different managerial behaviours than are apparent to supervisors (Simmons and Iles 2001). With customer-facing roles in particular, greater autonomy and the use of new communications technology may mean that more and more employees will have little contact with immediate superiors, subordinates or peers. Increasing levels of direct contact with internal and external customers able to provide input on such dimensions of performance as timeliness and quality of service also seem influential drivers of MSMR systems.

In the UK, Redman and Matthews (1997) found managers ranging from enthusiastic to sceptical, with the majority being 'relatively indifferent'; such managers were also sceptical about the use of MSMR systems to bring about change. Very little research, despite the apparent enthusiasm of organisations, has examined whether performance improves as a result of MSMR feedback, or generates development plans (De Nisi et al 2008).

In conclusion, there does seem to be a spread of Western-style PM systems to many other countries, even 'collectivist' and hierarchical ones like India and Mexico, especially in large IEs. However, this is most likely in more mature economies, and PM is more likely to show 'cross-vergence' or hybridisation with local patterns, rather than complete convergence or divergence (De Nisi et al 2008). Not all countries accept the peer evaluations implicit in 360-degree feedback, for example, and the more hierarchical the society, the less likely it is to accept upward feedback. Whether such systems are effective, or destructive, outside the USA (and perhaps western Europe) is a question for further research; its introduction may have unanticipated effects and demotivate rather than improve performance.

LEARNING SUMMARY

In this chapter we began by discussing the cornerstone of performance management, performance appraisal (now often not known by that term in many organisations, who prefer a term such as 'performance review', perhaps to reduce the 'assessor/judge' connotations of the word 'appraisal'). Appraisal as the review and assessment of performance plays a crucial role in IHRM by linking individual objectives and work behaviours to organisational, strategic aims and objectives, and by establishing a basis for identifying training and development needs and for establishing a framework for reward management. However, there are many issues that need to be resolved in performance management in IEs, such as what should be appraised and who should do the appraising.

In addition, the chapter discussed many issues of national difference – both cultural and institutional – that need to be taken into account in PM. In some more collectivistic cultures (for example Japan, China, the Middle East), individual appraisal, especially if linked to differential pay and to direct feedback and criticism, may be less culturally acceptable than group or team-based performance appraisal and management.

In terms of the 'what' of PM, there has been a move away from trying to assess personality traits (honesty, dedication, etc) to assessing either objectives/targets and their attainment (usually as set the previous year) or behaviours, usually in the form of competences/competencies. Both are useful, but complementary; whereas objectives may give feedback on what has been achieved, there are issues as to comparability over different sets of objectives and the contribution of an individual, rather than a team, to their achievement. Competencies allow feedback on how these objectives have been achieved; many organisations for this reason will use both frameworks in their performance management system.

In terms of 'who', the trend has been to move away from the boss as sole rater of performance to including other stakeholders: the individual appraisee, through 'self-assessment', and peers, customers, subordinates and others, such as superior levels, in the name of 360-degree feedback. However, 360-degree appraisal carries its own problems, and in the UK, as distinct from the USA, tends to be used for 'developmental' purposes rather than 'reward' purposes.

INTERNET RESOURCES

CIPD: http://www.cipd.co.uk/

CIPD surveys: http://www.cipd.co.uk/surveys

Society for Human Resource Management: http://www.shrm.org/

http://www.performance-appraisal.com/

www.worldatwork.org

CHAPTER 19

Global Reward Management, Organisational Benefits and Employer Branding

Paul Iles and Tingting Jiang

LEARNING OUTCOMES

By the end of this chapter, you should be able to:

- Identify the reward management objectives for IEs and employees in IEs.

- Critically analyse institutional and cultural influences on global reward management.

- Differentiate between the key components of a global reward management system.

- Critically evaluate different approaches and recent developments in global reward management, including merit and performance-related pay and executive compensation.

- Critically analyse employer branding in IEs and make recommendations for improvement to ensure success.

INTRODUCTION

In this chapter we discuss how international employees are attracted, retained and motivated through the instrumental and symbolic benefits and 'value' provided by both reward management strategies and employer branding. The chapter discusses reward management in a global context, particularly the objectives of international reward management and the different approaches taken by companies to this issue (especially in respect of expatriates and other staff on international assignments), along with their advantages and disadvantages. The chapter also discusses institutional and cultural influences on global reward strategies, especially in relation to merit/performance-related pay and executive compensation in a global context.

The issue of employer branding has also grown in importance, especially the concept of employer brand equity, and this is explored in relation to organisational attractiveness to both applicants and employees.

GLOBAL REWARD MANAGEMENT

Most classifications of reward management distinguish between financial and non-financial rewards; financial include both fixed (for example salary) and variable (for example performance-contingent) rewards. Non-financial includes recognition and training and development opportunities (though of course in practice these are intertwined – training may lead to promotion, for example). Do different rewards possess different motivational properties, and can they be used to achieve different performance objectives (Chiang and Birtch 2012: 543)? Is this true for global reward strategies? As we saw in Chapter 18, performance is increasingly multidimensional, with employees expected not just to perform in-role activities, but extra-role ones as well such as teamwork, cooperative behaviour, citizenship behaviour and emotional labour. What are the implications of different reward packages and components on these behaviours?

OBJECTIVES OF GLOBAL REWARD MANAGEMENT AND APPROACHES

In general, rewards are used to leverage human capital in a desired direction (Boxall and Purcell 2003) through their incentive power to elicit and reinforce behaviour and align the interests of employer and employee. Expectancy theory suggests that motivation is enhanced when behaviour results in valent outcomes (Porter and Lawler 1968); rewards can be used to support competitive strategies such as innovation, creativity or flexibility. Exchange theory suggests that when people participate in an economic exchange relationship, such as employment, financial and non-financial rewards affect calculations about the costs and benefits of the exchange. Social exchange theory predicts that reciprocity may follow if people perceive their needs are met. Do different cultural values and attributes influence individual work motives (such as transactional versus relational), reward expectations (such as direct or immediate compensation versus developmental rewards), attitudes towards one's self versus group (for example competition versus cooperation), and how employees perceive their employer's obligations in any exchange (Gerhart 2008b)?

This chapter addresses various questions in this field, such as:

- Do rewards effective in one country have the same effect in another (Chapter 2)?
- Will employees with different cultural orientations be motivated in different ways by identical rewards?
- Do rewards that work well in individualistic cultures also work in collectivist ones, or fail because, for example, they disrupt harmony?
- Do non-financial rewards such as family-friendly policies, parental leave or flexitime work better in 'feminine' countries such as Scandinavian ones?
- Can MNCs in one country successfully develop and implement reward packages that 'go against the grain' of local culture, or do they have to adapt them to local culture?
- Do US-centric theories of reward and motivation such as 'exchange theory' apply to less individualistic cultures (Chapter 8)?

- What are 'culture's consequences' for reward management (Hofstede 2001; Chiang and Birtch 2012)?

This issue is one area of research in IHRM on reward management (Parts 2 and 3); another, linked, area is on how to develop reward policies and practices for staff on international assignments. Here the initial focus has been on global compensation and expatriate pay/PCN compensation, but this has more recently been seen in other ways, for example:

- developing and reinforcing a global corporate culture
- acting as a source of corporate control
- and, with increasing concerns about executive pay, as a key component of corporate governance (Chapter 6) (Dowling et al 2008).

Outsourcing has introduced additional complexities, as have web-based HR information systems (HRIS) and the focus on performance metrics. There is a continuing need to balance a global reward strategy with local conditions (Chapter 3). This requires attention to employment and taxation laws, currency fluctuations and special allowances, often requiring advice from specialist consultancies.

The international orientations we discussed in Chapter 3 also relate to reward management. Some IEs export their home-country policies to maintain consistency (ethnocentric); others seek to adapt to local conditions (polycentric) or regional conditions (regiocentric). Others may seek to blend different policies and practices (geocentric).

Dowling et al (2008) argue that international reward policies need to:

- be consistent with the overall strategy, structure and business needs of the IE
- be able to attract and retain staff in areas of greatest need and opportunity
- facilitate the transfer of employees in the most effective manner
- give due consideration to equity and ease of administration
- meet employee needs for financial protection, advancement, career development, housing, education and recreation.

Of course, there may be contradictions and clashes between these objectives. Key components of an international reward programme, particularly for expatriates, include:

- *base salary*: payable in home- or local-country currency, and linked to the home country or an international rate; this acts as the foundation block for PCNs and TCNs
- *foreign service inducement hardship premium*: often expressed in percentage terms of base salary (for example 5–40%) and more commonly paid to PCNs than TCNs
- *allowances to encourage expatriation*: usually more common for PCNs rather than TCNs. Examples include cost of living allowances (may include housing, utilities, personal income tax); housing allowances (or company housing, help with former residence, etc); home leave allowances; education allowances for children; relocation allowances and perks (for example servants, cars, drivers),

spouse assistance allowances (for example employment opportunities for spouses)

- *benefits*: as 'transportability' of pensions and other social security benefits is often problematic (except within the EU), many PCNs remain under their home-country benefits plans; less planning is usually done for TCNs. Other benefits include vacations and special leave and emergency provisions, often additional in 'hardship' environments.

There are two main approaches to international reward policies, especially for expatriates:

- *The 'going rate' or 'market rate' approach*: here base salary is linked to the host-country salary structure; but are HCNs, expatriates of the same nationality, or of all nationalities, to be used as reference points? For low-pay countries, this may be supplemented by additional payments. Advantages include simplicity, equality with locals, identification with the host country and equity among different nationalities. Disadvantages include variation between assignments for the same employee, variation between expatriates of the same nationality in different countries and potential re-entry problems (Dowling et al 2008).
- *The balance sheet approach*: here the basic objective is to maintain the home-country living standard, plus a financial inducement; home-country pay and benefits are the foundations, with adjustments and financial incentives to make the package attractive. This is the most common system, being easy to communicate and providing equity between assignments and between expatriates of the same nationality, as well as facilitating re-entry. Disadvantages are that it can result in large disparities between expatriates of different nationalities, as well as between expatriates and locals, and may be quite complex to administer (Dowling et al 2008). Complexities arise over taxes and pensions in particular, as IEs operate in countries with very different tax rates. Tax equalisation, where firms withhold amounts equal to the home-country obligation of the PCN and pay all taxes in the host country, is the most common strategy here, as well as the use of specialist consultancies and agencies on taxation and international living and business costs, such as the Economist Intelligence Unit (http://www.economist.com/topics/economist-intelligence-unithttp).

Some IEs may seek to emphasise global mobility through a geocentric strategy; here remuneration is expressed in a major global or regional currency, for example the US dollar, euro. It seeks to develop a set of reward principles and practices that fit its global strategy and structure. Subsidiary managers may be granted autonomy to configure base pay, benefits and incentives in line with local standards, but core principles over performance-based recognition and reward differentiation remain consistent (Kramar and Syed 2012).

INSTITUTIONAL INFLUENCES ON GLOBAL REWARD MANAGEMENT

Management of reward – 'compensation' in the US literature – is subject to similar adaptation conditions and requirements as other areas of HRM in global contexts (Marin 2008). Global strategic alignment and adaptation to the cultural and institutional context are both objectives which require balancing to ensure the reward system is a key element in international success.

For Milkovich and Newman (2008) there are four key factors operating in international reward management: *institutional, economic, organisational* and *individual*. Each factor is composed of sub-factors; the institutional factors are affected by political and cultural traditions, social contracts and trade union power. In a global context, social contracts, trade unions, capital markets and ownership structure, management autonomy, and institutional and cultural frameworks are factors particularly important in accounting for variations in global reward practices.

Social contract issues refer to the relationships and expectations of the state, employers and employers' associations, and employees/employees' associations; as we saw in Chapter 1, these are key features of the institutionalist approach to 'national business systems', as people in different countries have different expectations of the roles of these institutions with respect to the reward system.

One example of the effects of the social contract in reward systems is the degree of *centralisation* within national reward frameworks. Some countries (for example USA, UK) use highly decentralised systems with minimal government intervention, while others (for example Sweden, Denmark) are much more centralised as 'national wage systems', with Japan and Germany in between, as the industrial *sector* is important here (Chapters 1 and 8). Related to this is the differing *presence of trade unions*; Sweden and Denmark have high union membership, the UK and USA low (Chapter 20). Even if trade union membership is low, for example France or Spain, collective agreements may still cover a majority of workers, affecting the autonomy of the organisation in establishing a reward system, as well as the level of involvement or resistance by employees.

Related to this is *social legislation*; the UK has the fewest legal requirements within the EU, whereas France and Germany are much more regulated, so that social costs as well as labour costs influence the reward system. *Ownership structures* also affect reward systems – for example, in South Korea a few families control most large corporations, while in Germany and Spain a small number of large banks are majority shareholders in large companies. Here incentives linked to share value or share purchase options may make less sense. Workers in private companies may have different expectations from employees in state-owned companies, preferring more performance-related rewards, as in China (Chapter 14). Managers have greater autonomy in decentralised systems such as the UK or USA in designing or modifying pay systems without the burden (or support?) of government and legislative intervention and trade union pressure, as in many EU countries. Reward decisions taken in headquarters can also influence local affiliate policies, even if not adapted to the local culture. See Case Study 19.1.

PAY IN JAPANESE RETAIL STORES IN CHINA

CASE STUDY 19.1

Gamble (2010) compared the HR policies and practices of three Japanese retail stores in China with their Japanese operations. One of the attractions offered to Chinese employees was greater job security than offered by Chinese organisations, though none explicitly offered lifetime employment. Chinese staff showed less loyalty than Japanese staff, and were more likely to leave for a higher salary or promotion. Promotion was faster than in stores in Japan, to prevent poaching, but slower than in comparable UK-owned stores, such as B&Q in China. The stores used the external labour market less than many Chinese companies.

The stores stressed monetary rewards and sanctions (for example fines) more than in Japan, with more use of

bonuses dependent on sales or customers served. However, while one company had retained seniority pay in Japan but did not use it in China, another was phasing it out in Japan but had introduced it in China to limit turnover and increase retention.

Questions

1   How would you analyse these cases from a national business systems framework (Chapter 1)?

2   How would you analyse them from a 'transfer' framework, such as neo-institutionalism (Chapter 1)?

3   How would you analyse them from a cultural framework (Chapter 2)?

CULTURAL INFLUENCES ON GLOBAL REWARD MANAGEMENT

In terms of *adaptation to local culture*, Marin (2008) reviews studies exploring links between the dimensions of national culture identified by Hofstede (2001) and the design of reward systems (Chapter 2). The claim is that these dimensions capture significant variations in values relating to work, in particular why certain rewards are valued over others. Preferences for the extent of individualisation in rewards, such as collective versus individual contracts, the criteria used to allocate rewards (for example seniority versus merit or performance) and attitudes to risk (for example fixed versus incentive rewards) seem to vary with culture (specifically, with individualism and uncertainty avoidance in the examples given above).

Countries with *high power distance* also tend to feature hierarchical systems with large differences in earnings reflecting differences in status and position; in high power distance, such as in many Asian, African and Latin American countries and cultures, people seek exchange-based security rather than self-development or autonomy and other non-financial rewards. Low power distance countries such as the Nordic countries tend to have more egalitarian systems.

Countries with high *uncertainty avoidance* scores, such as many Asian, African, Latin American and southern/eastern European countries, often have centralised, fixed pay systems linked to seniority and internal equity; they are less oriented to more risky, less predictable and less certain variable, as opposed to fixed, rewards. Low uncertainty avoidance cultures have more variable pay systems.

Individualist cultures (Chapter 2) prefer pay and other financial rewards to be based on individual performance; collectivists attribute greater importance to group harmony and relationships, and may see individual-based performance incentives as disruptive of these, in contrast to team-based incentives.

Highly *masculine* countries make less use of social benefits such as parental leave and flexitime, motivated more by achievement and material success; here financial rewards are more valued than non-financial ones. Feminine countries such as the Nordic ones are more likely to value flexible work, parental leave (for both genders), work–life balance and quality of life.

There is some evidence for such relationships. US executive compensation systems are more formally instituted, with large variable elements and high levels of salary compared with French or even Dutch systems. Total compensation, proportion of variable compensation and the compensation ratio of the CEO with respect to the lowest level seem linked to power distance, individualism and uncertainty avoidance, according to Tosi and Greckhamer (2004) using data from a Towers Perrin survey (quoted in Berrone and Otten 2008).

Contextual factors such as institutional and cultural aspects of the environment might constrain the use of certain reward practices by IEs or suggest caution over their use, because one would expect them to be more effective in some contexts than others. As Early and Erez (1997: 75) point out: 'attempts to transfer a reward system from one culture to another can result in a mismatch, and dissonant systems are likely to be ineffective and rejected'.

In terms of national differences in compensation, Marin (2008: 26–7) argues that the reward systems of different countries in different regions – Europe, America, Asia – 'clearly vary according to the cultural and institutional environment in which they are developed'. The USA has adopted an 'exchange' system, with a shorter-term vision and fewer guarantees of job security; compensation is linked to individual performance; and there are wide earnings disparities. East Asian countries (Japan, China) were more likely to design reward systems characterised by commitment and long-term loyalty, on both sides, emphasising length of service, fixed earnings, and internal rather than market orientation (though in Chapter 14 we noted rapid change in Chinese arrangements and the rise of performance-related pay systems; see Case Study 19.1). EU countries such as Spain or Germany (Chapter 8) are more likely to have regulated systems as a result of collective bargaining and state intervention, with greater employee protection through high fixed earnings, low performance-linked incentives and social benefits. Latin American countries such as Mexico (Chapter 12) are more likely to show informal systems displaying great inequalities between levels and predominantly fixed salaries; 'organisations are absorbed in their institutional environments, which in turn influence the compensation policies and practices adopted' (Marin 2008: 27).

However, this overstates the stability of reward systems; they are often changing rapidly, and not just in China. The compensation of executive board members in Germany has become a highly controversial topic since Vodafone's hostile takeover of Mannesmann in 2000 (Chapters 7 and 8). Based on panel data evidence of the 500 largest firms in Germany in the period 1977–2009, Fabbri and Marin (2012) found support for the *manager power* hypothesis for Germany; executives tend to be rewarded when the sector is doing well rather than the firm they work for. The *efficient pay* hypothesis was rejected, as CEO pay and the demand for managers increases in Germany in difficult times when the typical firm size shrinks. Domestic and global competition for managers has contributed to the rise in executive pay in Germany.

Chiang and Birtch (2012) found that individualism, masculinity, uncertainty avoidance and power distance affected perceptions of financial and non-financial rewards in a comparison of bankers in Hong Kong and Finland. Hong Kong respondents saw financial rewards and promotion as more effective motivators than non-financial ones, unlike Finns, who attributed greater value to non-financial and team-based incentives. Alternative working arrangements and training and development had stronger motivating effects for Finns, perhaps related to their higher 'femininity' scores. Finns also perceived group-based incentives to be more effective, contradicting assertions that collectivist Hong Kong was more likely to prefer group-based incentives. However, for the Finns, variable rewards were more important than fixed, in contrast to Hong Kong; perhaps recent economic crises had made security more valued here, showing the impact of short-term economic and labour-market factors as well as long-term cultural factors.

Other contextual factors (organisational, institutional and economic) also influenced and shaped reward–performance values, preferences and behaviours, such as the recent Asian economic crisis and lack of welfare net in Hong Kong, heightening the importance of financial rewards in Hong Kong. High, progressive income tax rates in Finland also reduced the overall appeal of financial rewards, while labour legislation on dismissal encouraged a longer-term view on the attractiveness of training and development.

This argues for *both cultural and institutional factors* needing to be taken into account in explaining the different salience and motivating potential of different rewards. Gerhart (2008a, 2008b), however, makes a number of criticisms with respect to culturalist claims with regard to the impact of national culture, pointing out problems with how culture has been measured in such studies (see criticisms of Hofstede in particular in Chapter 2). Many 'culture effect' sizes, if present, are very small, and studies have often failed to show that supposedly 'collectivistic' Chinese are any more likely to use 'equality' rather than 'equity' (contribution) rules in allocating rewards scenarios than individualistic Americans. A meta-analysis by Fischer and Smith (2003) of 14 different countries only found a very small positive effect, whereby collectivism was associated with 'equality' allocations. Studies of actual reward practice and its relationship to national culture (for example Schuler and Rogovsky 1998) also fail to take into account other important variables – countries differ not only in respect of culture, but in many other ways such as history, politics and institutions, making it difficult to know how much of the 'country' differences are due to national culture.

In most cases, 'what is actually estimated is instead the effect of country, which not only includes any national culture effect, but also other characteristics of countries' (Gerhart 2008b: 152). Gerhart (2008a, 2008b) argues that national culture is not as daunting a constraint as often claimed; current practices may not be optimal anyway, and local managers may use 'culture' as an alibi to protect local fiefdoms against head office interference. Gamble (2006) found Chinese workers in British-owned B&Q stores in China actually preferred the more performance-related reward systems offered there to local fixed-pay practices in Chinese stores (see Case Study 19.1). It may be that some employees actually prefer 'foreign' practices to local ones.

In addition, the organisation does not have to hire 'typical' local employees but those that fit country-atypical practices through selective hiring and retention, given cultural variability within as well as between countries. For example, companies in China and India may specifically seek out young locals educated in the West or in Western-oriented universities, rather than older locals with no such educational experience. Applicants to multinational rather than local firms may not be 'typical'; Lievens et al (2001) found that several personality characteristics moderated the effects of job/organisation attributes. Subjects high on conscientiousness preferred larger companies; subjects high on openness were more attracted to multinationals.

This point is particularly made in the *employer branding* literature; the impact and attractiveness of organisational and job characteristics are not the same for all applicants, such as young versus old employees. The 'issue of organisational attractiveness has also been framed into the broader framework of person–organisation fit' (Lievens et al 2002: 581). Schneider's (1987) 'attraction-selection-attrition' model has often been used in such research, as people are attracted to different types of organisations, depending on interests, personality and needs (for achievement, affiliation, power or stability, for example).

Generational diversity in work values is another significant issue here; again, like branding, it is a concept borrowed from the marketing literature, but increasingly applied to IHRM. Parry and Urwin (2011) paint a generally mixed picture of this idea, despite much magazine, consultancy and newspaper interest in the different generations in the working population (Veterans, Baby Boomers, Generation X, Generation Y, etc) offering advice on how to segment the workforce and how best to appeal to and manage each generation's different values or preferences at work, including how best to reward them (see http://somresearchinsights.com/2012/07/16/generational-differences-in-work-values-a-review-of-theory-and-evidence/).

Parry and Urwin (2011) present a critical review of the theoretical basis and empirical evidence for the popular practitioner idea that there are differences in how generations see values of work, such as concerns for status, pay, autonomy, work–life balance and freedom. Many studies fail to find predicted differences in work values, and often fail to distinguish between 'generation' and 'age' as possible causes of such observed differences through the use of cross-sectional research designs in most studies, mixing up generational, 'age cohort' and 'period' effects. A multitude of problems exist in disentangling cohort and generational effects from age effects as employees mature, and there is a lack of consideration for differences in national context, gender and ethnicity.

Most discourse on generational diversity has been in Western countries; generations need to be considered within national contexts, as generational effects are likely to be specific to national settings. We have already referred to rises in individualism in China (Chapter 14), Africa (Chapter 11) and the Middle East (Chapter 10). Whiteoak et al (2006) found younger UAE nationals to be more individualistic, but also more positive about the use of *wasta* to obtain a position.

There are also significant gender and personality effects, cutting across generations. Turban et al (2001) found elite Chinese college students more attracted to FIEs than local SOEs and to Western firms (Chapter 14). Individual differences moderated these effects, supporting person–organisation fit concepts, as the more risk-averse participants, with a lower need for pay, were more attracted to SOEs than FIEs. Chow and Ngo (2002) found significant gender similarities in Chinese student job preferences for advancement, compensation, learning and overseas opportunities, but some gender differences over job security, firm size and nationality of company/supervisor. Women were more likely to prefer FIEs as offering more rewarding, challenging but less secure careers than SOEs – perhaps because local SOEs were more likely to favour males than FIEs.

This discussion of possible generational diversity over attracting, retaining and motivating global employees leads us into a broader discussion of employer branding (EB).

RECRUITING, ATTRACTING AND RETAINING INTERNATIONAL EMPLOYEES: THE ROLE OF EMPLOYER BRANDING

It is often claimed that EB can help an organisation compete effectively for talent and enhance employee engagement, recruitment and retention if it is perceived positively by existing, potential and former employees as a good place to work. Most conceptions of EB stress both instrumental/financial and symbolic or non-financial rewards and benefits. The concept is linked to the notion of *brand equity* (BE), a measure of brand worth or value. BE evolved from concepts of 'brand image' in the 1980s when 'brand' value' became apparent in financial terms as the total value of a brand as a separable asset, that is, *brand value*, and a measure of the strength of consumers' attachment to a brand, that is, *brand loyalty* or *brand strength*. For Aaker and Joachimsthaler (2000: 17), BE is 'a set of *brand assets and liabilities* linked to a brand that add to or subtract from the value provided by a product or service to a firm and/or to that firm's customers'.

The concept of EB therefore represents a borrowing of a 'marketing' concept by HRM; for Lievens et al (2002: 581), 'a new and promising direction consists of applying marketing principles to the labour market shortage problems ... attracting and retaining employees have a lot of parallels with attracting and keeping customers to buy products or brands'. We will first explore how this concept has been used in employee recruitment and attraction, as 'brand image' seems particularly important to job applicants (Chapter 15).

For Allen et al (2007: 1704), 'future research may be able to draw more from the marketing literature on branding to explore the dynamics underlying the perception of organisational image'. Applicant attraction and intention to pursue employment in response to an organisational website depended on job information, and indirectly on organisational information. Attitudes about recruitment sources also influenced applicant attraction, and partly mediated the effects of organisational information: 'just as branding provides incremental preferences for an organisation's products or services beyond the attributes of these products or services, organisation branding may also provide incremental preferences for an organisation's employment opportunities beyond job and organisational attributes' (Allen et al 2007: 1697). For Wilden et al (2006), employment opportunities can be seen as products, and evaluations of them are based on such characteristics as salary, location and other job/organisational attributes, which cannot be directly observed, but need to be inferred through EB signals. Firms overcome uncertainties through purposive branding aimed at targeted job-seekers; EB thus helps establish the identity of the firm as an employer, including its values, systems and policies.

However, we can also view EB and organisational attractiveness (OA) not only in terms of applicants but also in terms of existing employees, linking it more closely to employee *retention and reward* as well as attraction, seeing EB in terms of 'the power that draws applicants' attention to focus on an employer brand and encourages existing employees to stay' (Jiang and Iles 2011: 101). OA has two dimensions: *internal attractiveness* (for existing employees) and *external attractiveness* (for external applicants). Supornpraditchai et al (2007) show that where employees perceive EB as having high equity, they are more able to deliver the company's brand promise to customers, and are more likely to stay with the company.

Lievens (2007: 62) found that instrumental attributes such as pay and benefits, job security and task diversity explained a greater variance in OA among actual applicants, as opposed to potential applicants or existing employees. For all groups, symbolic trait inferences such as prestige, excitement and ruggedness explained a similar portion of the variance over and above instrumental attributes. This research 'builds on conceptualisations of the employer brand as a package of instrumental and symbolic attributes ... [and] confirms the usefulness of the instrumental-symbolic framework as a conceptualisation of employer brands'.

For Wilden et al (2006), the extent to which the brand contributes to attracting and retaining employees affects its BE. Berthon et al (2005) explain EB as 'the envisioned benefits that a potential employee, or "internal customer", sees in working for a specific organisation' (151), mirroring the emphasis on *benefits* in many definitions of EB. OA is here again seen as 'an antecedent of the more general concept of employer brand equity' (153); the more attractive an employer is perceived to be, the stronger its EB. Drawing on Ambler and Barrow's (1996) distinction between 'psychological and economic' benefits, Berthon et al (2005) developed a five-factor scale for the measurement of OA (termed 'employer attractiveness'). These dimensions consisted of interest value, development value, social value, economic value and application value.

Figure 19.1 shows that the way different benefits – both intrinsic and extrinsic – are valued by applicants and employees leads to brand equity and affects both applicants' intentions to apply and employees' intentions to stay with an organisation. This suggests that financial rewards and benefits are important in retaining employees, but so are more symbolic benefits such as trust and feelings of belonging, as well as benefits such as training and development and intrinsic job interest. In India, Tymon et al (2010) draw attention to the importance of intrinsic rewards and employee engagement, involving meaningfulness, choice, progress and competence, in retaining knowledge workers in particular, even in challenging labour market environments.

Figure 19.1: Employer brand equity and organisational attractiveness

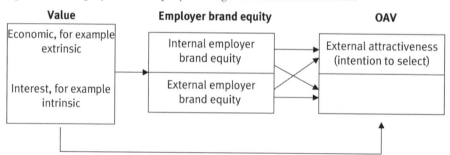

(based on Jiang and Iles 2011: 106)

There seem to be national and cultural differences in BE for employees, such as differential ratings of the benefits on offer. Young Chinese professionals in general rated personal interest, opportunities for applying knowledge and starting salary as the top three attractive job attributes (Fung et al 1996), with a preference for extrinsic rewards (Ding 1999). Companies offering generous compensation, training and development, and career opportunities are likely to be attractive to talented graduates. Hartmann et al (2010) found that Shanghai-based Western MNCs focused on building organisational cultures, supporting the development of personal relationships, and developing team spirit and commitment through joint sports activities, welfare and donation programmes, and other group events. Companies claimed it was very important to build belonging and pride to reduce employee turnover in China.

Y. Wang (2008) also found that emotional bonds with supervisors and co-workers were important determinants of organisational commitment in Chinese

FIEs, showing the importance of personal relationships and pleasant, healthy and harmonious working climates for Chinese employees, perhaps promoted through informal social events. Gamble and Huang (2008) also found that the organisational commitment of Chinese employees in an FIE (a British MNC retailer) was related to willingness to stay with the employer, but that, unlike in the West, this was not determined by a belief in company values and loyalty. Feelings of pride in working for the company were associated with a willingness to stay, perhaps because personal networks and relationships rather than 'company' values were more significant for Chinese employees. Job security and relationships with managers and co-workers were, however, significantly related to willingness to stay, again showing the importance of 'social values' to Chinese employees.

Let us now return to some studies of specific issues in global reward management, such as performance-related and merit pay and executive compensation.

PERFORMANCE-RELATED AND MERIT PAY AND EXECUTIVE COMPENSATION IN A GLOBAL CONTEXT

Here we discuss further two issues of great interest in discussions of global reward management, namely performance-related pay and executive compensation. Salimaki and Heneman (2008) point to global trends in reward management, such as moves from *job-based to person-based* rewards; *transferring social costs and risks* from the state or the organisation to the individual; and *threats to the psychological contract*.

The decentralisation of collective bargaining has led to more *individualised pay negotiations* and the spread of *pay for performance* schemes, though effectiveness and acceptance by different parties remain challenges. The *institutional context* is an important influence, such as the use of tax benefits to encourage profit-sharing in France, or the employment of employee stock ownership plans in Japan to encourage long-term commitment. The *cultural context* is also an important factor; masculinity is, as we saw (Chiang and Birtch 2012), often associated with the importance of financial, as compared with other, benefits; individualism is linked with a preference for individual-, rather than group-, based performance-related pay and less emphasis on need or relationships with co-workers; and uncertainty avoidance with seniority or skill-based compensation, offering more certainty and less variability or risk in pay.

Performance-related or merit pay refers to a policy where an organisation gives larger base salary increases to employees receiving higher performance (or merit) ratings than to employees receiving lower ratings (Gerhart and Trevor 2008). The intention is not only to motivate the current workforce (incentive effect) but also to increase the attraction and retention of high-performers (sorting effect). Such policies differ in terms of *pay level* (how much) and *pay basis* (how); organisations need to decide whether to pay the same, more or less relative to competitors, and what criteria to use on which to base decisions (seniority, performance, etc). Should a single performance criterion, or multiple criteria, be used?

Merit *bonuses* are different in not becoming part of the base salary; other pay-for-performance programmes include profit-sharing, stock plans, gainsharing, individual incentives and sales commissions. Here, measurement can be at the individual, plant or organisation level; it can use results or behaviour-oriented measures. Merit pay operates at the individual level and often uses behavioural measures. Many employees are covered by hybrid plans, mixing levels and measures.

The evidence for the effectiveness of merit/performance-related pay schemes is mixed; as Franco-Santos (2008: 41) points out, 'the effectiveness of an incentive system is closely related to the appropriateness of its performance measures'. If inappropriate measures are used, dysfunctional behaviour may result, as we saw in Chapter 18 on performance measurement, such as adverse effects on teamwork and the work climate.

Global organisations, especially geocentric ones, often seek to use a consistent set of performance measures in incentives, but this may not be appropriate; as Franco-Santos (2008: 51) argues, 'global organisations need to review the unique stakeholder profile and business model of each of the locations where they operate ... when using performance measures incentives as a management mechanism, global organisations should also take into consideration contextual factors such as national culture'. These factors influence the ways in which people perceive performance measurement and incentives (Chapter 2).

One area of current interest here is *executive compensation* in a global context, especially given recent shareholder revolts (the 'shareholder spring') over executive (especially chief executive) pay such as at WPP, the media giant, and rising concerns with ethical behaviour and CSR (Chapter 6). In the UK, FTSE100 chief executives in 2011 were awarded an average rise of 12 times at a time when earnings for the vast majority of people were stagnating: just over 200 times the average total pay in the private sector of just under •24,000 (Office for National Statistics). Basic pay for bosses of the UK's biggest companies rose 2.5%, but it was the variable elements of pay – so-called long-term incentive awards and deferred bonuses – that soared most. British owners and shareholders have become increasingly concerned about what they see as excessive pay increases for directors not justified by company performance, with a rise in the number of protest votes against remuneration practices at companies' annual meetings (Chapter 6). Governance reforms and insurer pressure may force all companies to disclose a single figure for realisable remuneration every year in their annual reports (http://www.bbc.co.uk/news/business-18407587).

As Haynes (2008: 86) points out, 'what contributes to the disparity in executive pay across countries is not merely to individual, firm or industry variables'. CEOs of firms of similar size in the same industry do not receive the same compensation, which is much higher in the USA than in other countries. *Institutional* factors (Chapter 1) such as legal and governance arrangements (for example the German requirement to have employee representatives on the board of large listed companies), ownership patterns, equity markets and the tax system all have an impact, as do cultural determinants. Uncertainty avoidance, affecting preferences for variable pay and its ratio to fixed pay, is one such cultural factor; higher uncertainty avoidance in the home country, as in Japan, is associated with higher ratios of fixed to variable pay and lower total CEO pay. The time horizon is another – short-term time horizon countries such as the USA focus on short-term goals, and high risk of turnover is associated with maximising CEO welfare. Egalitarianism is a third – more egalitarian home countries have higher ratios of fixed to variable pay within the CEO package and lower total CEO pay.

LEARNING SUMMARY

The chapter sought to identify the reward management objectives for IEs and employees in IEs and to critically analyse institutional and cultural influences on global reward management. It differentiated between the key components of a global reward management system, especially for expatriates and others on international assignments, and evaluated different approaches to global reward management, with their advantages and disadvantages.

The chapter also discussed the importance of both internal and external organisational attractiveness and employer branding, especially employment-based brand equity. It concluded by analysing recent developments in global reward management, with a particular focus on merit pay and performance-related pay systems, and the influence of institutional and cultural context on their effectiveness and acceptance. The issue of executive pay was also discussed under this heading.

INTERNET RESOURCES

PricewaterhouseCoopers: http://www.pwc.com/; http://www.pwc.com/gx/en/hr-management-services/executive-and-employee-rewards-attract-and-retain-key-staff.jhtml

ORCWorldwide: http://www.orcworldwide-ics.com/ and http://www.orcworldwide.com/ (from 2012 this is now **Mercer**: see http://select.mercer.com)

ECA International: http://www.eca-international.com/

http://www.citymayors.com/statistics/expensive-cities-world.html

Towers Perrin, now Towers Watson: http://www.towerswatson.com/ and http://www.towerswatson.com/about/

Economist Intelligence Unit: http://www.economist.com/topics/economist-intelligence-unit

CHAPTER 20

Employment Relations and Employee Voice in a Global Context

Paul Iles

LEARNING OBJECTIVES

By the end of this chapter, you should be able to:

- Discuss key issues in international employment relations and employee voice, and the policies and practices of IEs in this area.
- Examine key concerns for trade unions and their potential influence on ER.
- Critically analyse international developments and the role of international or transnational bodies such as the ILO and EU.
- Analyse differences between 'voluntarist' and 'mandatory' approaches to ER, with particular reference to contrasts between the UK and Germany.
- Critically discuss the effects of globalisation on global employment relations and the response of trade unions to economic and labour market policies and MNC policies, with particular reference to North America, western Europe, India, Africa (especially South Africa) and China.

INTRODUCTION

Comparative analysis can help us gain an understanding of the factors that shape employment relations in our own country. In this chapter we first discuss employment relations (ER) in a global context, analysing the ER policies of IEs in this area, the factors that influence them and the role of key actors such as the state, international bodies and trade unions in a comparative context. In particular, we look in more depth at ER in different systems, especially in voluntarist as opposed to mandatory systems, and the influences of globalisation on these, with particular reference to India and Africa, with a focus on South Africa. We also look in more depth at China, where the official union has lacked legitimacy in representing workers' interests and where spontaneous and self-organised strikes, demonstrations and collective bargaining in recent years show the potential for workers to develop free, independent associations.

INTERNATIONAL EMPLOYMENT RELATIONS

Wailes et al (2011: 1) draw attention to the ways in which 'globalisation is reshaping the employment relationship across companies, industries and countries'. Much interest has been over whether ER systems are 'converging' or remain divergent; national-level institutions remain strong determinants of ER systems, supporting a 'varieties of capitalism' (Hall and Soskice 2001) or national business systems approach (Chapter 1). National institutions tend to filter or refract common global economic pressures, so globalisation is unlikely to lead to convergence (for example union membership has declined in the USA and UK but held up in Scandinavia).

However, the 'varieties of capitalism' view (Hall and Soskice 2001) tends to identify just two institutional solutions to coordination –*liberal market economies* such as the US and UK, and *coordinated market economies* such as Germany and Japan. In Chapter 1, we referred to these as broadly 'voluntarist' or 'interventionist'. This, however, misses out most of the world, not neatly fitting into either category! Italy (and many other Mediterranean countries) fits neither model (Baccaro and Pulignano 2011). Change in the system – discussed in respect of VET in Chapter 1 – is also difficult to explain; we explore changes to the German ER system later (see also Chapter 8). Determinism – seeing the nation-state as hermetically sealed and leaving little scope for international factors, agency or politics – is also a problem, discussed in Chapter 3 with respect to the pragmatic adaptations made by Japanese firms in China, following neither purely Japanese nor Chinese models (Gamble 2010).

It is difficult to compare ER across national boundaries; concepts may change considerably when translated from one context to another (Dowling et al 2008). Concepts such as 'arbitration' or 'collective bargaining' (CB), for example, may mean different things: in China , 'collective consultation'; in the USA, local negotiations with a union in an organisation; in Germany, national or regional industry-level bargaining between an employers' association and an industrial trade union. ER systems cannot be understood without appreciating their historical origins and institutional context, which affect the structure of trade unions and other features of the ER system.

Poole (1986) identifies a number of influential factors affecting the ER system:

- mode of technology and industrial organisation
- methods of government regulation, such as interventionist versus voluntarist policies (discussed in relation to national HRD in Chapter 1)
- ideological divisions within the trade union movement, such as over religion or politics
- influence of religious organisations on trade union development
- managerial strategies for labour relations.

We explore some of these issues, particularly methods of regulation and managerial strategies, in North America and western Europe, before discussing ER issues in India, Africa (especially South Africa) and China.

In terms of *IHRM policy* (Chapter 3), MNCs often delegate responsibility for ER to the local subsidiary in a decentralisation policy or polycentric strategy (Perlmutter 1969), in contrast to reward management (Chapter 19), where geocentric, regiocentric or ethnocentric orientations are more common. However, some global coordination and monitoring is needed in order to make decisions on rationalisation, investment and location (Dowling et al 2008). How involved corporate HQ is depends on such factors as:

- the *degree of inter-subsidiary production integration*, such as in transnational sourcing using a global supply chain
- *nationality of ownership* of the subsidiary: US firms tend to be more centralised – a country of origin effect (Chapter 3)
- overall IHRM *orientation*: ethnocentric firms tend to experience more ER conflict, disregarding local norms and imposing a perceived 'foreign' system
- *subsidiary characteristics*: firms established through acquisition tend to have greater autonomy over ER, as in other IHRM policy areas; new and key subsidiaries attract more control, as does poor performance, a similar position to the use of expatriates (Chapter 15)
- *home product-market characteristics*: if home sales are small, it is more likely for the subsidiary to adapt to local ER norms and institutions
- *management attitudes towards unions*: union avoidance is characteristic of many US, but not German, firms; Japanese firms may not seek to impose 'enterprise unions', but often seek to negotiate with a single-table representative body, rather than several unions separately.

REGULATING EMPLOYEE VOICE

Hannon (2011) suggests that global competition has led managers to examine ways of increasing enterprise productivity and performance, including the introduction of schemes designed to enhance *employee voice* to increase commitment and decision-making input (Chapter 8). Employee voice is a general, overarching concept referring to the various ways in which employees take part in decision-making in organisations and the degree of influence they have (Hannon 2011: 230). It includes *employee participation* (power-sharing) and *employee involvement* (soliciting of employee views). Participation structures include collective bargaining by unions or works councils, constraining management freedom to make decisions. Unions can enhance social efficiency by the provision of 'voice' mechanisms to allow employees to express concerns and issues, providing a basis for fairer, more equitable and sustainable ER.

In contrast, involvement schemes such as quality circles or suggestion schemes tap into employee ideas to gain commitment and improve efficiency; but management remains the final decision-maker. Practices tend to be management-initiated and task- and performance-oriented, unlike the more power-centred issues addressed by participation mechanisms, such as wage levels, hours or redundancy packages. These are more often initiated by worker actions and initiatives or by government legislation. Involvement practices manifest direct employee involvement, and participation practices indirect involvement through elected or appointed representatives, such as union officials or works council representatives.

Figure 20.1 shows the level of involvement in some types of voice methods.

Figure 20.1: Level of voice in different methods

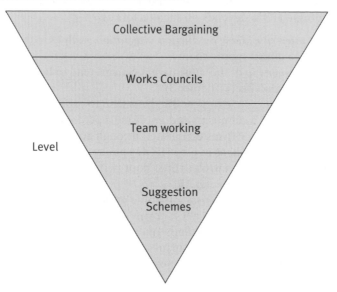

The *state* in various regions seeks to regulate employee voice: both the conditions under which labour power is sold and how it is used (Edwards 2003: 162), including programmes such as social security to guarantee basic living standards, imposition of age limits on employment and the operation of minimum wage legislation. It may also regulate the deployment of labour power through allocating union organisational rights, restricting working hours, initiating health and safety legislation, granting employment protection (including anti-discrimination and anti-harassment measures) and developing formal grievance proceedings.

Union structures themselves differ considerably – for example, *general* unions (open to all workers); *craft* unions (based on skilled groupings across industries); *industrial unions* (all grades in an industry); *conglomerate* unions (members in more than one industry); and *enterprise* unions (all enterprise members), common in Japan.

Unions may seek to influence IEs (Dowling et al 2008) by:

- *influencing wage levels* (contributing to MNC labour costs)
- *constraining their ability to vary levels of employment* (lobbying governments to introduce redundancy legislation and encouraging regulation by international bodies, to be discussed shortly)
- *hindering global integration efforts.*

National systems of *pay bargaining* influence the extent of pay inequality, with a strong relationship between density of union membership and compression of bottom-end earnings inequality (Vernon 2011). Collective bargaining constrains company and workplace reward structures, especially for non-managerial employees (Chapter 19). Multi-employer agreements, whether confederal or sectoral, do not dictate pay practices, but lay down minima; there is then typically much negotiation with unions or works councils at the level of the establishment.

Such influence has not, however, tended to block *pay for performance* (PfP) schemes (Chapter 19). Generally, unions have preferred competence pay schemes, as in Sweden, where pay increases with skill level or competence, but often concede some place for PfP if the basis for bonuses is transparent and objective, if the component is relatively small (for example less than 10%) and if implementation is subject to joint regulation. In some cases group-based or company-based PfP is preferred as less of a threat to union solidarity. However, unions at local levels may now be more sympathetic to individualised PfP as a complement to basic increases. Unions tend to be more accepting of *financial participation schemes* as a bonus, such as profit-sharing; this is less true of employee share-ownership schemes (ESOPs), however.

IEs influence ER through their:

- *financial resources*, such as ability to absorb losses in a specific subsidiary
- *alternative sources of supply*, for example dual sourcing, temporary switching of production to another subsidiary
- *ability to move facilities* to another country, for example 'off-shoring', as we saw in the BPO industry in India (Chapter 13)
- *remote locus of authority* – for example the corporate HQ may be in another country
- *production facilities in many countries*, which allow 'coercive comparisons', to play sites off against each other
- *ER expertise*
- *capacity to stage 'investment strikes'* by failing to invest, or withdrawing investment, in a particular country.

The union response has often been to:

- *form international secretariats*: loose confederations linking unions globally in particular industries and attempting to achieve transnational bargaining
- *lobby for national legislation* to prevent export of jobs through IE investment policies
- *lobby for international regulation* by international organisations via federations such as the European Trade Union Confederation (ETUC) and the International Federation of Free Trade Unions (ICFTU).

For example, Wailes et al (2011) draw attention to the accelerating development of *international framework agreements* (IFAs), voluntary agreements on minimum labour standards negotiated between global union federations and MNCs. This may also be influenced by NGOs putting pressure on companies through consumers (see Chapter 6 on CSR and Case Study 6.1, the Apple/

Foxconn case study, and Chapter 12 on Latin America). (See www.tuc.org.uk/international and www.etuc.org www.global-unions.org.)

REFLECTIVE ACTIVITY 20.1

1   What more can trade unions do in this area?

2   What problems or issues might they encounter?

This introduces the issue of how employee voice is *regulated internationally*.

The *International Labour Organization* (ILO) (www.ilo.org), established in 1919, was the first specialist agency of the United Nations in 1946 and works to gain recognition of the rights of workers to combine together and be represented in collective bargaining. It has developed a series of principles to be respected by all nations, such as freedom of association, the right to organise and collectively bargain, abolition of forced labour, and non-discrimination in employment, along with a set of voluntary guidelines for MNC activities. It is the main body for developing and enforcing minimum labour standards. If these are not in place, there may be a 'race to the bottom' and increasing inequality.

The ILO, composed of 177 member states, has representatives from governments, employers and employees. It sets two types of standards: *conventions*, legally binding treaties once ratified, and *recommendations*, advisory standards assisting the implementation of conventions. Collectively these are referred to as the International Labour Code. Details of ILO core standards and its Better Work programme can be found at http://www.ilo.org/global/lang--en/index.htm.

There are continuing breaches of these conventions, and problems in their implementation, but they ensure that employee participation through trade union-based collective bargaining is a relatively common feature of many national employment relations systems. The ILO has developed a 'Decent Work Agenda' in recognition of the growth of non-traditional forms of work and to integrate its programmes.

In addition, there are OECD/UN guidelines and codes of practice. The OECD (Organization for Economic Cooperation and Development, www.oecd.org), established in 1960, now consists of the leading 30 industrialised countries and has a series of directorates dealing with economic and social development, mostly engaged in research. However, it has developed a series of voluntary guidelines under the umbrella of a 'chapeau' agreement setting out recommendations on responsible conduct for IEs operating in or originating from OECD countries, often incorporated into domestic legal systems (see www.oecd.org/daf/investment/guidelines).

The World Trade Organization (WTO, www.wto.org) – another UN agency, established in 1996 to promote free trade and resolve trade disputes – has also had significant effects on ER (Chapters 3 and 14 in respect of HR transformations in China after accession in 2001). The WTO has not directly included labour standards in its rules or included social items as grounds for trade disputes, but it has recognised the ILO as the relevant competent body (Wailes et al 2011).

The European Union (EU) also engages in transnational regulation at the regional level through growing legislation on participation and voice. EU law has supremacy in a number of employment-related fields to do with information and consultation of employees if a majority of member states support the proposal. There are various directives on such areas as collective redundancies, transfers of undertakings, health and safety, information and consultation, and a directive on European works councils (EWCs) applied to companies with over 1,000 employees in at least two member states, even if the company originates from outside the EU. EWCs consist of employee representatives with such rights as the right to an annual general meeting and meetings in exceptional circumstances, and management is obliged to provide information on business, economic and investment plans, and proposed changes. Common minimum standards on participation apply across the EU, giving employees input and influence, but without – yet –leading to a common approach across the EU (Hannon 2011).

Some 'cooperative' or 'interventionist' countries (Chapter 1) such as Germany and Austria have been enthusiastic over these initiatives; more arms' length or 'voluntarist' ones such as the UK much less so. In addition, national governments have flexibility over how to bring binding EU directives into national legislation. In the UK there is a need for a 'trigger mechanism' to establish procedures for employee information and consultation, and permission to use direct, rather than indirect, methods of participation. Information may also often be presented late, and timely consultation may rarely happen.

For details of EU labour laws and relevant legislation, see http://ec.europa.eu/social/main.jsp?catId=157&langId=en.

Figure 20.2 shows the main parties involved in international ER.

Figure 20.2: Main parties in international ER

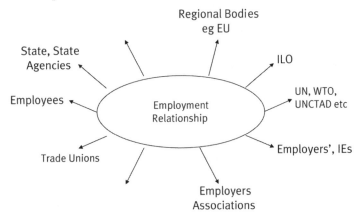

EMPLOYMENT RELATIONS IN DIFFERENT REGIONS

Here we look at employment relations issues and the role of trade unions in different regions: North America, western Europe and the EU, India, Africa (in particular South Africa) and China. In many developing countries unions may serve as campaigners to promote democracy, challenge authoritarian regimes and provide mechanisms for voicing concerns when formal political structures are only partly functional (Brewster and Wood 2007). They may also serve to protect democratic gains and help turn employers away from low-wage/low-skill employment models towards higher value-added and more cooperative employment relations frameworks characterised by high wages and high skills (Brewster and Wood 2007).

However, unions globally have faced many years of falling memberships and declining union density. They have also faced challenges of increasingly diverse workforces and less secure employment contracts in the face of employer demands for greater 'flexibility'. In some cases they have faced explicitly anti-union governments leading moves towards privatisation and labour market deregulation, though with uneven impacts (for example, union numbers have held up in Canada and Scandinavia, as well as in Brazil and South Africa).

In Chapter 1, we discussed national business systems and the difference between 'voluntarist' and 'interventionist' approaches to national HRD and VET systems. A similar distinction can be made over employment relations. In voluntarist systems, employers are fairly free to decide what practices to implement with respect to employee voice. In more interventionist systems, called *mandatory* by Hannon (2011), legislation often forces employers to adopt institutions or mechanisms for employee participation. Voluntarist systems include Anglo-Saxon 'common law' countries such as the USA and UK, favouring free market policies and an arms' length stance by government. They tend to have limited legal regulation, though EU legislation has changed this to some extent in the UK and Ireland. Indeed, it can be queried whether 'voluntarist' is now the appropriate term to describe the UK system. Marchington et al (2011: 44) point out the British state has historically been seen as *laissez-faire* or 'voluntarist' 'because of its comparatively low level of legal regulation of employment. But that characterisation is increasingly anachronistic as the state has increasingly sought to reconstruct ER institutions.' Though it has largely avoided intervention in employee rights, EU membership has brought legislation on health and safety, labour law, individual employment rights, and information and consultation rights.

In voluntarist systems, 'employee involvement' rather than participation is favoured. Mandatory systems oblige voice to be exercised through various institutions, more characteristic of many continental European countries, where it may sit alongside collective bargaining in a 'dual system' of ER. The ideal type here is often regarded as the Germanic system (see Chapter 8), which features works councils and rights to information, consultation and co-determination (joint decision-making) on many HR matters. There is also mandatory representation of employee interests on 'supervisory boards' of companies above a certain size; this appoints and oversees the activities of the management board and has directly elected employee representatives.

However, the situation in Germany, as discussed in Chapter 8, is changing, and it has recently moved towards a more flexible labour market (Keller and Kirsch 2011). Some companies have operated beyond industrial-level collectively bargained agreements, withdrawing from employers' associations to negotiate at company level. Others, such as McDonald's, have resisted the representation of employees in works councils.

Co-determination as a form of participation is a distinguishing feature of the German ER system at both workplace and company levels, with legally established rights for works councils – separate from unions, but with many works councillors coming from union members. However, one half of private sector employees are not now covered by them, a figure rising since the 1980s (especially in services, SMEs and in eastern Germany). Collective bargaining now mostly takes place at regional and industry levels, but the coverage rate of industry-level agreements has declined and there is an increasing 'tacit escape from collective agreements' (Keller and Kirsch 2011: 211). Though the German system has been characterised by this 'dual system' (collective bargaining and co-determination), only a minority of employees now enjoy both: 'the 'duality' of the German system, one of its fundamental characteristics, has gradually been weakened and is 'disintegrating' (212) in the wake of German reunification, changing modes of production, new forms of employment and Europeanisation and globalisation, becoming more similar to the Anglo-American model:

> Germany is no longer the prototypical example of highly regulated, well-integrated, consensus-driven employment relations … nevertheless, increasing heterogeneity … or even the dualisation between core and peripheral segments of employment is more likely than a wholesale convergence towards the Anglo-American model. (Keller and Kirsch 2011: 221)

In Chapter 8, we referred to this process of 'dualisation' as 'dual flexibility' (Eichorst 2012).

Hannon (2011) agrees that globalisation and competitive pressures have affected how German works councils work, but this has been uneven and contradictory. There is evidence of a decline in works council presence in companies, especially in services; employer disagreements with works councils over such areas as relocation, employment levels and outsourcing have grown; and councils have often made concessions over flexibility to secure jobs. However, trends towards negotiating employment conditions and practices at company or plant, rather than sectoral, level have also strengthened the role of works councils.

Case Study 20.1 illustrates some differences between the voluntarist British and the mandatory German systems, as well as the role played by the trade unions and supervisory boards in German companies.

ROVER, HONDA AND BMW

CASE STUDY 20.1

Adapted from Eckardt and Matthias (2003); http://en.wikipedia.org/wiki/MG_Rover_Group

BMW, the German car manufacturer, took over the British car manufacturer Rover in the 1990s. Land Rover was later sold to Ford and then sold on. The Jaguar and Rover name were sold to the Indian company, Tata Motors, and Rover cars to the Nanjing Automobile Group, badged under the MG brand name.

Cooperation between Rover's predecessor, British Leyland, and the Japanese producer Honda was established in 1979 (see Chapter 7 on alliances). Honda gained some control over Rover, especially in terms of quality and teamworking; Rover obtained the survival of the company and improvements in quality, working structures, HRM, productivity and costs. BAe (British Aerospace) bought Rover in 1988 and Honda acquired a 20% share in it in 1989. Honda later dissolved its four years of financial engagement with Rover by selling its stake when it was bought by BMW.

BMW initially acted very cautiously, sensitive to the different socio-cultural and national backgrounds of staff and emphasising the autonomy of Rover as an independent sister company. However, in 1999 the Rover crisis broke out, with disputes among BMW's leading managers and board members over future management and product policy against a background of slumping sales. The vice-president and chairman were ousted, the VP resigning when he didn't get a clear majority in the election for the new chairman. The new CEO mainly owed his appointment to the joint vote of the workers' representatives within the BMW supervisory board; it was an example of transnationally cooperating workers'

representatives affecting and co-determining the steering of an international company.

The company pursued short-term cost reduction, integration, standardisation and restructuring of the BMW directory board, with a stronger push to re-centralisation and globalisation. The Birmingham (Longbridge) plant was fitted up for new launches, and face-to-face mixed learning teams of Rover and BMW employees were established. BMW working structures, management culture and communication flows were introduced, and identical German managerial structures ('meister', process leader in assembly, team leader, manufacturing manager/area manager, technical director/ plant manager) established. The meister/production leader role was to control, lead and motivate workers by showing interest in each worker's behaviour and performance, using coaching and empowerment.

Rover structures were seen as outdated, with poor communication flows and weak middle management. Rover management behaviour was seen as arrogant (for example the predominance of written communication), leading to an emphasis on extrinsic motivation. The company also tried to combine opposed labour relation systems, 'British adversarial voluntarism' and 'German cooperative corporation'. The four most important British unions and their shop stewards had to adapt to the legally institutionalised German BMW works council system, representing mainly the IG Metall union. British shop stewards now faced new representation and negotiating structures and cultures based on cooperation ('co-management'), consultation and information. Some formerly 'isolationist' shop stewards became enthusiastic towards the German works council institution, but the relatively high information transparency between BMW management and the works council and demands for confidentiality often clashed with the intense and direct information flows between Rover shop stewards and employees.

In 2001 the family owner and banks insisted on selling the Rover division and Land Rover brand to Ford. Only the Mini brand, built in the Oxford plant, was to stay within the BMW group. When BMW sold off its interests, MG Rover was bought for a nominal •10 in May 2000 by a specially assembled group of businessmen, the Phoenix Consortium. In June 2004 Shanghai Automotive Industry Corporation signed a joint venture partnership to develop new models and technologies with MG Rover, with agreement between the two companies to create a joint venture company with shared production between the Longbridge site and locations in China.

MG Rover placed itself in administration on 8 April 2005; more than 6,000 workers at MG Rover lost their jobs, with 25,000 jobs reported lost in related supply industries. The principal remaining assets were sold to the Nanjing Automobile Group, which started shipping equipment from Longbridge to China and dismantling plant at Longbridge for reassembly in China. In August 2008, assembly at Longbridge began of a lightly revised

MG TF roadster for the European market from Chinese-built semi knock-down (SKD) kits.

One of the authors (Iles) was working with Rover on designing and delivering leadership programmes in the late 1990s when it was in alliance with Honda. It was interesting to observe its influence in such areas as common uniforms for all staff grades, common terms and conditions, eating areas, and common car-parking allocations, all contrary to conventional, hierarchical British practice. With the takeover by BMW, this rapidly changed; engineers were now informed that they were now the 'heart and soul' of the business, with grand offices to match, and soon went back to smart suits and ties! Another interesting contrast was in the backgrounds of the respective boards; while Rover only had one PhD (a mathematician, head of quality) on the board, and very few had engineering degrees, all BMW directors had PhDs in engineering, and the new CEO was a professor of engineering.

Questions

1   What does this case tell you about the different national business systems and cultures (Chapters 1 and 2) in the UK and Germany, and differences in the ER systems?

2   Analyse the role of trade unions and the supervisory board in this case.

EMPLOYMENT RELATIONS IN NORTH AMERICA

Briscoe et al (2012) identify a number of ER issues specific to North America, especially:

1   labour laws

2   unionisation

3   labour force values.

The US Government intervenes less to regulate the labour market than in many other regions, especially Europe. Labour laws are less intrusive, and the focus is more on the 'free market', with management given greater say over HR decisions and strategies. However, there are relatively strong federal and state laws giving employees protection against unfair, unsafe, unhealthy and discriminatory employment practices, particularly notable in the case of anti-discrimination and affirmative action laws protecting the rights of 'classified' workers (for example on race, gender, age grounds). US HRM has an important role to play in monitoring the legal and regulatory environment and reporting on the effectiveness of anti-discrimination and affirmative action legislation. The US trade union movement is currently split into two 'peak' federations (Katz and Colvin 2011).

For US labour laws see http://www.dol.gov/elaws/elg/

Canada is somewhat different; it is federal, bilingual and bicultural, with French-speaking Quebec following a more interventionist 'cooperative' system with more radical unions and greater union involvement in policy. The English-speaking 'rest of Canada' follows a more 'liberal market' model with more 'business-oriented' unions. In general, union membership and density is much higher than in the USA, the union movement has better links with the women's movement and other social movements, and employers are much less antagonistic to unions, preferring to work with them (Thompson and Taras 2011).

For Canadian labour laws see http://www.hrsdc.gc.ca/eng/labour/labour_law/index.shtml

Compared with many European countries, the US has relatively low levels of unionisation; membership was less than 12% in 2010 and 2011, but is much higher in the public sector at 37% (see http://www.bls.gov/news.release/union2.nr0.htm).

Membership has been declining for various reasons – shifts from manufacturing to service jobs, increases in white-collar jobs, greater interaction between management and staff, as well as federal and state laws and agencies providing some degree of employee protection. Briscoe et al (2012) do not mention the aggressive anti-unionism pursued by many employers (Katz and Colvin 2011). In most firms, unlike in Europe, employers have considerable autonomy in designing HR policies and practices to maximise shareholder value. Most US employees, as we saw in Chapters 2 and 8, are more individualistic than many others, and workforce HRM is more merit-based. Staffing policies are influenced by perspectives of 'employment-at-will' or 'hire and fire', enabling either party to terminate employment without advance notice, unlike in much of western Europe and elsewhere. The external labour market provides most staff recruits, unlike in Japan and parts of western Europe. Compensation is often based on merit-based or 'pay-for-performance' models, not seniority.

EMPLOYMENT RELATIONS IN WESTERN EUROPE AND THE EU

Briscoe et al (2012) identify three key employment relations issues for Europe, especially for the EU:

1 government regulations

2 labour unions

3 the flexibility–security nexus.

In terms of government regulations, European countries in general as compared with North America have relatively extensive government regulations in labour standards and legislation, shaping labour markets in such areas as employee rights, social security, healthcare, union negotiating rights, collective agreements and other aspects of the employment relationship, such as employment contracts, working time, and health and safety. All this limits (or does it support?) the HRM function's ability to decide on HRM policies.

There is greater government responsibility towards employee representation and protection in Europe in terms of collective bargaining, dialogue, wages and benefits, and working conditions, including at EU levels through the European Trade Union Confederation (ETUC). Many countries, and the EU itself, also provide works councils of employer and elected representatives of employees to cover such issues as employment protection, communications and employee interests over operational decisions; we discussed this extensively in relation to Germany.

The balance between the free trade rules of the EU (and global competition) to provide labour-market flexibility and deregulation on the one hand and employment protection and security on the other is shifting in Europe. Germany, France and Spain have made moves towards more flexible employment contracts, easing rules on hiring and firing and moving towards more part-time and temporary employment. Denmark is seen by some as offering a balance between flexibility and security (flexicurity) that may serve as a model for others, seeking to combine the flexibility of the UK labour market with the security and protection offered by other Nordic countries (Madsen et al 2011).

EMPLOYMENT RELATIONS IN INDIA

There is a large state presence in employee relations in India through a series of laws and institutions supporting collective bargaining and employee rights (Chapter 13). There is extensive use of complex legal means and interventions, such as the Industrial Disputes Act and Indian Labor Conference, though employers often evade these. Unionisation rates have slipped to below 10% of the total working population (Saini and Budhwar 2004).

Ratnam and Verma (2011: 349) claim that 'India has too many laws offering too little protection to too few who are mainly engaged in the formal/organised sector that accounts for barely 7% of the labour force'. They call for more training of those involved in labour administration and the labour judiciary, and greater awareness of alternative dispute-resolution procedures and arbitration. Given the cost of legal procedures, they also recommend people's labour courts closer to homes and workplaces. Fewer laws with better enforcement, elimination of multiple definitions across different legislations, clear rules on employee terminations (requiring government approval), and independent IR dispute-settlement machinery are also recommended.

We discussed the importance of the informal sector, and difficulties in organising it, in Africa (Chapter 11) and Latin America (Chapter 12), and will pursue this issue with respect to South Africa. Unions have also had little impact on MNCs operating in India, but are much stronger in Indian-owned firms and especially in the public sector.

EMPLOYMENT RELATIONS IN AFRICA, ESPECIALLY SOUTH AFRICA

Horwitz (2007) identifies key elements of employment relations in Africa in roughly chronological order from the nineteenth century:

- the colonial impact
- the role of nationalism post-independence
- post-colonial state formation and crisis
- structural adjustment programmes
- democratic reforms
- pressures for social partnership (Chapter 11).

For Brewster and Wood (2007), the general decline of organised labour following the economic crises of the 1970s represented only one of many pressures reforming employment relations in Africa. These crises weakened the ability of the state to enforce existing laws and bring in new employment relations legislation, resulting in wholesale job losses in the formal sector. The effects of neo-liberal reforms such as the structural adjustment programmes begun in the 1980s affected trade unions in several ways. Under-spending on education at all levels in many states caused skills bases to deteriorate, placing new entrants to the labour market in a weak position, lacking access to basic and technical education and weakening their bargaining position. Foreign competition and job losses greatly reduced the pool of potential union members. Alongside public sector job cutbacks, this damaged employees' bargaining position. Currency devaluations caused effective pay cuts, while the erosion of the state rendered labour laws difficult to enforce.

Social security provision tends to be negligible or non-existent, forcing individuals to sell their labour power at almost any cost and/or rely on extended, informal family-based networks of support, placing demands on those already in work (Chapter 11). The ability or will of governments to enforce age limitation and labour protection laws has also been eroded, while many informal sector workers operate beyond legal restrictions.

As a result, African unions have been forced on to the defensive. Many are losing members as casualisation and informalisation of labour grows; new entrants such as NGOs and social movements have also entered the ER arena, as have new, smaller trade unions (Kocer and Hayter 2011). In many African countries, a drift to one-party rule post-independence subsumed trade unions into transmitters of official government policy, not unlike China (Chapter 14). The 1990s, however, saw a return to multi-party democracy in many African states, as in Latin America (Chapter 12), and trade unions often played a key role in political protest movements. However, even in South Africa, the influential Congress of South African Trade Unions (COSATU) has failed to check the introduction of market-driven policies by the post-apartheid ANC Government, though it has with respect to privatisation in some instances.

Wood and Dibben (2008) discuss the role of COSATU, a 'super federation' launched in 1985 and perhaps the strongest African labour movement due to its role in the struggle against apartheid. Trade unions under apartheid were characterised by an exclusive 'racial Fordism' and the political exclusion of Africans. As apartheid began to end, COSATU rapidly expanded in the private sector in the 1980s and the public sector in the 1990s. Though active in resisting neo-liberal pressures, it has the potential to fragment along age, gender, skill level and ethnic lines. Brookes et al (2004) found continuing high levels of vertical and horizontal solidarity, but some cleavages linked to gender and ethnicity. Workers seemed generally appreciative of the 'strategic engagement' policy with the ANC (African National Congress) Government, with which (and the junior Communist Party) it had a formal partnership. Non-African members (for example 'coloured' and Indian) were more critical, as were female members of the catering workers union.

COSATU has generally failed to make strong headway among 'informal' and temporary workers, or with grassroots organisations representing these groups. Wood and Dibben (2008) found regular participation in union affairs, democratic accountability, participation in collective action and a strong commitment to the labour movement among members. Women were somewhat less active in union affairs, though levels of involvement were still high, and non-African workers were also less willing to participate in internal union affairs.

Buhlungu et al (2008) found that members still broadly supported the alliance with the ruling ANC, but COSATU faced challenges not only in opposing neo-liberal reforms sponsored by the ANC Government and in retaining and re-energising the rank and file after the struggle against apartheid, but also in reaching out to women and potential members in the informal sector and in other areas of insecure employment against a background of increasing unemployment (Buhlungu 2006; Buhlungu et al 2007).

REFLECTIVE ACTIVITY 20.2

What recommendations would you make to enhance unions' abilities to engage more effectively with women and especially with workers in the informal sector?

South African labour legislation is constitutionally quite 'labour-friendly', but accords organisational rights to 'representative' unions, rather than small players or 'breakaway' unions. In 2012 there was serious industrial unrest, especially in the mining industry (for example Lonmin, Impala Platinum), often led by new, more militant unions or by the workers themselves. Shop stewards from the giant National Union of Mineworkers (NUM) have been killed or threatened, and populists have portrayed the NUM leadership and COSATU as out of touch with the struggles of ordinary workers, sharply raising the issue of the legitimacy of the union leadership, as well as issues of the continuing power of capital in a highly unequal society (http://www.bbc.co.uk/news/world-africa-19635747).

However, African economic growth has been surprisingly high, leading to disposable incomes which might stimulate trade and employment creation, as might Chinese infrastructure investment (Chapter 11), leading to fertile recruitment grounds for African unions; in addition, collective bargaining is widening to include issues such as HIV/AIDS (Kocer and Hayter 2011).

EMPLOYMENT RELATIONS IN CHINA

ER in China show some similarities to South Africa, but in a more extreme form, such as the links between the 'official' trade unions and the 'party-state', issues of union legitimacy among members, difficulties faced by 'unofficial' trade unions, and union failure to combat state market-driven, neo-liberal policies. We discussed HRM in China in Chapter 14 and abuses of workers' rights in Chapter 6 over the Apple/Foxconn case. Cooke (2011a, 2012) points out that effective worker representation is often an aspiration rather than a reality in China, owing to flaws in the design and enforcement of labour regulations, the weak bargaining power of workers and the absence of effective organising bodies such as trade unions in the context of radical state-sector reform and the emergence of a market economy, leading to what Gamble (2010) refers to as 'de-institutionalisation'.

In general, labour standards established by laws and regulations in China in recent years 'are not markedly inferior to those of comparable countries and indeed many developed nations' (Cooney 2007: 674), with one major exception: the right to freedom of association. Rising levels of labour disputes since privatisation and marketisation have required the state to improve labour protection and labour standards, focusing mainly on individual rights around contracts, wages, conditions and social security. Collective rights to organise, strike and bargain are largely absent, making employee rights unenforceable or disregarded in many cases (as in the Apple/Foxconn case, Case Study 6.1). The Labour Law and Trade Union Law (1992) authorises unions at the enterprise level, but these are defined vaguely and abstractly as 'collective consultation'. This is defended as more culturally appropriate, reflecting 'harmony', not bargaining – before this the Communist party-state set terms and conditions unilaterally. Unions were given the official role of representing workers for consultation, a position reinforced and expanded in later laws to involve 'collective contracts', but without the right to independent organisation.

Only one *trade union* is recognised by the state: the All-China Federation of Trade Unions (ACFTU). This is usually seen as holding a weak position, with meetings held mainly to promote CCP messages and initiatives and to maintain stability and 'harmony'. Sometimes it has played a mediating or even peace-keeping/policing role in demonstrations and strikes, though it has played a role in skills training, employee representation and in promoting, drafting and monitoring labour legislation and the enforcement of labour regulations. It operates under the leadership of the CCP, which has suppressed any attempt by it to gain greater power and authority; this has also been true of independent unions. Local branches are partly funded by local government, which acts as a control, and senior officials are normally appointed by the CCP, rather than elected by members as the law stipulates. They are essentially managed as civil servants pursuing a government career.

All this has led to international criticism of union independence and legitimacy. Despite high and stable levels of membership in unionised workplaces (around 93% density), unions have difficulties in securing legitimacy with their own members. Women's membership is almost as high as men's; but as membership is virtually mandatory once a trade union unit is established, this is not a sign of union strength. Membership has expanded since 2005 with ACFTU's national recruitment drives aimed at migrant workers, officially classified as 'farmers', not 'workers', due to their rural administrative status. Organising this group became a priority with the expansion of FIEs and the market economy; private firms have often tried to resist union recognition here in many cases.

In enterprises there are union-guided 'Workers' Congresses' acting as official mechanisms of employee representation and participation in decision-making. These are often recognised by foreign firms to show compliance with labour laws (but without union recognition). Essentially these act as part of the HRM/welfare function.

However, Chinese workers are supportive of the idea of unions and collective bargaining, if critical of their leaders and organisations in practice as ineffective and powerless. Alternative forms of organising and representation have emerged, including legal centres (often union-supported), job centres/employment agencies, training centres (mostly aimed at laid-off SOE employees, rural migrants and disadvantaged groups) and the All-China Women's Federation. Founded in 1949 and the only official women's organisation at national level, this body has campaigned to defend women's equal employment rights and blocking 'women return home' proposals, but has had little impact in the private sector.

In addition, there has been a growth in self-organising, such as self-formed associations and networks, including those set up by migrant workers in informal employment, and numerous spontaneous strikes, protests and negotiations. These have taken place despite government suppression (though government is more willing to tolerate action against foreign MNCs in order to appease nationalist sentiment – currently expressed against Japanese control of various island groups), but such groups have been able in many cases to organise and mobilise labour laws to secure improvements in wages and benefits (as we saw in the Foxconn case in Chapter 6).

LEARNING SUMMARY

In this chapter we discussed key issues in international employee voice and employment relations and the policies and practices of IEs in this area. We analysed employment relations (ER) in a global context, discussing the IHRM policies of IEs, the factors that influence them, and the role of key actors such as the state, international organisations such as the ILO and EU, and trade unions in a comparative context. The chapter then examined key concerns for trade unions and their potential influence on IEs before analysing differences between 'voluntarist' and 'mandatory' approaches to ER, with particular reference to contrasts between the UK and Germany. The chapter also critically discussed the effects of globalisation on global employment relations and the response of trade unions to government economic and labour market policies and MNC policies, with particular reference to North America, western Europe, India, Africa (especially South Africa) and China.

Our focus on South Africa was on the response of trade unions there to various issues such as an alliance with the ruling party, the African National Congress, and towards the neo-liberal policies of deregulation, flexibility and privatisation pursued by the Government since the end of the apartheid regime of racial exclusion. We also explored new issues, such as the union response to the emergence of the informal economy. In looking in more depth in China, we examined how the official union has lacked legitimacy in representing workers' interests, and how spontaneous and self-organised strikes, demonstrations and collective bargaining in recent years show the potential for workers to develop free associations.

References

Aaker, D.A. and Joachimsthaler, E. (2000) *Brand leadership*. London: The Free Press.

Abdalla, I.S. (2006) *Human resource management in Qatar*. In: P.S. Budhwar and K. Mellahi (eds) *Managing human resources in the Middle East*, pp121–44. London: Routledge.

Abed, G.T. (2003) Unfulfilled promise: finance and development. (A quarterly magazine of the IMF). Available online at: http://www.imf.org/external/pubs/ft/fandd/2003/03/abed.htm.

Ablett, J., Baijal, A., Beinhocker, E., Bose, A., Farrell, D., Gersch, U., Greenberg, E., Gupta, S. and Gupta, S. (2007) The 'bird of gold': The rise of India's consumer market. *McKinsey Global Institute*. May.

Abrahamson, E. (1991) Managerial fads and fashions: The diffusion and rejection of innovations. *Academy of Management Review*. Vol 16, No 3. pp586–612.

Abramson, N.R., Keating, R.J. and Lane, H.W. (1996) Cross-national cognitive process differences: a comparison of Canadian, American and Japanese managers. *Management International Review*. Vol 36, No 2. pp123–47.

Abramson, N.R., Lane, H.W. and Takagi, H. (1993) A comparison of Canadian and Japanese cognitive styles: implications for management interaction. *Journal of International Business Studies*. Vol 24, No 3. pp575–87.

Abu-Doleh, J. and Weir, D. (2007) Dimensions of performance appraisal systems in Jordanian private and public organizations. *International Journal of Human Resource Management*. Vol 18, No 1. Special Issue: Managing human resources in the Middle East. pp75–84.

Adamsky, H. (2003) Talent management: Something productive this way comes. Available at: http:// www.ere.net/articles/db/76E79D059FEB4637A7F0FBD4439490C6.asp [accessed February 2008].

Adler, P. (1991) Culture shock and the cross-cultural learning experience. In: L. Fiber Luce and E.C. Smith (eds) *Toward internationalism: readings in cross-cultural communication*. Cambridge, MA: Newbury House Publishers.

Ahonen, M. (2008) Clarifying the stage of corporate branding research (1996–2007): a literature review and a classification. *Proceedings of the Australian and New Zealand Marketing Academy Conference ANZMAC, Sydney, Australia*, 1–3 December.

Ailon, G. (2008). Mirror, mirror on the wall: culture's consequences in a value test of its own design. *The Academy of Management Review.* Vol 33, No 4. pp885–904.

Akorsu, A.D. and Cooke, F.L. (2011) Labour standards application among Chinese and Indian firms in Ghana: typical or atypical? *International Journal of Human Resource Management.* Vol 22, No 13. pp2730–48.

Al-Arkoubi, K. and McCourt, W. (2004) The politics of HRM: waiting for Godot in the Moroccan civil service. *International Journal of Human Resource Management.* Vol 15, No 6. pp978–95.

Albert, M. (1993) *Capitalism against capitalism.* London: Whurr.

Ali, A. (1988) Scaling an Islamic work ethic. *Journal of Social Psychology.* Vol 128, No 5. pp575–83.

Ali, A. (1993) Decision-making style, individualism and attitude toward risk of Arab executives. *International Studies of Management and Organization.* Vol 23, No 3. pp53–74.

Ali, A. (2011) Talent management in the Middle East. In: H. Scullion and D. Collings (eds) *Global talent management*, pp155–77. Abingdon: Routledge.

Ali, A.J. and Al-Kazemi, A. (2006) Human resource management. In: P.S. Budhwar and K. Mellahi (eds) *Managing human resources in the Middle East*, pp79–96. London: Routledge.

Alimo-Metcalfe, B. and Alban-Metcalfe, R. (2001) The development of a new transformational leadership questionnaire. *Journal of Occupational and Organizational Psychology.* Vol 74, No 1. pp1–28.

Alimo-Metcalfe, B. and Alban-Metcalfe, R. (2011) Leadership in public and third sector organizations. In: J. Storey (ed.) *Leadership in organizations: current issues and key trends*, pp224–48. 2nd edition. London: Routledge.

Allen, D.G., Mahto, R.V. and Otondo, R.F. (2007) Web-based recruitment: effects of information, organization brand, and attitudes towards a web site on applicant attraction. *Journal of Applied Psychology.* Vol 92, No 6. pp1696–1708.

Allinson, C.W. and Hayes, J. (1996) The cognitive style index: a measure of intuition-analysis for organizational research. *Journal of Management Studies.* Vol 33, No 1. pp119–35.

Allinson, C.W. and Hayes, J. (2000) Cross-national differences in cognitive style: implications for management. *International Journal of Human Resource Management.* Vol 11, No 1. pp161–70.

Allinson, C.W., Armstrong, S.J. and Hayes, J. (2001) The effects of cognitive style on leader–member exchange: A study of manager–subordinate dyads. *Journal of Occupational and Organizational Psychology.* Vol 74, No 2. pp201–20.

Alon, I. and Higgins, J.M. (2005) Global leadership success through emotional and cultural intelligences. *Business Horizons.* Vol 48. pp501–12.

Al-Suleimany, M.S.M. (2009) *Psychology of Arab management thinking.* Oman: Trafford Publishing.

Alvesson, M. (1995) *Management of knowledge-intensive companies.* Berlin: de Gruyter.

Alvesson, M. (2011) De-essentializing the knowledge-intensive firm: reflections on sceptical research going against the mainstream. *Journal of Management Studies.* Vol 48, No 7. pp1640–61.

Alvesson, M. and Deetz, S. (2000) *Doing critical management research.* London: Sage.

Alvesson, M. and Sveningsson, S. (2003) Good visions, bad micro-management and ugly ambiguity: contradictions of (non-) leadership in a knowledge-intensive organization. *Organization Studies.* Vol 24, No 6. pp961–88.

Amankwah-Amoah, J. and Debrah, Y.A. (2011) Competing for scarce talent in a liberalised environment: evidence from the aviation industry in Africa. *International Journal of Human Resource Management.* Vol 22, No 17. 1 October. pp3565–81.

Ambler, T. and Barrow, S. (1996) The employer brand. *Journal of Brand Management.* Vol 4. pp185–206.

Ambrozheichik, G. (2011) Cultural profile of Russian leadership. *International Journal of Leadership Studies.* Vol 6, No 3. pp310–35.

Andonova, V., Gutierrez, R. and Avella, L.F. (2009) The strategic importance of close employment relations in conflict-ridden environments: three cases from Colombia. In: A. Davila and M.M. Elvira (eds) *Best human resource management practices in Latin America*, pp25–36. London: Routledge.

Appelbaum, E., Bailey, T., Berg, P. and Kalleberg, A. (2000) *Manufacturing advantage: why high performance work systems pay off.* Ithaca, NY: Cornell University Press.

Ardichvili, A. and Gasparishvili, G. (2001) Human resource development in an industry in transition: the case of the Russian banking sector. *Human Resource Development International.* Vol 4, No 1. pp47–64.

Ardichvili, A. and Kuchinke, K.P. (2002) Leadership styles and cultural values among managers and subordinates: a comparative study of four countries of the former Soviet Union, Germany and the US. *Human Resource Development International.* Vol 5, No 1. pp99–118.

Ardichvili, A., Zavyalova, E. and Minina, V. (2012) Human capital development: comparative analysis of BRICs. *European Journal of Training and Development.* Vol 36, No 2/3. pp213–33.

Argote, L., McEvily, B. and Reagans, S. (2003) Introduction to the special issue on managing knowledge in organizations: creating, retaining and transferring knowledge. *Management Science*. Vol 49, No 4. ppv–viii.

Arias-Galicia, L.F. (2005) Human resource management in Mexico. In: M.M. Elvira and A. Davila (eds) *Managing human resources in Latin America*, pp179–90. London: Routledge.

Armstrong, M. (2002) *Strategic human resource management*. London: Kogan Page.

Armstrong, M. and Baron, A. (2005) *Managing performance: performance management in action*. London: Chartered Institute of Personnel and Development.

Armstrong, S.J., Allinson, C.W. and Hayes, J. (2002) Formal mentoring systems: An examination of the effects of mentor/protégé cognitive styles on the mentoring process. *Journal of Management Studies*. Vol 39, No 8. pp1111–37.

Arthur, J.B. (1992) The link between business strategy and industrial relations systems in American steel minimills. *Industrial and Labor Relations Review*. Vol 45, No 3. pp488–506.

Arthur, J.B. (1994) Effects of human resource systems on manufacturing performance and turnover. *Academy of Management Journal*. Vol 37, No 3. pp670–87.

Ashour, A.S. (2004) Concept Paper 3: Integrity, transparency and accountability in public sector human resources management. RAB/01/006: Transparency in the Public Sector in the Arab Region. http://unpan1.un.org/intradoc/groups/public/documents/un/unpan015390.pdf

Ashton, C. and Morton, L. (2005) Managing talent for competitive advantage. *Strategic Human Resources Review*. Vol 4, No 5. July/August. pp28–31.

Avolio, B., Gardner, W., Walumbwa, F. and May, D. (2004) Unlocking the mask: a look at the process by which authentic leaders impact follower attitudes and behaviors. *Leadership Quarterly*. Vol 15, No 6. pp801–23.

Aycan, Z., Al-Hamadi, A.B., Davis, A. and Budhwar, P. (2007) Cultural orientations and preferences for HRM policies and practices: the case of Oman. *International Journal of HRM*. Vol 18, No 1. pp11–32.

Baccaro, L. and Pulignano, V. (2011) Employment relations in Italy. In: G. Bamber, R.D. Lansbury and N. Wailes (eds) *International and comparative employment relations: globalisation and change*, pp138–68. London: Sage.

Bach, S. (2005) *Managing human resources: personnel management in transition*, 4th edition. Oxford: Blackwell.

Backhaus, K. and Tikoo, S. (2004) Conceptualizing and researching employer branding. *Career Development International*. Vol 9, No 5. pp501–17.

Bakuwa, R. and Mamman, A. (2012) Factors hindering the adoption of HIV/AIDS workplace policies: evidence from private sector companies in Malawi. International Journal of Human Resource Management. Vol 23, No 14. 1 July. pp2917–37.

Banerjee, S. (2010) Governing the global corporation: A critical perspective. *Business Ethics Quarterly.* Vol 20, No 2. pp265–74.

Banerji, D. and Shah, R. (2012) India overtakes Japan to become third-largest economy in purchasing power parity. *Economic Times.* 19 April.

Barlow, G. (1989) Deficiencies and the perpetration of power: latest functions in management appraisal. *Journal of Management Studies.* Vol 26, No 5. pp499–517.

Barlow, L. (2006) Talent development: the new imperative? *Development and Learning in Organizations.* Vol 20, No 3. pp6–9.

Barney, J. (1991) Firm resources and sustained competitive advantage. *Journal of Management.* Vol 17, No 1. pp99–120.

Bartlett, C. and Ghoshal, S. (1989) *Managing across borders: the transnational solution.* Boston, MA: Harvard Business School Press.

Baruch, Y. (2001) Management in Israel. In: M. Warner (ed.) *IEMB management in Europe*, pp267–73. London: Thompson International.

Barzantny, C. and Festing, M. (2008) Performance management in France and Germany. In: A. Varma, P. Budhwar and A. DeNisi (eds) *Performance management systems: a global perspective*, pp147–67. London: Routledge.

Bass, B. (1985) *Leadership and performance beyond expectations.* Cambridge, MA: Harvard University Press.

Bass, B. (1990) *Bass and Stodgill's handbook of leadership.* New York: Free Press.

Bass, B. and Avolio, B. (1993) Transformational leadership: a response to critiques. In: M. Chemers and R. Ayman (eds) *Leadership theory and research: perspectives and directions*, pp49–80. San Diego, CA: Academic Press.

Bass, B. and Steidlmeier, P. (1999) Ethics, character and authentic transformational leadership behavior. *The Leadership Quarterly.* Vol 10, No 2. p181.

Becker, B.E. and Gerhardt, B. (1996) The impact of human resource management on organizational performance: progress and practice. *Academy of Management Journal.* Vol 39, No 4. pp779–801.

Bedward, D., Jankowicz, D. and Rexworthy, C. (2003) East meets West: a case example of knowledge transfer. *Human Resource Development International.* Vol 6, No 4. pp527–45.

Beechler, S. and Woodward, I. (2009) The global war for talent. *International Journal of Human Resource Management.* Vol 15. pp273–85.

Beer, M., Spector, B., Lawrence P.R., Quinn-Mills, D.Q. and Walton, R.E. (1984) *Managing human assets.* New York: The Free Press.

Bennis, W. and Nanus, B. (1985) *Leadership: the strategies for taking charge.* New York: Harper & Row.

Berger, LA. (2004) Creating a Talent Management System for Organizational Excellence: Connecting the dots in Berger LA & Berger DR (eds) The Talent Management Handbook Creating Organizational Excellence by Identifying, Developing and ptomoting your Best People. New York: McGraw Hill pp3-22

Berger, P.L. and Luckmann, T. (1967) *The social construction of reality: a treatise in the sociology of knowledge.* Harmondsworth: Penguin Books.

Berrone, P. and Otten, J. (2008) A global perspective on executive compensation. In: L.R. Gomez-Mejia and S. Werner (eds) *Global compensation: foundations and perspectives*, pp113–28. London: Routledge.

Berry, J.W. (1980) Acculturation as varieties of adaptation. In: A. Padilla (ed.) *Acculturation: theory, models and some new findings*, pp. 9–25. Boulder, CO: Westview.

Berry, J.W. (1997) Immigration, acculturation and adaptation. *Applied Psychology: An International Review.* Vol 46. pp5–68.

Bersin, J. (2007) *Enterprise learning and talent management.* Oakland, CA: Bersin and Associates, Industry Report.

Berthon, P., Ewing, M. and Hah, L.L. (2005) Captivating company: dimensions of attractiveness in employer branding. *International Journal of Advertising.* Vol 24, No 2. pp151–73.

Bevan, D. (2007) Ethics and HRM. In: J. Storey (ed.) *Human resource management: a critical text*, pp251–62. London: Thompson Learning.

Bhatnagar, J. (2007) Talent management strategy of employee engagement in Indian ITES employees: key to retention. *Journal of Employee Relations.* Vol 29, No 6. pp630–63.

Bhatnagar, J. (2012) Management of innovation: role of psychological empowerment, work engagement and turnover intention in the Indian context. *International Journal of Human Resource Management.* Vol 23, No 5. Special Issue: Human resource management in the new economy in India. pp928–51.

Bird, A. (1994) Careers as repositories of knowledge: a new perspective on boundaryless careers. *Journal of Organizational Behavior.* Vol 15, No 4. pp325–34.

Bird, A. and Fang, T. (2009) Cross-cultural management in the age of globalization. *International Journal of Cross Cultural Management.* Vol 9, No 2. pp139–43.

Bird, A. and Osland, J.S. (2004) Global competencies: an introduction. In: H. Lane, M. Maznevski, M. Mendenhall and J. McNett (eds) *Handbook of global management*, pp57–80. Oxford: Blackwell.

Biswas, S. and Varma, A. (2012) Linkage between antecedents of in-role performance and intention to quit: an investigation in India. *International Journal of Human Resource Management.* Vol 23, No 5. pp987–1005.

Black, J.S. (1989) Repatriation: A comparison of Japanese and American practices and results. *Proceedings of the Eastern Academy of Management Bi-annual International Conference.* Hong Kong. pp45–9.

Black, J.S. (2006) The mindset of global leaders: inquisitiveness and duality. In: W.H. Mobley and E. Weldon (eds) *Advances in global leadership*, pp181–200. Stamford, CT: JAI Press.

Black, J.S. and Gregersen, H.B. (1991) Antecedents to cross-cultural adjustment for expatriates in Pacific Rim assignments. *Human Relations.* Vol 44. pp497–515.

Black, J.S. and Mendenhall, M.E. (2007) A practical but theory-based framework for selecting cross-cultural training methods. In: M.E. Mendenhall, G.R. Oddou and G.K. Stahl (eds) *Readings and cases in international human resource management*, 4th edition, pp219–45. New York: Routledge.

Black, J.S., Mendenhall, M. and Oddou, G. (1991) Toward a comprehensive model of international adjustment: an integration of multiple theoretical perspectives. *Academy of Management Review.* Vol 16, No 2. pp291–317.

Blass, E. (ed.) (2009) *Talent management: cases and commentary*. Basingstoke: Palgrave Macmillan.

Blass, E., Knights, A. and Orbea, A. (2006) *Developing future leaders: the contribution of talent management, studying leadership, knowledge into action.* Fifth International Annual Conference on Leadership, Cranfield, 14–16 December.

Blyton, P. and Turnbull, P. (1992) *Reassessing human resource management.* London: Sage.

Bochner, S., McLeod, B. and Lin, A. (1977) Friendship patterns of overseas students: a functional model. *International Journal of Psychology.* Vol 12. pp277–97.

Boland, G., Sugahara, S., Opdecam, E. and Everaert, P. (2011) The impact of cultural factors on students' learning style preferences: a global comparison between Japan, Australia and Belgium. *Asian Review of Accounting.* Vol 19, No 3. pp243–65.

Bolden, R. (2011) Distributed leadership in organizations: a review of theory and research. *International Journal of Management Reviews.* Vol 13, Special issue. pp251–69.

Bolden, R., Petrov, G. and Gosling, J. (2008) Tensions in higher education leadership: towards a multi-level model of leadership practice. *Higher Education Quarterly*. Vol 62. pp358–76.

Bolden, R., Gosling, J., Marturano, A. and Dennison, P. (2003) *A review of leadership theory and competency frameworks*. Exeter: Centre for Leadership Studies, University of Exeter.

Bolino, M.C. (2007) Expatriate assignments and intra-organizational career success: implications for individual organizations. *Journal of International Business Studies*. Vol 38. pp819–35.

Bonache, J. and Brewster, C. (2001) Knowledge transfer and the management of expatriation. *Thuderbird International Business Review*. Vol 43, No 1. pp145–68.

Bond, M.H. (1988) Finding universal dimensions of individual variation in multicultural studies of values: the Rokeach and Chinese value surveys. *Journal of Personality and Social Psychology*. Vol 55, No 6. pp1009–15.

Boudreau, J. and Ramstad, P. (2005) Talentship, talent segmentation and sustainability: a new HR decision science paradigm for a new strategy definition. *Human Resource Management*. Vol 44. pp129–36.

Bourdieu, P. (1986) The forms of capital. In: J. Richardson (ed.) *Handbook for theory and research for the sociology of education*, pp241–58. New York: Greenwood.

Bourne, D. and Özbilgin, F. (2008) Strategies for combating gendered perceptions of careers. *Career Development International*. Vol 13, No 4. pp320–32.

Boxall, P. (1996) The strategic HRM debate and the resource-based view of the firm. *Human Resource Management Journal*. Vol 6, No 3. pp59–75.

Boxall, P. and Purcell, J. (2003) *Strategy and human resource management: management, work and organisations*. Basingstoke: Palgrave Macmillan.

Boxall, P. and Purcell, J. (2011) *Strategy and human resource management*. Basingstoke: Palgrave Macmillan.

Boxall, P., Ang, S.H. and Bartram, T. (2011) Analysing the 'black box' of HRM: uncovering HR goals, mediators and outcomes in a standardised service environment. *Journal of Management Studies*. Vol 48, No 7. pp1504–32.

Boyatzis, R.E. (1982) *The competent manager – a model for effective performance*. New York: Wiley.

Boyer, E. (1990) Letter to the editor. *Chronicle of Higher Education*. pB4.

Branine, M. (1996) Observations on training and management development in the People's Republic of China. *Personnel Review*. Vol 25, No 1. pp25–39.

Branine, M. and Analoui, A. (2006) Human resource management in Jordan. In: P.S. Budhwar and K. Mellahi (eds) *Managing human resources in the Middle East*, pp180–98. London: Routledge.

Bratton, J. and Gold, J. (1999) *Human resource management: theory and practice*, 2nd edition. Basingtoke: Macmillan Press.

Brewis, J. (2005) Othering organization theory: Marta Calás and Linda Smircich. *The Sociological Review*. Vol 53, No s1. Special Issue: Sociological Review Monograph Series: Contemporary Organization Theory. pp80–94.

Brewster, C (1995) Towards a European model of human resource management. *Journal of International Business Studies*. Vol 26, No 1. pp1–21.

Brewster, C. (2007a) HRM: the comparative dimension. In: J. Storey (ed.) *Human resource management: a critical text*. 3rd edition, pp197–214. London: Thomson Learning.

Brewster, C. (2007b) A European perspective on HRM. *European Journal of International Management*. Vol 1, No 3. pp239–59.

Brewster, C. and Wood, S. (2007) Introduction: comprehending industrial relations in Africa. In: G. Wood and C. Brewster (eds) *Industrial relations in Africa*. London: Palgrave.

Briscoe, D.R. and Schuler, R.S. (eds) (2004) *International human resource management*, 2nd edition. London: Routledge.

Briscoe, D., Schuler, R. and Tarique, I. (2012) *International human resource management: policies and practices for multinational enterprises*, 4th edition. London: Routledge.

Brislin, R.W. (1981) *Cross-cultural encounters*. London: Pergamon Press.

Brislin, R.W. (2000) *Understanding culture's influence on behavior*, 2nd edition. London: Thomson Learning Inc.

Brislin, R.W. and Pedersen, P. (1976) *Cross-cultural orientation programs*. New York: Gardner.

Broadman, H. (2007) *Africa's silk road: China and India's new frontiers*. Washington, DC: The World Bank.

Brookes, M., Hinks, T., Wood, G., Dibben, P. and Roper, I. (2004) Pulled apart, pushed together: diversity and unity within the Congress of South African Trade Unions. *Industrial Relations*. Vol 59, No 4. pp769–92.

Brookes, S. (2006) Out with the old, in with the new: why excellent public leadership makes a difference to partnership working. *British Journal of Leadership in Public Services*. Vol 2, No 1. pp52–64.

Brookes, S. (2008) Responding to the new public leadership challenge. Paper presented at Herbert Simon 2nd Annual Conference, Manchester, 16 April.

Brown, M.E., Treviño, L.K. and Harrison, D.A. (2005) Ethical leadership: a social learning perspective for construct development and testing. *Organizational Behavior and Human Decision Processes.* Vol 97, No 1. pp117–34.

Buckingham, M. and Vosburgh, R. (2001) The 21st century human resources function: it's the talent, stupid! *Human Resource Planning.* Vol 24, No 4. pp17–23.

Budhwar, P.S. and Debrah, Y.A. (eds) (2001) *Human resource management in developing countries.* London: Routledge.

Budhwar, P.S. and Khatri, N. (2001) A comparative study of HR practices in Britain and India. *International Journal of Human Resource Management.* Vol 12, No 5. pp800–26.

Budhwar, P.S. and Mellahi, K. (2006) *Managing human resources in the Middle East.* London: Routledge.

Budhwar, P.S. and Sparrow, P. (1997) Evaluating levels of strategic integration and devolvement of HRM in India. *International Journal of Human Resource Management.* Vol 8, No 4. pp476–94.

Budhwar, P.S. and Varma, A. (2010) Guests editors' introduction: emerging patterns of HRM in the new Indian economic environment. *Journal of Human Resource Management.* Vol 49, No 3. pp345–51.

Budhwar, P.S. and Varma, A. (2011) Emerging HR management trends in India and the way forward. *Journal of Organisational Dynamics.* Vol 40. pp317–25.

Buhlungu, S. (2006) *Trade unions and democracy: COSATU members and the democratic transformation of South Africa.* Johannesburg: HSRC Press.

Buhlungu, S., Wood, G. and Brookes, M. (2008) Trade unions and democracy in South Africa: union organizational challenges and solidarities in a time of transformation. *British Journal of Industrial Relations.* Vol 46, No 3. pp439–68.

Buhlungu, S., Daniel, J., Southall, R. and Lutchman, J. (eds) (2007) *State of the nation: South Africa.* Pretoria: HSRC Press.

Burda, M.C. and Hunt, J. (2011) *What explains the German labor market miracle in the great recession?* Centre for Economic Policy Research. DP8520. http://www.cepr.org/pubs/new-dps/dplist.asp?dpno=8520.

Burns, J. (1978) *Leadership.* New York: Harper & Row.

Burns, J.F. (1997) Lowest-caste Hindu takes office as India's President. *New York Times.* 26 July.

Business Standard. (2008) Indian employees most confident: Kenexa survey. http://www.business-standard.com/india/news/indian-employees-most-confident-kenexa-survey/343272/ [accessed 27 April 2012].

Buxton, C., Li, L. and Tantau, H. (2007) *Overcoming the challenges of recruiting and retaining talent in China's life science market.* Los Angeles, CA: Korn/Ferry International.

Cabrera, A. and Cabrera, E.F. (2002) Knowledge-sharing dilemmas. *Organization Studies.* Vol 23, No 5. pp687–710.

Caldwell, R.W. (2003) The changing roles of personnel managers: old ambiguities, new uncertainties. *Journal of Management Studies.* Vol 40, No 4. pp983–1004.

Caldwell, R.W. and Storey, J. (2007) The HR function: integration or fragmentation? In: J. Storey (ed.) *HRM: A critical text.* 3rd edition, pp21–38. Oxford: Blackwell.

Caligiuri, P. and Stroh, L. (1995) Multinational corporation management strategies and international human resources practices: bringing HRM to the bottom line. *International Journal of Human Resource Management.* Vol 6, No 3. pp494–507.

Caligiuri, P., Philips, J., Lazarova, M., Tarique, I. and Burgi, P. (2001) The theory of met expectations applied to expatriate adjustment: the role of cross-cultural training. *International Journal of Human Resource Management.* Vol 12, No 3. pp357–72.

Camps, J. and Luna-Arocas, R. (2012) A matter of learning: how human resources affect organizational performance. *British Journal of Management.* Vol 23, No 1. pp1–21.

Cappelli, P. (2008) *Talent on demand: managing talent in an age of uncertainty.* Boston, MA: Harvard Business School Press.

Cardon, P.W. and Bartlett, J.E. (2006) Evaluation of cross-cultural training: applying an evaluation model of human resource development. *Workforce Education Forum.* Vol 33, No 2. pp19–32.

Carlier, S.I., Consuelo, L.L. and Grau Grau, M. (2012) Comparing work–life balance in Spanish and Latin American countries. *European Journal of Training and Development.* Vol 36, No 2/3. pp286–307.

Carroll, A.B. (2001) Ethical challenges for business in the new millennium: corporate social responsibility and models of management morality. In: J.E. Richardson (ed.) *Business Ethics*, pp198–203. Guildord, CT: Dushkin/McGraw-Hill.

Casanova, L. (2005) Latin America: economic and business context. In: M.M. Elvira and A. Davila (eds) *Managing human resources in Latin America*, pp25–56. London: Routledge.

CEML (2002) *Managers and leaders: raising our game.* Report for the Council for Excellence in Management and Leadership, London.

Census of India. (2001) Government of India census 2001. http://censusindia.gov.in/ [accessed 24 April 2012].

Census of India. (2011) Government of India census 2011. http://censusindia.gov.in/ [accessed 24 April 2012].

Cerra, V. and Saxena, S.C. (2002) What caused the 1991 currency crisis in India? *International Monetary Fund Staff Papers.* Vol 49, No 3. pp395–425.

Chandra, V. (2012) Work–life balance: Eastern and Western perspectives. *International Journal of Human Resource Management.* Special Issue: Human resource management in the new economy in India. Vol 23, No 5. pp1040–56.

Chary, T.M. (2009) *India: nation on the move: an overview of the Indian people, culture, history, economy, IT industry and more.* Bloomington, IN: iUniverse.com.

Chatterjee, S.R. (2007) HRM in India: where from and where to. *Research and Practice in HRM.* Vol 15, No 2. pp92–103.

Chew, J. (2004) Managing MNC expatriates through crises: a challenge for international human resource management. *Research and Practice in Human Resource Management.* Vol 12, No 2. pp1–30.

Chhibber, P. and Kollman, K. (2004) *Formation of national party systems: federalism and party competition in Canada, Great Britain, India, and the United States.* Princeton, NJ: Princeton University Press.

Chiang, F.F.T. and Birtch, T.A. (2012) The performance implications of financial and non-financial rewards: an Asian Nordic comparison. *Journal of Management Studies.* Vol 49, No 3. pp538–70.

Chien, T-C. and McLean, G.N. (2011) Intercultural training for US business expatriates in Taiwan. *Journal of European Industrial Training.* Vol 35, No 9. pp858–73.

China Daily. (2002) Available at: http://www.chinadaily.com.cn/en/doc/ [accessed 8 May 2004].

Chow, I.H-S. (2004) The impact of institutional context on human resource management in three Chinese societies. *Employee Relations.* Vol 26, No 6. pp626–42.

Chow, I.H-S. and Ngo, H.S. (2002) Gender differences in job attribute preferences and job choice of university students in China. *Journal of Applied Business Research.* Vol 18, No 2. pp15–25.

CIPD. *The thinking performer concept.* London: Chartered Institute for Personnel Development. Available at: http://www.cipd.co.uk/about/profstands/thinkingperformer.htm [accessed 15 December 2010].

CIPD. (2007) *Talent: strategy, management, measurement.* London: Chartered Institute of Personnel and Development.

CIPD. (2009a) *Employer brand.* London: Chartered Institute of Personnel and Development.

CIPD. (2009b) *Talent management.* Factsheet. London: Chartered Institute of Personnel and Development.

CIPD. (2012) *Employee engagement.* Factsheet. London: Chartered Institute of Personnel and Development.

Ciulla, J.B. (2006) Ethics at the heart of leadership. In: T. Maak and N.M. Pless (eds) *Responsible leadership*, pp17–32. Oxford: Routledge.

Clarke, R. and Winkler, V. (2006) *Reflections on talent management.* London: Chartered Institute of Personnel and Development.

Coffield, F., Moseley, D., Hall, E. and Ecclestone, K. (2004) *Learning styles and pedagogy in post-16 learning: a systematic and critical review.* London: Learning and Skills Research Centre.

Cohen, W.M. and Levinthal, D.A. (1990) Absorptive capacity: a new perspective on learning and innovations. *Administrative Science Quarterly.* Vol 35. pp128–52.

Colbert, B.A. (2004) The complex resource-based view: implications for theory and practice in strategic human resource management. *Academy of Management Review.* Vol 29, No 3. pp341–58.

Collings, D. and Mellahi, K. (2009) Strategic talent management: a review and research agenda. *Human Resource Management Review.* Vol 19, No 4. pp304–13.

Collings, D., Scullion, H. and Morley, M. (2007) Changing patterns of global staffing in the multinational enterprise: challenges to the conventional expatriate assignment. *Journal of World Business.* Vol 42, No 2. pp198–213.

Collis, D.J. and Montgomery, C.A. (1995) Competing on resources: strategy for the 1990s. *Harvard Business Review.* Vol 73, No 4. July/August. pp118–28.

Constable, J. and McCormick, R. (1987) *The making of British managers.* London: British Institute of Management and Confederation of British Industry.

Cooke, F.L. (2004) Foreign firms in China: modelling HRM in a toy manufacturing corporation. *International Journal of Human Resource Management.* Vol 14, No 3. pp31–52.

Cooke, F.L. (2008a) A decade of transformation of HRM in China: a review of literature and suggestions for future studies. Presentation to HRM Conference, University of Manchester, April.

Cooke, F.L. (2008b) Performance management in China. In: A. Varma, P. Budhwar and A. DeNisi (eds) *Performance management systems: a global perspective*, pp193–209. London: Routledge.

Cooke, F.L. (2011a) Employment relations in China. In: G. Bamber, R.D. Lansbury and N. Wailes (eds) *International and comparative employment relations: globalisation and change*, pp307–29. London: Sage.

Cooke, F.L. (2011b) Social responsibility, sustainability and diversity of human resources. In: A. Harzing and A. Pinnington (eds) *International human resource management*, 3rd edition, pp583–624. London: Sage.

Cooke, F. (2011c) Talent management in China. In: H. Scullion and D. Collings (eds) *Global talent management*, pp132–54. Abingdon: Routledge.

Cooke, F.L. (2012) *Human resource management in China: new trends and practices*. London: Routledge.

Cooke, W., Macau, F. and Wood, T., Jr (2012) Brazilian management gurus as reflexive soft-HRM practitioners: an empirical study. *International Journal of Human Resource Management*. Vol 24, No 1. pp110–29.

Cooney, S. (2007) China's labour law, compliance and flaws in implementing institutions. *Journal of Industrial Relations*. Vol 49, No 5. pp673–86.

Cooper, D., Robertson, I.T. and Tinline, G. (2003) *Recruitment and selection: a framework for success*. London: Thomson.

Copeland, L. and Griggs, L. (1985) *Going international*. New York: Random House.

Corbin, J. and Strauss, A. (2008) *Basics of Qualitative Research*. 3rd edition. Thousand Oaks, CA: Sage.

Corbridge, S. and Pilbeam, M. (1998) *Employment resourcing*. London: Financial Times/Pitman.

Corkin, L., Burke, C. and Davies, M. (2008) *China's role in the development of Africa's infrastructure*. SAIS Working Papers in African Studies. Washington, DC: School of Advanced International Studies. Available at: http://www.sais-jhu.edu/sebin/e/j/CorkinetalWorkingPaper.pdf [accessed 11 December 2012].

Cox, T. and Nkomo, S.C. (1986) Differential appraisal criteria based on race of the rate. *Group and Organisational Studies*. Vol 11. pp101–19.

Crotty, J. and Rodgers, P. (2012) Sustainable development in the Russia Federation: the limits of greening within industrial firms. *Corporate Social Responsibility and Environmental Management*. Vol 19, No 3. pp178–90.

Cunningham, R.B. and Sarayrah, Y.K. (1993) *Wasta: the hidden force in Middle Eastern society*. Westport, CT: Praeger.

Cunningham, R.B. and Sarayrah, Y.K. (1994) Taming *wasta* to achieve development. *Arab Studies Quarterly*. Vol 16, No 3. pp29–39.

Curry, L. (1983) *Learning styles in continuing medical education*. Ottawa: Canadian Medical Association.

Czarniawska, B. (1997) Learning organizing in a changing institutional order: examples from city management in Warsaw. *Management Learning.* Vol 28, No 4. pp475–95.

Czarniawska, B. and Joerges, B. (1996) Travels of ideas. In: B. Czarniawska and G. Sevón (eds) *Translating organizational change*, pp13–48. Berlin: de Gruyter.

Dahl, S. (2004) *Intercultural research: the current state of knowledge.* Middlesex University Discussion Paper No. 26. London: Middlesex University Business School. Also available at: http://papers.ssrn.com/sol3/papers.cfm?abstract_id=658202 [accessed November 2005].

Dale, M. and Iles, P. (1992) *Assessing management skills: a guide to competencies and evaluation techniques.* London: Kogan Page.

Dalrymple, W. (1998) *From the holy mountain.* London: Flamingo.

Davenport, T.H. and Prusak, L. (1998) *Working knowledge: how organisations manage what they know.* Boston, MA: Harvard University Press.

Davila, A. and Elvira, M.M. (2007) Psychological contracts and performance management in Mexico. *International Journal of Manpower.* Vol 28. pp384–402.

Davila, A. and Elvira, M.M. (2008) Performance management in Mexico. In: A. Varma, P. Budhwar and A. DeNisi (eds) *Performance management systems: a global perspective*, pp115–30. London: Routledge.

Davila, A. and Elvira, M.M. (eds) (2009) *Best human resource management practices in Latin America.* London: Routledge.

Day, D. (2000) Leadership development: a review in context. *The Leadership Quarterly.* Vol 11, No 4. pp581–611.

Day, D., Gronn, P. and Salas, E. (2004) Leadership capacity in teams. *The Leadership Quarterly.* Vol 15, No 6. pp857–80.

D'Cruz, P. and Noronha, E. (2012) Cornered by conning: agents' experiences of closure of a call centre in India. *International Journal of Human Resource Management.* Special Issue: Human resource management in the new economy in India. Vol 23, No 5. pp1019–39.

Debrah, Y.A. (2007) Promoting the informal sector as a source of gainful employment in developing countries: insights from Ghana. *International Journal of Human Resource Management.* Vol 18, No 6. pp1063–84.

De Cieri, H., Sheehan, C., Costa, C., Fenwick, M. and Cooper, B. (2009) International talent flow and intention to repatriate: an identity explanation. *Human Resource Development International.* Vol 12, No 3. pp243–61.

Delamere, L., Diest, F. and Winterton, J. (2005) What is competence? *Human Resource Development International.* Vol 8. pp27–46.

Delaney, J.T. and Huselid, M.A. (1996) The impact of human resource management practices on perceptions of organizational performance. *Academy of Management Journal.* Vol 39. pp949–69.

Delery, J.E. and Doty, D.J.H. (1996) Models of theorizing in strategic human resource management: tests of universalistic, contingency, and configurational performance predictions. *Academy of Management Journal.* Vol 39. pp802–35.

Deng, P. (2012) The internationalization of Chinese firms: a critical review and future research. *International Journal of Management Reviews.* Vol 14, No 4. pp408–27.

DeNisi, A., Varma, A. and Budhwar, P.S. (2008) Performance management around the globe: what have we learned? In: A. Varma, P. Budhwar and A. DeNisi (eds) *Performance management systems: a global perspective*, pp254–62. London: Routledge.

Desai, R. and Taylor, D.W. (1998) Learning styles of accounting students in multi-cultural cohorts. *Asian Review of Accounting.* Vol 6, No 1. pp121–4.

DiMaggio, P. and Powell, W. (1983) The iron cage revisited: institutional isomorphism and collective rationality in organizational fields. *American Sociological Review.* Vol 48, No 2. pp147–60.

DiMaggio, P. and Powell, W. (1991) *New institutionalism in organizational analysis.* Chicago: University of Chicago Press.

DiMaggio, P. and Powell, W. (2002) The iron cage revisited: institutional isomorphism and collective rationality in organizational fields. In: C. Calhoun et al (eds) *Contemporary sociological theory*, pp175–92. London: Blackwell.

Ding, X. (1999) Twenty years through the eyes of Chinese youth: a survey. *ChinaToday.* May. p5.

Doh, J., Tymon Jr, W. and Stumpf, S. (2011) Talent management in India. In: H. Scullion and D. Collings (eds) *Global talent management*, pp113–31. Abingdon: Routledge.

Domsch, M. and Lidokhover, T. (eds) (2007) *Human resource management in Russia.* Aldershot: Ashgate.

Dorfman, P.W., Howell, J.P., Hibino, S., Lee, J.K., Tate, U. and Bautista, A. (1997) Leadership in Western and Asian countries: commonalities and differences in effective leadership processes across cultures. *The Leadership Quarterly.* Vol 8, No 3. pp233–74.

Dowden, R. (2009) *Africa: altered states, ordinary miracles.* London: Portobello Books.

Dowling, P.J., Festing, M. and Engle, A.D. (2008) *International human resource management*, 5th edition. London: Thomson Learning.

Dowling, P.J., Schuler, R.S. and Welch, D.E. (1994) *International dimensions of human resource management*, 2nd edition. Belmont, CA: Wadsworth.

Dulewicz, S.V. and Higgs, M.J. (2000a) Emotional intelligence: the key to future successful corporate leadership? *Journal of General Management*. Vol 25, No 3. pp1–14.

Dulewicz, S.V. and Higgs, M.J. (2000b) Emotional intelligence: a review and evaluation study. *Journal of Managerial Psychology*. Vol 15, No 4. pp341–68.

Duttagupta, R. (2005) *Identifying and managing your assets: talent management*. London: PricewaterhouseCoopers.

Earley, P.C. and Ang, S. (2003) *Cultural intelligence: individual interactions across cultures*. Stanford, CA: Stanford Business Books.

Early, P.C. and Erez, M. (1997) *The transplanted executive*. New York: Oxford University Press.

Eastwood, K. and Renard, M. (2008) Training the trainers: parlate Italiano? An experiential exercise in international human resources. *International Business and Economics Journal*. Vol 7, No 8. pp1–9.

Eckardt, A. and Matthias, K. (2003) The internationalization of a premium car producer: the BMW group and the Rover case. In: M. Freyssenet, K. Shimizu and G. Voplato (eds) *Globalization or regionalization of European car industry?*, pp170–97. Basingsoke: Palgrave.

Economist (2006) The search for Talent October 7th

Edstrom, A. and Galbraith, J. (1977) Transfer of managers as a coordination and control strategy in multinational organizations. *Administrative Science Quarterly*. Vol 22, No 2. pp248–63.

Edwards, G. (2011) Concepts of community: a framework for contextualizing distributed leadership. *International Journal of Management Reviews*. Vol 13, special issue. pp301–12.

Edwards, P. (ed.) (2003) *Industrial relations: theory and practice*, 2nd edition. Oxford: Blackwell.

Eichhorst, W. (2012) *The unexpected appearance of a new German model*. IZA Discussion Papers 6625. Bonn: Institute for the Study of Labor (IZA).

Eichhorst, W. and Marx, P. (2010) *Whatever works: dualisation and the service economy in Bismarckian welfare states*. IZA Discussion Papers 5035. Bonn: Institute for the Study of Labor (IZA).

Ejova, L. and Olimpieva, I. (2007) Professional training and re-training: challenges of transition (the case of the shipbuilding industry in St Petersburg, Russia). In: M. Domsch and T. Lidokhover (eds) *Human resource management in Russia*, pp209–26. Aldershot: Ashgate.

Elsaid, E. and Elsaid, A.M. (2012) Culture and leadership: comparing Egypt to the GLOBE study of 62 societies. *Business and Management Research*. Vol 1, No 2. pp1–13.

Elvira, M.M. and Davila, A. (eds) (2005) *Managing human resources in Latin America*. London: Routledge.

Endrissat, N., Muller, W.R. and Kaudela-Baum, S. (2007) En-route to an empirically-based understanding of authentic leadership. *European Management Journal*. Vol 25, No 3. pp207–20.

Engardio, P. and McGregor, J. (2006) Karma capitalism. *Bloomberg Businessweek*. 20 October.

Ensley, M.E., Hmieleski, K. and Pearce, C.L. (2006) The importance of vertical and shared leadership within new venture top management teams: implications for the performance of startups. *The Leadership Quarterly*. Vol 17, No 3. pp217–31.

Eraut, M. (2000) Non-formal learning, implicit learning and tacit knowledge in professional work. In: F. Coffield (ed.) *The necessity of informal learning*, pp12–31. Bristol: Policy Press.

Erdogan, B. and Liden, R.C. (2006) Collectivism as a moderator of responses to organizational justice: implications for leader–member exchange and ingratiation. *Journal of Organizational Behavior*. Vol 27. pp1–17.

European Commission (2011) *A renewed EU strategy 2011–14 for corporate social responsibility*. COM(2011) 681 final. 25.10.2011. Communication from the Commission to the European Parliament, the Council, the European Economic and Social Committee and the Committee of the Regions. Brussels: European Commission.

Evans, P. and Lorange, L. (1989) The two logics behind human resource management. In: P. Evans, Y. Doz and A. Laurent (eds) *Human resource management in international firms*, pp144–61. Basingstoke: Palgrave.

Evans, P., Pucik, V. and Barsoux, J.L. (2010) *The global challenge: frameworks for international human resource management*. London: McGraw-Hill/Irwin.

Evans, P., Smale, A., Bjorkman, I. and Pucik, V. (2011) Leadership development in multinational firms. In: J. Storey (ed.) *Leadership in organizations: current issues and key trends*, pp207–22. Abingdon: Routledge.

Eylon, D. and Au, K.Y. (1999) Exploring empowerment: cross-cultural differences along the power distance dimension. *International Journal of Intercultural Relations*. Vol 23, No 3. pp373–85.

Fabbri, F. and Marin, D. (2012) *What explains the rise in CEO pay in Germany? A panel data analysis for 1977–2009*. CESifo Working Paper Series 3757. Munich: CESifo Group.

Fajana, S., Owoyemi, O. and Elegbede, T. (2011) Human resource management practices in Nigeria. *Journal of Management and Strategy.* Vol 2, No 2. pp57–62.

Fan, Y. (2002) A classification of Chinese culture. *Cross Cultural Management.* Vol 7, No 2. pp3–10.

Fang, T. (2003) A critique of Hofstede's fifth dimension. *International Journal of Cross Cultural Management.* Vol 3, No 3. pp347–68.

Farndale, E., Scullion, H. and Sparrow, P. (2010) The role of the corporate HR function in global talent management. *Journal of World Business.* Vol 45, No 2. pp161–8.

Farnham, D. (2010) *Human resource management in context,* 3rd edition. London: Chartered Institute of Personnel and Development.

Feldman, D.C. and Thomas, D.C. (1992) Career management issues facing expatriates. *Journal of International Business Studies.* Vol 23, No 2. pp271–94.

Felstead, A., Gallie, D. and Green, F. (2002) *Work skills in Britain 1986–2001.* London: Department for Education and Skills.

Ferner, A. (1997) Country of origin effects in multinational companies. *Human Resource Management Journal.* Vol 7. pp19–37.

Fiedler, F.E. (1971) *Leadership.* New York: General Learning Press.

Fiedler, F.E. (1981) *Leader attitudes and group effectiveness.* Westport, CT: Greenwood Publishing Group.

Fincham, R. and Evans, M. (1999) The consultants' offensive: reengineering – from fad to technique. *New Technology, Work and Employment.* Vol 14, No 1. pp32–44.

Fischer, A.R. and Smith, P.B. (2003) Reward allocation and culture. *Journal of Cross-cultural Psychology.* Vol 34, No 3. pp251–68.

Fisher, A. (2005) Offshoring could boost your career. *Fortune.* Vol 151, No 2. p36.

Fitzgerald, S.P. (2000) Building personal and procedural trust through Sino-American joint ventures: the transfer of culturally embedded knowledge. Paper presented to the 7th International Conference on Advances in Management, Colorado Springs, USA, July.

Fitzsimons, D., James, K.T. and Denyer, D. (2011) Alternative approaches for studying shared and distributed leadership. *International Journal of Management Reviews.* Vol 13, special issue. pp313–28.

Fletcher, C. (1997a) Performance appraisal in context: organisational changes and their impact on practice. In: N. Anderson and P. Herriot (eds) *International Handbook of Selection and Assessment.* Chichester: John Wiley.

Fletcher, C. (1997b) *Appraisal – routes to improved performance*. London: Institute of Personnel and Development.

Fletcher, C. and Baldry C. (1999) Multi source feedback systems: a research perspective. In: C.L. Cooper and I.T. Robertson (eds) *International review of industrial and organisational psychology*, pp149–93. Chichester: John Wiley.

Fombrun, C., Tichy, N.M. and Devanna, M.A. (eds) (1984) *Strategic human resource management*. New York: Wiley and Sons.

Fox, K. (2004) *Watching the English: the hidden rules of English behaviour*. London: Hodder & Stoughton.

Francis, H. and Keegan, A. (2006) The changing face of HRM: in search of balance. *Human Resource Management Journal*. Vol 16, No 3. pp231–49.

Franco-Santos, M. (2008) Performance measurement issues, incentive application and globalization. In: L.R. Gomez-Mejia and S. Werner (eds) *Global compensation: foundations and perspectives*, pp41–56. London: Routledge.

Frank, A.G. (1998) *Re-Orient: global economy in the Asian age*. Berkeley: University of California Press.

Frear, K.A., Cao, Y. and Zhao, W. (2012) CEO background and the adoption of Western-style human resource practices in China. *International Journal of Human Resource Management*. Vol 23, No 19. Special Issue: Whither Chinese HRM? Paradigms, models and theories. pp4009–24.

Friedrich, P.F., Mesquita, L.F. and Hatum, A.O. (2006) The meaning of difference – beyond cultural and managerial homogeneity stereotypes of South America. *Management Research*. Vol 4, No 1. pp53–71.

Fung, C.K., Min, K.Z. and Yong, W.W. (1996) Job choice and job mobility for Chinese young

professionals. *Hong Kong Manager*. November–December. pp20–5.

Furnham, A. (2004) Performance management systems. *European Business Journal*. Vol 16, pp83–94.

Furnham, A. and Stringfield, P. (1993) Personality and occupational behaviour: Myers-Briggs Type Indicator correlates of managerial practices in two cultures. *Human Relations*. Vol 46, No 7. pp827–40.

Gamble, J. (2000) Localising management in foreign-invested enterprises in China: practical, cultural and strategic perspectives. *International Journal of Human Resource Management*. Vol 11, No 5. pp883–903.

Gamble, J. (2003) Transferring human resource practices from the United Kingdom to China: the limits and potential for convergence. *International Journal of Human Resource Management*. Vol 14, No 3. pp369–87.

Gamble, J. (2006) Introducing Western-style HRM practices to China: shopfloor perceptions in a British multinational. *Journal of World Business*. Vol 41, No 4. pp328–43.

Gamble, J. (2010) Transferring organizational practices and the dynamics of hybridization: Japanese retail multinationals in China. *Journal of Management Studies*. Vol 47, No 4. pp705–32.

Gamble, J. and Huang, Q. (2008) Organizational commitment of Chinese employees in foreign-invested firms. *International Journal of Human Resource Management*. Vol 19, No 5. pp896–916.

Gammack, J.G. and Stephens, R.A. (1994) Repertory grid technique in constructive interaction. In: C.M. Cassell and G. Symon (eds) *Qualitative methods on organizational research: a practical guide*. London: Sage.

Garavan, T.N. and Carberry, R. (2012) A review of international HRD: incorporating a global HRD construct. *European Journal of Training and Development*. Vol 36, No 2/3. pp129–57.

Gass, S. and Varonis, E. (1991) Miscommunications in nonnative speaker discourse. In: N. Coupland, H. Giles and J. Wiemann (eds) *Miscommunication and problematic talk*, pp121–45. Newbury Park, CA: Sage.

Gelfand, M.J., Erez, M. and Aycan, Z. (2007) Cross-cultural organizational behavior. *Annual Review of Psychology*. Vol 5, No 8. pp479–514.

Gerhart, B. (2008a) Cross cultural management research assumptions, evidence, and suggested directions. *International Journal of Cross Cultural Management*. Vol 8, No 3. pp259–74.

Gerhart, B. (2008b) Compensation and national culture. In: L.R. Gomez-Mejia and S. Werner (eds) *Global compensation: foundations and perspectives*, pp142–57. London: Routledge.

Gerhart, B. and Trevor, C.O. (2008) Merit pay. In: A. Varma, P. Budhwar and A. DeNisi (eds) *Performance management systems: a global perspective*, pp67–80. London: Routledge.

Gertsen, M. (1990) Intercultural competence and expatriates. *Journal of Human Resource Management*. Vol 4. pp341–61.

Gibb, C.A. (1958) An interactional view of the emergence of leadership. *Australian Journal of Psychology*. Vol 10, No 1. pp101–10.

Gilbert, K. and Gorlenko, E. (1999) Transplant and process-oriented approaches to international management development: an evaluation of British–Russian co-operation. *Human Resource Development International*. Vol 2, No 4. pp335–54.

Gill, J. and Johnson, P. (2010) *Research methods for managers*. London: Sage.

Glaser, B. (1978) *Theoretical sensitivity*. Mill Valley, CA: Sociological Press.

Gold, J., Holden, R., Iles, P.A., Stewart, J. and Beardwell, J. (eds) (2009) *Human resource development: theory and practice*. Basingstoke: Palgrave.

Goleman, D. (1996) *Emotional intelligence*. London: Bloomsbury.

Goleman, D. (2000) Leadership that gets results. *Harvard Business Review*. March–April.

Goleman, D., Boyatzis, R. and McKee, A. (2002) *Primal leadership: realizing the power of emotional intelligence*. Boston, MA: Harvard Business School Publishing.

Gomes, E., Angwin, D., Peter, E. and Mellahi, K. (2012) HRM issues and outcomes in African mergers and acquisitions: a study of the Nigerian banking sector pages. *International Journal of Human Resource Management*. Vol 23, No 14, Special Issue. pp2874–2900.

Goodall, K. and Warner, M. (1997) Human resources in Sino–foreign joint ventures: selected case studies in Shanghai compared with Beijing. *International Journal of Human Resource Management*. Vol 8, No 5. pp569–93.

Gordon, R.D. (2002) Conceptualizing leadership with respect to its historical-contextual antecedents to power. *The Leadership Quarterly*. Vol 13, No 2. pp151–67.

Gott, R. (2012) Chávez's economics lesson for Europe. *Guardian*. 16 May. http://www.guardian.co.uk/commentisfree/2012/may/16/hugo-chavez-lessons-europe-greece

Gouveia, V.V. and Ros, M. (2000) Hofstede and Schwartz's models for classifying individualism at the cultural level: their relation to macro-social and macro-economic variables. *Psicothema*, Vol 12 (supplement). pp25–33.

Government of People's Republic of China. (2006) Highlights of the 11th Five-Year Plan: Targets, Paths, and Policy Orientation. Quoted in: W. Dobson and A. Safarian (2008) The transition from imitation to innovation: an enquiry into China's evolving institutions and firm capabilities. *Journal of Asian Economics*. Vol 19, No 4. pp301–11.

Grachev, M.V. and Bobina, M.A. (2006) Russian organizational leadership: lessons from the GLOBE study. *International Journal of Leadership Studies*. Vol 1, No 2. pp67–79.

Graf, A. and Mertesacker, M. (2009) Intercultural training: six measures assessing training needs. *Journal of European Industrial Training*. Vol 33, No 6. pp539–58.

Grant, R.M.C. (1991) The resource-based theory of competitive advantage: implications for strategy formulation. *California Management Review*. Vol 33. pp114–35.

Grant, R.M., Almeida, P. and Song, J. (2000) Knowledge and the multi-national enterprise. In: C.J.M. Millar, R.M. Grant and C.J. Choi (eds) *International business: emerging issues and emerging markets*, pp102–14. Basingstoke: Macmillan.

Green, F., Ashton, D., James, D. and Sung, J. (1999) The role of the state in skill formation: evidence from the Republic of Korea, Taiwan and Singapore. *Oxford Review of Economic Policy*. Vol 15, No 1. pp82–96.

Greenhalgh, C. (2001) *Does an employer training levy work? The incidence of and returns to adult vocational training in France and Britain.* SKOPE Research Paper No. 14. Oxford: SKOPE.

Greenwood, R. and Hinings, C. (1996) Understanding radical organizational change: bringing together the old and new institutionalism. *The Academy of Management Review*. Vol 4, No 21. pp1022–54.

Grint, K. (1993) What's wrong with performance appraisals: a critique and a suggestion. *Human Resource Management Journal*. Vol 3, No 3. pp61–77.

Grint, K. (2005) *Leadership: limits and possibilities.* Basingstoke: Palgrave Macmillan.

Gronn, P. (2000) Distributed properties: a new architecture for leadership. *Educational Management and Administration*. Vol 28, No 3. pp317–38.

Gronn, P. (2002) Distributed leadership as a unit of analysis. *The Leadership Quarterly*. Vol 13, No 4. pp423–51.

Gronn, P. (2008) The future of distributed leadership. *Journal of Educational Administration*. Vol 46, No 2. pp141–58

Gronn, P. (2009) Leadership configurations. *Leadership*. Vol 5. pp381–93.

Groysberg, B., Nanda, A. and Nohria, N. (2004) The risky business of hiring stars. *Harvard Business Review*. May. pp93–101.

Gudykunst, W.B. and Hammer, M.R. (1983) Basic training design: approaches to intercultural training. In: D. Landis and R.W. Brislin (eds) *Handbook of intercultural training: issues in theory and design*, vol. 1, pp118–54. Elmsford, NY: Pergamon.

Gudykunst, W.B. and Hammer, M.R. (1988) Strangers and hosts: an uncertainty reduction based theory of intercultural adaption. In: Y. Kim and W.B. Gudykunst (eds) *Cross-cultural adaption*, pp106–39. Newbury Park, CA: Sage.

Guest, D.E. (1987) Human resource management and industrial relations. *Journal of Management Studies*. Vol 25, No 4. pp503–21.

Guest, D. (1990) Human resource management and the American dream. *Journal of Management Studies*. Vol 27. pp377–97.

Gullahorn, J.T. and Gullahorn, J.E. (1963) An extention of the U-curve hypothesis. *Journal of Social Issues*. Vol 19. pp33–47.

Guo, K., Iles, P.A. and Yolles, M. (2011) *Understanding organizational fitness: the case of China*. Charlotte, NC: Information Age Publishing.

Gurkov, I. and Zelanova, O. (2009) Managing human resources in Russia. In: M. Morley, N. Heraty and S. Michailova (eds) *Managing human resources in central and eastern Europe*, pp278–312. London: Routledge.

Gurkov, I. and Zelanova, O. (2012) Human resource management in Russian companies. *International Studies of Management and Organization*. Vol 41, No 4. pp66–80.

Gutierrez, B., Spencer, S.M. and Zhu, G. (2012) Thinking globally, leading locally: Chinese, Indian and Western leadership. *Cross Cultural Management*. Vol 19, No 1. pp67–89.

Guzzo, R.A., Noonan, K.A. and Elron, E. (1994) Expatriate managers and the psychological contract. *Journal of Applied Psychology*. Vol 79, No 4. pp617–26.

Hall, E.T. (1984) *The dance of life: the other dimension of time*. Garden City, NY: Anchor.

Hall, P.A. and Soskice, D. (eds) (2001) *Varieties of capitalism: the institutional foundations of comparative advantage*. New York: Oxford University Press.

Hamel, G. (1991) Competition for competence and inter-partner learning within international strategic alliances. *Strategic Management Journal*. Vol 12. pp83–103.

Hamlin, R., Ellinger, A. and Beattie, R. (2008) The emergent 'coaching industry': a wake-up call for HRD professionals. *Human Resource Development International*. Vol 11, No 3. pp287–305.

Hammer, M., Gudykunst, W. and Wiseman, R. (1978) Dimensions of intercultural effectiveness. *International Journal of Intercultural Relations*. Vol 2. pp382–93.

Hamori, M. and Koyuncu, B. (2011) Career advancement in large organizations in Europe and the United States: do international assignments add value? *International Journal of Human Resource Management*. Vol 22, No 4. pp843–62.

Handy, C. (1987*) The making of managers.* London: NEDO.

Hanley, A.G. (2010) Financing Brazil's industrialization. In: J. Horn, L.N. Rosenband and M.R. Smith (eds) *Reconceptualising the Industrial Revolution*, pp309–28. Cambridge, MA: MIT Press.

Hannon, E. (2011) International and comparative employee voice. In: T. Edwards and C. Rees (eds) *International human resource management: globalization, national systems and multinational companies*, 2nd edition, pp229–52. Harlow: Pearson FT Prentice Hall.

Haq, R. (2012) The managing diversity mindset in public versus private organizations in India. *International Journal of Human Resource Management*.

Vol 23, No 5. Special Issue: Human resource management in the new economy in India. pp892–914.

Harel, G. and Tzafrir, S.S. (2001/2002) HRM practices in the public and private sector: differences and similarities. *Public Administration Quarterly*. Vol 25. pp316–55.

Harris, A. (2007) Distributed leadership: conceptual confusion and empirical reticence. *International Journal of Leadership in Education*. Vol 10, No 3. pp315–25.

Harris, A. (2008) Distributed leadership: according to the evidence. *Journal of Educational Administration*. Vol 46, No 2. pp172–88.

Harris, A. (2012) Distributed leadership: implications for the role of the principal. *Journal of Management Development*. Vol 31, No 1. pp7–17.

Harris, H. and Brewster, C. (1999) The coffee machine system: how international selection really works. *International Journal of Human Resource Management*. Vol 10, No 3. pp488–500.

Harry, W. (2007) Employment creation and localization: the crucial human resource issues for the GCC. *International Journal of Human Resource Management*. Vol 18, No 1. Special Issue: Managing human resources in the Middle East. pp132–46.

Hartmann, E., Feisel, E. and Schober, H. (2010) Talent management of western MNCs in China: balancing global integration and local responsiveness. *Journal of World Business*. Vol 45, No 2. pp169–78.

Harzing, A.W. (2001) Of bears, bumble-bees and spiders: the role of expatriates in controlling foreign subsidiaries. *Journal of World Business*. Vol 36, No 4. pp366–79.

Hassan, A. (2012) Saudisation of industrial sector boosted. *Arab News*. 16 April.

Hassard, J., Morris, J. and Sheehan, J. (2002) The elusive market: privatisation, politics and state-enterprise reform in China. *British Journal of Management*. Vol 13, No 3. pp221–32.

Hassard, J., Morris, J. and Sheehan, J. (2004) The third way: the future of work and organization in a 'corporatized' Chinese economy. *International Journal of Human Resource Management*. Vol 15, No 2. pp314–30.

Haynes, K.T. (2008) Executive compensation in an international context: the role of formal and informal institutions. In: L.R. Gomez-Mejia and S. Werner (eds) *Global compensation: foundations and perspectives*, pp86–99. London: Routledge.

Hee, C.C.H. (2007) A holistic approach to business management: perspectives from the Bhagavad Gita. *Singapore Management Review*. Vol 29, No 1. pp73–85.

Heitzman, J. and Worden, R.L. (1995) *India: a country study*. Washington, DC: GPO for the Library of Congress.

Henderson, J. and Whitley, R. (1995) Dimensions of transformation in east-central Europe and Pacific Asia. *Proceedings of British Academy of Management Annual Conference*, Sheffield. pp180–86.

Hendry, C. and Pettigrew, A. (1990) Human resource management: an agenda for the 1990s. *International Journal of Human Resource Management*. Vol 1, No 1. June. pp17–43.

Herrera, J.M. and Erdener, C. (2009) Western ethical theories and their relevance to HRM in Latin America. In: A. Davila and M.M. Elvira (eds) *Best human resource management practices in Latin America*, pp157–69. London: Routledge.

Hiller, N.J., Day, D.V. and Vance, R.J. (2006) Collective enactment of leadership roles and team effectiveness: a field study. *The Leadership Quarterly*. Vol 17. pp387–97.

Hills, B. (2011) What the Indian call centre staff are really told about Australians. *Sunday Mail (Queensland)*. 23 July.

Hodgkinson, G.P. and Clarke, I. (2007) Exploring the cognitive significance of organizational strategizing: a dual-process framework and research agenda. *Human Relations*. Vol 60. pp243–55.

Hofstede, G. (1980) *Culture's consequences: international differences in work-related values*. Beverly Hills, CA: Sage.

Hofstede, G. (1984) *Culture's consequences: international differences in work-related values*. Thousand Oaks, CA: Sage.

Hofstede, G. (1987) The cultural relativity of organizational practices and theories. In: W. Dymsza and R. Vamberly (eds) *International business knowledge*. New York and London: Routledge.

Hofstede, G. (1991) *Cultures and organizations – software of the mind*. London: McGraw-Hill.

Hofstede, G. (1996) Riding the waves of commerce: a test of Trompenaars' 'model' of national culture differences. *International Journal of Intercultural Relations*. Vol 20, No 2. pp189–98.

Hofstede, G. (2001) *Culture's consequences: comparing values, behaviors, institutions, and organizations across nations*. 2nd edition. Thousand Oaks, CA: Sage.

Hofstede, G. (2002) Dimensions do not exist: a reply to Brendan Sweeney. *Human Relations*. Vol 55, No 11. pp1355–61.

Hofstede, G. (2011) Dimensionalising cultures: the Hofstede model in context. *Online Readings in Psychology and Culture, Unit 2*. Vol 2, No 1. p8.

Hofstede, G. and Bond, M.H. (1988) The Confucius connection: from cultural roots to economic growth. *Organizational Dynamics.* Vol 16, No 4. pp4–21.

Hofstede, G., Hofstede, G.J. and Minkov, M. (2010) *Cultures and organizations – software of the mind.* Revised 3rd edition. New York: McGraw-Hill.

Holden, N.J. (2002) *Cross-cultural management: a knowledge management perspective.* London: Prentice Hall.

Holden, N. and Tansley, C. (2007) 'Talent' in European languages: a philosophical analysis reveals semantic confusions in management discourse. Paper presented at Critical Management Studies Conference, Manchester Business School University of Manchester.

Holden, P.J and Cooper, C. (1994) Russian managers as learners: implications for theories of management learning. *Management Learning.* Vol 25, No 4. pp503–22.

Holehouse, M. (2012) Cost of scrapping foreign languages hits home. *Independent.* 10 April.

Holt, J., Purcell, W., Gray, S. and Pedersen, T. (2006) *Decision factors influencing MNEs' regional headquarters location selection strategies.* Copenhagen: Center for Strategic Management and Globalization.

Honey, P. and Mumford, A. (1982) *The manuals of learning styles.* Maidenhead: Honey Press.

Honey, P. and Mumford, A. (1996) *Managing the learning environment.* Maidenhead: Peter Honey Publications Ltd.

Honey, P. and Mumford, A. (2000) *The learning styles helper's guide.* Maidenhead: Peter Honey Publications Ltd.

Hong, J.F.L., Snell, R.S. and Easterby-Smith, M. (2006) Cross-cultural influences on organizational learning in MNCS: the case of Japanese companies in China. *Journal of International Management.* Vol 12. pp408–29.

Hooker, J. (2008) *Corruption from a cross-cultural perspective.* Pittsburgh, PA: Carnegie Mellon University.

Horwitz, F. (2007) Cross-continental trends and issues in employment relations in Africa. In: G. Wood and C. Brewster (eds) *Industrial relations in Africa,* pp219–34. London: Palgrave.

Horwitz, F.M. (2012) Evolving human resource management in Southern African multinational firms: towards an Afro-Asian nexus. *International Journal of Human Resource Management.* Vol 23, No 14. pp2938–58.

Horwitz, F.M., Kamoche, K. and Chew, I.K.H. (2002) Looking East: diffusing high performance work practices in the southern Afro-Asian context. *International Journal of Human Resource Management.* Vol 13, No 7. pp1019–41.

Horwitz, F., Nkomo, S.M. and Rajah, M. (2004) HRM in South Africa. In: K. Kamoche, Y. Debrah, F. Horwitz and G.N. Muuka (eds) *Managing human resources in Africa*, pp1–18. London: Routledge.

Hough, L.M. and Oswald, F.L. (2000) Personnel selection. *Annual Review of Psychology.* Vol 51. pp631–64.

Hourani, A. (1991) *A history of the Arab peoples.* London: Faber and Faber.

House, R. and Adtja, R. (1997) The social scientific study of leadership: quo vadis? *Journal of Management.* Vol 23, No 3. pp409–73.

House, R.J., Hanges, P.J., Javidan, M., Dorfman, P.W. and Gupta, V. (2004) *Culture, leadership, and organisations: the GLOBE study of 62 societies.* London: Sage Publications.

Huang, J. and Sisco, B.R. (1994) Thinking styles of Chinese and American adult students in higher education: a comparative study. *Psychological Reports.* Vol 74. pp475–80.

Huselid, M. (1995) The impact of human resource management practices on turnover, productivity, and corporate financial performance. *Academy of Management Journal.* Vol 38, No 3. pp635–72.

Huselid, M., Beatty, R. and Becker, B. (2005) A players or A positions? The strategic logic of workforce management. *Harvard Business Review.* Vol 83, No 12. pp110–17.

Hutchings, K. and Michailova, S. (2004) Facilitating knowledge-sharing in Russian and Chinese subsidiaries: the role of personal networks and group membership. *Journal of Knowledge Management.* Vol 8, No 2. pp84–94,

Hutchings, K. and Weir, D. (2006a) Understanding networking in China and the Arab world: lessons for international managers. *Journal of European Industrial Training.* Vol 30. pp272–90.

Hutchings, K. and Weir, D. (2006b) *Guanxi* and *wasta*: a comparative examination of the impact of internationalization and modernization on traditional ways of networking in China and the Arab world. *Thunderbird International Business Review.* Vol 48. pp141–56.

Hutchings, K., Metcalfe, B.D. and Cooper, B. (2010) Exploring Middle Eastern women's perceptions of barriers to, and facilitators of, international development. *International Journal of Human Resource Management.* Vol 21, No 2. pp61–83.

Hutchinson, S. and Purcell, J. (2007) Front line managers as agents in the HRM–performance causal chain: theory, analysis and evidence. *Human Resource Management Journal.* Vol 17, No 1. pp3–20.

IDS. (2003) *AstraZeneca Study.* Vol 748. April. pp10–16.

Iles, P.A. (1994) Diversity in selection practice: culture, context and congruence. *International Journal of Selection and Assessment.* Vol 2, No 2. pp11–14.

Iles, P.A. (2000) *Managing staff selection and assessment.* Buckingham: Open University Press.

Iles, P.A. (2007) Employee resourcing and talent management. In: J. Storey (ed.) *Human resource management: a critical text*, 3rd edition, pp133–64. Oxford: Blackwell.

Iles, P.A. and Feng, Y. (2011) Distributed leadership, knowledge and information management and team performance in Chinese and Western groups. *Journal of Technology Management in China.* Vol 6, No 1. pp26–42.

Iles, P.A. and Macaulay, M. (2007) Putting principles into practice – developing ethical leadership in local government. *International Journal of Leadership in Public Services.* Vol 3, No 3. pp15–28.

Iles, P. and Preece, D. (2006) Developing leaders or developing leadership? The Academy of Chief Executives Programmes in the north-east of England. *Leadership.* Vol 2, No 3. pp317–40.

Iles, P.A. and Robertson, I.T. (1989) The impact of personnel selection techniques on candidates. In: P. Herriot et al (eds) *Assessment and selection in organisations.* Chichester: John Wiley & Sons.

Iles, P.A. and Yolles, M. (2002a) Across the great divide: HRD, technology translation and knowledge migration in bridging the knowledge gap between SMEs and universities. *Human Resource Development International.* Vol 5, No 1. pp23–53.

Iles, P.A. and Yolles, M. (2002b) International joint ventures, HRM, and viable knowledge migration. *International Journal of Human Resource Management.* Vol 13, No 14. pp624–41.

Iles, P.A. and Yolles, M. (2003a) Complexity, HRD and organization development: towards a viable systems approach to learning, development and change. In: M. Lee (ed.) *HRD in a complex world*, pp25–41. London: Routledge.

Iles, P.A. and Yolles, M. (2003b) International HRD alliances in viable knowledge migration and development: the Czech Academic Link Project. *Human Resource Development International.* Vol 6, No 3. pp301–24.

Iles, P.A. and Yolles, M. (2006) Culture and transformational change with China's accession to the WTO: the challenge for action research. *Journal of Technology Management in China.* Vol 1, No 2. pp8–17.

Iles, P.A. and Zhu, X. (2012) Changing talent management practices and global talent management: a literature review and research agenda for the Mediterranean region. *Euromed Journal* (forthcoming).

Iles, P.A., Almhedie, A. and Baruch, Y. (2013) Managing HR in the Middle East: challenges in the public sector. *Public Personnel Management* (forthcoming).

Iles, P., Chuai, X. and Preece, D. (2010a) Talent management and HRM in multinational companies in Beijing: definitions, differences and drivers. *Journal of World Business*. Vol 45, No 2. pp179–89.

Iles, P.A., Meetoo, C. and Gold, J. (2010b) Leadership development. In: J. Gold, J. Stewart, P.A. Iles, R. Holden and J. Beardwell (eds) *Human resource development: theory and practice*. Basingstoke: Palgrave Macmillan.

Iles, P.A., Preece, D. and Chuai, X. (2010c) Is talent management a management fashion in HRD? Towards a research agenda. *Human Resource Development International*. Vol 13, No 2. pp125–46.

Iles, P.A., Ramgutty-Wong, A. and Yolles, M. (2004) HRM and knowledge migration across cultures: issues, limitations and Mauritian specificities. *Employee Relations*. Vol 26, No 6. Special issue on international HRM. pp643–62.

Institute of Management (1997) *A portrait of management development*. London: IoM.

International Journal of HRM. (2012) Special Issue: On managing human resources in Africa. No 14. pp2825–3046.

Isaacson, W. (2012) The real leadership lessons of Steve Jobs. *Harvard Business Review*. April.

Ituma, A., Simpson, R., Ovadje, F., Cornelius, N. and Mordi, C. (2011) Four domains

of career success: how managers in Nigeria evaluate career success. *International Journal of Human Resource Management*. Vol 22, No 17. pp3638–60.

Jackson, H.L. and Ones, D.S. (2007) Counterproductive leader behaviour. In: S. Werner (ed.) *Managing human resources in North America: current issues and perspectives*, pp114–26. London: Routledge.

Jackson, R. and Howe, N. (2004) *The graying of the middle kingdom*. Washington, DC: Center for Strategic and International Studies and the Prudential Foundation.

Jackson, T. (2001) Cultural values and management ethics: a 10 nation study. *Human Relations*. Vol 54, No 10. pp1267–1302.

Jackson, T. (2012a) Cross-cultural management and the informal economy in sub-Saharan Africa: implications for organization, employment and skills development. *International Journal of Human Resource Management*. Vol 23, No 14. pp2901–16.

Jackson, T. (2012b) Postcolonialism and organizational knowledge in the wake of China's presence in Africa: interrogating South–South relations. *Organization*.

Vol 19, No 2. pp181–204.Jain, H., Mathew, M. and Bedi, A. (2012) HRM innovations by Indian and foreign MNCs operating in India: a survey of HR professionals. *International Journal of Human Resource Management*. Vol 23, No 5. Special Issue: Human resource management in the new economy in India. pp1006–18.

Jaju, A., Kwak, H. and Zinkhan, G.M. (2002) Learning styles of undergraduate business students: a cross-cultural comparison between the US, India and Korea. *Marketing Education Review*. Vol 12, No 2. pp49–60.

Jankowicz, A.D. (1994) Holden and Cooper's 'Russian managers as learners': a rejoinder. *Management Learning*. Vol 25, No 4. pp523–6.

Jankowicz, D. (1999) Towards a meaningful HRD function in the post-communist economies of Central and Eastern Europe. *Proceedings of the Academy of Human Resource Development*. pp318–26.

Janney, J.J. and Gove, S. (2011) Reputation and corporate social responsibility aberrations, trends, and hypocrisy: reactions to firm choices in the stock option backdating scandal. *Journal of Management Studies*. Vol 48, No 7. pp1562–85.

Jiang, T.T. and Iles, P.A. (2011) Employer brand equity, organizational attractiveness and talent management in the Zhejiang private sector. *Journal of Technology Management in China*. Vol 6, No 1. pp97–110.

Jiminez, A. and Davila, J.C. (2009) Stakeholders' perspective and strategic human resource management: lessons from a Colombian case study. In: A. Davila and M.M. Elvira (eds) *Best human resource management practices in Latin America*, pp37–56. London: Routledge.

Johnson, S., Stewart, J., Gold, J., Iles, P.A. and Devins, D. (2008) *World class comparisons in HRD*. Leeds: Learning and Skills Council/Leeds Metropolitan University.

Joy, S. and Kolb, D.A. (2009) Are there cultural differences in learning style? *International Journal of Intercultural Relations*. Vol 33. pp69–85.

Judah, B., Kobzova, J. and Popescu, N. (2011) *Dealing with a post-BRICS Russia*. London: European Council on Foreign Relations.

Jung, C. (1923) *Psychological types*. London: Pantheon Books.

Kabaskal, H. and Bodur, M. (2002) Arabic cluster: a bridge between East and West. *Journal of World Business*. Vol 37, No 1. pp40–54.

Kabwe, C. (2011) The conceptualisation and operationalisation of talent management: the case of European internationally operating business. PhD thesis. University of Central Lancashire.

Kacmar, K.M., Bachrach, D.G., Harris, K.J. and Zivnuska, S. (2011) Fostering good citizenship through ethical leadership: exploring the moderating role of gender and organizational politics. *Journal of Applied Psychology*. Vol 96, No 3. pp633–42.

Kamoche, K. (1996) Strategic human resource management within a resource-capability view of the firm. *Journal of Management Studies*. Vol 33, No 2. pp213–33.

Kamoche, K. (1997) Competence-creation in the African public sector. *International Journal of Public Sector Management*. Vol 10, No 4. pp268–78.

Kamoche, K. and Newenham-Kahindi, A. (2012) HRM and knowledge appropriation: the MNC experience in Tanzania. *International Journal of Human Resource Management*. Vol 23. pp2854–73.

Kamoche, K., Chizema, A., Mellahi, K. and Newenham-Kahindi, A. (2012) New directions in the management of human resources in Africa. *International Journal of Human Resource Management*. No 14. Special Issue: On managing human resources in Africa. pp2825–34.

Kamoche, K., Muuka, G.N., Horwitz, F.M. and Debrah, Y.A. (2004) Preface. In: K. Kamoche, Y. Debrah, F. Horwitz and G.N. Muuka (eds) *Managing human resources in Africa*. London: Routledge.

Kanter, R.M. (1989) Becoming PALS: pooling, allying and linking across companies. *Academy of Management Executive*. Vol 3, No 3. pp183–93.

Kaplan, R. and Norton, D. (1996) *The balanced scorecard*. Boston, MA: Harvard Business School Press.

Kassem, M.S. (1989) Strategy formulation: Arabian Gulf style. *International Studies of Management and Organization*. Vol 19, No 2. pp6–21.

Katz, H.C. and Colvin, A.J.S. (2011) Employment relations in the United States. In: G. Bamber, R.D. Lansbury and N. Wailes (eds) *International and comparative employment relations: globalisation and change*, pp62–87. London: Sage.

Kauser, S. and Tleiss, H. (2011) The Arab woman manager: participation, barriers and future prospects. *Journal of International Business and Economy*. Vol 12, No 1. pp35–56.

Keesing, R.M. (1974) Theories of culture. *Annual Review of Anthropology*. Vol 3. pp73–97.

Kelemen, M. and Lightfoot, G. (1999) Discourses of entrepreneurship, pricing and control: the case of Romania. Presented to the British Academy of Management, September.

Keller, B.K. and Kirsch, A. (2011) Employment relations in Germany. In: G. Bamber, R.D. Lansbury and N. Wailes (eds) *International and comparative employment relations: globalisation and change*, pp196–223. London: Sage.

Kinnie, N., Hutchinson, S., Purcell, J., Rayton, B. and Swart, J. (2005). Satisfaction with HR practices and commitment to the organization: why one size does not fit all. *Human Resource Management Journal*. Vol 15, No 4. pp9–29.

Kirton M.J. (1976) Adaptors and innovators: a description and measure. *Journal of Applied Psychology*. Vol 61. pp622–9.

Kirton, M.J. (1994) *Adaptors and innovators: styles of creativity and problem-solving*. London: Routledge.

Kirton, M.J. (2003) *Adaption-innovation: in the context of diversity and change*. London: Routledge.

Kleymann, B. and Malloch, H. (2012) HRM and HRD as Bricolage: the making of 'The Godfather'. Presentation to CIPD Centres' Conference, York, UK, 21 June.

Kluckhohn, F.R. and Strodtbeck, F.L. (1961) *Variations in value orientations*. Evanston, IL: Row, Peterson.

Knights, D. and O'Leary, M. (2005) Reflecting on corporate scandals: the failure of ethical leadership. *Business Ethics: A European Review*. Vol 14, No 4. pp359–66.

Knights, D. and O'Leary, M. (2006) Leadership, ethics and responsibility to the Other. *Journal of Business Ethics*. Vol 67, No 2. pp125–37.

Kocer, R.G. and Hayter, S. (2011) *Comparative study of labour relations in African countries*. Amsterdam Institute for Advanced Labour Studies. Working Paper 116. December. http://www.uva-aias.net/uploaded_files/publications/WP116-Kocer,Hayter.pdf .

Kohls, L.R. (1984) *Survival kit for overseas living*, 2nd edition. Yarmouth, ME: Intercultural Press Inc.

Kolb, D.A. (1976) Management and the learning process. *California Management Review*. Vol 18, No 3. pp21–31.

Kolb, D.A. (1984) *Experiential learning: experience as the source of learning and development*. Englewood Cliffs, NJ: Prentice Hall.

Kolb, D.A., Boyatzis, R.E. and Mainemelis, C. (2001) Experiential learning theory: previous research and new directions. In: R.J. Sternberg and L.F. Zhang (eds) *Perspectives on thinking, learning, and cognitive styles*, pp227–47. Mahwah, NJ: Lawrence Erlbaum.

Kolman, L., Noordhaven, N.G., Hofstede, G. and Dienes, E. (2003) Cross-cultural differences in central Europe. *Journal of Managerial Psychology*. Vol 18, No 1&2. pp76–88.

Kostera, M. (1995) The modern crusade: missionaries of management come to eastern Europe. *Management Learning*. Vol 26, No 3. pp331–52.

Kostera, M. (2000) Reclaiming the voice: a reflection on some silenced ones. *Human Resource Development International*. Vol 3, No 1. pp9–13.

Kostova, T. (1996) Transnational transfer of strategic organizational practices: a contextual perspective. *Academy of Management Review*. Vol 24, No 2. pp308–25.

Kostova, T. and Roth, K. (2003) Social capital in multinational corporations and a micro–macro model of its formation. *Academy of Management Review*. Vol 28, No 2. pp297–317.

Kotter, J. (1990) *How leadership differs from management*. New York: Free Press.

Koubek, J. (2009) Managing human resources in the Czech Republic. In: M. Morley, N. Heraty and S. Michailova (eds) *Managing human resources in central and eastern Europe*, pp132–57. London: Routledge.

Kramar, R. and Syed, J. (2012) *Human resource management in a global context: a critical approach*. Basingstoke: Palgrave Macmillan.

Kume, T. (1985) *Managerial attitudes toward decision-making*. In: W.B. Gudykunst, L.P. Stewart and S. Ting-Toomey (eds) *Communication, culture, and organizational processes*, pp231–51. Beverly Hills, CA: Sage.

Kwok, L. and Silverman, R.E. (2012) Bio as Bible: managers imitate Steve Jobs. *Wall Street Journal*. 31 March.

Lane, C. (1992) European business systems: Britain and Germany. In: R. Whitley (ed.) *European business systems: firms and markets in their national contexts*, pp64–97. London: Sage Publications.

Lane, C. (2000) Globalization and the German model of capitalism—erosion or survival? *British Journal of Sociology*. Vol 51. pp207–34.

Lane, K. and Pollner, F. (2008) How to address China's growing talent shortages. *The McKinsey Quarterly*. Vol 3. pp33–40.

Latifi, F. (1997) Management learning in national context. Unpublished PhD thesis. Henley Management College.

Lawrence, P. (1990) *Management in the land of Israel*. Cheltenham: Stanley Thornes.

Lawton, A., Iles, P., Llewellyn, N., Macaulay, M. and Thompson, B. (2005) *Supporting monitoring officers*. London: Standards Board for England.

Lee, F. and Juda, A. (2004) A network of innovation. *Harvard Business Review*. Vol 82, No 4. p22.

Lee, S. (2003) How to understand intercultural conversation: a conversation analysis of non-native speakers in the United States. *International Area Studies Review*. Vol 6, No 2. pp65–83.

Legge, K. (1995). *Human resource management: rhetorics and realities.* London: Macmillan Business.

Leguizamon, F.A., Ickis, J.C. and Ogliastri, E. (2009) Human resource practices and business performance: Grupo San Nicolas. In: A. Davila and M.M. Elvira (eds) *Best human resource management practices in Latin America*, pp85–96. London: Routledge.

Leithwood, K., Day, C., Sammons, P., Harris, A. and Hopkins, D. (2006) *Successful school leadership: what it is and how it influences pupil learning.* Nottingham: NCSL/Dept for Education and Skills, University of Nottingham.

Lewin, K., Lippit, R. and White, R.K. (1939) Patterns of aggressive behavior in experimentally created social climates. *Journal of Social Psychology.* Vol 10. pp271–301.

Lewis, M.M. (2005) The drama of international business: why cross-cultural training simulations work. *Journal of European Industrial Training.* Vol 29, No 7. pp593–8.

Lewis, P. (2003) New China – old ways? A case study of the prospects for implementing human resource management practices in a Chinese state-owned enterprise. *Employee Relations.* Vol 25, No 1. pp42–66.

Lewis, R. and Heckman, R. (2006) Talent management: a critical review. *Human Resource Management Review.* Vol 16. pp139–54.

Li, H.Z. (1999) Communicating information in conversations: A cross-cultural comparison. *International Journal of Intercultural Relations.* Vol 23, No 3. pp387–409.

Libeskind, J.P., Oliver, A.L., Zucker, L. and Brewer, M. (1996) Social networks, learning and flexibility: sourcing scientific knowledge in new biotechnology firms. *Organization Science.* Vol 7, No 4. pp428–43.

Lievens, F. (2007) Employer branding in the Belgian army: the importance of instrumental and symbolic beliefs for potential applicants, actual applicants and military employees. *Human Resource Management.* Vol 46, No 1. pp51–69.

Lievens, F., Van Dam, K. and Anderson, N. (2002) Recent trends and challenges in personnel selection. *Personnel Review.* Vol 31, No 5. pp580–601.

Lievens, F., Decaesteker, C., Coetsier, P. and Geirnaert, J. (2001) Organizational attractiveness for prospective applicants: a person–organization fit perspective. *Applied Psychology: An International Review.* Vol 50, No 1. pp30–51.

Lievens, F., Van Keer, E., Harris, M. and Bisqueret, C. (2003) Predicting cross-cultural training performance: the validity of personality, cognitive ability and dimensions measured by an assessment centre and a behavior description interview. *Journal of Applied Psychology.* Vol 88, No 3. pp476–89.

Lincoln, Y.S. and Guba, E.G. (1985) *Naturalistic inquiry.* Beverly Hills, CA: Sage Publications, Inc.

Lindridge, A. (2005) Galton's problem. In: *The Blackwell Encyclopedia of Management.* Volume IV.

Littrell, L.N., Salas, E., Palye, M. and Riedel, S. (2006) Expatriate preparation: a critical analysis of 25 years of cross-cultural training research. *Human Resource Development Review.* Vol 5. pp355–88.

Litwin, G. and Stringer, R. (1968) *Motivation and organisational climate.* Boston, MA: Harvard University Press.

Liu, S. (2003) Cultures within culture: unity and diversity of two generations of employees in state-owned enterprises. *Human Relations.* Vol 56, No 4. pp387–41.

Lockwood, N. (2005) *Talent management overview.* Alexandria, VA: Society for Human Resource Management.

Loewe, M. et al (2007) *The impact of favouritism on the business climate. A study of wasta in Jordan.* DIE Studies 30. Bonn: German Development Institute.

Lofstrom, E. (2002) Person–situation interactions in SMEs: a study of cognitive style and sources of job satisfaction. In: M. Valcke and D. Gombeir (eds) *Learning Styles: reliability and validity.* Proceedings of the 7th Annual European Learning Styles Information Network Conference, 26–28 June, University of Ghent.

Loo, R. (2002) The distribution of learning styles and types for hard and soft business majors. *Educational Psychology.* Vol 22, No 3. pp349–60.

Loos, H. (2007) Tendencies of the Russian labour and recruitment markets – employment in a medium-sized IT company. In: M. Domsch and T. Lidokhover (eds) *Human resource management in Russia*, pp171–92. Aldershot: Ashgate.

Mabey, C. and Finch-Lees, A. (2008) *Management and leadership development.* London: Sage.

Madsen, J.S., Due, J. and Andersen, S.K. (2011) Employment relations in Denmark. In: G. Bamber, R.D. Lansbury and N. Wailes (eds) *International and comparative employment relations: globalisation and change*, pp224–51. London: Sage.

Mahapatro, B.B. (2010) *Human resource management.* New Delhi: New Age Management.

Makela, K., Bjorkmam, I. and Ehrnrooth, M. (2010) How do MNCs establish their talent pools? Influences on individuals' likelihood of being labelled as talent. *Journal of World Business.* Vol 45, No 2. pp134–42.

Malloch, H., Kleymann, B., Angot, J. and Redman, T. (2007) Les Compagnons du Devoir: A French Compagnonnage as an HRD system. *Personnel Review.* Vol 36. pp603–22.

Mangham, I.L (2004) Leadership and integrity. In: J. Storey (ed.) *Leadership in organizations: current issues and key trends*, pp41–57. London: Routledge.

Mangham, I.L. and Silver, D. (1986) *Management training: context and practice.* Bath: School of Management, University of Bath ESRC.

Marchington, M., Waddington, J. and Timming, A. (2011) Employment relations in Britain. In: G. Bamber, R.D. Lansbury and N. Wailes (eds) *International and comparative employment relations: globalisation and change*, pp36–61. London: Sage.

Marin, G.S. (2008) National differences in compensation: the influence of the institutional and cultural context. In: L.R. Gomez-Mejia and S. Werner (eds) *Global compensation: foundations and perspectives*, pp18–28. London: Routledge.

Marriott, P. (2002) A longitudinal study of undergraduate accounting students' learning style preferences at two UK universities. *Accounting Education: An International Journal.* Vol 11, No 1. pp43–62.

Martin, G. and Hetrick, S. (2006) *Corporate reputations, branding and people management: a strategic approach to HR* (Advanced HR Practitioner). Oxford: Elsevier Butterworth Heinemann.

Martin-Alcazar, F., Romero-Fernandez, P.M. and Sanchez-Gardey, G. (2008) Human resource management as a field of research. *British Journal of Management.* Vol 19, No 2. pp103–19.

Mashood, N., Verhoeven, H. and Chansarkar, B. (2010) *Proceedings of Annual Hawaii International Business Research Conference.* Available at: from http://www.wbiconpro.com/ [accessed 5 November 2010].

May, R.C. and Ledgerwood, R. (2007) One step forward, two steps back: negative consequences of national policy on human resource practices in Russia. In: M. Domsch and T. Lidokhover (eds) *Human resource management in Russia*, pp25–42. Aldershot: Ashgate.

May, R., Chan, A., Hodges, T. and Avolio, B. (2003) Developing the moral component of authentic leadership. *Organizational Dynamics.* Vol 32. pp247–60.

Mayo, A. and Lank, E. (1994) *The power of learning.* London: Institute of Personnel Management.

Mayrhofer, W. and Scullion, H. (2002) All equal? The importance of context empirical evidence about male and female expatriates from the German clothing industry. *International Journal of Human Resource Management.* Vol 3, No 5. pp815–36.

Mazdar, S. (2005) Subordinates information inquiry in uncertain times: a cross-cultural consideration of leadership style effect. *International Journal of Cross Cultural Management.* Vol 5, No 3. pp255–74.

Mbigi, L. and Maree, J. (1995) *Ubuntu: the spirit of African transformation management.* Johannesburg: Sigma Press.

McAdam, R. and Walker, T. (2003) An enquiry into balanced scorecards within best value implementation in UK local government. *Public Administration.* Vol 81, No 4. pp873–92.

McBeth, M. (2008) *The distributed leadership toolbox: essential practices for successful schools.* Thousand Oaks, CA: Corwin.

McCourt, W. and Ramgutty-Wong, A. (2003) Limits to strategic HRM: the case of the Mauritian civil service. *International Journal of Human Resource Management.* Vol 14. pp1–19.

McDonnell, A., Lamare, R., Gunnigle, P. and Lavelle, J. (2010) Developing tomorrow's leaders – evidence of global talent management in multinational enterprises. *Journal of World Business.* Vol 45, No 2. pp150–60.

McLean, G.N. (2004) National human resource development: what in the world is it? *Advances in Developing Human Resources.* Vol 6, No 3. pp269–75.

McNulty, Y. and Tharenou, P. (2004) Expatriate return on investment: a definition and antecedents. *International Studies of Management and Organization.* Vol 34, No 3. pp68–95.

McSweeney, B. (2001) The essentials of scholarship: a reply to Geert Hofstede. *Human Relations.* Vol 55, No 11. pp1363–72.

McSweeney, B. (2002) Hofstede's model of national cultural differences and their consequences: a triumph of faith – a failure of analysis. *Human Relations.* Vol 55, No 1. pp89–118.

McWilliams, A. and Siegel, D. (2001) Corporate social responsibility: a theory of the firm perspective. *Academy of Management Review.* Vol 26. pp117–27.

Mead, G.H. (1934) *Mind, self, and society.* Edited by Charles W. Morris. Chicago: University of Chicago Press.

Mead, R. (1994) *International management: cross-cultural dimensions.* Oxford: Blackwell.

Mehra, A., Smith, B.R., Dixon, A.L. and Robertson, B. (2006) Distributed leadership in teams: the network of leadership perceptions and team performance. *The Leadership Quarterly.* Vol 17. pp232–45.

Mellahi, K. (2006) Human resource management in Saudi Arabia. In: P. Budhwar and K. Mellahi (eds) *Managing human resources in the Middle East*, pp 97–120. London: Routledge.

Mellahi, K. and Budhwar, P.S. (2006) Human resource management in the Middle East: emerging models and future challenges for research and policy. In:

P. Budhwar and K. Mellahi (eds) *Managing human resources in the Middle East*, pp291–301. London: Routledge.

Mellahi, K. and Collings, D. (2010) The barriers to effective global talent management: the example of corporate elites in MNEs. *Journal of World Business*. Vol 45, No 2. pp143–9.

Mellahi, K. and Wood, G. (2002) *The ethical business: challenges and controversies*. Basingstoke: Palgrave Macmillan.

Mendenhall, M. and Oddou, G. (1985) The dimensions of expatriate acculturation: a review. Academy of Management Review. Vol 10, No 1. January. pp39–47.

Mendenhall, M. and Osland, J.S. (2002) An overview of the extant global leadership research. Symposium presentation, Academy of International Business, Puerto Rico, June.

Mendenhall, M., Kuhlmann, T., Stahl, G. and Osland, J. (2002) Employee development and expatriate assignments. In: M. Gannon and K. Newman (eds) *The Blackwell Handbook of Cross-Cultural Management*, pp155–83. Oxford: Blackwell Publishers.Mendenhall, M., Osland, J.S., Bird, A., Oddou, G.R. and Maznevski, M. (eds) (2008) *Global leadership: research, practice and development*. London: Routledge.

Mendenhall, M., Stahl, G., Ehnert, I., Oddou, G., Osland, J. and Kühlmann, T. (2004) Evaluation studies of cross-cultural training programs: a review of the literature from 1988–2000. In: D. Landis and J. Bennett (eds) *The handbook of intercultural training*. Thousand Oaks, CA: Sage.

Mendonca, M. (2001) Preparing for ethical leadership in organisations. *Canadian Journal of Administrative Science*. Vol 18, No 4. pp266–76.

Meredith, M. (2005) *The state of Africa: a history of fifty years of independence*. London: Simon & Schuster/The Free Press.

Metcalfe, B. (2006) Exploring cultural dimensions of gender and management in the Middle East. *Thunderbird International Business Review*. Vol 48, No 1. pp93–107.

Metcalfe, B.D. (2007) Gender and human resource management in Middle East. *International Journal of Human Resource Management*. Vol 18, No 1. pp54–74.

Metcalfe, B.D. (2011a) Gender, empowerment and development: a critical appraisal of governance, culture and national HRD frameworks in Arab Gulf states. *Human Resource Development International*. Vol 14, No 2. pp131–48.

Metcalfe, B.D. (2011b) Women, work organization and social change: human resource development in Arab Gulf states. *Human Resource Development International*. Vol 14, No 2. pp1–13.

Metcalfe, B.D. and Mnoumi, F. (2011) *Leadership development in the Middle East.* Cheltenham: Edward Elgar.

Metcalfe, B.D. and Mutlaq, L. (2011) Re-imagining the feminization of leadership in the Middle East. In: B.D. Metcalfe and F. Mnoumi (eds) *Leadership development in the Middle East*, pp328–70. Cheltenham: Edward Elgar.

Meyer, H.M., Kay, E. and French, J.R.P. (1965) Split roles in performance appraisal. *Harvard Business Review.* Vol 43. pp123–9.

Meyer, J. and Rowan, B. (1977) Institutionalized organizations: formal structure as myth and ceremony. *American Journal of Sociology.* Vol 83, No 2. pp340–63.

Meyer, K., Mudambi, R. and Narula, R. (2011) Multinational enterprises and local contexts: the opportunities and challenges of multiple embeddedness. *Journal of Management Studies.* Vol 48, No 2. pp235–52.

Mezias, J.M. and Scandura, T.A. (2005) A needs-driven approach to expatriate adjustment and career development: a multiple mentoring perspective. *Journal of International Business Studies.* Vol 36. pp519–38.

Michaels, E., Handfield-Jones, H. and Beth, A. (2001) *The war for talent.* New York: McKinsey & Company, Inc.

Milkovich, G. and Newman, J. (2008) *Compensation*, 9th edition. New York: McGraw-Hill.

Minbaeva, D. and Michailova, S. (2004) Knowledge transfer and expatriation in multinational companies. *Employee Relations.* Vol 26, No 6. pp663–79.

Minbaeva, D.B., Pedersen, T., Bjorkman, I., Fey, C.F. and Park, H.J. (2003) MNC knowledge transfer, subsidiary absorptive capacity, and HRM. *Journal of International Business Studies.* Vol 34, No 6. pp586–99.

Minkes, A.L., Smal, M.W. and Chatterjee, S.R. (1999) Leadership and business ethics: does it matter? Implications for management. *Journal of Business Ethics.* Vol 20. pp327–35.

Minkov, M. and Hofstede, G. (2012) Hofstede's fifth dimension: new evidence from the World Values Survey. *Journal of Cross Cultural Psychology.* Vol 43, No 1. pp3–14.

Mirvis, P.H. and Marks, M.L. (1992) *Managing the merger: making it work.* Englewood Cliffs, NJ: Prentice Hall.

Mishra, B.R. (2012) Infosys may give wage hike in October. *Business Standard.* 27 September.

Modaff, D.P., DeWine, S. and Butler, J. (2011) *Organizational communication: foundations, challenges, and misunderstandings*, 2nd edition. Boston, MA: Pearson Education.

Mohamed, M.A. and Mohamad, S. (2011) The effect of *wasta* on perceived competence and morality in Egypt. *Cross Cultural Management: An International Journal*. Vol 18, No 4. pp412–25.

Molinsky, A. (2007) Cross-cultural code-switching: the psychological challenges of adapting behavior in foreign cultural interactions. *Academy of Management Review*. Vol 32, No 2. pp622–40.

Morley, M., Heraty, N. and Michailova, S. (eds) (2009) *Managing human resources in central and eastern Europe*. London: Routledge.

Morley, M.J., Linehan, M. and Scullion, H. (2003) The management of expatriates: contemporary developments and future challenges. *Journal of Managerial Psychology*. Vol 18, No 3. pp174–84.

Morton, L., Ashton, C. and Bellis, R. (2005) *Differentiating talent management: integrating talent management to drive business performance*. London: CRF Publishing.

Muller, M. (1999) Enthusiastic embrace or critical reception? *Journal of Management Studies*. Vol 36, No 4. pp465–82.

Mumford, A. and Gold, J. (2004) *Management development: strategies for action*. London: Chartered Institute of Personnel and Development.

Muna, F. (1980) *The Arab executive*. London: Macmillan.

Muratbekova-Touron, M. (2011) Mutual perception of Russian and French managers. *International Journal of Human Resource Management*. Vol 22, No 8. pp1723–40.

Murphy, K.R. and DeNisi, A. (2008) A model of the appraisal process. In: A. Varma, P. Budhwar and A. DeNisi (eds) *Performance management systems: a global perspective*, pp81–96. London: Routledge.

Myers, I.B. (1962) *Manual: The Myers-Briggs Type Indicator*. Palo Alto, CA: Consulting Psychologists Press.

Namazie, P. (2003) Factors affecting the transferability of HRM practices in joint ventures based in Iran. *Career Development International*. Vol 8, No 7. pp357–66.

Namazie, P. and Frame, P. (2007) Developments in human resource management in Iran. *International Journal of Human Resource Management*. Vol 18, No 1. pp159–327.

Nambudiri, R. (2012) Propensity to trust and organizational commitment: a study in the Indian pharmaceutical sector. *International Journal of Human Resource Management*. Vol 23, No 5. Special Issue: Human resource management in the new economy in India. pp977–86.

Natesan, N.C., Keefe, M.J. and Darling, J.R. (2009) Enhancement of global business practices: lessons from the Hindu Bhagavad Gita. *European Business Review*. Vol 21, No 2. pp128–43.

Nell, P., Ambos, B. and Schlegelmilch, B. (2006) The benefits of hierarchy? – exploring the effects of regional headquarters in multinational corporations. *Advances in International Management*. Vol 24. pp85–106.

Newell, S. (1999) The transfer of management knowledge to China: building learning communities rather than translating Western textbooks? *Education and Training*. Vol 41, No 6/7. pp286–93.

Newell, S. (2005) Recruitment and selection. In: S. Bach (ed.) *Managing human resources: personnel management in transition*, 4th edition, pp115–47. Oxford: Blackwell.

Newell, S. (2009) Assessment, selection and evaluation. In: J. Lepold and L. Harris (eds) *The strategic managing of human resources*, 2nd edition, pp153–88. Harlow: Pearson Education.

Newell, S.M. and Shackleton, V. (2000) Recruitment and selection. In: K. Sisson and S. Bach (eds) *Personnel management: a comprehensive guide to theory and practice*, 3rd edition, pp111–36. Oxford: Blackwell.

Newton-Small, J. (2007) Obama's foreign-policy problem. *TIME*. 18 December. http://www.time.com/time/politics/article/0,8599,1695803,00.html.

Nonaka, I. (1991) The knowledge-creating company. *Harvard Business Review*. Vol 69. pp96–104.

Nonaka, I. (1994) A dynamic theory of organizational knowledge creation. *Organization Science*. Vol 5, No 1. pp14–37.

Nonaka, I. and Takeuchi, H. (1995) *The knowledge-creating company*. Oxford: Oxford University Press.

Oberg, K. (1960) Culture shock and the problem of adjustment in new cultural environments. In: G.R. Weaver (ed.) *Culture, communication and conflict: readings in intercultural relations*. Needham Heights, MA: Simon & Schuster Publishing.

OECD/UNDP (2006) Good governance for development in Arab countries: initiative steering group meeting at ministerial level: regional challenges and policy priorities/progress made in the field of civil service and integrity (Working Group 1). Sharm El Sheikh, Egypt, 19–20 May. www.oecd.org/dataoecd/36/8/36926998.pdf .

Offerman, L.R. and Hellman, P.S. (1997) Culture's consequences for leadership behaviour: national values in action. *Journal of Cross Cultural Psychology*. Vol 28, No 3. pp342–51.

O'Neill, J. (2011) *The growth map: economic opportunity in the BRICs and beyond.* London: Penguin.

Orru, M., Biggart, N. and Hamilton, G. (eds) (1997) *The economic organization of East Asian capitalism.* Thousand Oaks, CA: Sage.

Osland, A., Osland, J.S., Tanure, B. and Gabrish, R. (2009) Stakeholder management: the case of Aracruz Cellulose in Brazil. In: A. Davila and M.M. Elvira (eds) *Best human resource management practices in Latin America*, pp10–24. London: Routledge.

Osland, J.S. (2008) The multidisciplinary roots of global leadership development. In: M. Mendenhall, J.S. Osland, A. Bird, G.R. Oddou and M. Maznevski (eds) *Global leadership: research, practice and development*, pp34–63. London: Routledge.

Ovadje, F. and Ankomah, A. (2001) HRM in Nigeria. In: P.S. Budhwar and Y.A. Debrah (eds) *Human resource management in developing countries*, pp174–89. London: Routledge.

Özbilgin, M. and Healy, G. (2003) 'Don't mention the war' – Middle Eastern careers in context. *Career Development International.* Vol 8. pp325–7.

Özbilgin, M. and Syed, J. (2010) *Managing gender diversity in Asia: a research companion.* Cheltenham and New York: Edward Elgar Press.

Palrecha, R., Spangler, W.D. and Yammarino, F.J. (2011) A comparative study of three leadership approaches in India. *Leadership Quarterly.* Vol 23. pp146–62.

Parry, E. and Urwin, P. (2011) Generational differences in work values: a review of theory and evidence. *International Journal of Management Reviews.* Vol 13, No 1. pp79–96.

Pass, S. (2005) Missing links in the causal chain between HR practices and organisational performance. Paper presented to the CIPD Professional Standards Conference, Keele University, UK, May.

Paul, A.K. and Anantharaman, R.N. (2004) Influence of HRM practices on organisational commitment: a study among software professionals in India. *Human Resource Development Quarterly.* Vol 5, No 1. pp77–88.

Pauwe, J. (2004) *HRM and performance.* Oxford: Oxford University Press.

Pearce, C.L. (1997) The determinants of change management team effectiveness: a longitudinal investigation. Doctoral dissertation, University of Maryland, College Park, MD.

Pearce, C.L. (2004) The future of leadership: Combining vertical and shared leadership to transform knowledge work. *Academy of Management Executive.* Vol 18, No 1. pp47–57.

Pearce, C.L. and Conger, J.A. (eds) (2003) *Shared leadership: Reframing the hows and whys of leadership.* Thousand Oaks, CA: Sage.

Pearce, C.L. and Sims, Jr H.P. (2002) Vertical versus shared leadership as predictors of the effectiveness of change management teams: an examination of aversive, directive, transactional, transformational and empowering leader behaviors. *Group Dynamics.* Vol 6. pp172–97.

Pearce, C.L., Manz, C.C. and Sims, Jr H.P. (2008) The roles of vertical and shared leadership in the enactment of executive corruption: implications for research and practice. *The Leadership Quarterly.* Vol 19. pp353–9.

Perez Arrau, G., Eades, E. and Wilson, J. (2012) Managing human resources in the Latin American context: the case of Chile. *International Journal of Human Resource Management.* Vol 23, No 15. pp3133–50.

Perkmann, M. and Spicer, A. (2008) How are management fashions institutionalized? The role of institutional work. *Human Relations.* Vol 61, No 6. pp811–44.

Perlmutter, H. (1969) The tortuous evolution of the multinational corporation. *Columbia Journal of World Business.* Vol 1. pp9–18.

Perlmutter, H. and Heenan, D. (1979) *Multinational organization development.* Reading, MA: Addison-Wesley.

Petrovic, J., Harris, H. and Brewster, C. (2000) *New forms of international working.* Crème Research Report, 1/00. Cranfield: Cranfield School of Management, Cranfield University.

Pfeffer, J. (1998) *The human equation: building profits by putting people first.* Boston, MA: Harvard Business School Press.

Polanyi, M. (1966) *The tacit dimension.* London: Routledge & Kegan Paul.

Pollock, D.C. and van Reken, R.E. (2009) *Third culture kids: growing up among worlds.* London: Nicholas Brealey.

Poole, M. (1986) *Industrial relations: origins and patterns of national diversity.* London: Routledge.

Porter, L.W. and Lawler, E.E. (1968) *Managerial attitudes and performance.* Homewood, IL: Richard D. Irwin, Inc.

Prahalad, C.K. and Hamel, G. (1990) The core competencies of the organization. *Harvard Business Review.* Vol 68, No 3. pp79–92.

Preece, D. and Iles, P.A. (2009) Executive development: assuaging uncertainties through joining a leadership academy. *Personnel Review.* Vol 38, No 3. pp286–306.

Preece, D., Iles, P.A. and Chuai, X. (2011) Talent management and management fashion in Chinese enterprise: exploring case studies in Beijing. *International Journal of Human Resource Management*. Vol 22, No 16. pp3413–28.

Preece, D., Iles, P.A. and Jones, R. (2012) MNE regional head offices and their affiliates: talent management practices and challenges in the Asia Pacific. Paper submitted to the *International Journal of Human Resource Management*.

Pucik, V. (1988) Strategic alliances, organizational learning, and competitive advantage: the HRM agenda. *Human Resource Management*. Vol 27, No 1. pp77–93.

Pucik, V., Björkman, I., Evans, P. and Stahl, G. (2011) Human resource management in cross-border mergers and acquisitions. In: A-W. Harzing and A. Pinnington (eds) *International human resource management*, 3rd edition, pp119–52. Thousand Oaks, CA: Sage Publications.

Pulakos, E.D., Mueller-Hanson, R.A. and O'Leary, R.S. (2008) Performance management in the United States. In: A. Varma, P. Budhwar and A. DeNisi (eds) *Performance management systems: a global perspective*, pp97–114. London: Routledge.

Purcell, J. (1999) The search for 'best practice' and 'best fit': chimera or cul-de-sac? *Human Resource Management Journal*. Vol 9. pp26–41.

Purcell, J. and Ahlstrand, B.W. (1994) *Human resource management in the multi-divisional company*. Oxford: Oxford University Press.

Purcell, J., Hutchinson, S., Kinnie, N., Rayton, B. and Swart, J. (2003) *Understanding the people performance link: unlocking the black box*. London: Chartered Institute of Personnel Development.

Qiao, J. (2008) Leadership development programs: lessons learned from four case studies. 9th International Conference on Human Resource Development Research and Practice Across Europe, IESEG School of Management, Lille, France, May.

Rai, T.S. and Holyoak, K.J. (2009) Moral principles or consumer preferences? Alternative framings of the trolley problem. *Cognitive Sciences*. Vol 34, No 2. pp311–21.

Ram, S. (2010) India's next outsourcing wave. *Bloomberg Businessweek*. 9 March.

Ramsey, S.J. and Schaetti, B.F. (1999) Reentry: coming 'home' to the unfamiliar. Repatriates may feel like strangers in a strange land. *Mobility*. Employee Relocation Council. Available at: http://www.transitions-dynamics.com/reentry.html .

Ratnam, C.S.V. and Verma, A. (2011) Employment relations in India. In: G.J. Bamber, R.D. Lansbury and N. Wailes (eds) *International and comparative employment relations: globalisation and change*, pp330–52. London: Allen & Unwin/Sage.

Ray, T., Clegg, S. and Gordon, R. (2004) A new look at dispersed leadership: power, knowledge and context. In: J. Storey (ed.) *Leadership in organizations: current issues and key trends*, pp319–36. London: Routledge.

Redman, T. and Matthews, B.P. (1997) What do recruiters want in a public sector manager? *Public Personnel Management*. Vol 26, No 2. pp245–56.

Redman, T. and Snape, E. (1992) Upward and onward: can staff appraise their managers? *Personnel Review*. Vol 21, No 7. pp32–46.

Rees, C. and Edwards, T. (2009) Management strategy and HR in international mergers: choice, constraint and pragmatism. *Human Resource Management Journal*. Vol 19, no 1. pp24–39.

Rees, C.J., Mamman, A. and Bin Braik, A. (2007) Emiratization as a strategic HRM change initiative: case study evidence from a UAE petroleum company. *International Journal of Human Resource Management*. Vol 18, No 1. pp33–53.

Reiche, S. and Harzing, A-W. (2011) International assignments. In: A.W. Harzing and A. Pinnington (eds) *International human resource management*, 3rd edition. London: Sage Publications.

Resick, C.J., Hanges, P.J., Dickson, M.W. and Mitchelson, J.K. (2006) A cross-cultural endorsement of the concept of ethical leadership. *Journal of Business Ethics*. Vol 63. pp345–59.

Reuber, A. and Fischer, E. (1997) The influence of the management team's international experience on internationalization behaviors of SMEs. *Journal of International Business Studies*. Vol 28, No 4. pp807–25.

Richmond, A. (1993) Reactive migration: sociological perspectives on refugee movements. *Journal of Refugee Studies*. Vol 6. pp7–24.

Riding, R. and Rayner, S. (2002) *Cognitive styles and learning strategies: understanding style differences in learning and behaviour*, 5th edition. London: David Fulton.

Ritchie, J. and Spencer, L. (1994) Qualitative data analysis. In: A. Bryman and Burgess (eds) *Analysing qualitative data*, pp173–94. London: Routledge.

Riusala, K. and Suutari, V. (2004) International knowledge transfer through expatriates. *Thunderbird International Business Review*. Vol 46, No 6. pp743–70.

Robertson, I.T. and Iles, P.A. (1988) Approaches to managerial selection. In: C.L. Cooper and I.T. Robertson (eds) *International review of industrial and organizational psychology*. Vol 3. pp159–211. Chichester: John Wiley & Sons.

Robertson, I.T. and Smith, M. (2001) Personnel selection. *Journal of Occupational and Organizational Psychology*. Vol 74, No 4. pp441–72.

Robertson, I.T., Iles, P.A., Gratton, L. and Sharpley, D. (1991) The psychological impact of selection procedures on candidates. *Human Relations*. Vol 44, No 9. pp963–82.

Rodgers, H., Frearson, M., Gold, J. and Holden, R. (2003) *International comparator contexts: the leading learning project*. London: Learning and Skill Research Centre.

Roka, P. (2006) *Bhagavad Gita on effective leadership: timeless wisdom for leaders*. Bloomington, IN: iUniverse.com.

Rokhman, W. (2010) The effects of Islamic work ethics on outcomes. *Electronic Journal of Business Ethics and Organization Studies*. Vol 15, No 1. pp21–7.

Romani, L. (2011) Culture in international human resource management. In: A-W. Harzing and A.H. Pinnington (eds) *International human resource management*, 3rd edition, pp79–118. London: Sage.

Ronen, S. (1989) *Training the international assignee*. San Francisco: Goldstein.

Rosenthal, F. (1976) *Al-Biruni between Greece and India*. Edited by E. Yarshter. New York: Iran Center, Columbia University.

Ross, L., Rix, M. and Gold, J. (2005) Learning distributed leadership, part 1. *Industrial and Commercial Training*. Vol 37, No 3. pp130–37.

Rowley, C., Benson, J. and Warner, M. (2004) Towards an Asian model of human resource management? A comparative analysis of China, Japan and South Korea. *International Journal of Human Resource Management*. Vol 15, No 4. pp917–33.

Rugman, A., Verbeke, A. and Yuan, W. (2011) Reconceptualising Bartlett and Ghoshal's classification of national subsidiary roles in the multi-national enterprise. *Journal of Management Studies*. Vol 48, No 2. pp253–77.

Sachdev, S. (2006) International corporate responsibility and employment relations. In: T. Edwards and C. Rees (eds) *International human resource management: globalization, national systems and multinational companies*, pp262–82. Harlow: Pearson Education/FT Prentice Hall.

Sachdev, S. (2011) International corporate social responsibility and HRM. In: T. Edwards and C. Rees (eds) *International human resource management*, 2nd edition, pp253–71. Harlow: Pearson Education.

Sadler-Smith, E. (2006) *Learning and development for managers*. Oxford: Blackwell.

Sadler-Smith, E. and Tsang, F. (1998) A comparative study of approaches to studying in Hong Kong and the United Kingdom. *British Journal of Educational Psychology*. Vol 68. pp81–93.

Saini, D.B. and Budhwar, P. (2004) HRM in India. In: A. Varma and P. Budhwar (eds) *Managing human resources in Asia-Pacific*, pp113–40. London: Routledge.

Saka, A. (2004) The cross-national diffusion of work systems: translation of Japanese operations in the UK. *Organisational Studies.* Vol 25, No 2. pp209–28.

Salaman, G. (2004) Competences of managers, competences of leaders. In: J. Storey (ed.) *Leadership in organizations: current issues and key trends*, pp58–78. London: Routledge.

Salaman, G., Cameron, C., Hamblin, H., Iles, P.A., Mabey, C. and Thompson, K. (eds) (1992) *Human resource strategies: a reader.* London: Sage/Open University.

Salimaki, A. and Heneman, R.L. (2008) Pay for performance for global employees. In: L.R. Gomez-Mejia and S. Werner (eds) *Global compensation: foundations and perspectives*, pp158–68. London: Routledge.

Salovey, P. and Mayer, J.D. (1990) Emotional intelligence. *Imagination, Cognition and Personality.* Vol 9. pp185–211.

Sandler, S. (2006) Critical issues in HR drive 2006 priorities: # 1 is talent management. *HR Focus.* Vol 83, No 1. pp1–3.

Sarkar-Barney, S. (2004) The role of national culture in enhancing training effectiveness: a framework. In: E. Salas (ed.) *Advances in human performance and cognitive engineering research*, pp183–213. Amsterdam: Elsevier.

Sartorius, K., Merino, A. and Carmichael, T. (2011) Human resource management and cultural diversity: a case study in Mozambique. *International Journal of Human Resource Management.* Vol 22, No 9. pp1963–85.

Scarbrough, H. (2002) The role of intermediary groups in shaping management fashion: the case of knowledge management. *International Studies in Management and Organization.* Vol 32, No 4. pp87–103.

Schneider, B. (1987) The people make the place. *Personnel Psychology.* Vol 40. pp437–53.

Schuler, R.S. (2001) HR issues in international joint ventures and alliances. In: J. Storey (ed.) *Human resource management: a critical text*, 2nd edition, pp314–36. London: Thomson Learning.

Schuler, R.S. and Rogovsky, N. (1998) Understanding compensation practice variation across firms: the impact of national culture. *Journal of International Business Studies.* Vol 29, No 1. pp159–77.

Schuler, R.S., Dowling, P.J. and De Cieri, H. (1993) An integrative framework of strategic international human resource management. *Journal of Management.* Vol 19, No 2. pp419–59.

Schuler, R.S., Jackson, S.E. and Luo, Y. (2004) *Managing human resources in cross-border alliances.* London: Routledge.

Schwartz, S.H. (1990) Individualism–collectivism: critique and proposed refinements. *Journal of Cross Cultural Psychology.* Vol 21. pp139–57.

Schwieger, D.M., Csiszar, E.N. and Napier, N.K. (1993) Implementing cross-national mergers and acquisitions. *Human Resources Planning.* Vol 16, No 1. pp53–70.

Scullion, H. and Brewster, C. (2001) The management of expatriates: messages from Europe. *Journal of World Business.* Vol 36, No 4. pp346–65.

Scullion, H. and Collings, D. (2006) International talent management. In: H. Scullion and D. Collings (eds) *Global staffing*, pp87–116. New York: Routledge.

Scullion, H. and Collings, D. (eds) (2011) *Global talent management.* Abingdon: Routledge.

Scullion, H. and Starkey, K. (2000) In search of the changing role of the corporate human resource function in the international firm. *International Journal of Human Resource Management.* Vol 11, pp1061–81.

Scullion, H., Collings, D. and Caligiuri, P. (2010) Global talent management. *Journal of World Business.* Vol 45, No 2. pp105–8.

Selmer, J. (2006) Language ability and adjustment: Western expatriates in China. *Thunderbird International Business Review.* Vol 48, No 3. pp347–68.

Selmer, S. and Lam, H. (2004) Third-culture kids: future business expatriates? *Personnel Review.* Vol 33, No 4. pp430–45.

Sen, V. (2010) IBM, Accenture, Capgemini lock up employees to stop attrition. *TechEye.net.* 23 December. http://news.techeye.net/business/ibm-accenture-capgemini-lock-up-employees-to-stop-attrition [accessed 27 April 2012].

Shane, S.A., Venkataraman, S. and MacMillan, I. (1995) Cultural differences in innovation championing roles. *Journal of Management.* Vol 21. pp931–52.

Sharma, T., Budhwar, P.S. and Varma, A. (2008) Performance management in India. In: A. Varma, P.S. Budhwar and A. DeNisi (eds) *Performance management systems: a global perspective*, pp180–92. London: Routledge.

Shen, J. (2005) Towards a generic international human resource management model. *Journal of Organisational Transformation and Social Change.* Vol 2, No 2. pp83–102.

Shen, J. (2007) Labour contracts in China: do they protect workers' rights? *Journal of Organisational Transformation and Social Change.* Vol 4, No 2. pp111–30.

Shen, J., Edwards, V. and Lee, G. (2005) Developing an integrative IHRM model: the contribution of Chinese MNEs. *Asia Pacific Journal of Business Review.* Vol 11, No 3. pp365–84.

Shen, Y. and Hall, D. (2009) When expats explore other options: retaining talent through greater job embeddedness and repatriation adjustment. *Human Resource Management.* Vol 48, No 5. pp793–816.

Sherif, M.A. (1975) *Ghazali's theory of virtue*. Albany, NY: State University of New York Press.

Shutt, J., Iles, P.A., Chen, H. and Zhu, X. (2012) *Employability and entrepreneurship in Zhejiang Province*. Report to Prime Minister's Initiative 2. Leeds: British Council, Leeds Metropolitan University/Zhejiang University of Technology.

Silicon India. (2011) Cognizant caught poaching? 27 March. http://www.siliconindia.com/shownews/Cognizant_caught_poaching-nid-81118-cid-3.html [accessed 27 April 2012].

Simmons, J. and Iles, P.A. (2001) Performance appraisals in knowledge-based organisations: implications for management education. *International Journal of Management Education*. Vol 2, No 1. pp3–18.

Simmons, J., Iles, P.A. and Yolles, M. (2005) Identifying those on board 'the moving train': towards a stakeholder-focused methodology for organizational decision making. *Systems Research and Behavioral Science*. Vol 22, No 1. pp41–53.

Sims, R. (2000) Changing an organization's culture under new leadership. *Journal of Business Ethics*. Vol 25, No 1. pp65–78.

Sinha, V. (2012) India still the world's BPO hub. *Hindustan Times*. 8 April.

Skinner, B.F. (1953) *Science and human behavior*. New York: Macmillan.

Smircich, L. (1983) Concepts of culture and organizational analysis. *Administrative Science Quarterly*. Vol 28, No 3. pp339–58.

Smith, P. (2002) Culture's consequences: something old and something new. *Human Relations*. Vol 55, No 1. pp119–35.

Soderberg, A.M. and Holden, N. (2002) Rethinking cross-cultural management in a globalizing business world. *International Journal of Cross Cultural Management*. Vol 2, No 1. pp103–21.

Solitskaya, T. and Andreeva, T. (2007) Training and development of personnel in Russian companies. In: M. Domsch and T. Lidokhover (eds) *Human resource management in Russia*, pp193–208. Aldershot: Ashgate.

Som, A. (2008) Innovative human resource management and corporate performance in the context of economic liberalization in India. *International Journal of Human Resource Management*. Vol 19, No 7. pp1278–97.

Sparrow, P.R. (2007) Globalization of HR at function level: four UK-based case studies of the international recruitment and selection process. *International Journal of Human Resource Management*. Vol 5, No 18. pp845–67.

Sparrow, P. (2008) Performance management in the UK. In: A. Varma, P. Budhwar and A. DeNisi (eds) *Performance management systems: a global perspective*, pp131–46. London: Routledge.

Spillane, J.P., Halverson, R. and Diamond, J.B. (2004) Towards a theory of leadership practice: a distributed perspective. *Journal of Curriculum Studies*. Vol 36, No 1. pp3–34.

Srinivasan, V. (2012) Multi generations in the workforce: building collaboration. *Indian Institute of Management Bangalore*. Vol 24, No 1. pp48–66.

Srivastava, P. and Bhatnagar, J. (2008) Talent acquisition due to diligence leading to high employee engagement: case of Motorola India MDB. Conference paper at the Asian Pacific Researchers in Organisation Studies (APROS).

Stahl, G.K., Miller, E.L. and Tung, R.L. (2002) Toward the boundaryless career: a closer look at the expatriate career concept and the perceived implications of an international assignment. *Journal of World Business*. Vol 37, No 3. pp216–27.

Stewart, J.A. (2008) A blended action learning programme to develop cross-cultural skills for SME leaders. Paper presented to British Academy of Management, Harrogate, UK. September.

Stewart, J., Johnson, S., Iles, P.A., Gold, J. and Devins, D. (2008) *World class comparisons in HRD*. Research report. Leeds: Learning and Skills Council.

Storey, J. (ed.) (1989) *New perspectives in human resource management*. London: Routledge.

Storey, J. (1992) *Developments in the management of human resources*. Oxford: Blackwell.

Storey, J. (ed.) (2004) *Leadership in organizations: current issues and key trends*. London: Routledge.

Storey, J. (ed.) (2011) *Leadership in organizations: current issues and key trends*, 2nd edition. London: Routledge.

Stroh, L.K., Gregersen, H.B. and Black, J.S. (1998) Closing the gap: expectations versus reality among repatriates. *Journal of World Business*. Vol 33, No 2. pp111–24.

Sulieman, M. (1984) Senior managers in Iraqi society: their background and attitudes. Unpublished PhD thesis, University of Glasgow.

Suliman, A.M.T. (2006) Human resource management in the Arab Emirates. In: P.S. Budhwar and K. Mellahi (eds) *Managing human resources in the Middle East*, pp59–78. London: Routledge.

Sully de Luque, M.F. and Arbaiza, L.A. (2005) Human resource management in Peru. In: A. Davila and M.M. Elvira (eds) *Best human resource management practices in Latin America*, pp191–206. London: Routledge.

Sultan, N., Metcalfe, B.D. and Weir, D. (2011) Dealing with post-oil economies: towards knowledge-based economies: some examples from the Arab Middle East. In: N. Sultan, D. Weir and Z. Karake-Shalhoub (eds) *Managing people and wealth: the new post-oil Arab Gulf*, pp33–55. London: Al-Saqi.

Sultan, N., Metcalfe, B.D. and Weir, D. (2012) The 'future' cities of the Arabian Gulf: realities and aspirations. In: N. Sultan, D. Weir and Z. Karake-Shalhoub (eds) *Managing people and wealth: the new post-oil Arab Gulf*. London: Al-Saqi.

Supornpraditchai, T., Miller, K., Lings, I.N. and Jonmundsson, B. (2007) Employee-based brand equity: antecedents and consequences. *Proceedings of the Australia New Zealand Marketing Academy Conference, Dunedin, New Zealand.*

Tamkin, P. (2012) Leadership by design. *Strategic HR Review.* Vol 11, No 2. pp90–5.

Tang, T.L. and Ibrahim, A.H.S. (1998) Antecedents of organizational citizenship behavior revisited: public personnel in the United States and the Middle East. *Public Personnel Management.* Vol 27. pp529–49.

Tannen, D. (1981) Indirectness in discourse: ethnicity as conversational style. *Discourse Processes.* Vol 4. pp221–38.

Tansley, C. (2009) Concept borrowing to facilitate a multi-disciplinary approach to the theoretical development of talent management – the case of employer branding. Paper presented at the European Academy of Management Conference, Liverpool, May.

Tansley, C. (2011) What do we mean by the term 'talent' in talent management? *Industrial and Commercial Training.* Vol 43, No 5. pp266–74.

Tansley, C., Harris, L., Stewart, J. and Turner, P. (2007) *Talent management: understanding the dimensions.* London: Chartered Institute of Personnel and Development.

Tanure, B. (2005) Human resource management in Brazil. In: A. Davila and M.M. Elvira (eds) *Best human resource management practices in Latin America*, pp111–28. London: Routledge.

Tarique, I. and Caligiuri, P.M. (2004) Training and development of international staff. In: A.W. Harzing and J. van Ruysseveldt (eds) *International human resource management*, pp283–306. London: Sage.

Tarique, I. and Schuler, R. (2010) Global talent management: literature review, integrative framework, and suggestions for further research. *Journal of World Business.* Vol 45, No 2. pp122–33.

Tarique, I., Schuler, R.S. and Gong, Y. (2006) A model of multinational enterprise subsidiary

staffing composition. *International Journal of Human Resource Management.* Vol 17. pp207–24.

Tayeb, M.H. (1997) Islamic revival in Asia and human resource management. *Employee Relations.* Vol 19, No 4. pp352–64.

Taylor, S. (2005) *People resourcing*, 3rd edition. London: Chartered Institute of Personnel and Development.

Teclemichael Tessema, M. and Soeters, J.L. (2006) Challenges and prospects of HRM in developing countries: testing the HRM–performance link in the Eritrean civil service. *International Journal of Human Resource Management.* Vol 17, No 1, January. pp86–105.

Tempel, A. and Walgenbach, P. (2007) Global standardization of organizational forms and management practices? What new institutionalism and the business-systems approach can learn from each other. *Journal of Management Studies.* Vol 44, No 1. pp1–24.

The Economist. (2011) The hopeful continent: Africa rising. 3 December. http://www.economist.com/node/21541015 .

Thompson, M. and Taras, D.G. (2011) Employment relations in Canada. In: G. Bamber, R.D. Lansbury and N. Wailes (eds) *International and comparative employment relations: globalisation and change*, pp88–116. London: Sage.

Thomson, A., Mabey, C., Storey, J., Gray, C. and Iles, P. (2000) *Changing patterns of management development.* Oxford: Blackwell.

Thorne, A. and Gough, H. (1999) *Portraits of type: an MBTI research compendium*, 2nd edition. Gainesville, FL: Center for Applications of Psychological Type.

Thorpe, R., Gold, J. and Lawler, J. (2011) Locating distributed leadership. *International Journal of Management Reviews.* Vol 13, special issue. pp239–50.

Tlaiss, H. and Kauser, S. (2011) The importance of *wasta* in the career success of Middle Eastern managers. *Journal of European Industrial Training.* Vol 35, No 5. pp467–86.

Torrington, D. (1989) Human resource management and the personnel function. In J. Storey (ed.) *New perspectives in human resource management*, pp56–66. London: Routledge.

Tosi, H.L. and Greckhamer, T. (2004) Culture and CEO compensation. *Organization Science.* Vol 15, No 6. pp657–70.

Towers Perrin. (2004) *Look closer: Managing today's talent to create tomorrow's leaders.* June.

Treviño, L.K., Brown, M. and Hartman, L.P. (2003) A qualitative investigation of perceived executive ethical leadership: perceptions from inside and outside the executive suite. *Human Relations.* Vol 55, No 1. pp5–37.

Triandis, H.C. (1977) Theoretical framework for evaluation of cross-cultural training effectiveness. *International Journal of Intercultural Relations.* Vol 1. pp19–45.

Trompenaars, F. (1993) *Riding the waves of culture.* London: Nicholas Brealey Publishing.

Trompenaars, F. (1997) *Riding the waves of culture: understanding diversity in global business.* London: McGraw-Hill.

Trompenaars, F. and Hampden-Turner, C. (2003) *Riding the waves of culture: understanding cultural diversity in business.* London: Nicholas Brealey Publishing.

Trompenaars, F. and Woolliams, P. (2004) *Marketing across cultures.* London: Capstone.

Tulgan, B. (2001) *Winning the talent wars.* New York: W.W. Norton and Company.

Tung, R.L. (1981) Selection and training of personnel for overseas assignments. *Columbia Journal of World Business.* Vol 16, No 1. pp68–78.

Tung, R.L. (1998) American expatriates abroad: from neophytes to cosmopolitans. *Journal of World Business.* Vol 33, No 2. pp125–44.

Turban, D.B., Lau, C.M., Ngo, H.Y., Chow, H.I.S. and Si, S.X. (2001) Organizational attractiveness of firms in the People's Republic of China: a person–organization fit perspective. *Journal of Applied Psychology.* Vol 86, No 2. pp194–206.

Turnbull, S., Case, P., Edwards, G., Jepson, D., Schedlitzki, D. and Simpson, P. (eds) (2012) *Worldly leadership: alternative wisdoms for a complex world.* Basingstoke: Palgrave Macmillan.

Tymon, Jr, W.G., Stumpf, S.A. and Doh, J.P. (2010) Exploring talent management in India: the neglected role of intrinsic rewards. Journal of World Business. Vol 45, No 2. pp109-21.

Tzafrir, S., Meshoulam, I. and Baruch, Y. (2006) HRM in Israel. In: P. Budhwar and K. Mellahi (eds) *Managing human resources in the Middle East*, pp180–98. London: Routledge.

Ulrich, D. (1997) *Human resource champions: the next agenda for adding value and delivering results.* Boston, MA: Harvard Business School Press.

Ulrich, D. and Brockbank, W. (2005) *The HR value proposition.* Boston, MA: Harvard Business School Press.

USAID (2005) *Assessment of Ministry of Health human resource management policies and practices.* Jordan Human Resources Development Project Report No 5. http://dec.usaid.gov/exphtm/123005.htm .

Vaara, E., Sarala, R., Stahl, G. and Björkman, I. (2012) The impact of organizational and national cultural differences on social conflict and knowledge transfer in international acquisitions. *Journal of Management Studies*. Vol 49, No 1. pp1–27.

Vaiman, V. and Holden, N. (2011) Talent management's perplexing landscape in central and eastern Europe. In: H. Scullion and D. Collings (eds) *Global talent management*, pp178–93. Abingdon: Routledge.

Vaiman, V. and Vance, C. (2009) *Smart talent management: building knowledge assets for competitive advantage*. Cheltenham: Edward Elgar.

van de Vliert, E. and Smith, P.B. (2004) Leader reliance on subordinates across nations that differ in development and climate. *The Leadership Quarterly*. Vol 15. pp381–403.

Van Iddekinge, C.H., Roth, P.L., Raymark, P.H. and Odle-Dusseau, H.N. (2012) The criterion-related validity of integrity tests: an updated meta-analysis. *Journal of Applied Psychology*. Vol 97, No 3. pp499–530.

Van Renken, R.E. (2008) Obama's 'Third Culture' team. *The Daily Beast*. 26 November. http://www.thedailybeast.com/articles/2008/11/26/obamas-third-culture-team.html .

Varma, A., Budhwar, P. and DeNisi, A. (2008) Performance management around the globe: introduction and agenda. In: A. Varma, P. Budhwar and A. DeNisi (eds) *Performance management systems: a global perspective*, pp3–14. London: Routledge.

Vatchkova, E. (2009) Managing human resources in Bulgaria. In: M. Morley, N. Heraty and S. Michailova (eds) *Managing human resources in central and eastern Europe*, pp243–77. London: Routledge.

Vernon, G. (2011) International and comparative pay and reward. In: T. Edwards and C. Rees (eds) *International human resource management: globalization, national systems and multinational companies*, 2nd edition, pp206–28. Harlow: Pearson FT Prentice Hall.

Viswesvaran, C. and Ones, D.S. (2000) Perspectives on models of job performance.

International Journal of Selection and Assessment. Vol 8. pp216–26.

Voros, J. and Schermerhorn, J. (1993) Institutional roles in higher education for business and management in Hungary. *Management Education and Development*. Vol 24, No 1. pp70–82.

Wachira, F.N. (2010) Improving the management of human resources in the public service through application of information and communication technologies (ICTs). Paper presented to the Africa Public Service Human Resource Management Network. Cotonou, Benin.

Wailes, N., Bamber, G.J. and Lansbury, R.D. et al (2011) International and comparative employment relations: an introduction. In: G. Bamber, R.D. Lansbury and N. Wailes (eds) *International and comparative employment relations: globalisation and change*, pp1–35. London: Sage.

Wall, B. (1994) U.S. Expats Seem Ill-prepared for UK Culture. *USA Today*. 16 September. pA2.

Walter, A. and Zhang, X. (eds) (2012) *East Asian capitalism: diversity, continuity and change*. Oxford: Oxford University Press.

Wang, G. (2008) National HRD: new paradigm or reinvention of the wheel? *Journal of European Industrial Training*. Vol 32, No 4. pp303–16.

Wang, G. and Swanson, R. (2008) The idea of national HRD: an analysis based on economics and theory development methodology. *Human Resource Development Review*. Vol 7, No 1. pp79–106.

Wang, H.K., Tseng, J.F. and Yen, Y.F. (2012) Examining the mechanisms linking guanxi, norms and knowledge sharing: the mediating roles of trust in Taiwan's high-tech firms. *International Journal of Human Resource Management*. Vol 23, No 19. Special Issue: Whither Chinese HRM? Paradigms, models and theories. pp4048–68.

Wang, Y. (2008) Emotional bonds with supervisor and co-workers: relationship to organizational commitment in China's foreign-invested companies. *International Journal of Human Resource Management*. Vol 19, No 5. pp916–31.

Wang-Cowham, C. (2007) The transfer of HR knowledge in MNCs in China: The perspective of Chinese HR managers. PhD thesis. Manchester: Manchester Metropolitan University.

Wang-Cowham, C. (2011) Developing talent with an integrated knowledge-sharing mechanism: an exploratory investigation from the Chinese human resource managers' perspective. *Human Resource Development International*. Vol 14, No 4. pp391–407.

Wanous, J.P., Poland, T.D., Premack, S.L. and Davis, K.S. (1992) The effects of met expectations on newcomer attitudes and behaviors: a review and meta-analysis. *Journal of Applied Psychology*. Vol 77. pp288–97.

Ward, C. and Kennedy, A. (1999) The measurement of sociocultural adaptation. *International Journal of Intercultural Relations*. Vol 23. pp659–77.

Ward, C., Bochner, S. and Furnham, A. (2001) *The psychology of culture shock*, 2nd edition. London: Routledge.

Warner, M. (2002a) Conclusion: the future of Chinese management. *Asia Pacific Business Review*. Vol 9. pp205–23.

Warner, M. (2002b) Globalization, labour markets and human resources in Asia-Pacific economies: an overview. *International Journal of Human Resource Management*. Vol 13. pp384–98.

Warner, M. (2004) Human resource management in China revisited: introduction. *International Journal of Human Resource Management*. Vol 15. pp617–34.

Warner, M. (2008) Reassessing human resource management 'with Chinese characteristics': an overview. *International Journal of Human Resource Management*. Vol 19. pp771–801.

Warner, M. (2012) Whither Chinese HRM? Paradigms, models and theories. *International Journal of Human Resource Management*. Vol 23, No 19. Special Issue: Whither Chinese HRM? Paradigms, models and theories. pp3943–63.

Warner, M. and Goodall, K. (2009) *Management training and development in China*. Abingdon: Routledge.

Warner, M., Wong, L. and Lee, G. (2002) Editorial. *International Journal of Human Resource Management*. Vol 13, No 3. pp379–83.

Waxin, M.F. and Panaccio, A. (2005) Cross cultural training to facilitate expatriate adjustment: it works. *Personnel Review*. Vol 34, No 1. pp51–67.

Weber, M. (1978) *Economy and society*. Los Angeles: University of California Press.

Weir, D.T.H. (1998) The fourth paradigm. In: A. Al-Shamali and J. Denton (eds) *Management in the Middle East*, pp60–76. Kuwait: Gulf Management Centre.

Weir, D. (2000a) Management in the Arab world: a fourth paradigm? In: A. Al-Shamali and J. Denton (eds) *Arab business: the globalisation imperative*. Kuwait: Arab Research Centre.

Weir, D.T.H. (2000b) Management in the Arab world. In: M. Warner (ed) *Management in emerging countries: regional encyclopaedia of business and management*, pp291–300. London: Business Press/Thomson Learning.

Weir, D.T.H. (2003) Human resource development in the Middle East: a fourth paradigm. In: M. Lee (ed.) *HRD in a complex world*, pp69–82. London: Routledge.

Weir, D. and Hutchings, K. (2005) Cultural embeddedness and contextual constraints: knowledge sharing in Chinese and Arab cultures. *Knowledge and Process Management*. Vol 12, No 2. pp89–98.

Weir, D. and Hutchings, K. (2009) Modernisation and internationalisation of business and management in the Middle East: is *wasta* still relevant? *Academy of Management Conference Proceedings*, Academy of Management, Atlanta, USA.

Weisbord, M. (1987) Productive workplaces. San Francisco, CA: Jossey Bass.

Wendt, H., Euwema, M.C. and van Emmerik, H. (2009) Leadership and team cohesiveness across cultures. *The Leadership Quarterly*. Vol 20. pp358–70.

Wenger, E. (2000) Communities of practice and social learning systems. *Organization*. Vol 7, No 2. pp225–46.

Werner, S. (ed.) (2007) *Managing human resources in North America*. London: Routledge.

West, M., Borrill, C., Dawson, J., Scully, J., Carter, M., Anelay, S., Patterson, M. and Waring, J. (2002) The link between the management of employees and patient mortality in acute hospitals. *International Journal of Human Resource Management*. Vol 13, No 8. pp1299–1310.

Whitaker, B. (2009) *What's really wrong with the Middle East?* London: Saqi Books.

Whiteoak, J., Crawford, N. and Mapstone, R. (2006) Impact of gender and generational difference in work values and attitudes in an Arab culture. *Thunderbird International Business Review*. Vol 48, No 1. pp77–91.

Whitley, R. (1999) *Divergent capitalisms: the social structuring and change of business systems*. Oxford: Oxford University Press.

Wilden, R., Gudergan, S. and Lings, I.N. (2006) Employee-based brand equity. *Proceedings of the Australia New Zealand Marketing Academy Conference*. Brisbane, Australia.

Wilkinson, B., Gamble, J., Humphrey, J., Morris, J. and Anthony, D. (2001) The new international division of labour in Asian electronics: work organization and human resources in Japan and Malaysia. *Journal of Management Studies*. Vol 37, No 8. pp675–95.

Williams, M. (2000) *The war for talent: getting the best from the best*. London: Chartered Institute of Personnel and Development.

Wilson, B. (2008) Hidden dragons. *People Management*. 7 August. p1.

Wilson, D. and Stupnytska, A. (2007) *The N-11: more than an acronym*. Global Economics Paper No. 153. Goldman Sachs. http://www.chicagobooth.edu/alumni/clubs/pakistan/docs/next11dream-march%20%2707-goldmansachs.pdf .

Witkin, H.A. (1978) *Cognitive styles in personal and cultural adaptation*. Worcester, MA: Clark University Press.

Witkin, H.A. and Goodenough, D.R. (1981) *Cognitive style: essence and origins*. New York: International Universities Press.

Wocke, A. (2007) Building flexibility into multi-national human resource strategy: a study tour of four South African multi-national enterprises. *International Journal of Human Resource Management*. Vol 18, No 5. pp829–44.

Wocke, A. and Klein, S. (2007). Emerging global contenders: the South African experience. *Journal of International Management.* Vol 13, No 3. pp319–37.

Woldu, H. with Budhwar, P. (2011) Cultural value orientations of the former communist countries: a gender based analysis. *International Journal of Human Resource Management.* Vol 22. pp1365–86.

Wood, G. and Brewster, C. (eds) (2007) *Industrial relations in Africa.* London: Palgrave.

Wood, G. and Dibben, P. (2008) The challenges facing the South African labour movement: mobilization of diverse constituencies in a changing context. *Industrial Relations.* Vol 63, No 4. pp671–93.

Wood, S. and Mellahi, K. (2001) HRM in South Africa. In: P.S. Budhwar and Y.A. Debrah (eds) *Human resource management in developing countries*, pp222–37. London: Routledge.

World Bank (2007) *The environment for women's entrepreneurship in the Middle East and North Africa region.* Washington, DC: The World Bank.

World Bank (2011) *Women, business and the law: removing barriers to economic inclusion.* Washington, DC: IFC/The World Bank.

World Bank (2012) *Knowledge assessment methodology 2012.* Available at: www.worldbank.org/kam .

Wright, C. (2008) Reinventing human resource management: business partners, internal consultants and the limits to professionalization. *Human Relations.* Vol 61. pp1063–86.

Wright, P.M. and McMahan, G.C. (2011) Exploring human capital: putting human back into strategic human resource management. *Human Resource Management Journal.* Vol 21, No 2. April. pp93–104.

Wright, P.M., McMahan, G.C. and McWilliams, A. (1994) Human resources and sustained competitive advantage: a resource-based perspective. *International Journal of Human Resource Management.* Vol 5. pp301–26.

Wu, M.Y. (2006) Hofstede's cultural dimensions 30 years later: a study of Taiwan and the United States. *Intercultural Communication Studies.* Vol XV, No 1. pp33–42.

Yahiaouni, D. and Zoubir, Y.H. (2006) Human resource management in Tunisia. In: P.S. Budhwar and K. Mellahi (eds) *Managing human resources in the Middle East*, pp233–49. London: Routledge.

Yakubovich, V. and Kozina, I. (2007) Recruitment at Russian enterprises. In: M. Domsch and T. Lidokhover (eds) *Human resource management in Russia*, pp153–70. Aldershot: Ashgate.

Yamazaki, Y. (2005) Learning styles and typologies of cultural differences: a theoretical and empirical comparison. *British Journal of Intercultural Relations.* Vol 29, No 5. pp521–48.

Yolles, M. and Iles, P.A. (2006) Exploring public–private partnerships through knowledge cybernetics. *Systems Research and Behavioral Science.* Vol 23. pp1–22.

Yousef, D.A. (1997) Satisfaction with job security as a predictor of organizational commitment and job performance in a multicultural environment. *International Journal of Manpower.* Vol 19, No 3. pp184–94.

Yousef, D.A. (1998) Predictors of decision-making styles in a non-Western country. *Leadership and Organizational Development Journal.* Vol 19, No 7. pp366–73.

Yousef, D.A. (2000) Organizational commitment as a mediator of the relationship between Islamic work ethic and attitudes toward organizational change. *Human Relations.* Vol 53, No 4. pp513–37.

Yousef, D.A. (2001) Islamic work ethic – a moderator between organizational commitment and job satisfaction in a cross-cultural context. *Personnel Review.* Vol 30, No 2. pp152–69.

Yukl, G. (1999) An evaluation of conceptual weaknesses in transformational and charismatic leadership theories. *The Leadership Quarterly.* Vol 10, No 2. pp285–305.

Yukl, G. (2010) *Leadership in organizations,* 7th edition. New York: Pearson Prentice Hall.

Zack-Williams, T. and Mohan, G. (2005) Africa from SAPS to PSAPS: plus ca change plus c'est la même chose. *Review of African Political Economy.* Vol 32, No 106. pp501–3.

Zander, U. and Kogut, B. (1994) Knowledge and the speed of the transfer and imitation of organizational capabilities: an empirical test. *Organization Science.* Vol 6, No 1. pp76–92.

Zhu, C. and Dowling, P. (2001) Contextual variables and their impact on HRM in China. Presented at Global HRM Conference, Barcelona, Spain. June.

Zhu, C.J. and Nyland, C. (2004) Marketization and social protection reform: emerging HR issues in China. *International Journal of Human Resource Management.* Vol 15, No 4/5. pp853–77.

Zhu, C.J., Zhang, M. and Shen, J. (2012) Paternalistic and transactional HRM: the nature and transformation of HRM in contemporary China. *International Journal of Human Resource Management.* Vol 23, No 19. Special Issue: Whither Chinese HRM? Paradigms, models and theories. pp3964–82.

Zorob, A. (2012) Research perspectives after the Arab Spring: economics / political economy of the Middle East and North Africa. In: J. Gertel and A-L.

Amira Augustin (eds) *Realigning power geometries in the Arab world, conference reader*, pp403–8. 24–26 February. Leipzig.

Index